GW00498912

London's Hidden Walks 4

by Stephen Millar

Volume 4

London's Hidden Walks 4

Written by Stephen Millar
Photography by Stephen Millar,
additional photographs by Charlie Repp
Edited by Eve Kershman
Book design by Lesley Gilmour and Susi Koch
Illustrations by Lesley Gilmour and Hannah Kershman

All rights reserved. No part of this publication may be
reproduced, stored in a retrieval system or transmitted in any
form or by any means electronic, mechanical, photocopying,
recording or otherwise without the prior consent of the publishers
and copyright owners. Every effort has been made to ensure the
accuracy of this book; however, due to the nature of the subject,
the publishers cannot accept responsibility for any errors which
occur, or their consequences.

Published in 2022 by
Metro Publications Ltd,
www.metropublications.com

Metro® is a registered trademark of Associated Newspapers
Limited. The METRO mark is under licence from Associated
Newspapers Limited.

Printed and bound in Turkey. This book is produced using
paper from registered sustainable and managed sources.

© 2022 Stephen Millar
British Library Cataloguing in Publication Data. A catalogue
record for this book is available from the British Library.

ISBN 978-1-902910-68-0

For the kids

Note: Larger maps of each walk are available to download and print. Just visit our website **www.metropublications.com**

CONTENTS

Introduction 1

Area Map 2

1. **Pimlico Walk** **5**

2. Kentish Town Walk 35

3. **Oxford Street Walk** **61**

4. Primrose Hill Walk 99

5. St John's Wood Walk........................127

6. **Earl's Court Walk** **157**

7. Fulham Town Walk 187

8. **Clapham Walk** **215**

9. Tooting Walk...................................241

10. Peckham Walk 263

11. Leamouth Peninsula 289

12. **Lost City** **313**

Index 342

Acknowledgements

This book is dedicated to those who have walked routes in volumes 1-3. Some have managed to do all the routes, covering – in total – a few hundred miles. Over the years I've had the pleasure of getting to know many of London Hidden Walks' readership and I want to thank some of them including: Jane Sheehan, Keri Lloyd, Jill Rock, Alan Roberts, Nicola Bielicki, Stacey Reed, Michael Barrie, Luke Billingham, Gordon Mackay, Bitu Williams, Simon Drury, Torben Betts, Tim Chesher, David Bishop, Graeme Light, Phil Rider, Nick Eastwell, Giacomo Peirano, Philip Davidson, Adam Perfect, Bob and Janet Mapleson, Farhan Mannan and Maria Robinson. Some have since become friends and ventured out on new trial walks. Steve Magee deserves particular thanks, having volunteered to walk the new routes in volume 4 with me and his feedback was very helpful, as was his knowledge of good pubs along the way. When the book was finally finished, it was left to stalwart readers, Alison and Jim Martyn, to try the new walks and provide valuable corrections and suggestions.

I also set up a 'meetup' group online, inviting people to come along on a few of the new walks in this book. I wanted to mention some of the people who joined me on the walks: Anna, Dalton and his daughters Iris and Anna, Prisha, Farhan, Kevin, Aaron, Dalton, Claire, Diane, Mast, Yuri, Anya, Yola, Roberta, Vian, Bea, Adam and Liz, Michael, Mel, Judith, Alan and Michael, Columba, Bob, Janet, Julie and Nida. It has been fascinating to meet people who have arrived in the city from around the world, all interested in getting to know London a little better.

Finally, a big thank you to everyone at Metro for their continued support and enthusiasm, which has helped make this new book into such an attractive addition to the series.

St Dunstan-in-the-East

Introduction

Whilst planning this new volume, I started by looking at a giant map of London and became aware of the many parts of the city that were unknown to me. Exploring new areas such as Peckham, Clapham, Pimlico and Tooting, has been a real joy. I also made the surprising decision to include Oxford Street, to reveal its hidden secrets, often missed by the hordes of busy shoppers.

The new walks revealed lots of fascinating stories. I discovered the intrigues of spies and fascists in Pimlico. In Earl's Court I visited the hotel where the assassin of Martin Luther King Jr. laid low, and in the Square Mile explored the ruins of Shakespeare's parish church. In Clapham there are secret tunnels and the site of a murder that drew attention to the teenage menace of the Teddy Boys. Kentish Town has its own secrets, including a pipe carrying one of London's lost rivers and a plaque in memory of a much loved family pet – Boris the cat. Visiting St John's Wood you can walk in the footsteps of The Beatles on that famous Abbey Road crossing and discover a centuries-old chapel hidden within the grounds of a hospital. My personal favourite is the Leamouth Peninsula – a strip of land that seems never to have been inhabited and can claim to be one of London's 'hidden' gems.

As with previous books, I have tried to find unusual and less-visited places, away from the usual tourist trail. The routes are designed to give you time to understand a little more about our urban environment, something most of us are too busy to appreciate. The walks also take you to parts of the city you would never have thought of visiting without this book in hand.

All these routes are stand-alone walks, so you can enjoy them without having tried the earlier volumes. I hope in the course of your travels, even the most seasoned urban explorer will discover a few surprises and delights. If you spot anything I have missed or a building that has disappeared, please do let me know.

Stephen Millar
stephenwmillar@hotmail.com

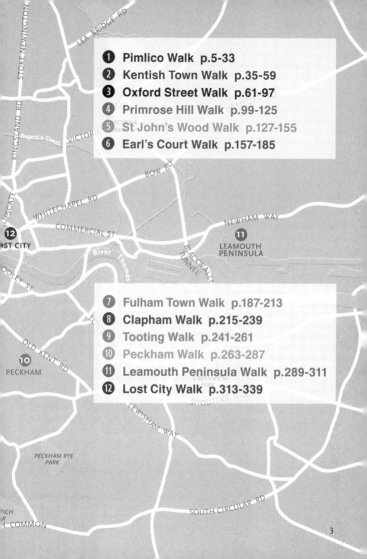

1 **Pimlico Walk** p.5-33

2 **Kentish Town Walk** p.35-59

3 **Oxford Street Walk** p.61-97

4 **Primrose Hill Walk** p.99-125

5 St John's Wood Walk p.127-155

6 **Earl's Court Walk** p.157-185

7 **Fulham Town Walk** p.187-213

8 **Clapham Walk** p.215-239

9 **Tooting Walk** p.241-261

10 Peckham Walk p.263-287

11 **Leamouth Peninsula Walk** p.289-311

12 **Lost City Walk** p.313-339

1 Pimlico Walk

Pimlico

1. Eduardo Paolozzi Ventilation Shaft
2. Plaque to Major Wingfield
3. Cabman's Shelter
4. Ventilation Shaft
5. Laurence Olivier's childhood home
6. St Saviour's Church

7. Former Bomb Site
8. Young England Kindergarten
9. Plaque to Francis Crick
10. St George's Square Garden
11. Grosvenor Road
12. River Tyburn Plaque
13. Pimlico Gardens
14. Westminster Boating Base
15. Dolphin Square
16. Former Wharves
17. Claverton Street
18. Churchill Gardens Estate
19. Thomas Parade
20. Former King William IV
21. Grosvenor Canal
22. Western Pumping Station
23. Peabody estate
24. Former 18th Century Distillery
25. Holy Apostles Catholic Church
26. Crime Scene at 36 Alderney Street
27. Plaque to Jomo Kenyatta
28. St Gabriel's Church
29. 33 Warwick Square
30. Warwick Square
31. Rank Foundation Offices
32. Ecclestone Square
33. Plaque to Winston Churchill
34. Maltese Religious Order
35. Ecclestone Square Mews
36. Marquis of Westminster
37. Lillington and Longmoore Estate
38. St James the Less Church

Pimlico Walk
Start/Finish: Pimlico Tube Station
Distance: 3.3 miles

This walk begins at Pimlico underground station. Exit the station towards the Tate to visit an often overlooked piece of public art by ❶ **Eduardo Paolozzi** (1924-2005). Installed in the early 1980s, this striking structure is functional too, as it encloses equipment used to cool the underground station below. Paolozzi came from Leith in Scotland, the son of Italian immigrants, and is regarded today as one of the pioneers of the pop art movement in Britain. He's responsible for many pieces of public art in London and beyond.

Follow Lupus Street west towards the spire of St Saviour's. Look out for a blue plaque outside the home of ❷ **Major Walter Clopton Wingfield** (1833-1912) at 33 St George's Square. This army officer is regarded as the father of lawn tennis. Whilst the game was played before he became involved, Wingfield is credited with codifying the game as it is played today, and obtained a patent for the rule book in 1874. He lived here for the last 10 years of his life.

Passing this house, on the left is the church of **St Saviour's Pimlico** and on the right a ❸ **cabman's shelter** dating from 1893. The Cabmen's Shelter Fund was set up in 1875 to build shelters for cabmen (originally in charge of horse-drawn hansom cabs) who otherwise had little opportunity to rest while on duty. Those behind the fund were teetotalers who wanted to provide an alternative to the local pub. There were once over 60 shelters in London, serving hot food and non-alcoholic drinks. The few remaining shelters are still run by the fund.

4

5

7

If you look to the north of the shelter you will see an odd little building which stands over a ❹ **Ventilation Shaft** used for the Victorian underground line far below. It is certainly needed as recent tests show London's underground stations have a level of pollution 30 times higher than the capital's busiest roads.

Just a short way along Lupus Street at number 22 is the ❺ **childhood home of** actor **Laurence Olivier** (1907-89). He came here in 1912, aged just five, when his father Gerard became the assistant rector at St Saviour's church nearby. Whilst Olivier found his father a rather cold fish, his father's performance in the pulpit had a profound effect on the young Laurence. The actor later recalled 'when to drop the voice, when to bellow about the perils of hellfire, when to slip in a gag, when suddenly to wax sentimental... The quick changes of mood and manner absorbed me, and I have never forgotten them'.

As you cross to visit the church, it is worth reading a little about the history of Pimlico. For centuries the area remained an undeveloped open space – marshy and prone to flooding from the Thames. It was part of the Manor of Ebury until 1677, when the heiress of that manor, Mary Davies (aged 12), married Sir Thomas Grosvenor. This partnership meant the manor became part of the famous Grosvenor Estate. Although the area that is now called Pimlico was sold off by the Second Duke of Westminster in 1953.

The man who really created the Pimlico you see today was the builder Thomas Cubitt

(1788-1855). Cubitt became the preferred builder for the great landowners, who wanted to transform their semi-rural landholdings around London into new suburbs. Cubitt's vast army of builders ripped up fields and old agricultural tracks, transforming whole districts into squares and roads lined with elegant buildings. Aside from Pimlico, Cubitt was also responsible for developing much of Bloomsbury and Belgravia.

In 1835, the Grosvenor family commissioned the already renowned Cubitt to create the streets you are standing on today. By the mid-1860s much of Pimlico had been laid out and the market gardens that once supplied Londoners with fruit and vegetables had long since disappeared to make way for the fine houses and squares.

❻ St Saviour's was built in 1864 to a design by Thomas Cundy Jr. The church authorities were determined to make sure the residents of this new suburb were not tempted to forget about their faith, or stray to a rival organisation, so the creation of a grand church like this carried a clear message.

Aside from the Olivier connection, tennis pioneer Major Walter Clopton Wingfield worshipped here, and author Compton Mackenzie, best known for *Whiskey Galore*, was married in the church.

The school and playground opposite the church were the site of four substantial buildings that were destroyed during the Blitz. The extensive grounds of Pimlico Primary School are a reminder of this **❼ Former Bomb Site** and how devastating World War II was for London. Most people know of the destruction of the East End but Westminster and Pimlico were also heavily bombed during the Blitz.

11

Right beside the church is the **❽ Young England Kindergarten**. Lady Diana Spencer (1961-97) was working here as a teacher's assistant when she became engaged to Prince Charles in 1981. She left the job soon after the paparazzi began camping outside the school in the hope of catching a picture of the future Princess. After the tragic death of Diana on the streets of Paris, a bench was erected outside the school that fondly remembers 'Miss Diana'.

Continue down the west side of St George's Square, stopping outside **number 56** to see a **❾ plaque commemorating scientist Francis Crick** (1916-2004). A Nobel laureate, he co-wrote with James Watson the famous paper of 1953 that explained the double-helix structure of the DNA molecule. Crick lived here between 1945 and 1947, when he was working for the Admiralty research department developing mines that could be used against German minesweepers.

Another famous resident of the Square was Bram Stoker (1847-1912), author of the Gothic-horror classic *Dracula* (1897). He died, possibly due to contracting syphilis, whilst living at number 26 on the Square.

Unlike many squares in London, you can enter the huge **❿ St George's Square Garden** – not a bad spot for a picnic in good weather. Diana Spencer no doubt came here with children from the kindergarten to enjoy a sunny afternoon, before she had to worry about the papparazi that were to plague her for the rest of her life in the limelight.

Cubitt opened the garden to new residents in 1854 and during World War II an air raid shelter was constructed on the north side, which is now covered over by plants.

Continue south. This is one of three grand squares in Pimlico designed by Cubitt, – you will visit the other two later on. The style of building favoured by Cubitt and seen here – tall, Italianate terraces, with a painted stucco façade – is common throughout Pimlico. The style is certainly impressive, but blander and more uniform than the houses produced in the earlier Regency period.

Pimlico never acquired the cachet of Belgravia and the opening of Victoria Station in 1860, surrounded by railway lines and smoke-belching engines, diminished the desirability of the area. By 1900 parts of Pimlico were becoming shabby, and many streets once inhabited by the wealthier classes became home to hotels, shops and social housing (including Peabody Estates seen later). Damage caused by World War II bombing gave Westminster City Council the opportunity to build new council estates that contrast sharply with the grand houses built by Cubitt.

Continue south until you reach ⓫ **Grosvenor Road**, named after the great estate headed today by Hugh Grosvenor, the 7th Duke of Westminster. The Grosvenor family sold their Pimlico landholdings in 1953, but the Grosvenor Group retain substantial interests in other parts of London and beyond, which are worth, by most recent estimates, over £12 billion. The south side of the Square used to open onto the River Thames and until the 1870s had its own pier where boats docked.

Metal staircase down to the river bed where
the Tyburn outflow point can be observed.

Cross over and bear left until you see a gap in the buildings. There is a **⓬ plaque** here marking where the **River Tyburn** has its outflow into the Thames. This 'lost' London river runs south from Hampstead, and by the time Cubitt began building modern Pimlico, had been covered over and diverted into sewer pipes.

The final stretch leading up to here was called the King's Scholars Pond Sewer (as it passed by the King's Scholars of nearby Westminster School). The two buildings on either side – Rio Cottage and Tyburn House – were used by those operating the sluice gate that helped control the sewer. If you are brave (and careful) there is a metal staircase leading down to the river bed to see the outflow point. There is also a plaque that lists several of the places the Tyburn river runs through before reaching this point.

Walk along the Thames Path, with superb views of South London. The Nine Elms area on the other side of the river has been transformed in recent years, looking suspiciously more like Singapore or Hong Kong than London. You soon reach **⓭ Pimlico Gardens**. It lies opposite the US Embassy across the river in Nine Elms. The Embassy was controversially moved here in recent years from its previous site in Grosvenor Square. Former President Donald Trump was not a fan of the move, in 2018 describing the new site as 'lousy' and 'horrible'.

Pimlico Gardens is small but charmingly lush and contains a statue of William Huskisson (1770-1830), the statesman whose political career was unfortunately overshadowed by the fact he is the first person in history to be killed by a train. He was run over by Robert Stephenson's revolutionary *Rocket* locomotive at the

opening of the Liverpool and Manchester Railway. Huskisson was attempting to cross the tracks to meet the Duke of Wellington when he misjudged the train's speed and instead met his maker.

Next door is the ⑭ **Westminster Boating Base**, which is home to a charity that teaches water sports on the Thames and is also popular with celebrities. Among the notables who have dabbled in the waters is actress Angelina Jolie, who learnt to canoe here before playing Lara Croft in *Tomb Raider* (2001).

Exit the Gardens and cross over the road to reach ⑮ **Dolphin Square**. The Square has been the scene of so many scandalous stories over the years that the BBC in 2015 asked whether it was 'the UK's most notorious address?'.

The Square was built in the mid-1930s, but a century before, this was the site of Cubitt's construction yard. For decades this was a hive of activity with hundreds of workers carrying the materials that would shape Pimlico's streets. Much of the gravel and soil that helped lay strong foundations in the marshy land of Pimlico was brought here after being excavated during the construction of St Katharine Docks, so this walk takes you over part of London's East End as well.

Once Cubitt and his builders were finished in Pimlico, the yard was closed and in 1859 the vast area was acquired for the Royal Army Clothing Store. Hundreds of seamstresses worked here making uniforms for the Army – uniforms that would have turned up in every far-flung part of the British Empire.

When the uniform factory was closed, the site was cleared and Dolphin Square was built between 1935 and 1937. The name derives from the water-pumping machine nicknamed 'the dolphin' that once stood here. The flats were designed to provide reasonably priced homes for the middle classes and cater also for the growing demand for apartment blocks with a high standard of amenities and services.

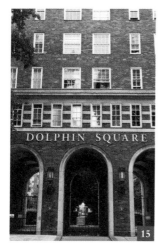

Given Dolphin Square's proximity to Westminster, it has always attracted politicians, and at any one time, there are dozens of MP's and members of the House of Lords residing in flats here. However, other residents have also frequently brought the Square into the glare of the media. The British Fascist leader Oswald Mosley was arrested at his apartment on the square in 1940. The arrest saved him from any conflict with the Free French and De Gaulle who were based here during World War II, alongside intelligence officer Maxwell Knight. Knight recruited author Ian Fleming and was said to have been the inspiration for 'M' in Fleming's Bond novels.

Other spies and safe houses were based here, including double-agent John Vassall who was exposed as a Soviet spy in 1962. Mandy Rice-Davies and Christine Keeler — key figures in the Profumo affair that also involved a Russian spy — also shared a flat here. Other prominent former residents include Princess Anne, Harold Wilson, and William Joyce — the Nazi propagandist better known as 'Lord Haw-Haw',

15

You can walk through the entrance of the square to see the lovely gardens inside, irrigated from the site's own artesian well.

When finished, continue westwards. In the late 19th century the land to your left, beside the Thames, was the site of several **16 wharves** where goods and passengers could connect with riverboats. To the right of the road were residential streets and (given Pimlico's modern-day appearance) a surprising amount of industry and commercial premises: factories, a distillery, a sawmill, engine works, furniture warehouses and mineral waterworks. With so little business of this kind in London today, it seems almost inconceivable that Pimlico was once a place of industry.

Keep walking west, passing **17 Claverton Street** on the north side. This street is associated with a famous scandal, The Pimlico Poisoning Mystery of 1886. A resident of this street, Thomas Bartlett, died in mysterious circumstances and traces of chloroform were found in his stomach. The authorities believed his wife had poisoned him but she was acquitted at the end of the well publicised trial.

On the north side is the **18 Churchill Gardens Estate**. It was built between 1946 and 1962 and contains over 35 blocks of residential housing. During World War II German bombing destroyed much of the housing in this southern part of Pimlico, as well as the industrial enterprises previously found here. The estate – designed by Philip Powell and Hidalgo Moya – was regarded as an innovative and pioneering attempt to deal with the post-war housing problem in this part of London, and many other estates built in the capital followed the example set here.

The contrast between the estate and the wealthy residents of Dolphin Square is a sharp one. *The Telegraph*, in 2003, reported 'it's unlikely many Dolphin Square residents walking out of the prestigious complex in Pimlico turn left into Churchill Gardens council estate'. The two developments stand almost cheek by jowl, but in terms of the class and incomes of the residents, they remain worlds apart with very little interaction

between Dolphin Square and those that live in the surrounding estates.

Continue along with the Thames on your left. On the right side is ⑲ **Thomas Parade** (numbers 105-109) which has an unusual history. Before Cubitt, a stone merchant named John Johnson tried to develop this area in 1817, but he only managed to build these houses before giving up due to opposition from local businesses. Compare these houses from the early 1800s to those Cubitt produced in the rest of Pimlico in later decades. Old maps show a small inlet named Johnson Dock that went a short way up here from the Thames.

Soon you will see the ⑳ **former King William IV Pub** that dates from the mid-19th century. This is where – according to *The Telegraph* – 'notorious Chelsea football hooligans once gathered to get tanked up before accosting rival fans at Stamford Bridge'. The pub and its hooligans have now disappeared, but the pub's signage remains.

Continue for a few minutes under the railway bridge to see on the right the truncated remains of the ㉑ **Grosvenor Canal**. Before the canal, the Chelsea Waterworks Company was based here. Founded in 1723, it was set up to supply fresh water (as far as that was possible given it came from the Thames) to the new districts being built in this part of London and beyond. Utilising an existing creek, the company constructed huge ponds to collect the water, and old maps show the east side of Pimlico to be a miniature version of Venice, punctuated by market gardens

When the lease expired, the Grosvenor family decided to develop the creek into a proper canal that stretched from here for less than a mile to an inland basin. This allowed coal to be brought down the Thames and then brought inland, to be used in the many grand houses built on land owned by the Grosvenor Estate. The canal was first used in 1824 and ended at a huge water basin. The latter would later be filled in to become the site of Victoria station (built in the late 1850s). Over time the canal was shortened and used for moving rubbish rather than valuable goods before it eventually closed.

Retrace your steps, passing the impressive Grade II listed **㉒ Western Pumping Station** on the left. It was built in 1875 and used as part of the capital's sewage system. The striking Italianate-style chimney is 82 metres high.

22 Western Pumping Station

Carry on, taking a left up Lupus Street and walk a short way into Turpentine Lane. To your left are the distinctive buildings of one of the **❷ Peabody estates**, this one dating from 1876. The Peabody Trust was founded in 1862 by the American millionaire George Peabody (1795-1869) to help London's poor find decent accommodation. Regarded as the father of modern philanthropy, his legacy is not just the thousands of Peabody Trust residential properties in London and elsewhere in Britain, but dozens of other museums, schools, universities and libraries throughout America that benefitted from his donations. Look out for the small memorial garden.

Turpentine Lane is one of only a handful of streets or lanes in the whole area covered by this walk that retain their names from Pimlico's rural past. Cubitt cared little for tradition and often changed old names – for example, Willow Walk became today's Warwick Way, whilst today's Lupus Street follows the route of the old Cross Lane.

Before Cubitt, this part of Pimlico was dominated by the Chelsea Waterworks Company, and also a white lead factory and distillery. To the north were osier beds where willows were planted that could later be used for basket making and fish traps.

Return to Lupus Street and bear right into Churchill Gardens Road and through the Churchill Gardens estate mentioned earlier. Soon you will see a green space on your right. This stands approximately on the site of where a vast **❷ Distillery** was based

24

Churchill Estate

Narrow path

in the early 18th century. This was also the site of the Belgrave Dock in the late 19th century – another major part of London's infrastructure now lost and confined to the history books.

Immediately opposite the area of grass, head north up a narrow road (with playing pitches on your right). At the end turn left then right along a narrow path that leads you back onto Lupus Street. This street is named after Hugh Lupus, Earl of Chester (c.1047-1101). He came to England with William the Conqueror and was known as Hugh the Fat (in French, Hugh le Gros) or Hugh the Wolf (Lupus being Latin for wolf). The Grosvenors trace their family history back to Gilbert Grosvenor (le grosveneur – or master of the hunt), who was the nephew of Hugh Lupus.

Follow the map turning into Sutherland Street and bear right onto Gloucester Street. Continue along, passing the stucco-fronted houses so typical of Cubitt's Pimlico.

Turn left into Winchester Street to see the ㉕ **Holy Apostles Catholic Church** on the left. The first Catholic church in Pimlico was founded in 1917 in Claverton Street (passed earlier) but was destroyed by German bombing in 1941. The congregation spent a further 16 years trying to find the church a new permanent home, eventually coming here in 1957. The church was finally built, ironically, on a vacant World War II bomb site.

Pass the church, turning right into Sussex Street. After two blocks you cross Alderney Street. The GCHQ employee (since branded "spy") Gareth Williams (1978-2010) lived at number 36 on this street. On 23rd August 2010, it became a **26** **crime scene** when his body was found in unusual and suspicious circumstances. Following a week of absence from work, police visited Williams' flat and discovered his naked body, inside a travel bag, padlocked from the outside. The Metropolitan Police, MI6 and other British intelligence services, as well as the FBI, were involved in the investigation and the whole incident remains shrouded in mystery over a decade later. In 2015 there were allegations of Russian involvement and in 2021, new forensic evidence surfaced. The truth – at least publicly – may never be known.

Next up is Cambridge Street, **number 95** was the **27** **home of Jomo Kenyatta (1891-1978), first President of Kenya**, in the 1930s. During this period he was heavily involved in the anti-imperialist movement, meeting with Mahatma Ghandhi when he visited London. He was also put under surveillance by the security services. At one stage Kenyatta fell behind with his rent and made some money playing a tribal leader in the film *Sanders of the River (1935)*. This is how the future president became friends with the film's star, the American singer Paul Robeson. Kenyatta's four years at this address before his rise to power is now marked with a blue plaque.

Warwick Square

To your right is the **28** **Gothic-style St Gabriel's Church**. Dating from the early 1850s, it was funded by a grant of £5,000 from the Duke of Westminster and designed by Thomas Cundy Jr. (1790-1867), who was surveyor of the Grosvenor Estates for 41 years. Cundy also designed St Saviour's seen earlier, and many other buildings here and in Belgravia for Cubitt. Cundy's father (Thomas Snr.) also worked for the Grosvenor estate and was closely involved in the development of Bloomsbury and Belgravia.

The unusual building on the corner (beside the church, facing St George's Drive) is **29** **number 33 Warwick Square.** It dates from 1859 and was commissioned by Scottish painter James Rannie Swinton (1816-88) and is described as being the first in London to combine an artist's studio with a gallery and home. It was lavishly furnished, with a ballroom and domed glass ceiling. The legendary American dancer Isadora Duncan (1877-1927) had a studio inside.

Continue north, to reach **30** **Warwick Square** – one of the great but unfortunately private squares of Pimlico. It is the third of Cubitt's squares in Pimlico alongside St George's (already visited) and Ecclestone Square (seen shortly). Built on the site of a market garden, the square was laid out in 1843, and the houses bordering it were completed by the 1860s. The quality of the houses here meant it was known by some as South Belgravia, although that suggests wishful thinking on the part of certain residents envious of their more illustrious neighbours.

27

The west side of the Square, at number 12, is home to a charity named the **31 Rank Foundation**, which emerged from the film empire of James Arthur Rank (1888-1972). At its height in the mid-20th century it employed 31,000 people rivalling Hollywood studios. J. Arthur Rank was a major philanthropist, a commitment stemming from his strong Methodist beliefs. He used to walk around his garden each morning declaring 'I am in films because of the Holy Spirit'. It was profits from some of Britain's greatest films such as *Brief Encounter*, *The Red Shoes*, *Henry V*, *The Ipcress File* and *Carry on Dick* that funded the foundation's charitable work.

ECCLESTON
SQUARE SW1
CITY OF WESTMINSTER

32

Look out for coal-hole covers on the pavement. These were used from the mid-19th century to mid-20th century. The covers were removed when coal was dropped down into cellars underneath neighbouring houses. Clean air legislation in the 1950s largely killed off the domestic coal trade, but many people continue to 'spot' these distinctive designs produced by local companies. One enthusiast for these urban oddities is Labour politician Jeremy Corbyn.

34

33

Continue along St George's Drive to reach **32 Ecclestone Square** – the third of Cubitt's grand Pimlico squares. It is named after the village of Ecclestone, part of the Duke of Westminster's landholding in Cheshire. The village has a population of less than 300 people – far fewer than live here. The award-winning garden at the square's centre is unfortunately only for residents.

35

35

On the south side at number 34 is where ㉝ **Sir Winston Churchill** lived with his wife between 1909 and 1913. His first two children (Diana and Randolph) were born here. The Labour Party and Trades Union Congress were based on Ecclestone Square in the 1920s, and the famous General Strike of 1926 was planned here, amid the Georgian grandeur of Pimlico.

London is full of unusual institutions, one being found at number 9 – home to the ㉞ **Maltese religious order of the Franciscan Sisters of the Heart of Jesus**. Founded in Malta in 1877, the Sisters now have sites in locations worldwide; including Jerusalem, Italy, Brazil, Ethiopia and Pakistan. The President of Malta made an official visit to these premises in 2019.

Retrace your steps slightly and walk down Warwick Way, heading left into ㉟ **Ecclestone Square Mews**. Follow it down to see some of the charming Mews houses. Originally these were built to stable horses and provide accommodation for servants, normally located directly behind the grand houses that owned the mews. Exit along Warwick Place North back onto Warwick Way. The latter

follows the route of the old Willow Walk, an ancient track that ran alongside Pimlico farmland, long before Cubitt transformed the area.

At the end of Warwick Way head right along Belgrave Road, passing the north side of Warwick Square. On your left you'll shortly pass the ㊱ **Marquis of Westminster**, a great Victorian pub and a reminder of the Grosvenor family's influence on Pimlico. It is named after Hugh Grosvenor (1825-99), 1st Duke of Westminster, ironically a teetotaller and supporter of the temperance movement. He shut down nearly 40 pubs on his land in Mayfair. When he died the Duke was thought to be the richest person in Britain, a reputation his descendants have managed to live up to.

From here turn up Churton Street – full of upmarket shops, delis and bars – to reach Tachbrook Street. This lies on the route of the King's Scholars Pond Sewer that ran right through the land here and represented the last leg of the now lost Tyburn River (whose outflow point you visited earlier).

Follow right along the curve of the road and as you continue along Tachbrook Street, you'll find the ㊲ **Lillington and Longmoore Estate** to your left. Whilst the Grosvenor family were the main landowners in Pimlico, the area to the east came into the hands of Henry Wise (1653-1738), a royal gardener, in the late 17th century. He also owned land in Warwickshire, and many of the streets developed by Cubitt in Pimlico took their names from villages there (Tachbrook, Moreton, Lillington).

The area was increasingly run down during the first part of the 20th century and suffered considerable damage from German bombing during World War II. Around 400 houses and flats were later demolished to make way for the new estate. You will see the great contrast between the red brick estate on the left and Victorian houses on the right. The Lillington Gardens Estate was built in phases between 1964 and 1968, whilst the smaller Longmore Estate was completed by 1980.

Continue along Tachbrook Street, and turn left into Moreton Street, stopping at **38** **St James the Less**. Dating from 1861, this was described by Pevsner as 'one of the finest Gothic revival churches anywhere'. It was designed by George Edmund Street (1824-1881), a prominent figure in the Victorian Gothic Revival movement and best known for the Royal Courts of Justice on the Strand. Today the church is notable for being the only Victorian building in this part of Pimlico to survive the war.

The post-war years must have been difficult for many residents of Pimlico, with houses destroyed and ongoing food, clothing and fuel shortages. This inspired the famous Ealing comedy *Passport to Pimlico*

(1949), starring Stanley Holloway and Margaret Rutherford. In the film, set just after the war, a German bomb explodes uncovering a cellar with a medieval charter revealing Pimlico to be legally part of Burgundy. Residents declare independence and so avoid rationing and other British privations. The authorities eventually force the 'Bergundians' to lay aside their claim, but not before many comic episodes take place. Ironically, some scenes were filmed in Lambeth.

The origin of the name Pimlico is obscure. It may be connected to Ben Pimlico, a 16th-century brewer and publican in Hoxton or (more romantically) to the Pamlico tribe of America whose timber might have been brought to a wharf nearby during the 17th century. The first use of the name was recorded in 1626.

Retrace your steps and continue down Tachbrook Street and take time to enjoy the market that has been here for many years and still boasts a fishmonger, fresh fruit and veg, as well as the more common street food traders. The walk concludes back at Pimlico underground station which only opened in 1972, and stands approximately where the ancient White's Bridge ran across King's Scholars Pond. ●

VISIT...

St Saviours Church (see p.11)
St. George's Square, SW1V 3QW
www.stsp.org.uk

Tate Britain
Millbank, SW1P 4RG
www.tate.org.uk

Pimlico Gardens (see p.15)
SW1V 3QP

James the Less Church (see p.31)
4 Moreton Street, Pimlico,
SW1V 2PS
www.sjtl.org

EAT / DRINK...

Tachbrook Street Market
(see p.32)
42 Tachbrook Street, SW1V 2JS

Morpeth Arms
58 Millbank, SW1P 4RW
www.morpetharms.com

Tachbrook Street Market

Greek Orthodox Cathedral of St Andrew

2 Kentish Town Walk

Hampstead
Heath

Gospel Oak

Tufnell Park   TUFNEL

38

37

36   LADY SOMERSET ROAD

39

40   RAVELEY ST

OSPRINGE ROA

FORTESS ROAD

COUNTESS ROAD

35

34

33   31

32   42

30   41

43

29

28

LEIGHTON ROAD

Kentish Town

27

1

2

ISLIP STREET

22

CAVERSHAM ROAD

GRAFTON ROAD

25   3

GALSFORD STREET

21

19   20

24

5   4

KENTISH TOWN ROAD

Kentish Town West

18   17

6

7

PATSHULL ROAD

Talacre
Gardens

MARSDEN ST

23

LAWFORD ROAD

PRINCE OF WALES ROAD

8

PRINCE OF WALES RD

9

16

ROCHESTER RD

15

CASTLE RD

ROCHESTER PL

HARMOOD STREET

CASTLEHAVEN RD

14

13   12   WILMOT PL

ROYAL COLLEGE STREET

HARTLAND ROAD

KENTISH TOWN ROAD

HAWLEY RD

11

IVOR ST

CHALK FARM ROAD

10

Camden Road

MALDEN ROAD

Kentish Town

1. Kentish Town Station
2. The Oxford Tavern
3. Gaisford Street
4. Patshull Road
5. Blustons
6. Owl Bookshop
7. Former Palace Cinema
8. The Abbey Tavern
9. Greek Orthodox Cathedral of St Andrew
10. Castle's Traditional Pie & Mash shop
11. The Old Eagle
12. Reed's Place
13. Creation Studios
14. Disused tube station
15. Castle Road
16. Kelly Street
17. Former Public Baths
18. The Grafton
19. Perren Street
20. No 23 Ryland Road
21. Brinsmead Piano Factory
22. The College Francais Bilingue de Londres
23. Hope Chapel
24. Plaque to 'Boris the Cat'
25. Rio's 'Relaxation Spa'
26. Old Dairy Mews
27. Former Electric Alhambra
28. Assembly House
29. Saint Espresso & Kitchen
30. Kentish Delight kebab shop
31. Former public toilet
32. The Bull & Gate
33. The Forum
34. Former Tally Ho
35. The Maple Building
36. College Lane
37. Little Green Street
38. Fleet River water pipe
39. Plaque to Kwame Nkrumah
40. Junction Tavern
41. Piano Works Apartments
42. The Pineapple
43. Falkland Place

Kentish Town Walk
Start/ Finish: Kentish Town Station
Distance: 3 miles

The walk begins from ❶ **Kentish Town Station**. As you step out onto Kentish Town Road look back at the distinctive oxblood tiled frontage of the building. The station dates from 1907 and the façade is typical of the work of Leslie Green (1875-1908). The prolific underground station designer and architect worked himself into an early grave but dozens of underground stations remain as a testament to his skill. Leave the station and head left (southwards) down Kentish Town Road.

For many centuries Kentish Town was a small hamlet outside London that grew up in the shadow of St Pancras Church nearby. The church was damaged by flooding from the Fleet River, and so a chapel of ease was built near here in the 13th century for local worshippers. A few cottages, and later inns, sprung up, alongside the bank of the famous Fleet River. The river once dominated the landscape but gradually the pressure of urbanisation forced it underground. The origin of the district's name is most probably linked to the river, a corruption of the old English words 'Ken-ditch' meaning 'bed of a waterway'.

As you walk along Kentish Town Road you will soon realise Kentish Town is a busy place – one that has been considerably gentrified in recent years, but which retains a fair amount of its traditional character. There are a mix of mediocre 20th century buildings sitting beside much grander Victorian architecture – an example of the latter being ❷ **The Oxford Tavern**, found just a short way down on the left by Islip Street. In the 17th and 18th centuries wealthy people began to build country houses in the area, then surrounded by hay fields and farms, with the River Fleet running right through the middle. Beside the pub is Islip Road,

where – on 4 July 1937 – around 6,000 fascists assembled under the leadership of Oswald Mosley. Many locals protested against the march and several arrests were made. The British Union of Fascists eventually made their way to Trafalgar Square.

The River Fleet starts in two places, one on Hampstead Heath, the other in Highgate. Long ago built over, the two tributaries of the Fleet converge just to the north of here and continue underground right under the feet of Londoners before emptying into the Thames at Blackfriars. It is hard to imagine in the modern age how important it was for Londoners of the past to be near to water as it was used for drinking, washing, disposing of waste, the transportation of goods and the powering of industries. Sadly, there is little to remind visitors to Kentish Town of the underground river, but you will see some evidence of the Fleet along this walk.

Continue along Kentish Town Road, which just like many other British shopping streets is dominated by tattoo parlours, charity shops and tanning salons nestling beside more upmarket cafés and delis. In the past, there was a pub on most street corners but in recent years many have closed.

On the left, you pass ❸ **Gaisford Street**, named after Thomas Gaisford (1779-1855), Dean of Christ Church, Oxford. The College was a major landowner in the area for a considerable time and many streets such as Busby Place, Caversham Road, Islip Street, and Wolsey Mews are named after places or people connected to

the College. The College was bequeathed the estate by clergyman Robert South, and from the 18th century developed its lands for residential and commercial purposes, transforming the rural landscape. The college sold the estate in 1955, and these days the only reminders of Oxford's influence on Kentish Town are the Oxford pub, street names and an archive kept by Christ Church, Oxford. Later on in the walk you will see part of Kentish Town owned by a Cambridge college.

Continue down Kentish Town Road, passing ❹ **Patshull Road**. The road was built on land owned by the Earls of Dartmouth and is named after Patshull Hall near Wolverhampton, acquired by the family in the mid-19th century. Some of the most expensive properties in Kentish Town are found here, and the general area has recently attracted famous names including actor Charles Dance and journalist Jon Snow.

On the right, look out for ❺ **Blustons** (opposite Patshull Road), a local institution with period signage that opened in the 1930s selling clothes. Now occupied by a charity, it is an example of how old frontages can be retained.

A few doors down on the right is the excellent ❻ **Owl Bookshop** which is always worth a browse. Immediately past Tesco Express, there is another reminder (number 197) of the golden age of the cinema as this innocuous building was once home to ❼ **The Palace** that opened in 1913.

After a short walk, you pass ❽ **The Abbey Tavern** on the left. A pub since the 1860s, it is just one of the many Victorian boozers for which Kentish Town is known. In 1824 Mary Shelley, author of Frankenstein and wife of the poet Percy Shelley, moved into Bartholomew Place, which stood very near here. Unfortunately, Kentish Town has found it hard to shrug off her description of the place as an 'odious swamp', even though it still had open fields and orchards nearby at the time of her residency.

Shortly you will find **❾ the Greek Orthodox Cathedral of St Andrew**. The building originated in 1885 as an Anglican church dedicated to St Barnabas and was later converted in 1957 for use by the Greek community. Inside you will find one of the most beautiful and dramatic interiors of any church in London.

Continue down Kentish Town Road, bearing left and following the map for a short excursion over the border into the Republic of Camden. Continue along Royal College Street to see **❿ Castle's Traditional Pie and Mash shop** – don't forget to buy some jellied eels. This is a rare reminder of a long past age when Londoners flocked to such places. Retrace your steps, passing **⓫ The Old Eagle** – a lovely Camden pub that has not changed in decades and is worth a stop for a pint before you go on.

Shortly on the right, passing the Garden Centre ghost sign, walk up **⓬ Reed's Place** – a quiet, pretty road of old 19th-century cottages that is the first of many tranquil spots you will visit on this walk.

Return to the junction, with **⓭ Creation Studios** down below occupying what was originally a toilet. On the other side are what you will recognise as the oxblood tiles of a **⓮ tube station**, except this has long stopped being used for that purpose. It began as South Kentish Town station when it opened in 1907 and was yet another design of Leslie Green. However, the station was never popular and it closed just 17 years later and is currently a branch of Cash Converters.

The station featured in a 1951 short story by Sir John Betjeman named 'South Kentish Town' which centres on an 'income tax official' named Basil Green who, taking the tube home, accidentally gets out at the deserted ghost station when the driver stops here and opens the doors to check a fault on the line. The hapless Basil is left stranded here and Betjeman's story begins with the opening line 'This is a story about a very unimportant station on the underground railway in London'.

Stop at the entrance to ⓯ **Castle Road**. When Kentish Town was still a rural idyll, the Castle Inn stood here, which is said to date back to the reign of King John. It is long gone, having been demolished in 1849, but many of the surrounding roads lie on the former gardens of the famous old inn. It is said Lord Nelson lived at the inn for a while. Between 1775 and 1800 the population of the local St Pancras parish jumped from 600 to 32,000, evidence of the huge urbanisation that was taking place at that time.

Continue north, turning left onto ⓰ **Kelly Street**. Kelly Street and nearby Castlehaven Road date from the 1850s, the decade that saw the Fleet River and many ponds along its route covered over. The arrival of the railways from the 1860s saw the area decline in social standing, becoming more working class as wealthier residents moved elsewhere.

New industries moved here too. Kentish Town became famous for its piano manufacturers but was also home to makers of false teeth, metal workers, furniture manufacturers and many other trades. These industries thrived until the 1920s after which time the area began a slow, steady decline, only reversed in recent years.

Look out for Mario's Café on the right, a local institution immortalised in the 1993 song 'Mario's Cafe' by London group Saint Etienne ('Rainy café, Kentish Town, Tuesday, /Joking around, still digging that sound'). Originally called Church Street, it was re-named after local housing developer John Kelly in 1870. Walk a

16

17

18

19

hundred yards or so to see the pretty pastel-coloured houses which were originally home to the many workers in the local piano factories. No one knows why residents began to make such an effort to paint their houses this way, but it seems to have started in the 1960s.

Kelly Street with its charming houses is typical of the gentrification that has transformed many parts of Kentish Town. In the late 1990s houses sold here for under £100,000, whereas in recent years they are more likely to sell for ten times that amount. This is a far cry from when the social reformer Charles Booth visited the street in the Victorian Age, describing it as the area's 'worst street for immorality'.

At the end of Kelly Street turn right into Castlehaven Road, heading north to reach Prince of Wales Road. Directly opposite are the huge ⓱ **former public baths** that were opened in 1900. They were part of a drive by the authorities in the Victorian and Edwardian age to provide amenities for ordinary people who often had no running water or bathroom at home. Today it is a sports centre. In the 1970s the area to the west of here (around Talacre Gardens) was an important place within London's squatting scene. The since demolished Prince of Wales Crescent was once a squat, former occupants included the innovative film-makers John 'Hoppy' Hopkins and Sue Hall and future pop star Boy George. It was a creative, bohemian scene that has now disappeared.

Cross over and just to the left, walk a short way down Grafton Road, looking out for the old sign for 'Public Washhouse' and 'Ladies Baths', as well as '1st Class men' and '2nd Class Men'. Not only were men and women separated, but there were first and second class entrances that demonstrated the class distinctions of the time. Back on the corner is another great local Victorian pub, ⓲ **The Grafton**. It has a lovely roof terrace and is worth a visit even just to get a better view of the former baths.

Pass the pub, heading down Prince of Wales Road and then turn right onto Ryland Road. A short way up on the left is ⓳ **Perren Street**. At the end is a building that is a relic of Kentish Town's industrial past. This was once home to the Imperial Works where pianos and organs were manufactured.

Continue up Ryland Road. A few properties on this road still have World War II Anderson Shelters now repurposed as garden sheds. The novelist Fay Weldon (b.1931) used to live at ㉑ **number 23 Ryland Road** in the 1980s. The north end of the Road is dominated by another late 19th century, red-brick building which originally served as the ㉑ **Brinsmead Piano Factory**. John Brinsmead & Sons ceased manufacture in 1919, but the luxury flats that now occupy the site still bear the Brinsmead name.

Head left up Grafton Road – stopping on Wilkin Street on the left to get another view of the old piano factory.

Piano factory from the back

Follow the map onto Holme Road, past the now closed George IV Pub, to reach ㉒ **The College Francais Bilingue de Londres** on your right. This French school opened in 2011 to cater for the explosion of demand from London's then-growing French community, many working in the financial services sector of the City. It is housed in an old school that dates from 1874, significant as it was one of the schools built following the ground-breaking Education Act of 1870. This act established State-funded education for ordinary people.

Turn left down Willes Road and walk for a few minutes (crossing over Inkerman Road) to reach the old public baths seen earlier. Many of these surrounding streets were laid out after the Crimean War, when the developers hoped to appeal to people's sense of patriotism. The Battle of Inkerman took place in 1854 and Willes is named after a General who fought in the Crimea.

23

24

26

former Jolly Angler

Opposite is the striking ❷❸ **Hope Chapel** which dates from the 1870s and is home today to the Church of Christ. The modest, plain interior is worth a visit if open.

Take the road immediately on the left to walk along Anglers Lane. This is just one of several local streets whose names are a reminder of the age when the Fleet River flowed above ground. On the right are more large-scale buildings once used for industrial production and – inevitably – converted into apartments and studios.

Just by the junction with Raglan Street (named after another Crimean military General), at number 24 Anglers Lane, see if you can spot ❷❹ **a strange memorial plaque** which reads 'Boris the cat lived here 1986-1996'. Apparently, Boris used to sit by the wall and had a fierce temper. No ordinary London cat in recent times has such a public memorial – so he must have been quite a character.

Continue on to re-join busy Kentish Town Road. On the right at the junction is a branch of Nandos, housed in what was once a great pub called the Jolly Anglers. It retains some of its original pub features including the tiling and elaborate lettering for Reid's Brewery, a bygone producer of beer.

Carry on passing at number 239 ❷❺ **Rio's 'Relaxation Spa'** – a remnant from this part of London's sleazier past, when there were many more massage parlours in this area and Camden, most of which have disappeared in the gentrification of the last 20 years. The hidden delights of Rio's features in Suzanne Portnoy's popular erotic memoir *The Butcher, The Baker, The Candlestick Maker* (2006).

A little further on the left you pass ❷❻ **Old Dairy Mews**, once home to a milk depot, and before that the Vicarage Farm Dairy – another sign that Kentish Town was once a rural idyl.

Soon you pass a branch of Iceland that retains part of the façade of an old cinema: the ❷❼ **Electric Alhambra**. It opened in 1911, at the very beginning of the age of cinema. In those days many locals were poor and crowded the cinemas, not only to enjoy the new and revolutionary form of entertainment, but because they provided a warm place to spend a few hours on a winter's day.

Continue to walk back up Kentish Town Road, going north until you pass ㉘ **the Assembly House**. An old inn stood here, where travellers would assemble before heading further out of London – many hoping for safety in numbers as a protection against highwaymen. In 1850 one traveller described it as 'The old Assembly House of very long standing was held in great repute, being a pleasant distance from London, when those who sought a Country Walk could meet there with every enjoyment a Country Inn could supply'. The current building is a late 19th-century construction on the same site as the original.

Just up on the right, at number 296, is ㉙ **Saint Espresso & Kitchen**. The basement here has old cells from the former Police station, where in the past drunks would be kept until they sobered up. Legend has it that the Fleet River used to flood the floor of the cells – something that presumably helped sober up the inhabitants.

Just past here on the left at number 381 is ㉚ **the Kentish Delight** kebab shop. Surprisingly, it featured in Taylor Swift's video for her song *End Game*, released in early 2018.

At the junction, look out for another ㉛ **former public toilet** that has been converted – in this case into a cool underground bar. Bear left onto Highgate Road, and just a short way along is another great Kentish Town boozer ㉜ **the Bull &Gate** (which also features in Swift's video). This is also where Coldplay played when they were still largely

unknown. A review of the gig in NME helped launch a career that has made them global superstars. Further along is ㉝ **The Forum**, one of London's most famous music venues. This Art Deco beauty was originally a cinema when first opened in 1934.

Opposite the Forum is the site of the ㉞ **former Tally Ho pub**, recently demolished to make way for the modern 'Tally Ho Apartments'. The pub that stood here is credited as the birthplace of the 'pub rock' movement that began in the early 70s. Bands such as Ian Dury's Kilburn and the High Roads, Eddie and the Hot Rods, Nick Lowe and Dr Feelgood gained a loyal following here, helping provide an alternative to Prog Rock and performing with an energy that would inspire Punk.

Continue along Highgate Road, broadly following the route of one branch of the Fleet River. On the left is ㉟ **The Maple Building**. Maple & Co was once a leading furniture maker with retail premises on Tottenham Court Road. The company's expensive, hand-crafted wooden furniture fell out of fashion after World War II and the building has in recent times been converted into flats and offices.

Now head right onto Lady Somerset Road, and almost immediately walk left up the narrow ㊱ **College Lane** – perhaps one of the most unexpected thoroughfares in North London.

This tiny lane contains many of the oldest buildings in Kentish Town and dates from the 1780s. By numbers 13 and 14 is a plaque commemorating the fallen of World War I, said to be the only memorial of its kind to be found on a residential house in London. It remembers ten local men who died in Flanders and Northern France, although it is almost illegible today. One man, Lieutenant-Sergeant Alfred Stanton, died from his wounds at the end of the war in October 1918.

Keep going, and soon you will reach on the left ㊲ **Little Green Street**. This charming, narrow lane also contains houses from the late 18th century, a rare example of such a complete Georgian terrace in London. It has a peculiar claim to fame as The Kinks filmed an early promotional film for their song *Dead End Street* here in 1966. The band dressed up as undertakers and Ray Davies later recalled how the BBC disliked the early video thinking it was in bad

taste. Just to the north of here was Highgate Road Station that closed in the early 20th century.

Now head away from Little Green Street (turning right) through the Ingestre housing estate and along Ingestre Road. On the left, behind railing, is a railway line. Continue along until you reach a pedestrian bridge going over the railway line (a sign for the Ingestre Estate should be to your rear). If you walk up the steps and carefully look over to the left, you should see an ugly pipe at ground level. This contains the famous **❸ Fleet River** and takes it southwards. Local kids who would go on to form the pop group Madness used to hang around near here breaking into freight trains.

Go back along the bridge and bear right, still walking along Ingestre Road to join Burghley Road – named after William Cecil, 1st Baron Burghley (1520-98). For four decades he served as the closest adviser to Queen Elizabeth I and attended St John's College, Cambridge. St John's owned an estate around here and named many streets after distinguished people associated with the college. You turn right now, passing number 60 where there is a **❸ blue plaque that remembers Kwame Nkrumah** (1909-72), first President of Ghana. He lived here in the 1940s and was a prominent figure in the campaign for Ghana's independence from British rule.

Continue along, and soon you meet Lady Somerset Road. Turn left to walk uphill to reach Fortess Road, named after Fortys or

Fortess Field, a nearby meadow. **40 The Junction Tavern** on the corner is yet another imposing Victorian pub, dating from 1885.

Turn right onto Fortess Road, walking back towards the heart of Kentish Town. Look out for the Ford Maddox Brown plaque at number 58. On your left walk down Fortess Grove, a narrow street with pretty houses and yet another old piano factory on the corner. In 1901 the Piano Journal described Kentish Town as: '...that healthful suburb dear to the heart of the piano maker'.

Retrace your steps to Fortess Road, passing the **41 Piano Works Apartments** on your left, located on the site of a former piano factory. T. & G. Payne came here in 1899, and their pianos won a prestigious gold medal at the Glasgow Exhibition in 1904.

Shortly you reach Falkland Road on your left and walk up this street, well-known for its pretty multi-coloured houses. Turn left on Leverton Street where you can find **42 The Pineapple** – one of the best pubs in London. It is a great place to rest and treat yourself near the end of this walk.

When finished, retrace your steps but when on Falkland Road, turn left down narrow ⑬ **Falkland Place**. This also featured in the Taylor Swift video mentioned before and is a picturesque place. It is named after Lucius Carey, 2nd Viscount Falkland (1610-1643) who studied at St John's College, Cambridge. Cary's title refers to Falkland in Scotland. He was an author and politician, whose brilliant career was cut short when, aged just 33, he died fighting for Charles I at the Battle of Newbury. It also serves as another reminder of the landholdings of St John's College in Kentish Town. The colleges of Oxford and Cambridge today hold billions of pounds of property in London and elsewhere, much of it bequeathed by former students in past centuries.

At the bottom of Falkland Place turn right onto Leighton Road and then at the end you arrive at Kentish Town Road. Turn left, returning to the station where this walk ends. ●

VISIT...

Greek Orthodox Cathedral of St. Andrew (see p.43)
124 Kentish Town Road,
NW1 9QB

EAT / DRINK...

Castles Traditional Pie and Mash Shop (see p.43)
229 Royal College Street,
NW1 9LT

The Pineapple (see p.57)
51 Leverton Street, NW5 1AG
www.thepineapplepubnw5.com

The Junction Tavern (see p.57)
101 Fortess Road, NW5 1AG

Knowhere Special
The Basement, 296 Kentish Town
Road, NW5 2TG
www.knowherespecial.co.uk

The Old Eagle Pub (see p.43)
251 Royal College Street,
NW1 9LU

SHOP...

Owl Bookshop (see p.41)
207-9 Kentish Town Road,
NW5 2JU
www.owlbookshop.co.uk

London College of Fashion, see p 79.

FASHION

3 Oxford Street Walk

Oxford Street

1. Marble Arch
2. Tyburn Roundel
3. The Cumberland Hotel
4. The Annunciation Marble Arch
5. Old Quebec Street
6. Marks & Spencer
7. Orchard Street
8. Portman Square
9. Selfridges
10. Henry Holland
11. The Lamb & Flag

12. Gee's Court
13. Stratford Place
14. Stratford House
15. London Kabbalah Centre
16. Plaque to Martin Van Buren
17. Marylebone Lane
18. John Lewis
19. Holles Street
20. Cavendish Square
21. Barbara Hepworth Sculpture
22. London College of Fashion

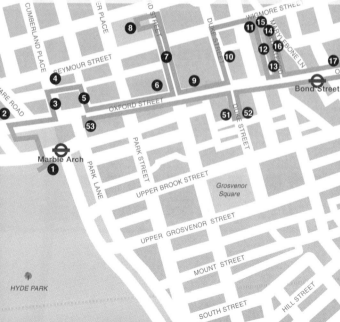

23 Oxford Circus
24 Former Peter Robinson Store
25 AIR Studio
26 200 Oxford Street
27 Market Place
28 Thomas de Quincey
29 Princess's Theatre
30 Adam and Eve Court
31 Plaque to William Coleridge
32 100 Club
33 Bradley's Spanish Bar
34 Odeon (former UFO Club)
35 Horse Shoe Brewery
36 Site of Gallows
37 Flying Horse
38 Oxford Music Hall

39 Soho Square Murder
40 Radha-Krishna Temple
41 Plaque to William Blake
42 Plaque to Percy Shelley
43 Marquee Club
44 Marks & Spencer (Pantheon)
45 219 Oxford Street
46 Oxford Circus LU
47 Regent Hall
48 Hanover Square
49 Former HMV
50 South Molten Street
51 Brown Hart Gardens
52 Ukrainian Catholic Cathedral
53 Former Sitar Shop

Oxford Street

Start/Finish: Marble Arch
Distance: 3.75 miles

The walk begins by Marble Arch station, at the western end of Oxford Street. Many people would rather visit the dentist than spend more time on Oxford Street than is strictly necessary. As well as being the busiest shopping street in Europe, it has been described as the most polluted street in the world. Historically, it's been plagued by street crime and cyclists are killed by vehicles far too often. Visitors have to navigate half a million daily visitors, nearly all looking to shop in around 300 shops. But the street contains some remarkable history, so – brace yourself – you may be one of the very few people here for a reason other than shopping.

Use the pedestrian crossing to visit ❶ **Marble Arch** itself. The arch was designed by John Nash (1752-1835), the architect who arguably did more than any other to shape the development of Regency London. It is constructed of white Carrara marble and is thought to have been influenced by the Arch of Constantine in Rome.

It originally stood at the entrance to Buckingham Palace from 1827, however as the palace was rebuilt and expanded in later years, the arch was moved to another location in 1851 and only came here in the 1960s. It is now rather sadly marooned on this busy traffic

island. Traditionally, only members of the Royal family, the King's Troop and the Royal Horse Artillery are allowed to travel through the arch but nowadays the gates are open to all. It contains three small rooms that were for many years used by the police. Look closely and you can see tiny doorways on the outside.

Look out for the superb details on the gates – often missed by passersby. Marble Arch stands at what was once the junction of two great Roman roads. Watling Street headed north (the route of Edgware Road)

to St Albans, whilst Colchester Road headed to the West Country. A mysterious ancient stone – possibly dating from Roman times – and known as Oswald's Stone, was propped against Marble Arch until it was stolen in 1869.

To the right of the Marble Arch was the largest free-standing bronze sculpture in London – *Still Water* by Nic Fiddian-Green. The graceful form of a horse's head pausing to drink water provided a moment of calm in amongst the chaos of Oxford Street.

It was moved in 2020 to accommodate the Marble Arch Mound, an initiative after lockdown to bring tourism back to Oxford Street. The installation of the mound was met with public ridicule after £6 million were spent on the 25-metre high artificial hill. The *Still Water* sculpture can now be found a short walk away at Achilles Way.

Cross back over and follow the map down Bayswater Road to see a ❷ **roundel** on the pavement by the road junction that marks the site of Tyburn Tree. This was the main execution site in London from the late 12th century until 1783, and by some estimates, 50-60,000 people were brutally executed here. Many were dragged to this spot from Newgate Prison, the route lined by drunken, baying Londoners eagerly waiting to see the execution. After the execution, many would try to touch the corpse for luck, the hangman later selling the executed prisoner's clothes and the noose.

The name of the gallows came from the Tyburn village that once stood here, itself named after the Tyburn brook. A tributary of the River Westbourne, one of London's many 'lost' rivers that have been forced underground. The Westbourne – now largely contained in underground pipes – starts in Hampstead, emptying into the Thames by Chelsea.

Before walking down Oxford Street, walk up a short way to the grand 1930s façade of The Hard Rock Hotel – formerly ❸ **The Cumberland Hotel** on Great Cumberland Place. Jimi Hendrix was a regular in the last years of his eventful life. He checked into a suite here on September 6, 1970, paying £17 a night, just a week after playing a famous set at the Isle of Wight festival. He died just a few days later in a hotel in Notting Hill, but the Cumberland was listed as his residence on the death certificate.

The BBC recorded his final radio session in his suite (room 507) just before his death, it being broadcast for Radio One's *Scene and Heard*. Other stars who have stayed here include Bob Dylan, Diana Ross and Buddy Holly.

Just a little further north, up Great Cumberland Place (not visited but at number 51) is where pop star Madonna lived in recent years. In 2008, the council's noise team turned up after neighbour's complained about noise from an after-gig party being held there. The *Daily Mail* reported George Michael and Stella McCartney to be among the guests. Less fun was had in 2011 when a 'delusional fan' broke into her home causing the star great distress, which she described at the intruder's subsequent trial.

Cumberland Place was laid out in the 1770s and named after the Duke of Cumberland (1721-90), son of George II. He became known as the Butcher of Culloden after his victory in 1746 over the Jacobite army of Bonnie Prince Charlie.

Just after the hotel turn right on Bryanston Street to stop at a dramatic looking church called **❹ The Annunciation Marble Arch**. This is the first of many striking buildings dotted along or near to Oxford Street and rarely noticed by shoppers.

The first church was built here in 1787 and named the Quebec Chapel, probably to honour General Wolfe's capture of Quebec a few years earlier. The current building dates from just before World War I, and on the day of its dedication in June 1914, the ceremony overseen by the Bishop of London was apparently a tense one.

The church authorities feared suffragettes were planning to disrupt the ceremony and a report at the time read: 'The talk of the crowd... was to the effect that it was feared that some of the "wild women" might make a "scene" or a "succession of scenes" that even the outward and visible grandeur of the worthy Head of the Church in London might not avail to quench the ardour of perverse and unruly females, married, or otherwise'.

If you are lucky enough to be here when the church is open, do make the effort to visit the magnificent interior (open Mon-Fri and Sun 11am- 3pm).

Pass the church and turn right up **5 Old Quebec Street** – typical of many owned by the Portman Estate. The estate is one of London's great private landowning dynasties. In the capital alone they control 110 acres of some of the most expensive real estate in the world. You will read more about the history of the Portman Estate shortly.

When you reach Oxford Street again turn left and stay on that the north side (you will visit the south side later). Oxford Street stands on the route of an ancient Roman road and has had many names over the centuries including 'the way to Uxbridge', 'the Road to Oxford' and 'Tyburn Way'. In the first few decades of the 18th century it become widely known as Oxford Street, probably because it led to Oxford, but perhaps due to the fact that the land on the north side was purchased in 1713 by the 2nd Earl of Oxford.

In the 18th century this was not a shopping utopia (or hell), but a far less salubrious area, particularly on account of the prostitutes and criminals who were attracted by the Tyburn gallows. Thomas Pennant, the 18th-century traveller, described the area as 'a deep hollow road and full of sloughs; with here and there a ragged house, the lurking place of cut-throats'. The double gated Tyburn Turnpike was then situated near here, controlling traffic and charging travellers.

Cross Portman Street. The land around here was originally owned by the Knights of St. John of Jerusalem, and later leased to Sir William Portman in the 1530s. His descendants oversaw the development of the area in the 18th century, part of London's gradual spread westwards at the time. The grand centre piece is Portman Square, to the north of here, that was laid out in the 1760s.

Today the Portman Estate is a trust that benefits around 130 people within an extended family group, and is currently headed by billionaire Christopher Edward Berkeley Portman, 10th Viscount Portman (b.1958). Notable buildings within the Estate include Selfridges on Oxford Street (seen shortly).

This part of London is owned by several great estates founded by some of England's great aristocratic families. On this walk you pass near three: the Portman Estate, The Howard de Walden Estate (which own much of the land to the north of Oxford Street) and the Grosvenor Estate, whose holdings extend from the south side. Many of the streets and squares you pass today are named after these aristocratic families, their various titles and other properties in London and elsewhere.

Soon you reach two of the great flagship stores that transformed Oxford Street in the late 19th century from a relative backwater to London's greatest shopping district. The first ❻ **Marks & Spencer** traces its history back to 1884 when it was founded in Leeds by a Russian born refugee named Michael Marks who founded a humble Penny Bazaar. He was joined in the business by Thomas Spencer, and the company went from strength to strength. The Marble Arch branch opened in 1930 and if you look up you can see the Art Deco style of 'M' and 'S' intertwined.

After M&S is the curiously named ❼ **Orchard Street**. It is named after Orchard Portman, a village of 150 people in Somerset, that was once owned by the Portman Estate. Sir William Portman, who bought the lease to the estate in the 1530s, came from the village.

Walk up Orchard Street, after a few minutes reaching ❽ **Portman Square** – the centrepiece of the private Portman Estate. The main office of the estate lies at number 40 on the south side. Sadly, like many squares in London you cannot enter the garden at the centre unless you are a resident.

8 *Portman Square*

Return to Oxford Street to reach arguably the greatest department store ever to open in Britain – the monumental ❾ **Selfridges**. Opened in 1909, it revolutionised British retailing. Founder, Harry Gordon Selfridge (1858-1947), learnt the art of retailing in America. Realising Brits were better at making things than selling them, he decided to invest his fortune in a vast new shopping emporium on what was already the city's busiest shopping street. Large crowds came from the very start, the owner possessing a genius for promotion.

So much has happened at Selfridges over the years that books have been written about the store. A popular television series *Mr Selfridge* ran for four series from 2013, and its 40 episodes only covered 20 years from 1908, focussing on Harry Gordon Selfridge's love affairs, and the extraordinary highs and lows of his career.

Some of the more fascinating things that have taken place here include the use of secret equipment in the basement to scramble telephone conversations between Roosevelt and Churchill during World War II – conversations that changed the direction of world history. John Lennon and Yoko Ono visited the store in July 1971 so that Yoko could sign copies of her book *Grapefruit*, the event attracting widespread publicity and large crowds. Selfridges also boasted the seismograph that recorded earthquakes around the world during the 1930s and 40s. Mr Selfridge was a great publicist who in 1909 put on display Louis Blériot's monoplane after the Frenchman famously flew across the Channel. The department store also gave the first public demonstration of John Logie Baird's 'shadowgraphs' in 1925, that was the precursor to television.

Oxford Street – and Selfridges in particular – fascinated maverick punk pioneer Malcolm McLaren (1946-2010), perhaps best remembered as the manager of the Sex Pistols. In the late 60s, he was an art student and member of a radical group aligned to the Situationist movement which undertook provocative acts to encourage social change. McLaren and the group came to Selfridges in 1968 to cause chaos. McLaren, dressed as Santa Claus, handed out the store's toys to kids whilst leaflets were given out proclaiming 'Christmas: it was meant to be great but it's horrible'. McLaren

would later recall 'on Oxford Street I saw that modern life had been reduced to the spectacle of a commodity. Oxford Street has always seemed to me to be a strange paradise of joy'.

The event influenced McLaren's life, and he used provocation to further the careers of his bands such as the Sex Pistols and Bow Wow Wow. He even made a film titled *The Ghosts of Oxford Street* (1991) that explored the darker side of this area, including the myth that a street of ghostly shops lies underneath the road, the stories of prostitutes who once sold

themselves to passersby and the spirits of those killed on Tyburn Tree. McClaren also revealed that his mother was a lover of a former owner of Selfridges.

Walk up Duke Street to the corner with Barrett Street, where the ❿ **Henry Holland pub** stands. The Red Lion pub stood here from the late 18th century until it was destroyed by a V2 rocket at this junction on 6 December 1944. The explosion killed 18 people in the street and others in the canteen at Selfridges. It was one of many terrible attacks inflicted on Oxford Street and the surrounding area during World War II. The worst was probably on 17-18 September 1940 when dozens of shops were badly damaged and four of the biggest department stores – including Selfridges and John Lewis – were set ablaze. It is said H. Gordon Selfridge cried when he saw the damage, which included a window in the store that had been signed by famous visitors over previous decades.

Continue down Barrett Street to reach James Street, full of nice restaurants, bars and boutiques. On one corner is a great old London boozer – ⓫ **the Lamb & Flag** – which is a good place to enjoy a pint. A pub has stood here since 1777 and the current building dates from 1890 and was once a place favoured by anarchists for their meetings.

Enter **St Christopher's Place**, one of the most charming quarters you will visit during the walk. It used to be a terrible slum and was later redeveloped for social housing by the founder of the National Trust, Octavia Hill. In the late 1960s, it was still run-down but was transformed into what you see today by a property developer named Robert Spiro.

Turn right down the increasingly narrow ⓬ **Gee's Court** before exiting the tiny entrance back onto Oxford Street.

Continue along, turning up ⓭ **Stratford Place**. This is another reminder of the area's cosmopolitan flavour, given it is home to the High Commissions of Tanzania and Botswana. Walk up to the end to see ⓮ **Stratford House**, built in the 1770s for Edward Stratford, 2nd Earl of Aldborough.

It is a magnificent example of a Regency period house in London, tucked away from the fumes of Oxford Street. It once belonged to a son of Tsar Nicholas I of Russia, and today is home to the Oriental Club.

The club was founded in 1824 by the Duke of Wellington – its first and only President – and other notable figures with connections to India and the East. The founders described its purpose to attract 'noblemen and gentlemen associated with the administration of our Eastern empire...'. The club is a legacy of the days when Britain ruled India and other large parts of the world, and still remains very much part of the 'Establishment'. Before Stratford House was built, a bridge over Tyburn Brook stood near here.

Stratford Place is also the site of the ⓯ **London Kabbalah Centre**, whose reported regulars in recent years have included Gwyneth Paltrow and Madonna. In 2015, the Evening Standard reported how 36-hour chanting sessions were causing tensions with neighbours. Look for a plaque outside number 15 commemorating former resident **Edward Lear** (1812-1888), the poet, painter and traveller who is best remembered today for his nonsense poetry.

There is another plaque outside number 7 for  **US President Martin Van Buren** (1782-1862). An American whose first language was Dutch, he served as ambassador to Britain in the early 1830s and would serve as the eighth President of the United States between 1837-41. Van Buren was one of the founders of the Democratic Party.

Return to Oxford Street, passing ⑰ **Marylebone Lane**. In John Rocque's famous 1746 map of London, nearly all the land on the north side of Oxford Street which you have just walked past is shown as comprising of open fields. Indeed, up to this point Rocque names the road as 'Tiburn Road', with Oxford Street only being used for the route east of Marylebone Lane. The map shows the land to the north and east of Marylebone Lane as increasingly developed, with grand new streets and squares being laid out to attract the wealthier classes. This tide of urbanisation would soon ensure the remaining fields to the west were built over.

In 1746, however, Marylebone Lane still led through fields to Marylebone, a small village whose name is a contraction of 'St Mary at the bourne'. St Mary's was the church in the village, standing by the Tyburn 'bourne' – or stream. Around 90 acres of land around here is owned by the Howard de Walden Estate and said to be valued at over £3 billion.

This Estate has its origins in 1708 when John Holles, 1st Duke of Newcastle, purchased the Manor of Marylebone in 1708. His wife was Lady Margaret Cavendish (hence Cavendish Square) and his daughter Lady Henrietta Cavendish Holles. The latter married the 2nd Earl of Oxford (mentioned earlier), and the lands later passed by marriage to the Duke of Portland, becoming part of the Portland Estate (not to be confused with the Portman Estate). It later passed to another Duke of Portland's sister who was the widow of Lord Howard de Walden – giving her name to the Howard de Walden Estate.

The current holder of the barony is Hazel Czernin, 10th Baroness Howard de Walden. Her father – the 9th Baron – was a hugely

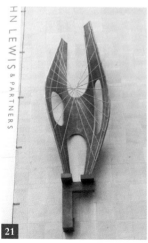

wealthy racehorse owner who almost changed world history when he accidentally ran into Adolf Hitler with his car whilst living in Munich in the early 1930s. He later met Hitler at the opera and introduced himself, recalling that the Nazi leader 'was quite charming to me for a few moments'. Hazel Czernin's son is film producer Peter Czernin, responsible for movies such as *In Bruges* and *Three Billboards Outside Ebbing, Missouri*.

Continue eastwards to reach **⓲ John Lewis**, founded on Oxford Street as a drapery shop by John Lewis (1836-1928) in 1864. Lewis was a difficult character, prone to temper tantrums and sacking workers on the spot. It was only after his death that the company adopted a worker-cooperative ethos for which it is now famous. The store has a roof garden that is open in the summer months, as well as a café with great views over Oxford Street.

When writer George Orwell, who worked nearby, walked past the burnt out shell of John Lewis during the Blitz, he thought the piled up shop mannequins looked like corpses. John Lewis remained a bombsite until 1954.

View from John Lewis's Roof Garden

As you leave John Lewis you reach ⓳ **Holles Street**, named after the Duke of Newcastle mentioned earlier. Further up this street is ⓴ **Cavendish Square** – again named for one of the ancestors of the de Walden family. Look back to see ㉑ **Barbara Hepworth's** sculpture titled *Winged Figure* (1963) that hangs on the side of the store. Hepworth (1903-75) was known for her Modernist sculptures and had an international reputation.

Lord Byron, one of the most famous poets of the Romantic age, was born at 16 Holles Street on 22 January 1788 and was baptised in the old parish church of Marylebone. He became both enormously famous and controversial during his short life, eventually leaving Britain to travel extensively in Europe and take part in the Greek War of Independence against the Turks. He died during his time in Greece aged just 36.

Be careful here – between 2005 and 2013 this junction was the most dangerous place for pedestrians in the whole of Britain, one of three streets off Oxford Street that ranked highly in national figures for accident hotspots.

Walk on, passing the ㉒ **London College of Fashion** on the left. Former students here include shoe designer Jimmy Choo, model Alex Wek, and S Club 7 singer Rachel Stevens. Soon you reach ㉓ **Oxford Circus**, a place best avoided if you suffer from agoraphobia.

The junction dates from the early 1820s and was called Regent Circus North (Piccadilly Circus was originally Regent Circus South). To the south runs Regent Street, completed in 1825 and designed by architect John Nash. Named for George, the Prince Regent (later George IV), it was originally intended to form part of a grand thoroughfare linking Carlton House in Pall Mall with Regent's Park. By the 1890s maps still referred to this junction as Regent Circus, but the public had begun to refer to it instead as Oxford Circus and the name stuck.

Cross over (carefully...), still heading eastwards. On the corner is the former flagship store of ㉔ **Peter Robinson** – once a grand department store chain founded by Peter Robinson (1804-1874). Robinson was one of the men who helped turn Oxford Street into a great shopping thoroughfare. John Lewis used to work for him before founding his own store. Dating from 1924, half of the frontage of this grand building was destroyed during a terrible German bombing raid on 17th September 1940 – the same raid that damaged four of the biggest department stores in Oxford Street.

On April 30th 2007, Kate Moss caused chaotic scenes here as thousands gathered to see the supermodel pose in the window of the Topshop store on this site wearing a red dress. She was unveiling her fashion collection that had been produced in partnership with controversial billionaire Sir Philip Green, owner of Topshop.

Just past here at number 214, once stood ㉕ **AIR Studios**. George Martin, the legendary producer to the Beatles, left EMI in the late 60s and started his own independent recording company – Associated Independent Recording (or AIR). The studio here opened in 1970 on the 4th

floor, and Paul McCartney, Ringo and many other famous artists were regulars here. McCartney was at AIR on the day Lennon was killed in 1980 and when leaving made his often quoted (and misunderstood) comment 'It's a drag' to the press when pressed for his reaction by the awaiting press. AIR moved away from here in 1991.

㉖ **Number 200** is another grand building from the 1920s, long home to C&A. During the war its basement was used by the BBC and writer George Orwell made broadcasts here for the Indian Section of the BBC between 1941 and 1943.

Carry on, taking a small detour up Market Court and then up to ㉗ **Market Place**. The information boards will tell you about the long-lost Oxford Market which was founded in the 1720s to provide meat, fish and vegetables for those living in the newly developed streets and squares (particularly Cavendish Square). Stallholders were located within a wooden market building, and it was named for the 2nd Earl of Oxford who whose family owned land here. It continued to operate until around 1880.

If you look at one of the trees beside the information board, you will see the metal grill at pavement level has the sign 'Great Portland Estates'. This is one of Britain's biggest real estate companies that acquired many properties originally owned by the Dukes of Portland.

Follow the map, walking along Market Place, and then go right down Great Titchfield Street to join Oxford Street again.

There is a sad story associated with this spot. **28** **Essayist Thomas de Quincey** (1785-1859) is best known for his book *Confessions of an English Opium Eater* (1821), a frank account of his years as an addict. After running away from school, he ended up in a relationship with 'noble minded' Ann, a 15-year-old prostitute on Oxford Street. He wrote of how 'for many weeks I had walked at nights with this poor friendless girl up and down Oxford Street or had rested with her on steps and under the shelter of porticos'.

Leaving her to find some money, they agreed 'on the fifth night from that, and every night afterwards, she would wait for me at six o'clock near the bottom of Great Titchfield Street, which had been our customary haven'. However, he never found her again, and the thought of what might have happened to his young love haunted him for the rest of his life.

Cross Winsley Street, near to the former site of the **29** **Princess's Theatre**. The original theatre opened in the late 1830s and named after Princess (later Queen) Victoria. It was rebuilt many times, and for much of its life was used for opera, and then – under Charles Kean – became famous for its productions of Shakespearian plays, employing famous actors such as Ellen Terry. The theatre closed in 1902 and was finally demolished in 1931.

As you continue down Oxford Street it might not be obvious to you, but you are in fact walking on a road that ends in Wales. This is part of the A40 that runs for over 260 miles between London – via Oxford – and the coastal town of Fishguard. The fairly tacky souvenir shops trace their origins to the late 19th century when Oxford Street became less residential and more retail focused – attracting drapers,

furniture stores, carriage manufacturers and cobblers. The crowds of shoppers attracted street vendors selling tourist souvenirs, and also less salubrious visitors – pickpockets, prostitutes and confidence tricksters. To this day you can often see characters doing the three-card trick under the watchful eye of their lookouts and pop-up shops selling counterfeit perfumes.

On your left is ㉚ **Adam and Eve Court**, named after the Adam and Eve tavern that occupied a rural location here until it disappeared in the 1740s. In the brutal world of the 18th century, a prizefighter named Figg kept an establishment near to here, and locals used to say 'Long live the great Figg, by the prize-fighting swains/Sole monarch acknowledged of Marybone plains'. Men and women both fought here, and one advert described how 'Mrs Stokes, the City Championess, is ready to meet the Hibernian Heroine at Figg's'. Animal fighting and other cruel sports also attracted people to Figg's. Today a pub named the Adam & Eve just up the Court is a much more subdued descent of this old tavern.

Walk on, passing Berners Street where poet ㉛ **Samuel Taylor Coleridge** (1772-1834) lived at number 71 for a couple of years, and then you come to the iconic ㉜ **100 Club** at number

100. Live music has been played here since 1942, mainly jazz in the early years. During World War II the club was used as a bomb shelter and frequented by American GIs, and great musicians such as Glenn Miller, Benny Goodman and Art Pepper. Later Billie Holliday, Muddy Waters and Louis Armstrong would perform here.

However, the 100 Club really became famous with the explosion of Punk, particularly when in September 1976 bands such as The Clash, The Damned, the Sex

Pistols and Siouxie and the Banshees all played here. Over the years many high-profile names have played 'secret' gigs at the club including Paul McCartney (who performed a benefit for the club when threatened with closure), The Rolling Stones, Primal Scream and Oasis. Sex Pistol, Sid Vicious once threw a glass here that shattered, blinding a young woman, and on another night, he attacked music journalist Nick Kent with a bicycle chain.

Walk past the 100 Club and, to get a short break from the bustle, turn left up narrow Hanway Street. On the left is ㉝ **Bradley's Spanish Bar** – a hidden delight that is a friendly place for a drink and which boasts an excellent vinyl jukebox. Its name was adopted in the 50s when bullfighting was all the rage – although strangely, it does not serve Spanish food.

Continue to reach Tottenham Court Road, turn left and walk for a short way to reach ㉞ **the Odeon** – formerly the site of the UFO club in the late 60s. In the building that used to stand here at number 31, counterculture figures John 'Hoppy' Hopkins and producer Joe Boyd ran a club in the basement that became the coolest in Britain. Pink Floyd was the house band, and others who played here include Soft Machine, Arthur Brown and Procol Harum. The coolest hippies in London would flock here to take in avant-garde performances, cutting edge bands and – of course – indulge in illicit substances. The establishment and the press hated the place, and it closed shortly after a *News of the World* exposé was published in July 1967.

37

Retrace your steps, passing Hanway Street and continuing to the junction of Tottenham Court Road and Oxford Street. The whole area here has dramatically changed in the last few years with the Crossrail project. Excavations that took place as part of the building work uncovered Roman pottery, 18th-century cellars, and all manner of artefacts.

The junction on the northeast corner was once the location of the **35 Horse Shoe Brewery**, founded in 1764 and named after the nearby Horseshoe tavern. It became one of the largest producers of porter beer in London and remained in operation until 1921 – a reminder that before the age of department stores, McDonald's and Starbucks, this part of central London was once highly industrialised.

The London Beer Flood took place at the brewery in 1814. The tragedy, which killed eight people, resulted after a vat burst. Thousands of gallons of porter flooded the brewery but also the cellars of neighbouring buildings, causing people to drown in beer.

Between the Middle Ages and the 15th century, the junction here was the location of a **36 gallows** where prisoners were executed.

Start to walk westwards back along Oxford Street, looking out on the corner for the **37 Flying Horse pub**. It dates back to at least 1790 and – incredibly – is the last remaining pub on the whole length of Oxford Street.

The Primark store stands approximately where the **38 Oxford Music Hall** stood, opened in 1861 by Charles Morton – the 'father of the halls'. It attracted the greatest stars of the era, including Marie Lloyd. Like many music halls, it suffered from the rise of the cinema after World War I, and the theatre was closed in 1926, with a Lyons' Corner House replacing it.

To your left lie a number of streets leading to the heart of Soho, for centuries the heart of bohemian life in London and from where sub-cultures such as the Mods and New Romantics have emerged. Soho Street leads down to **39 Soho Square**, and it was in a building just here, on the corner of Oxford Street, that a gruesome murder took place in June 1860.

That month the London *Evening Standard* reported on how 'much excitement prevailed in Oxford Street near Soho Square' after the body of a young woman was discovered in a blood-stained lodging room. Her 'head was found in a cupboard, some of her limbs were observed to have been cut, as with a saw'. The police realised the murder was connected to a French tailor, Antonio D'herard, who had committed suicide in Hyde Park a few days before. It turned out the woman was his 'very beautiful' young English wife, Caroline.

D'herard's corpse was found to have the words 'death to an unfaithful woman' inked onto his chest, along with a likeness of Napoleon. He left a blood-stained letter that complained of Caroline's violent temper and described his own disgrace after having been previously imprisoned for hitting her. Their final quarrel in their Oxford Street lodging rooms would lead to both their deaths, and the tragedy was reported in many newspapers around the world.

Walk back down Soho Street and on your left is the ⑩ **Radha-Krishna temple**, located at Govinda's restaurant. This has been here for over 50 years and Beatle George Harrison co-signed the original lease. You can go into Govinda's and ask to visit the temple next door. Followers of the movement can often be seen walking up and down Oxford Street.

Return to Oxford Street and soon you pass Poland Street. It was laid out in the 1680s, and is therefore a century older than many of the streets you passed on the north side of Oxford Street. It was named after the King of Poland tavern once found here, and a pub of the same name was another casualty of the Blitz in 1940. If you are interested in Britain's great poets, you may wish to take a detour down Poland Street to see where ⑪ **William Blake** (1757-1827) lived at number 28 and ⑫ **Percy Shelley** (1792-1822) at number 15.

Near to the corner of Oxford Street and Poland Street, at number 165, is the location of the original ⑬ **Marquee Club** between

1958 and 1964. Originally a coffee shop and jazz club beneath a cinema, the venue became an iconic part of the early 60s pop and rock scene. This early incarnation of the club is best-known for being where the Rolling Stones made their debut on 12 July 1962.

Just before the gig, the band called up *Jazz News* to try and get a listing. When asked for the band's name, they panicked, having not yet chosen one, and worried about running up a large phone bill. They spied *The Best of Muddy Waters* record on the floor, the first track of which was *Rollin' Stone*. Keith later recalled, 'The cover is on the floor. Desperate, Brian, Mick and I take the dive. The Rolling Stones Phew!! That saved sixpence'. The night is said to have ended badly when local mods attacked the audience. The Marquee club later moved to nearby Wardour Street.

Next door is another **44 Marks & Spencer**. If you look up at the 1930 façade, you can see a sign spelling out 'The Pantheon'. This name commemorates a grand entertainment venue built by James Wyatt in the early 1770s and designed to attract wealthy patrons who visited London's pleasure gardens. For a while, it was the most talked-about place in London, partly because of its huge scale and dome – said to be based on the ancient Roman Pantheon in Rome. The opening night in January 1772 attracted eight dukes and duchesses, ambassadors and many of the highest ranks of society.

Despite hosting masquerades, balls, and concerts, the Pantheon was never a great success. It was later used for operas, suffered a fire and was rebuilt, and became a showroom in the early 20th century. The buildings were demolished in the 1930s to make way for the M&S store which opened in 1938. This fine building was designed by Robert Lutyens, son of the renowned architect Sir Edwin Lutyens.

Walk on, stopping outside **45** **219 Oxford Street** (on the junction with Hills Place) – a narrow building that dates from 1951. The plaques on the exterior make little sense until you realise they celebrate the Festival of Britain that took place that year on the South Bank. The bottom plaque shows the Royal Festival Hall, the next up the Festival's logo, and at the top the Skylon and Dome of Discovery which featured at the Festival.

Just before you reach Oxford Circus again, look out for the tiled exterior of **46** **Oxford Circus underground station** on the left. The distinctive oxblood red-tiled façade was designed by the prolific underground architect Leslie William Green (1875-1908). In recent years the number of people visiting this busy underground station have averaged between 80 and 90 million per annum.

45

Take care crossing Oxford Circus and continue westwards. On the left (number 275) is the fairly non-descript entrance of **47 Regent Hall** (look for the Salvation Army sign). This hall, formerly an ice skating rink, was bought in 1882 by William Booth, founder of the Salvation Army, and became known as the 'Rink'. For decades, bands and choirs performed here, and behind the modest entrance is an auditorium that can seat 550 people. It is a fantastic place to visit to get away from the crowds and has a café too.

Just afterwards is Harewood Place which leads you down to **48 Hanover Square**. This was laid out during the late 1710s as the city spread westwards. It is loyally named after the Hanoverian monarchy, with its first incumbent being George I. See if you can spot one of the last remaining green cabmen's shelters. These were built in 1875 after a fund was set up to provide horse-drawn hansom cab drivers with somewhere to rest and refuel, as well as avoid going to the pub on duty! They have since been used more recently by black cab drivers.

Return to Oxford Street. Charles Dickens used to live nearby, and his writing was likely influenced by the story of a spinster named Miss Mary Lucrine. She lived somewhere on Oxford Street and, having been 'met with disappointment in matrimony' in early life, she vowed to 'never see the light of the sun!'. She shut herself inside her house for years, and even kept her windows covered. She died in 1778, and if her story was well

47 Regent Hall

known enough to be printed in the 19th century, it is likely Dickens would have come across it. Mary Lucrine definitely resembles the character of Miss Havisham in *Great Expectations* (1861).

Continue to reach what was, until fairly recently, the ❹❾ **HMV** shop at number 363. The original shop was opened by Sir Edward Elgar in 1921, although is most famous for the visit by Beatles manager Brian Epstein in February 1962. At that time, Epstein was desperate – the Beatles had so far failed to attract interest from London's record companies, and Epstein was close to giving up. He visited HMV with the intention of turning a Beatles demo tape into a record. The tape was initially made for Decca, who famously rejected it, and Brian was led upstairs to the office of a music publishing company. There, he made contact with George Martin of Parlophone Records (and later AIR records). Within a few days, the Beatles would audition for Martin and secure the record deal that would change their fortunes, and pop culture, forever.

Walking on, turn left down Davies Street and then into ❺⓿ **South Molten Street** for a small detour. This Mayfair street is very upmarket, full of posh restaurants, modelling agencies, art galleries, antique shops and boutiques. Perhaps surprisingly, Labour giant and trade union leader Ernest Bevin (1881-1951) lived at number 34 (there is a blue plaque). Additionally, number 17 was another of the poet William Blake's residencies.

Back on Oxford Street, return to Duke Street and follow the map to see on your right a rather unusual building. The ornate façade gives no clue that it serves a very practical purpose as an **electricity substation**. Taking the steps to the building's roof there is a further surprise in the form of **51** **Brown Hart Gardens**. This Italian-style paved gardens were originally designed in 1903 by Stanley Peach. Following 20 years of closure, the gardens were returned to their majestic splendour and reopened to the public in 2007 (visit brownhartgardens.co.uk).

While exploring the gardens take some time to admire, on the other side of Duke Street, the magnificent **52** **Ukrainian Catholic Cathedral** which has been based here since 1967. The building was originally the home of a Free Chapel congregation that was founded by Queen Matilda in 1148. They had formerly worshipped near the Tower of London but moved to Weighhouse Street in the late 19th century. The church was clearly very popular at the time as this ornate building was designed by the renowned architect, Alfred

Waterhouse. The building remains an impressive site and can hold up to 900 Worshippers. In October 1940 a bomb fell on the chancel during a communion service, killing the minister's wife and injuring one other person.

Return to Oxford Street observing the grand department stores mentioned earlier from a different perspective. On the corner at Marble Arch is another Beatles connection as it was from a **53 Sitar Shop** here that George Harrison bought a sitar in 1965. He played it in the recording of *Norwegian Wood*, having been inspired by the Indian musicians who were part of the band's film *Help* (1965). The Beatles were the first Western band to issue a record featuring a sitar and many other 60s bands followed their example. On that musical note, this walk ends, and you can return to Marble Arch underground station. ●

VISIT...

Annunciation Church (see p.68)
Bryanston Street, W1H 7AH
www.annunciationmarblearch.org.uk

The Photographers' Gallery
16-18 Ramillies Street, W1F 7LW
www.thephotographersgallery.org.uk

Selfridges (see p.72)
400 Oxford Street, W1C 1JS
www.selfridges.com

Wallace Collection
Hertford House, Manchester
Square, W1U 3BN
www.wallacecollection.org

EAT / DRINK...

John Lewis Rooftop Cafe
(see p.78)
300 Oxford Street, W1C 1DX
www.johnlewis.com

Lamb and Flag Pub (see p.75)
24 James Street, W1U 1EL

Bradley's Spanish Bar (see p.85)
42-44 Hanway Street, W1T 1UT
www.bradleysspanishbar.com

4 Primrose Hill Walk

Primrose Hil

1. Chalk Farm Underground Station
2. Railway Bridge
3. Primrose Hill Railway Station
4. The Pembroke Castle
5. The Lansdowne
6. Edis Street
7. The Engineer
8. Regent's Canal
9. Primrose Hill Primary School
10. Coal Hole Covers
11. Utopia Village
12. Princess of Wales
13. Plaque to W.B. Yeats
14. Primrose Hill Studios
15. The Old Piano Factory
16. Primrose Hill Community Association
17. H.G. Wells' Former Home
18. Chalcot Square
19. Plaque to Sylvia Plath
20. Plaque to Dr José Rizal
21. Paddington Film Location
22. Boris Johnson's Childhood Home
23. Apex of Primrose Hilll
24. Former Zoological Garden
25. Sigmund Freud's home
26. Barrow Hill Reservoir
27. St Edmund's Terrace
28. Shakespeare's Tree
29. Plaque to Friedrich Engels
30. The Queen's
31. St George's Mews

ETON AVE

N

W E

S

WILLOWS ROAD

ADELAIDE ROAD

LOWER MERTON RISE

KING HENRY'S ROAD

BRIDLEY ROAD

WADHAM GARDENS

ELSWORTHY ROAD

25

AVENUE ROAD

BROXWOOD WAY

TOWNSHEND RD

QUEEN'S

ST E

CHARLBERT STREET

MACKENNAL ST

ST JO

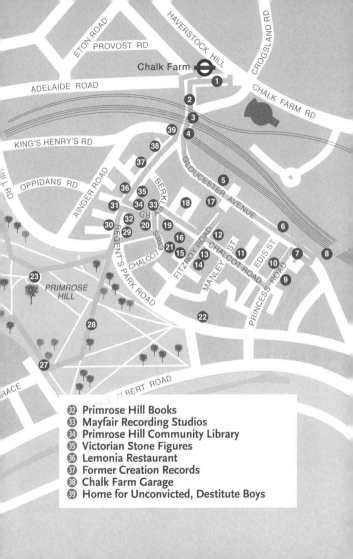

32 Primrose Hill Books
33 Mayfair Recording Studios
34 Primrose Hill Community Library
35 Victorian Stone Figures
36 Lemonia Restaurant
37 Former Creation Records
38 Chalk Farm Garage
39 Home for Unconvicted, Destitute Boys

Primrose Hill Walk

Start/Finish: Chalk Farm Underground
Distance: 2.9 miles

This walk starts from ➊ **Chalk Farm underground station** and explores Primrose Hill – one of the most pleasant, and desirable residential areas in London. Before you leave the station, look out for the oxblood red tiles – a sign that this is another design by Leslie Green (1875-1908). The prolific underground architect died at the age of just 33, after working himself into an early grave. This Grade II listed building opened just a year before his death and has the longest façade of any of his stations.

Follow the map along Regent's Park Road to reach a ➋ **Railway Bridge** over the line that feels more like a border point between (relatively) scruffy Camden and the 'urban village' of Primrose Hill. It was on this bridge that the young poet, Ted Hughes, passed a man with a fox cub under his coat. The encounter, including the man's words 'You can have him for a pound', was immortalised in Hughes's poem *Epiphany*.

➌ **Primrose Hill Railway Station** used to stand just to the left of the bridge. It opened in 1855 and had a number of different names over the years (Hampstead Road, Chalk Farm), before taking the name Primrose Hill station until its closure in 1992. The shop on the left, as you start to cross the bridge, was originally part of the old station building.

Once over the bridge ➍ **The Pembroke Castle** welcomes you to Primrose Hill. This legendary pub opened in the early 1860s largely to slake the thirst of the thousands of labourers that arrived in London to build the railway.

In Camden and Primrose Hill, pubs sprung up to cater for these new arrivals – the Scots frequenting the Edinboro Castle, the Irish drinking in the Dublin Castle, the English favouring the Windsor Castle, and the Welsh, having exceptional taste, came here to the Pembroke Castle. (The Edinboro Castle and Dublin Castle are still open today in Camden). Likewise, The Pembroke Castle remains a popular pub with a pleasant terrace – although working-class manual workers are today a rare sight.

Head left down Gloucester Avenue to see the pristine, superb houses that attract so many wealthy residents to Primrose Hill. The world famous photographer, David Bailey, was one of the first celebrities to make Gloucester Avenue his home at the height of his fame in the 1960s. Thirty years later, the 'Primrose Hill Set' made the area famous, attracting paparazzi by the scooter load. Centring around celebrities such as Sadie Frost, Rhys Ifans, Jude Law and Kate Moss, most lived in the area, hosting parties and frequenting many of the local pubs. Primrose Hill has remained fashionable, with more recent residents including Jamie Oliver, Robert Plant, Daniel Craig, Alan Bennett, Joan Bakewell and Stefano Gabbana.

This was once an area of dense forest. The ancient trees were gradually cut down during Tudor times to make way for a modest hamlet, and in the 15th century the first reference to 'primrose' was recorded. The name probably derives from the wild flowers that grew in the surrounding meadows.

As late as the early 19th century, you would have seen open fields and just a few small buildings. The Chalk Farm Tavern was the only place of any significance (the site of which is visited later). But London was expanding with its population and as the 19th century continued, local landowners – Eton College and Lord Southampton – exchanged or sold their land to allow developers to build new suburban streets. As a result, nearly all of the buildings you will see today were built in the first half of Victoria's reign between 1840-1875.

Many street names are associated with Eton – for example King Henry's Road (Eton was founded by Henry VII) and Oppidans Road (Eton has its Oppidan scholars).

On the left you pass another famous Primrose Hill pub – **5** **The Lansdowne**. The current upmarket establishment opened in 1992. However, the first pub on the site dates back to the early 1860s, and was also popular with railway workers. It is named after the Marquess of Lansdowne who was given his title in 1784, after successfully negotiating peace terms with the new American Republic. In the 1960s striptease artists appeared here at lunchtime – today you are more likely to see a hedge fund manager or celebrity.

Continue along Gloucester Avenue. Despite the 'urban village' tag for Primrose Hill, it was never really a village; going from fields and meadows with a solitary tavern to a planned, suburban district in just a few short years. Whilst the new suburb of Primrose Hill started off as an upmarket residential area, the pollution from the railway on the north side, resulted in this part of the development becoming run down over the years.

Houses began to be converted into flats, and railway workers and navvies frequented the pubs. It was only from the 1960s, when trains became electric, that localised pollution was reduced. The area once again began to attract wealthy, middle-class families who could not afford St John's Wood or Chelsea. They found bargains here, often converting buildings back into use as family homes. Today, houses on this road can sell for over £6 million.

On the right you pass **6** **Edis Street**, originally called Eton Street in the 19th century, when Eton College's ownership of

land was much more evident. You will see some upmarket shops and boutiques that are a feature of Primrose Hill, the locals often opposing the arrival of chain stores.

Historically, one of the main employers in the area, apart from the railway companies, was the Electric Telegraph Company that once stood on the Avenue. Many others were employed by local piano manufacturers (the locations of which are seen later).

Just ahead is ❼ **The Engineer**. When moving to London to live in a grotty street in Camden in the early 90s, I occasionally ventured over the border into Primrose Hill for a pint. The Engineer felt like a world away from my local in Camden, and even the landlady was posh – the daughter of Laurence Olivier. It remains a charming, upmarket pub.

Walk a little further to the ❽ **Regent's Canal** down below. Like the railway lines you have passed, it creates another border that helps make Primrose Hill seem quite cut off from the rest of London. It was finished in 1820 and runs for nearly nine miles across London, from Paddington to Limehouse. In the late 19th century a brewery was located on the south side of the bridge.

Retrace your steps to head down Princess Road. As a child Boris Johnson lived here with his family for around two years from 1970. On the left is ❾ **Primrose Hill Primary School** that opened in 1885. You can still see the original stone entrance signs for 'boys', 'girls' and 'infants'.

Past pupils here include politicians Boris Johnson (Conservative) and Ed Miliband (Labour), writer Zoe Heller and director Sam Mendes. Miliband, Heller and Mendes were in the same class. This is clearly not your average inner city primary school.

In 2012 Johnson, in *The Telegraph*, wrote about Miliband – 'I'm sorry to say it, but my old school chum isn't PM material... Ed and I were at the same superb school – Primrose Hill Primary School, Camden, a coincidence that he is curiously disinclined to mention'. Three years later Johnson was still mentioning the school – telling one crowd 'You might as well talk about the sinister grip of Primrose Hill primary school on British politics'.

Look out on the pavement for **10** **circular coal hole covers** through which coal used to be poured, arriving in the cellars of neighbouring houses. The covers bear the name of their manufacturer and their own unique design.

Take the next right along Chalcot Road, originally St George's Road in the 19th century. On the right is **11** **Utopia Village**, which stands on the site of a 19th-century piano factory – one of many that used to be found in this part of London. Whilst hard to imagine now, before the plush eateries and boutiques dominated Primrose Hill, this area was a place of industry.

Chalcot was the name of the local manor in this area and Chalk Farm is a corruption of this name, rather than a reference to any chalk underneath your feet.

If you have resisted a drink so far, you may be tempted by the ⑫ **Princess of Wales**, dating from the 1860s. Its name celebrated the marriage of Princess Alexandra to the Prince of Wales (later Edward VII). It has a small garden featuring Banksy-esque murals. The pub stands on the junction with Fitzroy Road, named for Charles FitzRoy, 3rd Baron Southampton (1804-1872), the former landholder here. The surname FitzRoy is traditionally given to illegitimate children of British monarchs. In this case the Baron is a descendant of Henry FitzRoy, the illegitimate son of Charles II and his mistress Barbara Villiers.

Turn left here, to find at number 23 a ⑬ **Blue Plaque** commemorating the boyhood home of the great Anglo-Irish poet **W.B. Yeats** (1865-1939). Yeats preferred his mother's family home in Sligo and wrote of the capital 'This melancholy London. I sometimes imagine the souls of the lost are compelled to walk through its streets perpetually'. One such soul is fellow poet **Sylvia Plath** (1932-1963) who moved to the house after separating from Ted Hughes and took her own life here on 11th February 1963. Later you will see the home Plath shared with Hughes on Chalcot Square.

A little further along on the left is the entrance to ⑭ **Primrose Hill Studios**. They were completed in 1877 and contained 12 studios, cementing the area's association with artists. Designed in an Arts & Crafts style, they were once used by the illustrator Arthur Rackham and conductor Henry Wood. This was also the last major development in Primrose Hill, all the other streets on the walk having been completed in the previous 25 years.

On the other side of Fitzroy Road is a fine looking building that looks different to anything else you will see on the walk. In the late 19th century this was the location of ⑮ **Piano Makers, John and James Hopkinson**. The building is a rare physical reminder that Primrose Hill was once well known for the manufacture of pianos with a still existent sign for 'The Old Piano Factory'.

Next door, walk down Hopkinsons Place to reach the ⑯ **Primrose Hill Community Association**. If it is open, pop in and have a look around. The centre is proof that despite the affluent surroundings, the area does have a real sense of community. Upstairs there is a board listing donations to the centre, including famous locals such as Alan Bennett, Andrew Marr, Mary Portas, Jon Snow and Camilla Guinness.

Return to Chalcot Road and follow the map to see where ⑰ **H.G. Wells** lived between 1888-89 on the (north) side of Fitzroy Road (number 12). It is thought he began *The War of the Worlds* whilst living here with his aunt, and Primrose Hill features in the novel.

Continue along Chalcot Road and turn right to reach ⑱ **Chalcot Square** (originally St George's Square). With its pastel coloured houses, this is one of the prettiest spots in Primrose Hill.

There's a ⑲ **Blue Plaque** remembering **Sylvia Plath** at number 3, where she lived in a cramped top floor flat with her husband, Ted Hughes, between 1960-1. The unhappy family did not stay together for long, but it was a productive time for Plath. Here she wrote a volume of poetry, *The Colossus*, and her only novel, *The Bell Jar*. At the same time, she was taking care of her children and dealing with her troubled marriage.

They later rented the flat to friends, Assia and David Wevill. It was Hughes' affair with Assia that led to the breakdown of the marriage and Plath's move to Fitzroy Road – seen earlier in the walk. When her children unveiled a plaque to their mother on Chalcot Square, her daughter Frieda was asked why they had not done the same on Fitzroy Road, and she replied 'My mother died there – but she had lived here'.

Follow the map from the Square along Chalcot Crescent, another of the most picturesque streets in Primrose Hill. There is a ⑳ **Blue Plaque to Dr José Rizal** (1861-96) at number 37 on the Crescent. Rizal was a writer and poet, and his works helped inspire a revolution by Filipinos against Spanish Rule. He was executed by the Spanish aged just 35 and today Filipinos still come to this spot to pay homage to a national hero. Whilst the Philippines managed to escape rule from Spain in 1898, it went on to fight another bloody war of independence against the United States that cost hundreds of thousands of lives. The United States eventually granted independence to the Philippines in 1946.

Continue along the Crescent to the house at number 30. This served as the exterior of the ㉑ **Brown's family home** in the recent *Paddington Bear* films. (In the Paddington books the Browns live in the fictional Windsor Gardens). Chalcot Square and other nearby streets also feature in the films.

Retrace your steps slightly to walk up Rothwell Street and at the end you finally reach Primrose Hill. The walk will now take you around the park, although you may wish to shorten your journey and continue through Primrose Hill from **Shakespeare's Tree** (p.118).

Before you enter the park on your left is Regent's Park Road running alongside. Further down the road and off the route of the walk is number 60, which was the ㉒ **childhood home of Boris Johnson**. Despite Mr Johnson's public aversion to the 'metropolitan elite', his former home is a grand Georgian terrace dating from the 1820s. Screenwriter Lukas Heller (father of Zoe, mentioned earlier) lived at the same address in the 1960s. He wrote the screen adaption of *Whatever Happened to Baby Jane?* (1962), *The Flight of the Phoenix* (1965) and *The Dirty Dozen* (1967).

You now enter the park. Head towards the ㉓ **high point of Primrose Hill**, an observation spot that offers arguably the best view in North London. The park has inspired generations of poets, writers, photographers and musicians almost too numerous to mention. It became a public park after being bought from Eton College in 1841.

Beat poet Allen Ginsberg wrote *Primrose Hill Guru* after a visit here in May 1965. He was in London for a seminal poetry reading at the Albert Hall that is often regarded as the catalyst for the counterculture movement of the late 1960s.

A poet from a very different time – William Blake – also came here, writing of

'The fields from Islington to Marybone
To Primrose Hill and Saint John's Wood
Were builded over with pillars of gold
And there Jerusalem's pillars stood'.

From this viewpoint, follow the map to see more of the park.

Luckily for present day visitors, an ambitious plan in the early 19th century to build a mammoth pyramid shaped cemetery on this site was rejected. The man campaigning for the site, George Carden, calculated the pyramid would hold 5,167,104 bodies, but the then landowner, Eton College, blocked the plan.

In 1967, Paul McCartney was walking his dog Martha here when he was surprised by the sudden appearance of a man. It inspired the Beatles' classic *The Fool on the Hill*. Another dog-walk here with the sun coming out is said to have inspired *Getting Better*, which appeared on the *Sgt. Pepper's Lonely Hearts Club Band* album.

Not to be outdone, in November 1966 The Rolling Stones came here at 5.30 in the morning with legendary photographer Gered Mankowitz. The result was a seminal, blurry shot of the band that was used for the cover of their album *Between the Buttons*.

Continue walking around the park. The north-west corner was the site of a **24** **zoological garden** in the 19th century, and nearby was the Eton & Middlesex Cricket Ground which opened in 1857, and later moved westwards as streets were laid out nearby.

On the northwest side is Elsworthy Terrace, that leads onto Elsworthy Road. The founding father of Psychoanalysis, **Sigmund Freud**, briefly lived at **㉕** **39 Elsworthy Road** in 1938 after fleeing the Nazi occupation of Vienna. Freud soon moved to Maresfield Gardens in Hampstead (where the Freud Museum is now based) and continued to work right up until his death from cancer in 1939.

Back on the hill, as you start to reach the south side, behind trees is the **㉖** **Barrow Hill Reservoir** – it is hard to see because of the foliage. The original reservoir was constructed in the 1820s, and held water from the Thames that was pumped up from Hammersmith. There was once an actual Barrow Hill here, but it was levelled to make way for the reservoir.

Not far from the reservoir site used to be a ditch where the body of magistrate Sir Edmund Berry Godfrey was discovered in October 1678. He had been murdered and his body dumped there. The crime caused a sensation in London at the time as it was believed he was killed by Catholics who were plotting against the King. The murder whipped up an anti-Catholic frenzy in the capital, and three men were hanged by the hill after pleading guilty.

Just past here is the end of **㉗** **St Edmund's Terrace**. In H.G. Wells' book, *The War of the Worlds*, this is the setting for the climax of the novel, where the hero approaches what he soon realises are the doomed Martian killing machines on Primrose Hill. *'I hurried through the red weed that choked St. Edmund's Terrace...and emerged upon the grass before the rising of the sun'.* Soon he sees *'the tattered red shreds of flesh that dripped down upon the overturned seats on the summit of Primrose Hill'.* As mentioned earlier, Wells lived on Fitzroy Road, so knew Primrose Hill well.

On the south side of the park is a playground, laid out on the site of a 19th-century gymnasium. Like the cricket ground, it was designed for the residents of the new streets being laid out on all sides.

In the mid-1840s Primrose Hill was talked about briefly as a potential site for the Great Exhibition, which eventually took place in Hyde Park in 1851.

The Hill was later selected for siting gun batteries during World War II. After the war the guns were removed and squatters occupied the army huts.

Walk up the path to see an oak tree known as **28 Shakespeare's Tree**. In the past Primrose Hill was used as a meeting place for ordinary people, including many radical groups such as the Chartists (10,000 met here in September 1856, demanding democratic reform).

In the 19th century, Shakespeare became very popular amongst sections of the working-class, keen on self-improvement, and around 100,000 attended the planting of an oak tree here in 1864 to mark 300 years since the Bard's birth. The event also involved speeches supporting Giuseppe Garibaldi, the Italian nationalist, who spent time in Britain that same year and inspired many radicals. The current oak tree replaced the original in 1964.

If you come here at the time of the autumn equinox, you are likely to see dozens of druids in white robes celebrating. They have been coming here since 1792 (a few years after the Ancient Order of Druids was founded in Soho). Poet and artist William Blake was one of their number. He wrote 'I have conversed with the – Spiritual Sun – I saw him on Primrose Hill'.

The prophetess Mother Shipton (1488-1561) spent much of her life in a cave from

where she made numerous prophesies that were later published. One prophesy was that when London surrounds Primrose Hill, the streets of the capital would run with blood. Thankfully, despite London extending in all directions beyond Primrose Hill, Mother Shipton's prophesy has yet to come true.

Return to the entrance to the Park and walk along Regent's Park Road. On the right at number 122 is where ㉙ **Friedrich Engels** lived with Lizzie Burns after moving to London from Manchester in 1870. Engels continued to support his great friend Karl Marx (living nearby) financially and emotionally, and so in a practical way made a huge contribution to the birth of Communism as a world-changing ideology.

Opposite is ㉚ **The Queen's pub**, an excellent watering hole that serves good food. Celebrities are often spotted here, from actor Gerard Butler to Liam Gallagher of Oasis fame. He was even captured on Google Street View sitting outside having a quiet pint.

31

Almost directly beside the pub (on the same side) walk through the small entrance way to visit the pretty **31 St George's Mews**, where horses and carriages were once kept.

Walk along Regent's Park Road, passing one of London's best independent bookshops – **32 Primrose Hill Books** (number 134 Regent's Park Road – on the right). In 2019, the then Home Secretary Priti Patel made a speech criticising the 'north London metropolitan liberal elite', prompting the *Guardian* to examine where the 'elite' could be found. This bookshop featured in the article and was described as a place that had 'long been a browsing place for the intellectuals who moved to this pretty Georgian neighbourhood in the 1960s and 70's and where Boris Johnson's father Stanley once had an account'.

ST. GEORGE'S MEWS NW1

31

Follow the map down Sharples Hall Street. Number 11A was the location of **33 Mayfair Recording Studios** after it moved here in 1981 from South Molton Street, Mayfair. Whilst in Primrose Hill artists such as Pink Floyd, David Bowie, U2, Radiohead, George Michael, Tina Turner and Madonna came here to record. The studio eventually closed in 2008.

Another musical connection was the great rock photographer Allan Ballard who had his studio nearby. Musicians such as Bob Marley, Billy Idol, Marc Bolan and Status Quo were known to have visited his studios to have their picture taken.

SHARPLES HALL STREET

33

PRIMROSE HILL BOOKS

32 Primrose Hill Books

Next door is another sign of the 'village' feel of the area – the ㉞ **Primrose Hill Community Library**. It came about after Camden Council planned to close a local library, and Primrose Hill residents – led by figures such as Dame Joan Bakewell and Alan Bennett – ran a campaign to set up a community-run alternative. It now has around 100 volunteers.

Return to Regent's Park Road and continue along, passing upmarket independent cafés, restaurants and shops that draw the celebrities that live in the area. Look out for old ㉟ **Victorian stone figures of humans and animals** – above a number of shop fronts (for example outside number 152).

When Starbucks tried to open a branch here in 2002, 1,300 objections were received by the council. Powerful forces (and celebrities) were mobilised and, at the time of publication, you will find no Starbucks in Primrose Hill.

Greek restaurant ㊱ **Lemonia** at number 89 is one of the best loved eateries in Primrose Hill, run by the same family since 1979. It also stands on the site of the Chalk Farm Tavern that was for many years the main feature of the area before it became a 19th century suburb. Its neighbour, Chalcot Farm, operated here for hundreds of years and they would have stood alone, surrounded by fields and country lanes, until the mid-19th century.

The tavern was famous for its wrestling competitions, sports events, shooting grounds and pleasure gardens. Gentlemen

also came here to take part in duels, having breakfast in the Tavern before trying to kill or maim each other. It was common for the dead or injured losers of the duel to be brought for medical examination at the Tavern afterwards.

In 1832, the 'melancholy suicide of an artist' took place at the Tavern. Charles Horme, 49, a painter, was down on his luck, and went to the Tavern. He drank gin before a waiter found him dead 'having swallowed a quantity of laudanum'.

In 1860, the Tavern advertised its Gardens, boasting a 'Chinese orchestra...36 feet high...together with a Leviathan Platform capable of accommodating 1,000 persons....unrivalled Vaulters and Trampoline Performers...A race with two balloons...and a superb display of Fireworks at 10 o'clock'. It seems doubtful any pub in Primrose Hill today could compete with that offering.

An advert for the sale of the Tavern in 1809 included 12 acres of 'rich meadow land laying immediately around' and also a tea garden. This gives some sense of how rural Primrose Hill still was at that time.

In the 1970s it was rebranded Pub Lotus, an early theme pub celebrating Lotus sports cars. Unsurprisingly, this was not very successful and it became the Chalk Farm Tavern once again, before closing in 1990.

One long-term resident who lived near here after World War II remembered a very different way of life in Primrose Hill. It was more bohemian, with students and artists living beside working-class residents, many with jobs in local factories and workshops. There was a significant Greek and Irish presence, but also Italians, and sometimes tensions between different ethnic groups would boil over.

Continue along, passing a single-storey building (number 109A) that was home to Alan McGee's **37 Creation Records** in the mid 1990s when their biggest act, Oasis, were at their zenith. Beside this is the beautiful frontage of the former **38 Chalk Farm Garage** with its ghost sign.

On the corner, ahead on the left, is a remaining building from the **39 Home for Unconvicted, Destitute Boys** that dominated this side of Regent's Park Road after it was opened in 1868. Hundreds of destitute boys came here to be trained for jobs in its bakery, printing shop and other trade crafts until the school closed in 1920. Many learnt musical instruments so they could join army bands when they left, often travelling the Empire in service.

From here you can cross back over the bridge and retrace your steps out of Primrose Hill to Chalk Farm station. ●

VISIT...

London Zoo
Outer Circle, NW1 4RY
www.zsl.org/zsl-london-zoo

EAT / DRINK...

Pembroke Castle Pub (see p.103)
150 Gloucester Avenue,
NW1 8JA

Lansdowne Pub (see p.105)
90 Gloucester Avenue,
NW1 8HX
www.thelansdownepub.co.uk

The Engineer Gastropub
(see p.107)
65 Gloucester Avenue, NW1 8JD
www.theengineerprimrosehill.co.uk

The Princess of Wales
(see p.109)
22 Chalcot Road, NW1 8LL
www.lovetheprincess.com

Lemonia Greek Restaurant
(see p.122)
89 Regents Park Road,
NW1 8UY
www.lemonia.co.uk

SHOP...

Primrose Hill Bookshop
(see p.120)
134 Regent's Park Road,
NW1 8XL
www.primrosehillbooks.com

5 St John's Wood Walk

St John's Wood

1. St John's Wood Underground Station
2. Eyre Court
3. All Saints Church
4. Marlborough Road Underground Station
5. Pembroke Terrace
6. George Eliot Primary School
7. Boundary Road
8. Site of Carlos the Jackle Attack
9. Plaque to George Frampton
10. St John's Wood Barracks
11. Ordnance Arms
12. St Marylebone Almshouses
13. Former Star
14. Townshend Estate
15. RAK Studios
16. The Ivy
17. Barrow Hill Road
18. Cabmen's Shelter
19. Gardens of St John's Wood Church
20. St John's Wood Church
21. Danubius Hotel
22. Lord's Cricket Ground
23. Clergy Orphan School for Boys
24. Cavendish Avenue
25. Plaque to Billy Fury
26. Hidden Chapel
27. Edward Onslow Ford Monument
28. Abbey Road Studios
29. Alma Square
30. Abercorn Place
31. St Mark's, Hamilton Terrace
32. Abercorn Close
33. Violet Hill Gardens
34. New London Synagogue
35. Stephen Spender's Home
36. The American School
37. Langford Court

KING'S HENRY'S RD

THE REGENT'S PARK

TO TRAINS

St John's Wood Walk

Start & Finish: St John's Wood underground station
Distance: 4 miles

This walk starts at ❶ **St John's Wood underground station**. Before you leave the station, notice the impressive tiling at platform level depicting London landmarks and people, including Thomas Lord (after whom nearby Lord's Cricket ground is named). These are the work of Harold Stabler (1872-1945) and date from the 1930s. He designed many now-iconic posters for the London Underground, and other works of art produced by him are found in the Louvre and the V&A.

As you exit the station onto Finchley Road, stop for a moment. If you stood at this exact spot in 1795 you would have been surrounded by St John's Wood farm and very little else, other than fields and open countryside. Everything you see today has sprung up since then, creating a district that is amongst the most prestigious in London.

From the station head north up Finchley Road, stopping for a moment to see ❷ **Eyre Court** on the left. It dates from around 1930 and is typical of the Art Deco style residential blocks which are found throughout St John's Wood. These attracted wealthy residents who wanted space but were not able to afford the large, detached villas that had been built in the area during the 19th century. Look for the old fashioned 'Eyre Court' signage at the entrances, designed to be lit up to attract taxi drivers when needed by residents.

In medieval times this area was part of the Great Forest of Middlesex and the Manor of Lilestone. The Manor was given to the legendary Knights Templar in 1238, whose Order was dissolved after they fell from favour with Pope Clement V. The land was later passed to the Knights of the Order of St John of Jerusalem in 1328 – hence why this area became known as St John's Wood.

The name Eyre Court has an interesting history. During the English Reformation, the land was acquired by the Crown and its oak trees were felled for use in the construction of ships and royal palaces. The merchant, Henry Samuel Eyre, bought 500 acres in 1732. Another section to the west was bequeathed to the Harrow school, and another substantial area was owned by the Dukes of Portland. By 1800 the Harrow, Eyre and Portland estates had begun to develop housing and other buildings in St John's Wood. The Eyre Estate still exists to this day, the family retaining an interest in some of the most expensive real estate in London.

Continue up Finchley Road. On the right – just below Queen's Terrace – is the former site of ❸ **All Saints Church.** Long-demolished, it was once the parish church of a substantial part of St John's Wood. As the estate owners began to develop the district, fields were ripped up and replaced by villas, terraces, new roads and churches. Several religious denominations founded churches here, keen to ensure the new residents wouldn't be allowed to forget their faith.

Stop at the junction with Queen's Grove. On the northeast corner is the former **4 Marlborough Road Underground station**. This operated from 1868 until 1939, originally part of the Metropolitan and Saint John's Wood Railway. Along with Lord's Station (seen later), it closed after suffering a long decline due to growing competition from buses, and the opening of St John's Wood station. In more recent years the building has been used for other purposes, including as a restaurant.

Opposite the old station is **5 Pembroke Terrace**. Look for the sign above displaying a coat of arms with the letters 'St M B C'. This stands for St Marylebone Borough Council – a long lost administrative district of London that existed between 1900 and 1965. St Marylebone is named after an old chapel of St Mary that stood by the River Tyburn – or 'bourne' – hence 'St Mary by the bourne'. The blue and white waves in the coat of arms you can see on the frontage represent the waves of the River Tyburn. The flowers of the design are connected to the tale that when St Mary's tomb was opened, a lily and a rose were found inside. As you continue the walk you will see other examples of good-quality social housing built by this lost borough council in the mid-20th century (look out for the coat of arms).

On the other (west) side of the old tube station and Finchley Road is **6 George Eliot Primary School** (hidden behind Beachcroft Academy). Its name recalls the author – whose real name was Mary Anne Evans (1819-1880) – one of many prominent writers, artists and musicians who settled in the new leafy, residential streets of St John's Wood during the 19th century.

Follow the map, continuing up Finchley Road.

During World War II, St John's Wood suffered significantly. In post-war maps, all the houses on the east side of your location (along The Marlowes) are shown as 'ruins'. Many residents moved away and for years large sections of St John's Wood remained dilapidated. It was only from the 1960s that the area once again began to regenerate into the upmarket district you see today.

Turn right onto **7** **Boundary Road**, so-named because it marked the boundary between the City of Westminster and the Borough of Camden. Head south on St John's Wood Park road, then stop at the junction with Queen's Grove. This is one of the most expensive residential streets in the area, and individual properties have sold for up to £18 million in recent years. You may see private security personnel patrolling up and down, and on my last visit, I was questioned several times by security guards as I took photos – but never saw a single policeman. Evidently, the super-wealthy have taken control of their own streets.

In many ways, nothing has changed – as evidenced when you stop outside number 48 Queen's Grove. This was where **8** **Venezuelan Ilich Ramirez Sanchez** – better known as the terrorist **Carlos the Jackal** – arrived on the evening of 30 December 1973 and

knocked on the door. His target was Edward Sieff, president of Marks & Spencer and vice-president of the British Zionist Federation. Sieff's butler opened the door, and the Jackal pushed his way in and ran upstairs, firing a single shot at Sieff in his bathroom. Sieff's teeth partially deflected the bullet, and when the Jackal's revolver jammed the terrorist fled. Sieff survived, but for the Jackal this signalled the start of a long terrorist career. At the time of writing, he is in a French prison after being captured by French agents in 1994.

You may wish to also walk down to number 32 which was once occupied by sculptor  **Sir George Frampton** (1860-1928), and marked by an **English Heritage blue plaque**. Frampton is perhaps best known today for his sculpture of Peter Pan in Kensington Gardens that was commissioned by J.M. Barrie. Frampton was also associated with the so-called 'St John's Wood Clique' – a group of artists who lived, worked and socialised in the area during the 1860s to 1880s. They helped create the bohemian reputation St John's Wood once enjoyed.

Walk down Ordnance Hill, passing the former site of the  **St John's Wood Barracks** on the right, which once played a major part in the history of this district. The first military presence in the area was in 1804, during the Napoleonic Wars, when the Corps of Gunner Drivers were billeted in St John's Wood. The Board of Ordnance then decided to set up a permanent base just to the north of the farm, leasing land from the Eyre family. In the 1820s the Cavalry Riding Establishment moved into the barracks, to be followed in later years by several other regiments until 1880, when the Royal Horse Artillery moved in.

They stayed here until 2012, for many years taking part in a Christmas ride around St John's Wood. This all came to an end when the site was sold by the Eyre Estate to Malaysian billionaire Ananda Krishnan for £250 million. The troop moved to Woolwich, and the district's long connections with the army came to an end.

Continue down Ordnance Hill, named after the Ordnance Board responsible for the original barracks, and pass the ⑪ **Ordnance Arms** – a great Victorian-era pub that dates from the 1850s. In 1942-3 it was briefly closed because of Blitz damage.

On my last visit, a local told me *Queen* frontman Freddie Mercury used to visit his good friend and disc jockey Kenny Everett who lived in St John's Wood, and that some of the scenes for the hit film *Bohemian Rhapsody* (2019) were filmed nearby.

Head east along Acacia Road, lined with fine houses built in the 19th century as St John's Wood attracted wealthy families seeking an escape from the smog and crowded streets of central London. At the junction with Woronzow Road is a house that in recent years sold for £16 million. Turn right onto Woronzow Road and then you meet St John's Wood Terrace where you turn right again.

Shortly on the right are ⑫ **St Marylebone Almshouses**. Count Simon Woronzow (1744-1832) served as Russian ambassador in London for many years before retiring to St John's Wood. He left money to build almshouses for the elderly, and the original building was completed in 1837. The object was 'to afford an asylum and means of support to aged and decayed parishioners of St Marylebone, and their widows, who are of good character and industrious reputation...who, by unexpected reverses, or the failure of their accustomed means of support, have fallen from a state of respectability into indigence, but have not had recourse to Parochial Relief'. The almshouses were rebuilt in the mid-1960s. The Russian connection with St John's Wood continues to this day, as the larger homes have proved popular with those who have made their fortunes during the Putin era.

Walk along St John's Wood Terrace. On the left-side are good examples of utilitarian and functional council-built housing that stand in sharp contrast to some of the ivy-clad villas seen already.

12

Turn left into Charlbert Street, passing on the corner a restaurant that from the 1820s until fairly recently used to be the ⑬ **Star public house**, 'the local' for Paul McCartney, Dustin Hoffman and Liam Gallagher of Oasis when they lived nearby.

This part of St John's Wood was once called Portland Town after the Duke of Portland who owned an estate here. Several terraces were built in this area, usually of a lower standard than the developments elsewhere on the Eyre and Harrow estates. By the 20th century, many of the terraces in Portland Town were regarded as slums and were eventually replaced by apartment blocks along streets such as Allitsen Road. If you stop at the junction with Allitsen Road you will see the frontage of the ⑭ **Townshend Estate** with the distinctive 'St M B C' lettering and coat of arms seen earlier on in the walk.

Soon you reach the site of the legendary ⑮ **RAK Studios**, with plaques for Hot Chocolate's Errol Brown and Mickie Most, who founded RAK in 1976. Originally an artist who was part of Britain's rock 'n' roll scene in the 1950s, Most became a producer who helped break acts such as The Animals, as well as managing acts alongside Led Zeppelin manager Peter Grant. The studios occupy a former Victorian schoolhouse. Artists such as David Bowie, Paul McCartney, Michael Jackson, Whitney Houston, Pink Floyd and the Arctic Monkeys have recorded here. This is also where the Pogues recorded 'Fairytale of New York' in 1987 (although Kirsty McColl's contribution was recorded separately by the song's producer, and her husband, Steve Lillywhite).

Retrace your steps to continue along Allitsen Road and reach St John's Wood High Street. This road is peppered with the sort of shops and cafés you might expect to see in one of the more expensive parts of London. If you have time, it is worth a stroll up and down the High Street and you may even spot a few of the many local celebrities. On the corner is **16 The Ivy St John's Wood** – a branch of the famous restaurant in central London.

When finished in the High Street follow the map passing **17 Barrow Hill Road** – its name may have its origins in a Barrow Hill which is mentioned in a Saxon charter of AD986. The old English 'baeruwe' meant a grove or wood. Walk right down Wellington Place, named after the Duke of Wellington whose victories against Napoleon caused many roads then being constructed to be named after him.

You will pass one of the few remaining **18 cabmen's shelters** in London. They were provided by the Cabmen's Shelter Fund, set up in 1874 by the Earl of Shaftesbury and others to help

cabmen and try and prevent them from spending too much time in the pub. Such shelters used to be ubiquitous in London, but now only about a dozen are left.

Go through a gate to enter the ⑲ **Gardens of St John's Wood Church**. This is a magnificent place for a wander and a picnic. There is a wildlife area on the northeast side and a mass of gravestones that add to the atmosphere. There are information boards on the history of a number of other interesting burials, including Private Samuel Godley (1781-1832), who fought at the Battle of Waterloo, and religious visionary Joanna Southcott (1750-1814).

Southcott was born in Devon, and in middle age claimed to be receiving apocalyptic dreams in which she was one of the Women of the Apocalypse referred to in the Book of Revelations. She became a religious prophetess who claimed to be pregnant with a messenger from God, and she attracted thousands of supporters including the poet Lord Byron. She left a mysterious box that she said contained secrets and should only be opened in the presence of 24 bishops of the Church of England – a state of affairs that has given rise to great speculation (and numerous newspaper articles) in later years.

When finished continue through the Gardens to visit the ⑳

church itself. It is one of the few buildings to still exist from the period in the early 19th century when this district was still largely rural. It was designed by Thomas Hardwick as a chapel of ease to the main parish church of St Marylebone and was completed in 1814. The site of the church was once a plague pit.

What was originally a chapel became a parish church after the existing church – St Stephen's on Avenue Road – was damaged during World War II. It contains several monuments to people connected to the East

20

India Company that once ran a considerable part of the British Empire. Paul McCartney married Linda Eastman at Marylebone Register Office on 12 March 1969, and afterwards, the couple came to this church where the marriage was blessed. None of the other Beatles attended, the band was then breaking up and relations between them were at an all-time low.

If you stand at the entrance of the church, just to the south of the roundabout opposite is the ㉑ **Danubius Hotel**. This stands approximately on the site of Lord's underground station which opened in 1868 (like Marlborough Road tube station seen earlier). Originally known as St John's Wood station, it was closed in 1939 and later demolished.

Walk around the corner a little to get a view of ㉒ **Lord's Cricket Ground**. Thomas Lord opened his first cricket ground in 1787 in what is now Dorset Square, later moving to St John's Wood in 1814 when the area was still largely undeveloped. It is famously home to the MCC – or Marylebone Cricket Club – and is regarded as the home of world cricket. If you have time the MCC Museum is worth a visit but check their website beforehand as opening times can vary.

The area between Lords and Wellington Road was once the site of the ㉓ **Clergy Orphan School for Boys** which looked after fatherless children of Anglican clergymen. The school was based here from 1812 until 1855 when it moved to Canterbury. Now known as St Edmund's School, Canterbury, past pupils include actor Orlando Bloom and novelist Lawrence Durrell.

Follow the map up Wellington Road, then take a left down Wellington Place. Bear right into ㉔ **Cavendish Avenue**. As you enter Cavendish Avenue, stop at the first on the left, number 19. This eleven-bed property was once the home of Labour MP, journalist and broadcaster Woodrow Lyle Wyatt (1918-97). He was close friends with many famous figures such as Queen Elizabeth, the Queen Mother, Rupert Murdoch and Margaret Thatcher. He became one of Thatcher's most trusted advisers, and she was a regular visitor here. Wyatt's daughter Petronella (1968) followed her father's footsteps by becoming both a journalist and close friend of the leader of the Tory party. In her case, it was Boris Johnson, with whom she had a four-year affair until 2004. Johnson has

another link with Cavendish Avenue as he lived here for a while as a child at his grandparents' house, just after his family returned from America in 1969.

Number 7 has been the main London residence of Paul McCartney since he bought it for £40,000 in March 1966. It was just a walk away from the famous EMI studios on Abbey Road (seen later) and Paul was then going out with Jane Asher. The other Beatles were moving out of London, but Paul was closely involved in the counter-cultural scene then at its height in the city. He famously had a geodesic dome built in the garden for meditation where he kept a bed Groucho Marx had originally given to Alice Cooper. His famous guests are too numerous to mention, and several Beatles songs were written here. According to Rock lore, in 1971 when a High Court judgement confirmed the dissolution of the Beatles, John, George and Ringo drove in Lennon's car to this spot and Lennon then climbed over the wall and threw two bricks through a window (Paul was on his farm in Scotland).

Continue up Cavendish Avenue, looking out for the **blue plaque** that commemorates another rock star – ㉕ **Billy Fury** – who lived at number 1. Fury (1940-83) and his other fellow stars of the late '50s were part of the first British wave of rock'n'roll. However, this

first wave was short-lived and for a while, it seemed this youth movement might just be a passing fad. Fury's neighbour McCartney and the Beatles would, however, trigger off a new rock and pop musical revolution from 1963 that would change the world.

You reach Circus Road. The name is the only reminder of an ambitious plan by the Eyre family to build a Circus development on the site. A map of London dated 1806 even showed the 'proposed British Circus – 1¹/₄ miles in circumference. Pleasure Ground 42 Acres'. The heart of the development would have stood to the northwest of where St John's Wood underground station is today. Sadly, the economic downturn caused by the Napoleonic Wars prevented what would have been one of the strangest developments in London.

In the Regency period, St John's Wood offered a discreet home to many high-class courtesans and mistresses. The most famous was Harriet Howard (1823-1865), who ran away from home with a jockey to live in London aged 15. She lived on Circus Road in some splendour and is best known for becoming the mistress of Napoleon III of France and acquiring the title Countess de Beauregard.

On the other side is the Hospital of Saint John and Saint Elizabeth, now a private hospital and hospice. It was founded in 1856 by an order of nuns who worked with Florence Nightingale during the Crimean War. Old maps show a convent on the site, but the nuns have long gone. It contains a beautiful **26 hidden chapel** used for services by the Knights of the Hospitallers – the modern-day descendants of the Knights of St John who once owned the land here and gave the district its name. To reach the chapel, you must go through the main entrance located on Grove End Road, so

follow the map (left up Wellington Road and left again at Grove End Road). At the reception ask if you can see the chapel – it is well worth the effort.

After the chapel, return to Grove End Road and then head north up Abbey Road, so-named because it led to an abbey that once stood in Kilburn to the north of here. You pass a memorial to the prominent Victorian sculptor ㉗ **Edward Onslow Ford** (1852-1901) who died in Acacia Road in St John's Wood.

Soon you see the world-famous ㉘ **Abbey Road Studios** and 'that' zebra crossing.

The studios were opened in 1931 by the Gramophone Company, later EMI. The first recording made here was 'Land of Hope and Glory' with the orchestra conducted by Sir Edward Elgar. Other great artists who have recorded here include Yehudi Menuhin, Richard Tauber, Paul Robeson, Glenn Miller, Tony Bennett, Cliff Richard and the Shadows, Pink Floyd, Kate Bush, U2 and Lady Gaga.

However, it was the Beatles who made the studio famous and why tourists and fans from around the world still gather here to write graffiti and pose crossing the most famous zebra crossing in the world. On the 8 August 1969, the Beatles were photographed

27

by Iain Macmillan crossing the road. He only took ten photos in ten minutes, with one chosen by McCartney to grace the cover of *Abbey Road* – the band's eleventh and penultimate album.

In 2019, an unofficial re-staging of the crossing took place to celebrate the 50th anniversary of the shoot, modern-day members of tribute bands taking the place of the Fab Four. There is some doubt about whether this is the true location of the crossing in 1969 – however best not to mention this to any fans risking the anger of drivers to have their photo taken in homage to the fab four.

Follow the map down Hill Road and along the edge of **㉙ Alma Square** to reach number 11. Now a private residence, this was once a pub called the Heroes of Alma. The Beatles, The Seekers, Manfred Mann, Pink Floyd, Queen and the Hollies would all come here in the 1960s during breaks in recording at Abbey Road. No doubt the recording of some of the greatest songs in history were discussed here over a few pints.

Continue along Nugent Terrace and then left onto **㉚ Abercorn Place**. This is one of several roads named after former governors of Harrow School when the Harrow Estate was developed into residential streets in the 19th century (in this case the Duke of Abercorn).

Harrow School was founded in 1572 by John Lyon. Famous alumni include Sir Winston Churchill, Nehru, Lord Byron, and Benedict Cumberbatch. Lyon bought land here in around 1580 for £660, and land holdings in St John's Wood continue to generate income 450 years later for the John Lyon's Charity which spends around £10 million per annum on charitable causes.

Turn left down Abercorn Place heading for the church spire and now getting a clear view of why a few streets around here have 'hill' in their name. On the corner is **㉛ St Mark's, Hamilton Terrace** (named for Harrow school governor Charles Hamilton). It was consecrated in 1847, and was built 'to cater for the new villa dwellers who came to live on this previously rural fringe of London'.

ABERCORN
PLACE NW8

CITY OF WESTMINSTER

30

Canon Robinson Duckworth served here and had a distinguished career, including officiating at the funeral of Charles Darwin in 1882. However, he is perhaps best known for being part of a seemingly innocuous boating expedition in Oxford on 4 July 1862. Those in the boat included a young girl named Alice Liddell and Duckworth's friend, the Reverend Charles Dodgson. Dodgson was inspired by the boat trip and Alice to write the Alice in Wonderland books using the name Lewis Carroll. Duckworth was also immortalised as the character Duck in one of Lewis Carroll's stories.

When finished at the church, walk back along Abercorn place, stopping to see the pretty mews of ㉜ **Abercorn Close** on the right. Turn left up Violet Hill, passing some pastel-coloured dwellings and pretty 19th-century houses that are now shops.

At the end turn onto ㉝ **Violet Hill Gardens**, opened by Queen Elizabeth the Queen Mother in 1952. The name helped inspire the pop band Coldplay who wrote a song entitled *Violet Hill* which was released in 2008. It includes the lines:

"I took my love down to violet hill, There we sat in snow, All that time she was silent still, Said if you love me, won't you let me know?"

When finished, walk up Abbey Gardens to reach Abbey Road again. Turn left, stopping to see the impressive-looking ㉞ **New London Synagogue** at the junction with Marlborough Place. This building has been a

synagogue since 1882. The Beatles attended a memorial service here for their manager Brian Epstein in 1967, his death contributing to the group's demise. The synagogue has also had other famous visitors including the musician Jacqueline du Pré, who performed here.

Turn right up Marlborough Place then take a left onto Loudon Road. It is said that Thackeray based his famous character Becky Sharp from *Vanity Fair* (1863) on a woman named Mary Baker who lived on this street.

Turn left to visit number 15 Loudoun Road where for many years the poet **35** **Stephen Spender** lived with his pianist wife **Natasha Litvin**. It was an unconventional marriage – Spender was homosexual, and Litvin was pursued for many years by writer Raymond Chandler. Stephen's son, Matthew, has written a fascinating account of life here – *A House in St John's Wood: In Search of My Parents* (2015).

The Spenders were at the heart of the literary and artistic world, and regular guests included figures such as Christopher Isherwood and W.H. Auden. Many would love to have been a fly on the wall at the dinner party here in 1955 when Ian Fleming (creator of Bond) met Raymond Chandler (creator of Philip Marlowe). Chandler praised Fleming's Bond novel *Casino Royale*, and Fleming later pressed him for an endorsement for another Bond book – *Live and Let Die* – to help 'make the fortune which has so far eluded me'.

Turn to walk down the east side of Loudoun Road, passing on your left **36** **The American School in London**, founded

at another site in 1951 by an American journalist to teach the US curriculum. The school has had many famous visitors over the years including Presidents Truman, Reagan, Clinton and Obama; Margaret Thatcher and Elton John. The original school had 13 students while today it has over 1,300.

Opposite the school is Langford Place. Walk down here and see some beautiful houses that have been the homes in the past of many artists and actors. On the right is the private **Langford Court**. George Orwell lived here in 1941 after being kicked out of his previous flat by his landlord, H.G. Wells. Wells believed that Orwell and his wife had been talking about him behind his back. Orwell later invited Wells to dinner in an attempt to patch things up.

Retrace your steps up to Loudoun Road and turn right, where you soon reach Grove End Road. Turn left and continue on until you reach St John's Wood underground station, where this walk ends. ●

VISIT...

'Hidden Chapel', Hospital of St. John and St. Elizabeth (see p.145)
60 Grove End Road, NW8 9NH
www.hje.org.uk

St. Johns Wood Church and Gardens (see p.140)
Lord's Roundabout, NW8 7NE
www.stjohnswoodchurch.org.uk

EAT / DRINK...

Ordnance Arms Pub (see p.136)
29 Ordnance Hill, NW8 6PS

The Ivy (see p.139)
120 St. Johns Wood High Street, NW8 7SG
www.theivystjohnswood.com

Duke of York
2 St Anne's Terrace, NW8 6PJ
www.thedukeofyork.com

Panzer's Deli & Café
13-19 Circus Road, NW8 6PB
www.panzers.co.uk

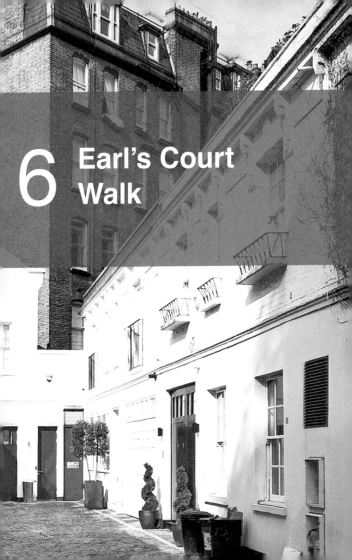

6 Earl's Court Walk

GLOUCESTER

Earl's Court

1. Earl's Court Station Entrance
2. 'Tardis' Telephone Box
3. Hogarth Road
4. 19th-Century Cottages
5. The King's Head
6. Former Village Blacksmith
7. Builder's Ghost Sign
8. Plaque to Willie Rushton
9. Child's Walk
10. Child's Place
11. Spears Mews
12. Plaque to Benjamin Britten
13. Plaque to Alfred Hitchcock
14. Former MI5 Headquarters
15. Gaspar Mews
16. Courtfield Gardens
17. Laverton Mews
18. Hesper Mews
19. Plaque to Howard Carter
20. Bramham Garden
21. High Commission of St Lucia
22. Former Lloyd-Webber Flat
23. Sir John Gielgud's Childhood Home
24. Bousfield Primary School
25. Plaque to Jenny Lind
26. The Boltons
27. St Mary The Boltons
28. Coleherne Court
29. Brompton Library
30. The Bolton
31. The Pembroke
32. Location for *An American Werewolf in London*
33. The Troubadour
34. Finborough Road
35. Brompton Cemetery
36. Earl's Court Square
37. Plaque to Hattie Jacques
38. Former Earl's Court Exhibition Centre
39. Earl's Court Hotel
40. Plaque to Norman Lockyer
41. Old Manor Yard
42. Former Earls Court House

South Kensington

GARDENS

TONS
ROAD
GILSTON ROAD
REDCLIFFE ROAD
ROAD

GARDENS
RDENS

FULHAM ROAD

OLD CHURCH STREET

ELM PARK ROAD

KING'S ROAD

Earl's Court Walk

Start/ Finish: Earl's Court Underground Station
Distance: 3.3 miles

The walk begins at Earl's Court underground station. If you stood here as late as 1830, in front of you would have been just a handful of streets, the site of the station occupied by Earl's Court Farm and an old manor house nearby. On all sides beyond were fields, market gardens, and – in the distance – the villages of Old Brompton to the east, North End to the west, and Chelsea to the south.

The station stood on the site of Earl's Court Farm, and on the walk, you will initially explore some of the very old streets that were found in Earls Court Village before the whole area was developed for housing in the second half of the 19th century. That development led to the area's reputation for having a transient population, dominated by hotels and with a slight air of seediness. On this walk, you will see a surprising side to this fairly unloved and often unnoticed part of London.

The ❶ **station entrance** you see today is the second site – the original station was opposite, opening in 1871. Made of wood, it burnt down a few years later, and a new station entrance was constructed on the current site. In 1911, the first escalators on the underground were installed here, but travellers were nervous about this novelty. A one-legged man named Bumper Harris was hired to travel up and down on them to show they were safe.

Before you leave the station, look out for ❷ **the blue 'Tardis' telephone box**. This is not one of the famous police telephone boxes dating from the 1930s, but a modern creation placed here in 1996. It was part of an attempt to reduce crime in the area, particularly after sex workers and drug dealers moved here when King's Cross was redeveloped. It was the first new police telephone box to be installed since 1969.

11-12 HOGARTH PLACE

TEL : 020 7373 8304

MANILA *Super Market*

MANILA SUPERMARKET LTD

Cross over from the station, heading up
❸ **Hogarth Road**, full of restaurants, estate
agents and small shops. Earl's Court has long
been a home for migrants – Belgians fleeing
the fighting in their homeland during World
War I, Poles who could not return home after
World War II, Arabs, Lebanese, and – perhaps
most famously – Australians, in the 1960s
and 70s. Earl's Court is today the centre of
the British Filipino community, and you are
at the heart of a small group of streets known
as 'Little Manila', which includes shops like
the **'Manila' Super Market**.

By 1830, the old village consisted of only
a few cottages, mainly on Earl's Court Road
(then Earl's Court Lane), and a few smaller
lanes such as Hogarth Road. Look out
on the left for some early ❹ **19th-century
cottages** (9-15 Hogarth Place). They are
completely different to the tall, imposing
Victorian terraces you will see later that date
from the 1860s onwards and which, within
20 years, would transform Earls Court
village into a suburban sprawl of streets,
squares and crescents.

Bear left down Hogarth Place where at
the end is one of the best pubs in the area –
❺ **The King's Head**. In the 1950s-70s many
Australians ended up in Earl's Court, often
travelling in campervans through Asia and
Europe before finding accommodation in the
cheap hostels, hotels and YMCAs that are still
so evident here. The campervans would then
be sold on the street to those embarking on
their own adventures, with many Australians
staying and finding jobs in London.

Kenway Road

The King's Head was popular with Australians during this heyday, and it is claimed former pub manager Bruce Newton coined the phrase 'Kangaroo Valley'. It also served its beer cold – a key to attracting Aussies, and a rarity in London at that time. Regulars included Barry Humphries, who worked at *Private Eye* and later became famous as Dame Edna. The pub claims that one Australian regular, after a renovation in 1971, paid for the old interior to be sent over to his home in New South Wales.

Earl's Court, and its old-style boozers, feature heavily in Patrick Hamilton's classic book *Hangover Square* (1941). Subtitled 'A story of Darkest Earl's Court', it is set just before World War II, and follows a group of hard-drinking characters inhabiting the pubs and threadbare flats of the area. Hamilton had first-hand experience having lived in Earl's Court, and it was not far from here that he was hit by a car in 1932, suffering horrible injuries. The pain only exacerbated Hamilton's alcohol dependency, but he perfectly captured the run-down nature of the area in the mid-20th century, writing 'To those whom God has forsaken is given a gas-fire in Earl's Court'.

In *Hangover Square* the main character is George Harvey Bone, an unstable drinker who is infatuated with an actress living on Cromwell Road. It is thought that the King's Head is the inspiration for one of Bone's regular drinking holes in the novel.

From the pub take a short walk down Kenway Road to see pretty houses from the early 1800s when this was just a village. Number 21 is the **former** site of the **6 Village Blacksmith**. Looming above the houses, a little further along, look out for the old wall advertisement – or **7 Ghost Sign** – for a local builders and decorators. The south side of Kenway Road has at the time of writing a Filipino Restaurant (Lutong Pinoy) – worth a visit if you want to experience some of the hospitality of this community in Earl's Court.

Retrace your steps and walk down Wallgrave Road, full of quaint, two and three storey multi-coloured houses. Number 9 has a **8 Blue Plaque** commemorating the cartoonist, satirist and co-founder of *Private Eye*, **Willie Rushton** (1937-1996).

Carry along, bearing left on Redfield Lane to rejoin Earls Court Road. The fields that would have once lain behind the houses of Hogarth Road, Kenway Road and Child's Street (seen shortly) were developed for housing from the 1860s. Within 20 years the area had been transformed, and the layout of Earl's Court on maps from the 1880s is essentially the same as you see today.

Redfield Lane

Child's St

The Royal Borough of Kensington and Chelsea

CHILD'S WALK. S.W.5

9

10

To see more of the village's original streets, turn left onto **Child's Street** which contains original workmen's houses and cottages from the early part of the 19th century. It is named after Samuel Childs and his family who helped develop part of this area. About halfway down on the right is narrow ❾ **Child's Walk** which is worth a look.

Continue along Earls Court Road, and turn left onto ❿ **Child's Place** to see some other cottages dating from the earlier part of the 19th century. Retrace your steps and cross over Earls Court Road to reach ⓫ **Spear Mews**. Here you'll find attractive houses that once served as horse stables, along with servants' quarters for those working for the bigger houses nearby – all part of the redevelopment of the area in the late 19th century.

In medieval times the aristocratic De Vere family owned around 770 acres of London, including this area. Aubrey de Vere became the Earl of Oxford in 1141, and the De Vere's land was run from a courthouse, the origin of the name Earl's Court.

In 1604, the manor was purchased by Sir Walter Cope, and later passed to the Henry Rich family, Earls of Warwick and Holland, who were also lords of the manor here. In 1728, Earl's Court Manor passed onto William Edwardes, later the first Lord Kensington. In the second half of the 19th century, the old village was redeveloped into a suburb to attract London's growing middle-class with the construction of tall, terraced houses, along with mews streets containing servants quarters and stables.

Billboard by Zaha Hadid Design

However, Earl's Court never reached the grandeur of Belgravia or Mayfair. By the early 20th century the big houses began to be subdivided into flats, or converted into hotels. The typical resident was now a lower-middle-class clerk who worked in an office in the City, although Earl's Court did attract its fair share of writers, artists and other interesting characters as you will discover along the walk. Today, houses in this mews that were once inhabited by servants sell for around £2 million.

Walk through the Mews and turn up Templeton Place, heading northwards past typical Victorian and Edwardian terraced houses, of the kind constructed all over suburban London. Soon you reach Cromwell Road, a busy route that marks the northern boundary of Earl's Court. During and after World War II, the Polish Government in Exile was based not too far from here, and many Poles settled in Earl's Court – hence the area's nickname: the 'Polish Corridor'.

Head eastwards, passing an unusual curved digital billboard – one of the few designs of the architectural practice of Zaha Hadid, to be found in London. The curved metal structure is an impressive work that stands over nine metres high. It is impossible for passing motorists to miss, with its 26 metre-long digital screen projecting advertising and TFL updates. As a pedestrian, you will be blissfully unaware of the advertising and can appreciate the curved form of the design.

Fans of Patrick Hamilton may be interested to know he lived just north of here at 134 Earls Court Road, and the car crash that changed his life took place near Logan Place.

Number 173 Cromwell Road has a **⑫ Blue Plaque** remembering composer **Benjamin Britten** (1913-76). He lived here from 1931 when it was a boarding house (his sister lodged here too). His constant piano playing caused friction with other lodgers – little did they appreciate a free concert from someone who would become one of the nation's greatest modern composers. Britten and his sister moved away in 1935, the composer remarking 'anything to get away from boarding houses'.

Look out on this stretch for old fashioned doorbells which still display signs for 'servants' and 'visitors' (for example outside number 169). A reminder of how the divide between classes at that time was much more evident than today, despite differences in wealth between the richest and poorest perhaps being no less extreme.

Continue along to number 153, the home of film director **⑬ Alfred Hitchcock** (1899-1980) which is marked by another **blue plaque**. He lived here after his marriage in 1926 and stayed throughout his rise to stardom in British cinema before moving to Hollywood in 1939.

Patrick Hamilton and Hitchcock have a connection as the author wrote the play *Rope* in 1929. It centres around two undergraduates who try to execute the perfect murder. In 1948, Hitchcock adapted it into a film of the same name, starring James Stewart.

Continue along Cromwell Road. The name of the road was chosen by Prince Albert, husband of Queen Victoria, and thought to be because Oliver Cromwell (or perhaps his son) lived in a house near here. Why a member of the monarchy would have chosen to remember the name of someone involved in the execution of Charles I is unclear.

Further along at 124-126 was the site of the intelligence service **⑭ MI5's Headquarters** in the 1930s. At that time, the Soviet Russians were one of their chief targets.

Retrace your steps, turning down Courtfield Gardens and pausing at **⑮ Gaspar Mews** on the right. This is one of many mews you will see on the walk that once were essential to those living in the surrounding terraces. An early resident of Earl's Court was James Gunter, who made a fortune as a confectioner and caterer. He bought fields in Earls Court, Chelsea and Fulham in the early 1800s, and the family house in Earl's Court was called Currant Jelly Hall. Between the mid-1860s and 1890s, approximately 60 acres around Earls Court were developed by his sons, James and Robert.

Several street names remember the Gunter family – the wife of Robert Jr. had connections to Gledhow Hall in Yorkshire, giving rise

to nearby Gledhow Gardens, whilst Robert Jr. represented Barkston and Knaresborough in Yorkshire as MP (hence Barkston Gardens and Knaresborough Place).

Continue along to reach **⑯ Courtfield Gardens**, one of several private gardens in Earl's Court that were originally used by the wealthy Victorian families that had moved into a grand terraced house but who had no back gardens. Follow the map to walk along Courtfield Gardens and reach Laverton Place, where you turn left.

SPAR
S. SW.5

Gaspar Mews

Moving on, stop to see more examples of mews – first ⓱ **Laverton Mews** then ⓲ **Hesper Mews**. Opposite at number 19 Collingham Gardens there is a ⓳ **blue plaque** commemorating Egyptologist **Howard Carter** (1874-1939) where he lived for much of the 1920s with his brother. Carter, who discovered the tomb of Tutankhamun in 1922, became globally famous after the find and so must have been a local celebrity when he returned to this address. He spent his later years between Egypt and his flat in Kensington.

When he died in 1939 his executors discovered 18 antiquities from Tutankhamun's tomb which were discreetly sold to the Metropolitan Museum and later returned to the Egyptian Museum in Cairo.

Continue along to the elegant, Victorian era ⓴ **Bramham Gardens**. Houses have sold here for over £8 million in recent years, and flats can cost over £4 million – a sign that Earls Court is as exclusive as Mayfair or Chelsea in certain areas. One of the apartments was the home of socialite and 90's 'It girl', Tara Palmer-Tomkinson (1971-2017). At the height of her success as a model she was famed for her billboard lingerie adverts which reportedly stopped traffic. She became a celebrity, with paparazzi following her eventful private life. Sadly, her later years were plagued by ill health and she took her own life here in February 2017 at just 45 years of age.

Follow the map, turning left into Bolton Gardens and looking out for an impressive building that today houses the ㉑ **High Commission of St Lucia** – a welcome break from the repetitive terraced houses.

Cross over to take a short detour to 10 Gledhow Gardens where ㉒ **Andrew Lloyd-Webber** once lived in a basement flat, and where he wrote the music for *Jesus Christ*

Superstar in 1964. Actor **㉓ Sir John Gielgud** was born at number 7 Gledhow Gardens in 1904 and lived here as a child.

Return to Bolton Gardens and walk south to Boltons Place. On the right is **㉔ Bousfield Primary School**. This stands on the site of the family home of writer Beatrix Potter (1866-1943). Best known for books such as *The Tale of Peter Rabbit*, she was born in the house and lived here until her marriage in 1913. By all accounts, she had an unhappy, lonely childhood here. The house was destroyed by German bombing during World War II.

Opposite the school spot the **㉕ blue plaque** that remembers the Victorian singing sensation **Jenny Lind** (1820-87). The 'Swedish nightingale' wooed audiences around the world and was an internationally famous opera singer. She recently became much better known to contemporary audiences after her character featured heavily in the hit film *The Greatest Showman* (2017).

Continue onwards. We are now straying from Earls Court into Chelsea to visit **㉖ The Boltons**. Laid out in the shape of a lens, it is among the top five most expensive streets in Britain – with number 20 being sold for £54 million in 2012. Today this is the favoured location of the super-rich – hedge fund managers, aristocrats, Middle Eastern oil sheikhs and billionaires. In the 1950s, the suave American actor and Anglophile **Douglas Fairbanks Jr.** lived at number 28 and had an active social life, entertaining the Queen and Prince Philip here. Other

Bramham Gardens

27

27

past residents include Madonna and Jeffrey Archer. The area is likely named after William Bolton, who bought land in this area in 1795. He later sold the land to James Gunter – mentioned earlier.

London has always had extremes of wealth on display and when the Boltons were laid out, its residents were just over a five-minute walk from the Workhouse of St George Hanover Square (where the Chelsea & Westminster Hospital is today).

The centre of the Boltons is dominated by the church of ㉗ St Mary The Boltons, consecrated in 1850. This was originally a farm and market gardens. George Godwin was responsible for developing houses here including the church.

You may wish to walk along the other side of the Boltons to visit the church or admire the other grand residences, however when finished follow the map down Tregunter Road and then right, up Little Boltons where at the top, on the left, is ㉘ Coleherne Court.

Lady Diana Spencer lived in a flat here (number 60) between 1979 and 1981. It had been bought for her by her mother. The red-brick and Portland stone mansion block was built at the very start of the 20th century. Diana's flat cost £50,000 in 1979, and after Diana married Prince Charles, her mother sold it for double that amount. Today, flats here are worth well over £1 million. During her engagement to Charles, the paparazzi were ever-present on the street, beginning Diana's long, complicated and ultimately tragic relationship with the British press.

Now you reach Old Brompton Road and turn left (westwards). On the right is **㉙ Brompton Library**, which Diana used when living at Coleherne Court.

At the next junction you'll find a charming pub called **㉚ The Bolton**. It was originally built as a hotel of the same name in 1892 and later became an Irish-themed pub. The journalist and playwright Keith Waterhouse (1929-2009) was a regular here in the last few years of his life. Like Patrick Hamilton, Waterhouse managed to combine a love of pub life with a prolific literary career. His most famous work was the novel *Billy Liar* (1959), but his career included a film script for Alfred Hitchcock, and writing for television shows such as *Worzel Gummidge*. Waterhouse was also a columnist for the *Daily Mail* and *Daily Mirror*. He had a reputation as a drinker but believed that God had blessed him with the gift of the delayed hangover, allowing him to get up the next morning and start writing. One obituary noted that 'despite his considerable income, he lived in modest circumstances, shunning a Mayfair address for Earls Court'.

Cross over the road and continue westwards for a few minutes to reach **31 The Pembroke Pub** on the left-hand side. This used to be The Coleherne Arms, that was popular with the gay community from the 1950s. The old name still survives on the stone tablet at roof level. The pub also has the misfortune to have been frequented by three serial killers: Dennis Nilsen, Michael Lupo and Colin Ireland. It is known for certain that Lupo (in the late 80s) and Ireland (in the early 90s) picked up some of their victims at the Coleherne, and it is possible Nilsen also came here for the same reason. Wharfedale Street, behind the pub, was a well-known cruising zone, particularly after the Coleherne had shut for the night.

Fans of the horror film **32 An American Werewolf in London** (1981) might be interested to know that 64 Coleherne Road, just south of the pub, was used as the location for Jenny Agutter's flat in the film.

Next door – at 263-267 Old Brompton Road – is another legendary London venue – **33 The Troubadour**. One of the original 1950s coffeehouses, it became a key venue during the folk revival of the late 50s and 60s. Bob Dylan played here in 1962, as did Paul Simon three years later (he later returned to America and recorded again with Garfunkel). Other musical legends who played here include Jimi Hendrix, Joni Mitchell, Elton John, Charlie Watts, Jimmy Page and Robert Plant. From the world of British folk, performers here include Sandy Denny, Bert Jansch and Linda Thompson. Look out for a photo of

the venue taken in the 1950s by L. Ron Hubbard, founder of Scientology. He spent time in London during that decade while trying to build his worldwide religious movement.

Just along from here is **㉞ Finborough Road** where Conservative MP and minister David Mellor owned a flat in the early 1990s. It became the centre of tabloid frenzy in 1992 when Mellor was discovered to be having an affair with actress Antonia de Sancha. He later resigned and the scandal contributed to the demise of John Major's government. The most remembered detail of the scandal – aside from the headline 'from toe job to no job..' – was the tabloid story that Mellor wore his beloved Chelsea shirt in bed. A detail that Mellor has always denied.

Continue along, and if you have time, visit **㉟ Brompton Cemetery** – one of the most atmospheric places in London. It has a stunning variety of tombs, sculptures and memorials, dating from 1840. Hundreds of notable people are buried here – perhaps the most famous being the suffragette Emmeline Pankhurst and cricketer John

Emmeline Pankhurst's grave

Wisden. Names of the deceased were also used by local Beatrix Potter for characters in her books: Mr Nutkins, Mr McGregor, Jeremiah Fisher and even Peter Rabbit.

When finished continue up Warwick Road – named after the Earls of Warwick who owned lands here – and turn into **36 Earl's Court Square**. Look out for the ornate façade of Langham Mansions on the right – a good example of the upmarket apartment blocks built in the 1890s and where today flats cost well over £1 million. Originally the building offered residents use of a communal billiard and reading room.

The square was built on the site of Rich Lodge and surrounding market gardens, and in the early 1800s became part of the Edwardes Estate. The houses on the square were built in the 1870s with the garden at its centre being tended to by its own full-time gardener until 1939. Around the Square you will see an interesting contrast between the Italianate-style, white stuccoed terraces on the north, east and west sides, and the more interesting Flemish red-brick houses to the south. The houses became dirty in the years after construction due to London's smog, and after World War I most were painted white for the first time to make them more presentable.

The census of 1891 shows that the houses were then owned by single families, which had more servants living in them than family members. However, records also show that many houses remained vacant for several years after they were built, and

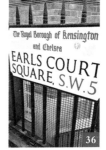

were later used as boarding houses, schools, hotels or converted into flats – developers having failed to attract enough wealthy families. During World War II the southern part of the gardens housed huge water tanks, and the cast-iron railings were taken away for scrap metal. Numbers 25-27 on the north side were destroyed by a German bomb in 1942, only the exterior from the original building remains.

Whilst the largest properties here can sell for nearly £6 million, the Square still has echoes of the darker side of Earl's Court as immortalised by Patrick Hamilton. In January 2014, Robert Richard Fraser viciously murdered Columbian, sex worker Maria Duque-Tunjano in a flat on the northeast side of the Square. Maria had been working as an escort from the flat, and using her earnings to support her family back home. Fraser was later diagnosed as suffering from paranoid schizophrenia and detained indefinitely at Broadmoor Hospital.

The streets around here can feel a little soulless and it is hard to get a sense of community, but one way is to visit the modest but vibrant farmer's market that is held by the Square every Sunday. There is also a plaque stating 'I am a refugee' commemorating pop star **Rita Ora** (b.1990) who moved to London as a child after her family escaped Kosovo during the conflict in the early 1990s. The plaque can be found on the wall of the nearby St Cuthbert with St Matthias Primary School where she was a pupil.

After walking around the square, continue up Warwick Road. Turn right, passing Eardley Crescent where at number 67 you will find a **37** **Blue Plaque** to comedy actress **Hattie Jacques**. She lived here from 1945 until her death in 1980 and is best known for her roles in 14 *Carry On* films. Her husband John Le Mesurier – who also lived here with her – appeared in more than 120 films before finding national treasure status as Sergeant Wilson in *Dad's Army*.

Continue on, and shortly on the left is the site of the former **38** **Earl's Court Exhibition Centre** (opposite the drum-shaped underground station). It closed in 2014, ending Earl's Court's long history as a venue for major events. Unique concerts took place here such as David Bowie performing as Ziggy Stardust and Pink Floyd playing *Dark Side of the Moon*, while this was also the venue for annual events like the Motor Show where many famous cars were ceremonially unveiled.

In the 19th century, the growth of the railway in west London created a wasteland in this area. An entrepreneur named John Robinson Whitley developed the land for use as a showground in the 1880s. In the 1930s new owners built a vast exhibition centre, opening here in 1937, later joined by another sister building which was opened by Princess Diana in 1991.

This long history came to an end when owners – Capco – decided to demolish the exhibition complexes and build residential properties. This has still to be completed, and controversy rages about what will happen to the site, with considerable opposition from locals who fear their estates are going to disappear.

The land to the west of here is the site of one of London's 'lost' rivers – The Counter's Creek. Starting in Kensal Green, it flowed

through here before running alongside Brompton Cemetery and then emptying into the Thames by Chelsea. The lower two miles of the creek disappeared into the Kensington Canal that was developed by Lord Kensington in the 1820s. However, the canal could not compete with the rise of the railways and was taken over by a railway company in 1839. Most of the canal was filled in and a railway line built over the route. The only remnant of the canal to be found today is at Chelsea Creek.

Retrace your steps to walk up Penywern Road. Number 35-37 was once the ㊴ **Earl's Court Hotel**, which played a small part in one of the most tragic events of the 1960s. On 4 April 1968, the civil rights leader Martin Luther King was assassinated by an escaped convict named James Earl Ray (1928-1998) while King was at a motel in Memphis, Tennessee. The FBI launched its biggest ever manhunt and the assassin went on the run, arriving in London on a false Canadian passport. Earl Ray stayed in a number of places including – on 28 May 1968 – room 54 of Earl's Court Hotel. The receptionist Jane Nassau later stated: 'I recognised his southern drawl and wondered why he had a Canadian passport'. He was arrested at Heathrow Airport, and swiftly returned to the American authorities. Earl Ray was subsequently found guilty and died in prison aged 70.

Continue along Penywern Road passing number 16 – home to ㊵ **Norman Lockyer** (1836-1920) marked with a **blue plaque**. Lockyer was a scientist credited with discovering the gas 'helium' and also founded the journal *Nature*.

Follow the map to Earl's Court Road and turn left until you reach ㊶ **Old Manor Yard**. This was the site of the old manorial court that contributed to this district's name. Lovers of grammatical problems can debate for eternity whether it is Earls Court or Earl's Court but life is too short. A manor house also stood near here, which along with the farm was demolished in the mid-1860s when the original Earl's Court Station was constructed.

Opposite once stood **42 Earls Court House**, built in 1772 and owned by Scottish surgeon Dr John Hunter (1728-1793). He pioneered research into gunshot wounds and venereal disease but is perhaps most famous for his vast collection of stuffed animals. He also kept live animals on the site, including lions, leopards, zebras, ostriches and a bull (which he used to wrestle). His collection, which included the skeleton of the 'Irish giant' Charles Byrne, later became the basis of the Hunterian Museum which you can visit in London. In the 19th century, Hunter's former residence became a 'mad house' for young women of wealthy families before being demolished in 1886. You are now by the underground station where this walk ends. ●

VISIT...

St Mary the Boltons Church (see p.176)
8 The Boltons, SW10 9TB
www.stmarytheboltons.org.uk

Brompton Cemetery (see p.179)
Fulham Road & Old Brompton Road, SW10 9UG
www.brompton-cemetery.org.uk

EAT / DRINK...

The King's Head Pub (see p.163)
17 Hogarth Road, SW5 0QT
www.kingsheadearlscourt.co.uk

North Lodge Café
Brompton Cemetery North Lodge.
Lillie Road, SW5 9JE
www.cooksandpartners.co.uk

The Troubadour Cafe (see p.178)
265-7 Old Brompton Road, SW5 9JA
www.troubadourlondon.com

7 Fulham Town Walk

Fulham Town Walk

1. World War II Pillbox
2. Plaque to Frederick Richard Simms
3. Fulham Vestry Wharf
4. Putney Bridge
5. Bishops Park
6. Sculpture Garden
7. Spanish Civil War Memorial
8. Ferry Steps
9. Fielder's Meadow
10. Fulham Football Club
11. Water Fountain
12. Bishop's Garden Tea House
13. Fulham Palace
14. Walled Garden
15. All Saint's Fulham
16. Sir William Powell Almshouses
17. Numbers 5 & 6 Church Gate
18. The Temperance
19. King's Arms
20. The Golden Lion
21. Victorian School Building
22. Fulham Pottery Kiln
23. Fulham House
24. Eight Bells
25. Hurlingham Books

FINLAY STREET

STEVENAGE ROAD

ELLERBY

10

9

Bishops Park

River Thames

PUTNEY EMBANKMENT

Leader's Gardens

PUTNEY EMBA

SWATERS PLACE

FESTING ROAD

ASHLONE ROAD

ROTHERWOOD ROAD

BENDEMEER RD

GLADWYN RD

GLENDARVON ST

LOWER RICHMC

LOWER RICHMOND ROAD

THORPE ST

WYMON

STANBRIDGE RD

FARLOW RD

ROSKELL RD

SALVIN ROAD

PUTNEY EMBA

FELSHAM ROAD

Tey Brook

Fulham Walk
Start/Finish: Putney Bridge Underground Station
Distance: 1.75 miles

Confidence

For a walk concerned with Fulham, this walk starts – perhaps confusingly – at Putney Bridge underground station. Putney is south of the Thames, but the station was built on the north side of Putney Bridge in 1880. The Victorians, rather oddly, named the station after the borough beyond the bridge. If you've travelled here by tube, before you leave the station, look towards the end of the platform for the remains of a ❶ **World War II Pillbox**. It was part of a largely forgotten 'Stop Line' – a defensive ring of fortifications built around London in the expectation of an imminent German invasion. The station was originally called Putney Bridge & Fulham, then was renamed Putney Bridge & Hurlingham in 1902. It only changed to its present name in 1932.

Leave the station and bear left towards the railway bridge, looking out for a blue plaque that remembers this spot as being where ❷ **Frederick Richard Simms** (1863-1944) had his first workshop. In the 1890s Simms acquired rights to the petrol engine from Daimler, and used the engines in the riverboats he built here, demonstrating his motorised vessels on the Thames. Realising the potential for land-based transport, he became an early pioneer in Britain's burgeoning car industry. Simms co-founded what became the Royal Automobile Club, and was the first to use the words 'motorcar' and 'petrol'.

Walk down the path signposted just before the bridge on the right (under the blue plaque) and soon you reach the footpath parallel to the Thames where you turn right.

What constitutes Fulham can be confusing. In the past, it was simpler and maps of the 18th-century show this area was still mostly fields, whilst hugging the land near the Thames is Fulham Old Town. To the north and east, across the fields, are places that developed separately – the villages of Parsons Green, Walham Green and North End. To the southeast of here was a largely deserted marshland – Sands End.

The name Walham Green has largely disappeared from use, the village became a suburb during the 19th century. The village centre was where Fulham Broadway stands today. For many this remains the heart of modern Fulham, rather than the historic Old Town you will mainly visit today.

Look out for a floor mosaic depicting the Oxford and Cambridge Boat Race which starts near here. The race has been held nearly every year since it began in 1829.

As you walk along the Thames Path, on the right is an inlet of water that was once part of ❸ **Fulham Vestry Wharf**. It was used for river transport to and from the malt house that stood next door in the late 19th century. The Swan Inn was also nearby, frequented by the ferrymen who plied their trade from medieval times. Continue along the path, to reach ❹ **Putney Bridge** which you pass underneath.

You now reach the entrance to ❺ **Bishops Park**, which opened in 1893 using land granted to the public by the Church. It is worth stopping to read a little more about the history of the area.

Putney Bridge

Bazalgette Stone

Ranelagh Gardens

The Bishops of London acquired the manor of Fulham in 704AD. The earliest settlement was a tiny fishing village, first recorded in 1391, that lay between here and Fulham High Street. The most important buildings – both seen later – were All Saints Parish church (dating from the 13th century) and the adjacent Fulham Palace that for around 12 centuries served as the residence for the Bishops of London. Archaeological discoveries have unearthed evidence of Neolithic (3000 BC), Iron Age (800-43AD) and Roman (200-500 AD) settlements in the area.

For many centuries ferrymen operated here, and unsurprisingly they fought hard against the proposal to build a bridge. Their efforts were, however, in vain and a wooden bridge was erected in 1729. The original bridge began at the bottom of the High Street – about a hundred yards from the Putney Bridge you see today. The ferrymen disappeared, and instead, tolls were collected from those using the new bridge, then known as Fulham, not Putney, Bridge. The only other bridge in central London at that time was London Bridge.

In 1739 three Army officers were lucky to escape with a fine of 20 guineas for a 'riot and assault...on the persons of the toll men by beating them in a most cruel and inhuman manner'. The Bishop of London and his household were exempt from bridge tolls, although for years this led to unscrupulous travellers claiming they were connected to the Bishop.

The bridge you see today was completed in 1886. It was designed by the great civil engineer, Sir Joseph Bazalgette (1819-91), best known for his transformation of London's sewer system. You can see a commemorative stone in his memory at the foot of the bridge. It is the only bridge in England to have churches on either end (All Saints on the north side, St Mary's on the south). The construction of the first bridge attracted more people to the village. Over time grand houses were built near the shoreline, most of which have now been lost. Ranelagh Gardens, the road which leads up to the station, is named after one of these – Ranelagh House. To the east of the station is a rare survivor – Hurlingham House, now an exclusive private sports club and for many years the most famous place in the world for lovers of polo.

Mary Wollstonecraft (1759-97), a pioneering feminist, tried to commit suicide from the original bridge in 1795, having been abandoned by her lover, who eloped with an actress. Had she succeeded, her daughter Mary Shelley (1797-1851) would not have been born, and the world would not have enjoyed her Gothic masterpiece, *Frankenstein*.

At the beginning of the park, you can also see All Saints church which we will explore later on. There is a map of the park and an information board listing its main features. By the entrance look out for the ❻ **Sculpture Garden** and Rose Garden. Continue further into the park to see the ❼ **Spanish Civil War Memorial** which remembers 37 residents of Hammersmith and Fulham who died fighting in the International Brigade against Franco's forces in the Spanish Civil War. You may wish to explore the Park at your leisure, but to follow this walk continue, or return to, the path by the Thames.

If you have seen the horror film *The Omen* (1976) this walk under tall London Plane trees may seem eerily familiar, as scenes from the film were shot here. This is always a very popular place to watch the beginning of the Boat Race each year, and normally about 250,000 spectators crowd the banks of the Thames.

Over on the south side of the Thames, you should be able to spot a series of boat clubs. Even after the ferrymen disappeared from the river, mucking about on the water in this part of London remained an important pastime.

You will reach a break in the embankment wall with some ❽ **steps leading down to the Thames** and the word 'Ferry' visible. This does not refer to the historic ferry that operated between Putney and Fulham, but a later service that ran between Bishops Park and a location near Putney. It operated from when the embankment wall was completed in the early 1890s, right up until the 1950s. It was once very popular with football supporters who arrived in their hundreds on the penny ferry to see Fulham F.C. play. This was also once known as the Bishop's Stairs as the barge belonging to the Bishop of London would pull up here, transporting clergymen between Fulham Palace and central London.

While Putney Bridge is often assumed by many people to be the official start of the world-famous Boat Race between Oxford and Cambridge, the actual starting point is the University Boat race stone on the south bank of the Thames, directly opposite the steps.

On the south side of the Thames, you also should be able to see the outflow of one of London's little known rivers – the Beverley Brook. It rises about 9 miles away in Worcester Park.

You can either continue along a little further and cut through the open space known as ❾ **Fielders Meadow**, or walk more centrally through the Park and pass the lake. Either way, you should end up in the south-east corner of the Park, exiting onto Stevenage Road to reach Craven Cottage, home of ❿ **Fulham Football Club**.

Opened in 1896, the stadium was later rebuilt to a design by Archibald Leitch, responsible for more than 20 other football grounds in Britain, including Glasgow Rangers' Ibrox Stadium. The capacity here is currently only around 25,000 – a small ground for a club with such a pedigree.

The club was founded in 1879, originally as Fulham St Andrew's Church Sunday Football F.C., and linked to St Andrew's, Fulham Fields (on Star Road). The club became professional in 1898, and later attracted great players such as Johnny Haynes, George Cohen, Bobby Robson, Bobby Moore, and Alan Mullery. There is a statue of Haynes (1934-2005) outside. The 'Maestro' spent 18 years at Fulham, and in the early 1960s became the first football player to earn the princely sum of £100 a week.

George Best had a short but memorable spell at Fulham in the mid-1970s, sometimes turning up late for training after a late night out. One teenage trainee at the club remembered the manager Bobby Campbell 'would give [Best] a rollicking and send him into Bishops Park' where jumpers were put down for goalposts and the legendary player would 'dribble around a few willing kids and score a few, while dodging women pushing prams'.

Former owner of the club Mohamed Al-Fayed (b.1933) was friends with Michael Jackson and after his death, erected a statute of the singer outside Harrods. After Al-Fayed sold Harrods, he moved the statue to Craven Cottage in 2011 but it was not well received by fans (even though Jackson had attended a game here). It was removed once more when Fulham F.C. was sold to a new owner in 2013.

Craven Cottage is named after a house built here in 1780 by William Craven, sixth Baron Craven and not the earlier royal hunting lodge that once stood on this site. The grand house was later destroyed by fire in 1888.

Flooding was a major problem for many parts of Fulham, but this was alleviated by the construction of the embankment you saw earlier. It was built in the 1890s by Joseph Mears, whose sons Joseph and Gus were responsible in 1905 for founding another great London football club – Chelsea F.C. Gus Mears had bought Stamford Bridge athletics stadium in 1904 and offered it to Fulham F.C., they turned him down so Mears decided to found his own football team. He could not call his new team Fulham (even though Stamford Bridge was in the district) so he took the name of neighbouring Chelsea.

Retrace your steps along Stevenage Road. To your left are rows of pleasant, semi-detached Victorian houses, but as late as the 1890s there was nothing here but open fields – a reminder of how much London has spread in a relatively short period. Re-enter the park and walk along the path on the south side (parallel to Stevenage Road).

You will soon encounter the ⑪ **water fountain** which requires you to step on a footplate to pump up the water. It was made by the Murdock Supply Company in Cincinnati in the United States. There is no date of manufacture, but the Murdock company was founded in 1853 and is still making public fountains today.

You can stop at the ⑫ **Bishop's Garden tea house** if you need a break. There is also a farmer's market in the Park every Sunday, which is a pleasant distraction if you happen to be exploring Fulham when the market is open.

Continue along and through the gates on the left to reach **⑬ Fulham Palace**. There is a superb moat that dates from the 14th century. Maps of the late 19th century still show the moat being full of water, but in the 1920s it was filled with debris from building firms at the request of the Bishop of London – a controversial move that annoyed many residents and was discussed in Parliament. The moat was nearly a mile in length, making the Palace the largest domestic moated site in Medieval England. It was fed by the water from the Thames controlled by a sluice gate and the winding mechanism is still visible in the Palace grounds.

Enter the grounds of Fulham Palace, an often overlooked treasure of London. Bishop Waldhere first took possession of the site in around 700 AD, and Bishops lived here for around 12 centuries. For many years it was used as a summer retreat, and often the Bishop and his household would come here to escape the plague or other pestilence that regularly afflicted London's inhabitants. The Palace stopped being used as a residence in 1973 when Bishop Stopford retired.

As Lord of the Manor, the Bishop of London wielded enormous power over the lands of Fulham and beyond. His appointees presided over the manorial court that decided many local disputes, landholding claims, and petty crimes. The Bishop was also entitled to rents, farm produce, fish from the Thames and a share of the fees earned by the ferrymen and livestock. However, he also had responsibilities, including maintaining

bridges and ditches. The Bishop of London retained the title of Lord of the Manor right up until 1868, powers then exercised by the parish vestry before Fulham Borough Council was created.

When the Thames froze over in 1789, villagers from Fulham and those to the south of the Thames would meet on the frozen surface and play games, whilst Bishop Beibly Porteus and his wife walked across the ice to Putney. Porteus was the first American to serve as Bishop of London. The post has historically been fraught with danger, vulnerable to the dramas of national life. Bishop Edmund Bonner, a Catholic, was imprisoned by Edward VI and Nicholas Ridely was burned at the stake by Queen Mary.

Bonner was a particularly nasty individual, keeping religious prisoners at the Palace where they suffered torture. The Bishop's ghost is said to haunt the area north of the courtyard. Another Bishop, William Juxon, was with Charles I on the scaffold in Whitehall when the King was executed in 1649. The office of Bishop of London was abolished between 1646-60, during Oliver Cromwell's brief reign as Lord Protector.

The names of all 132 Bishops of London reflect the history of England itself; in the early centuries the names are Saxon – Ecgwulf, Eadgar, Osmund, whilst after 1066 many reflect Norman or French influence – Robert de Sigillo, William of Sainte-Mere-Eglise. By the 18th century, the names are much more 'English' – for example, John Robinson, Thomas Sherlock. These Bishops regularly received Royal visitors, including Henry III, Elizabeth I, James I and Charles I.

As you explore the Palace and its grounds, you will notice it is a mix of styles including Georgian and Gothic Revival dating from the 15th to the 20th centuries. The Great Hall dates from 1495 and the superb ⑭ **Walled Garden** and surrounding gardens are a real highlight. Now covering 13 acres, the gardens originally spread out over 36, enclosed by what was once the longest moat in England. In the late 17th-century Bishop Henry Compton famously planted trees and plants brought to England for the first time from the New World.

Fulham Palace is open daily but visiting times can vary according to the season. It is best to check the website (www.fulhampalace.org/visit/opening-times/).

14

When finished at the Palace, return to Bishops Park and continue to walk towards the prominent spire of the church of All Saints Fulham. Alternatively, a nicer route is to continue through the garden and at the east side, exit through a small gate that leads to the church – however this is not always open.

You should now be at **⓯ All Saints Fulham**. The view of the church and Palace is little changed from that which greeted early visitors to the Manor of Fulham arriving by ferry, or later crossing the bridge.

The first mention of a church in Fulham dates from 1154, but the 15th-century Kentish ragstone tower is now the oldest part of the building. By the late 19th century, the medieval church was too small for the local congregation, and prone to flooding. As a consequence, in 1880, the decision was made to demolish much of the church, and architect Sir Arthur Bloomfield (1829-99), son of Bishop of London Charles Bloomfield, was commissioned to design the new building. Sir Arthur was a prolific architect, responsible for dozens of other churches in Britain, and even a cathedral in Guyana. The new church sympathetically incorporated the late medieval stone tower.

If the church is open, look out for some fine memorials including the Legh Memorial to Lady Margaret Legh who died in 1603. The figure of Lady Margaret wears Elizabethan dress and holds two swaddled children who died in infancy. She was married to a Member of Parliament and had 9 children before she died aged just 33. There is another memorial to Sir William Butts (d.1545) who was chief physician to Henry VIII. He even made it into Shakespeare's play, Henry VIII.

> "Butts: I'll show your Grace the strangest sight –
> King: What's that Butts?
> Butts: I think your Highness saw this many a day.
> King: Body o'me, where is it?"

There is also a memorial attributed to the famous craftsman Grinling Gibbons to Lady Dorothy Clarke (d.1695). Her husband was Secretary of War under Charles II and died fighting in a naval battle against the Dutch Navy.

Outside the main entrance turn right and then the last path on the left to find the tomb of Granville Sharp (d.1813), one of the key forces behind the anti-slavery movement in England, and the founding father of Sierra Leone. A superb musician, his bass voice was described by George III as 'the best in Britain'. He wittily signed his name 'G#'. Eleven Bishops of London are also buried in this churchyard.

Like Bishops Park, the church also features in the horror film, *The Omen*. The famous scene where a priest is impaled by a falling lightning conductor was shot here.

From the church enter Church Gate. On the right is the site of the old vicarage that stood here for over 500 years. This would once have been a tranquil place, but the widening of the nearby road in 1906 brought the traffic much closer and disturbed the Vicar's peace. This led to a successful campaign to demolish the original building and move the vicarage, and the Vicar, to a more peaceful location.

On the left-hand side are the charming **16 Sir William Powell Almshouses**, comprising of 12 flats. The original almshouses were founded in 1680 for 12 poor widows. The current Gothic-style structure dates from 1869 and is the third building to occupy the site. It is named after Sir William Powell (1624-80), an MP who owned nearby Munster House. Powell's home was one of many grand houses found in Fulham in the years before the railway and underground turned this area into another London suburb.

Further along, on the left, you see some 18th century housing at **⑰ Numbers 5 and 6 Church Gate**, giving you an idea of how old Fulham Town once appeared. Look for the rare insurance firemark, or symbol, for the 'Hand in Hand Fire & Life Insurance Company' that was founded in 1696 and was in its day the oldest fire insurance company in the world. For 135 years the company ran its own fire brigade and firemarks like this would have shown the firefighters that the hapless house owner did indeed have insurance.

Continue along Church Gate to reach Fulham High Street. One publication from 1878 described the High Street as having 'the dull, sleepy aspect of a quiet country town: many of the quaint old red-brick houses, with high-tiled roofs, carry the mind of the observer back to times long gone by.'

Stop at the inappropriately named **⑱ The Temperance pub** on the corner. Ironically this was originally the Grade II listed Temperance Billiard Hall – the second example found in this book (the other is in Clapham). Built in 1910, it was part of an attempt by the powerful temperance movement to get drinkers out of pubs and into dry billiard halls where they could play games and hopefully avoid the evils of alcohol. The words 'Temperance Billiard Hall' are still to be seen in the mosaic glass above the pub entrance

The railways came to Fulham in the late 19th century with Putney Bridge Station opening in 1880. This helped transform a sleepy village into yet another London

suburb, and the growing population needed new forms of entertainment. Near here stood the Fulham Theatre which opened in 1897, with a plush interior designed in the style of Louis XIV. Later called 'the Grand', at its peak, it could accommodate over 2,000 people. However, like many such establishments, it suffered due to competition from the new medium of cinema. It finally closed in 1950 and was later demolished. The Grand Theatre site is now a glass-fronted office block called Riverbank House.

Opposite The Temperance is the **19** **King's Arms**, a rare reminder of old Fulham Town. The building dates from 1888, but is the third structure on this site, its origins going back to the time of Henry VIII. At that time it was a coaching inn, serving those travelling between London and Southampton. Look out for the original brewery brickwork tiled arch to the right of the entrance.

You are now on Fulham High Street. In the days of the Manor of Fulham there were two courts – the Court Leete (for more minor matters) and the Court Baron. The courts did not have a dedicated building and met in the open air, at a local church, or in the King's Arms. Locals found guilty of an offence could find themselves put into a cage, the stocks or even whipped (the stocks and whipping-post were located nearby).

From the pub turn left and continue a short way up Fulham High Street to arrive at ⑳ **The Golden Lion**. Rebuilt in 1836, this was originally a Tudor building that was used as a private residence, and then later a coffee house before becoming a pub.

Legend has it that the cellar of the old house was used by Bishop Bonner as a dungeon in the 16th century. During the reign of Queen Mary, Bonner had many Protestants tortured and years later a workman discovered both a gridiron and human remains in a dark recess of the cellar.

The origin of the name Fulham is not entirely clear – perhaps derived from the Saxon word 'Fullenham', or "Foulenham," meaning 'the habitation of birds, or place of fowls'. Alternatively, it may be because someone called Fulla owned the land here, marking it as Fulla's settlement.

Just past here is an elegant ㉑ **Victorian school building**, and the old parish workhouse built in the 1770s once stood not far from here. A whipping post and stocks stood on the northeast corner of the High Street until the mid 19th century.

This area also has a Shakespearean connection as Henry Condell (1576-1627), who acted alongside the great playwright, lived for a time in Fulham to escape the plague. Condell is now remembered because he and another member of Shakespeare's company, John Heminges, published the famous First Folio in 1623, an act which ensured Shakespeare's brilliance would never be forgotten. Condell died in Fulham, aged 51, wearing the ring that Shakespeare had left him in his will.

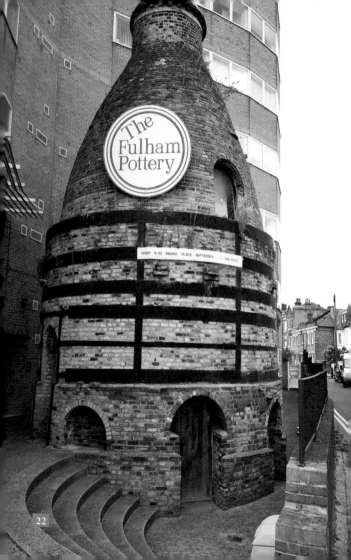

The
Fulham
Pottery

SHOP 8-10 INGATE PLACE BATTERSEA · 720 0005

22

Now turn and retrace your steps before heading left down New Kings Road. After a few minutes, you will see on the left ㉒ **The Fulham Pottery Kiln** (on Burlington Road). This once famous pottery was opened by John Dwight in 1672 and specialised in salt glaze ceramics. Dwight had 'discovered the mystery of the stone or Cologne wares hitherto made only in Germany'. The solitary kiln is all that remains of what was once a huge enterprise. It continued in use under a variety of different owners well into the 20th century.

After the Fulham Pottery kiln, cross the New Kings Road and take the footpath to the right of the Majestic wine store. At the end of the path turn right along Station Approach to reach Fulham High Street.

On the corner is ㉓ **Fulham House**, which dates from the early 1800s. Now occupied by the army, an older building on this site was called Passors after a local family who lived here during the reign of Edward III (a passator was a term for ferryman).

The house was later owned by Sir Thomas Whyte who served as Lord Mayor of London and founded St John's College, Oxford. The site's military connections began in 1904 when the building was taken over by the Territorial Army, and during World War I the Cyclist Battalion was based here.

Continue to the neighbouring ㉔ **Eight Bells** public house – a great place for a drink as you near the end of this walk. Founded in 1629, this is another remnant from the Old Fulham Town. The pub was popular with those travelling across the old bridge which was located at the end of the High Street. When the first bridge was demolished, the current Putney Bridge was located further to the west, leaving the Eight Bells in a back street, surviving on its charm and loyal customers.

In 1729 two additional bells were acquired by All Saints church, so the pub is probably named in celebration of this 'upgrade'. In the early 19th century a spinster once lived near here and was known as the 'old coffin woman'. Her fear of a pauper's funeral caused her to keep a coffin in her room, said to be fitted out as a cupboard for more practical use and regularly oiled.

Next door is a real Fulham treat – ㉕ **Hurlingham Books**. It claims to be the oldest independent bookshop in London, having been opened by Ray Cole in 1968. It is an atmospheric place, where bookworms will feel very much at home, browsing among the towering bookshelves.

When finished, walk down Ranelagh Gardens to reach Putney Bridge station again, where this walk ends. ●

VISIT...

Fulham Palace (see p.201)
Bishop's Avenue, SW6 6EA
www.fulhampalace.org

All Saints Church (see p.205)
Pryor's Bank, SW6 3LA
www.allsaints-fulham.org.uk

SHOP...

Hurlingham Books (see p.212)
91 Fulham High Street, SW6 3JS
www.hurlinghambooks.com

EAT / DRINK...

Temperance Pub (see p.207)
90 Fulham High Street, SW6 3LF
www.craft-pubs.co.uk/
thetemperancefulham

King's Arms (see p.208)
425 New King's Road, SW6 4RN
www.kingsarms-fulham.co.uk

The Golden Lion (see p.209)
57 Fulham High Street, SW6 3JJ
www.thegoldenlionfulham.co.uk

RANELAGH
GARDENS SW 6

1 Fulham High Street S.W.6

25

8 Clapham Walk

Clapham Walk

1. Clock Tower
2. Former Shelter
3. Venn Street
4. Clapham Picturehouse
5. 'The Majestic' building
6. Art Deco Building
7. Shelter entrance
8. Former Temperance Billiard Hall
9. Former Clapham Public Hall
10. The Railway Tavern
11. Gauden Road
12. The Socialist Party Office
13. Gillette Ghost Sign
14. West Indian Ex Services Association
15. Clapham Tap
16. The Pipeworks Building
17. Oddfellows Hall
18. Grafton Square
19. Ebenezer Strict Baptist Church
20. Clapham Manor Estate
21. St Paul's Clapham
22. Eden Community Garden
23. Former African Academy
24. Turret Grove
25. Rectory Gardens
26. The Metalworks
27. Queen Anne Buildings
28. The Polygon Buildings
29. Old Fire Station
30. Omnibus Theatre
31. Graham Greene (former home)
32. Charles Barry (former home)

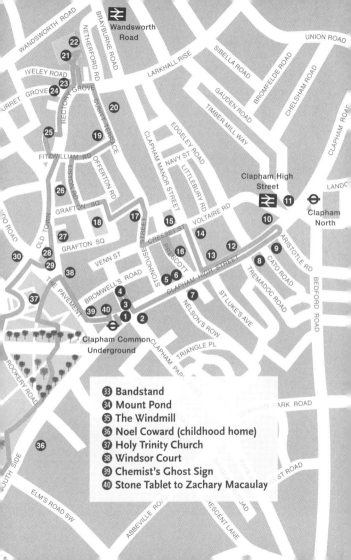

WANDSWORTH ROAD

BRAYBURNE ROAD

NETHERFORD RD

UNION ROAD

Wandsworth Road

WANDSWORTH ROAD

IVELEY ROAD

LARKHALL RISE

SIBELLA ROAD

BROMFELDE ROAD

CHELSHAM ROAD

GROVE

RECTORY GROVE

CUBITT TERRACE

GAUDEN ROAD

TIMBER MILL WAY

CLAPHAM ROAD

URRET GROVE

FITZWILLIAM RD

LISTON RD

OFFERTON RD

EDGELEY ROAD

CLAPHAM MANOR STREET

NAVY ST

LITTLEBURY RD

VOLTAIRE RD

Clapham High Street

CLAPHAM ROAD

LANDO

Clapham North

GRAFTON SQ

CRESSET ST

PRESCOTT

ARISTOTLE RD

CATO ROAD

TREMADOC ROAD

BEDFORD ROAD

GRAFTON SQ

VENN ST

BROMWELL'S ROAD

THE PAVEMENT

CLAPHAM PARK ROAD

CLAPHAM HIGH STREET

NELSON'S ROW

ST LUKE'S AVE

ST LUKE'S AVE

Clapham Common Underground

TRIANGLE PL

CLAPHAM PARK ROAD

ROOKERY ROAD

SOUTH SIDE

ELM'S ROAD SW

ABBEVILLE ROAD

CRESCENT LANE

ST ROAD

33 Bandstand
34 Mount Pond
35 The Windmill
36 Noel Coward (childhood home)
37 Holy Trinity Church
38 Windsor Court
39 Chemist's Ghost Sign
40 Stone Tablet to Zachary Macaulay

Clapham Walk
Start/Finish: Clapham Common Underground
Distance: 3 miles

This walk starts at Clapham Common underground station. It explores a little of Clapham High Street, then heads into the historic heart of Clapham village, before returning to the Common.

Just outside the station look out for the ❶ **Clock Tower** which was unveiled by the Mayor of Wandsworth in 1906. It used to be situated elsewhere and was moved here to make way for the station booking office. Cross over to the entrance to Clapham Park Road to see the external remains of a ❷ **former deep-level shelter**. During the war, the Government built eight such shelters in London that were linked to existing underground stations. Each shelter comprised of two tunnels around 370 metres long and could hold around 8,000 people.

The grand plan was eventually to link these shelters by tunnels that would form new express tube lines, however, this never materialised after the war. Deep-level shelters were also built at Clapham North and Clapham South stations, and from 1944 were used by the public during air raids. Today the deep-level complex is used by the world's first underground vertical farm and you can contact the owners who arrange visits for the public (growing-underground. com). Another deep-level shelter at Clapham South (not visited on this walk) was used to house members of the Windrush Generation who had arrived in Britain as immigrants from the West Indies – this can also be visited through the London Transport Museum (ltmuseum.co.uk/whats-on/hidden-london/clapham-south).

Pause at ❸ **Venn Street**. It is named after Henry Venn (1725-97), a leading light and founder of the famous 'Clapham Sect' who you will come across at different points

along the walk. The Clapham Sect was a close-knit group of evangelical Christians who were active in the late 18th and early 19th centuries. Their strong belief that religious and moral principles should be reflected in public affairs saw them become incredibly influential in British life. Many lived in Clapham and worshipped at Holy Trinity church (seen later). The best-known member of the group was William Wilberforce and he, along with many others, spearheaded the movement to abolish slavery.

The Venn Street market takes place every Saturday between 10am and 3pm. This is also the home of the ❹ **Clapham Picturehouse**, occupying a site that was once horse stables, and later the Electric Picture Palace that opened in 1910.

Continue along Clapham High Street which first appears on a map in 1745, and contains an interesting mix of different architectural styles ranging from the late 18th century onwards.

In recent years Clapham has become considerably gentrified, earning it the alternative name 'Clahm' (mocking its new posh inhabitants). It is therefore hard to imagine that in the years following World War II, there was still a fair amount of industry in Clapham High Street and the surrounding area. This included the Wellington

Tube Works, Stonehouse Electrical Works, a cardboard box factory, and manufacturers of bicycles, and engineering equipment. These businesses sat alongside churches of various denominations and cinemas that have also since disappeared. Maps of this era show several sites marked as 'ruins' – a reminder that Clapham suffered badly during the Blitz.

Opposite Sainsbury's, look up to see ❺ **'The Majestic' building**. Today this is home to Infernos nightclub (one journalist has joked 'You can't call yourself a true

Claphamite unless you've been to/been sick in/been barred from Infernos'). It was used for scenes in *The Inbetweeners Movie* (2011). The Majestic cinema was built in 1914 (there used to be four on the High Street). It was capable of seating an astonishing 3,000 people, and remained a cinema until 1960, before becoming a recording studio where artists as diverse as David Bowie, Brian Eno, Adam Faith and the Sex Pistols recorded. If you walk down Stonehouse Street you will see another side of the original cinema.

For another example of architectural history, on the same side as Infernos look out for the McDonalds. It is housed in an **6 Art Deco building** dating from 1932 that was originally a branch of Marks & Spencer. Many of the other shops and restaurants you will pass

here occupy buildings that were originally used as domestic houses, often dating from the 19th century. Look out for the later ground level extensions that were added for commercial purposes.

Up ahead, on the other side, you'll see a drum-shaped building. This is the other **7 entrance to the deep-level shelter** you visited earlier, and where the tours by the underground farm start. Looking back to where the walk started, you can get an idea of the length of the shelter.

Continue along, stopping at number 47 – the unusual looking **8 former Temperance Billiard Hall**, dating from 1910. It is a reminder of the power of the Temperance movement during the early 20th century. The movement sought to lure ordinary people away from Clapham's pubs, and by 1939 there were around 50 such billiard halls in London. It is currently occupied by a firm of architects. A similar hall can be seen in the Fulham walk.

Stop next at **number 35**, which boasts a grand entrance with the date 1911 above the doorway. This was originally ❾ **Clapham Public Hall**, but is now used for rehearsals by the Royal Shakespeare Company.

Walk a little further to reach ❿ **The Railway Tavern**. This is a great Victorian pub dating from the mid 19th century, its name reminding visitors that Clapham was utterly transformed by the creation of new transport systems in the 19th century. First came the horse-drawn buses in the 1830s, followed by horse-drawn trams, then the railway (nearby Clapham High Street station opened in 1862 and Clapham Junction station opened the next year), and later on the underground.

Just past the Tavern on the left is ⓫ **Gauden Road**. If you want to take the detour, number 47 is where a remarkable life came to a tragic end. Vera Menchik was born in Russia in 1906, and after the Revolution came to England with her mother and sisters. Taught to play as a child by her father, she became the greatest female chess player of her age, a world champion in 1927 who would defend her title six times. On 26 June 1944, a German V-1 rocket hit Gauden Road, killing Vera, one of her sisters and her mother.

Cross to the side opposite the RSC building and retract your steps to ⓬ **The Socialist Party of Great Britain office** at number 52, seemingly at odds with the image of 'Clahm' and the expensive restaurants and cafés nearby. The Socialist Party office has been here since 1951, long before Clapham

became the middle-class enclave it is today. It featured in the news in 2015 after reports emerged that the party's assets had – perhaps ironically – been considerably swelled by Clapham's booming property prices. To date, the party has resisted continued attempts by property developers to sell up.

Having explored the High Street a little, it is time to retrace your steps before heading towards the heart of old Clapham. This road roughly follows an ancient Roman military road that ran between London and Chichester. Follow the map, taking care not to miss the **13 Gillette ghost sign** (beside numbers 90-92). See if you can spot the numerous other ghost signs along Clapham High Street.

Head north up Clapham Manor Street, laid out by the prolific builder, Thomas Cubitt (1788-1855). Look out for the fine 19th-

century terraced houses, and the ⑭ **West Indian Ex Services Association building**. The Association was founded in 1972 to support West Indians and their families who had served in the armed forces. On the right is Bicycle Mews, named after the Claude Butler Cycle Works once situated near here.

Turn left on Cresset Street, passing the excellent late Victorian ⑮ **Clapham Tap pub** on the corner. When you pass Prescott Place take a short detour to see ⑯ **The Pipeworks building** – another reminder of the industrial nature of old Clapham. Continue along Cresset Street, turning right by The Stonehouse pub on the corner then up Stonehouse Street and along a path.

On the left, stop outside ⑰ **Oddfellows Hall**. Dating from 1852, this was originally used by the Ebenezer Strict Baptists (the 'Ebenezer Cottage' sign can still be seen). It was taken over in 1908 by the Oddfellows, a once prolific friendly society movement that emerged from the old trade guilds, but which is now largely forgotten. Hundreds of Oddfellows halls, pubs and other buildings used to operate throughout Britain, and members could (for a modest contribution) receive benefits that were vital in the days before the Welfare State. The movement faded during the 20th century, but the local group still meets here and The Oddfellows friendly society (based in Manchester and established in 1810) has over 300,000 members. The building is also used by the Shambhala Meditation Centre.

Continue down Belmont Road to reach ⑱ **Grafton Square**. Squares like this are less common south of the river and this one is a welcome change from the uniform street layout of Clapham. The Square dates from 1847, an era when developers were still building large houses for the wealthy classes flocking to Clapham. However, within a few years, the district's good transport links to central London would increasingly attract more modest residents such as clerks who could commute to their insurance office in the city with relative ease. This new kind of resident became immortalised as 'the man on the Clapham Omnibus' and would have lived in the smaller, terraced houses you passed earlier. Unlike many other London Squares, the central garden is open to the public.

Continue up Liston Road then turn right onto Fitzwilliam Road and follow the map up Cubitt Terrace. Look for the ⑲ **Ebenezer Strict Baptist Church** on the corner that dates from 1861 and the pretty cottages opposite. This street's name is another reminder of

the influence of the builder Thomas Cubitt on Clapham. He lived here and was responsible for developing Clapham Park to the southeast of the Common. Thomas, along with other members of the Cubitt family, are better known for their work in Bloomsbury, Belgravia and Pimlico, and arguably as a family did more than any other in history to shape the physical appearance of the capital as we see it today.

Continue along Cubitt Terrace, looking out for the contrast between the cottages and the **⓴ Clapham Manor Estate** on your left – an example of the social housing built in London in the decades following World War II.

Turn left and walk up Rectory Grove to reach **㉑ St Paul's Clapham**.

The name Clapham was derived from the old English words for a short hill ('clopp') and a village ('ham' – hence the word 'hamlet'). The village was first mentioned in the time of King Alfred, and in the 11th century, the manor was owned by a Danish nobleman. For centuries it remained an insignificant Surrey village centred around where St Paul's is today – a world away from the busy metropolis. However, in the 17th century, particularly after the Great Plague of 1666, many wealthy residents of London moved here. The famous diarist Samuel Pepys was one of these new arrivals, spending the last few years of his life in Clapham before his death in 1703.

The original parish church on this site, known as Holy Trinity, was built as far back as

21

21

22

23

the 12th century, situated beside the old manor house of Clapham. By the 18th century, the church was not in a good state, and many of the key figures in Clapham society were now living in grand houses constructed by the Common. As the focus of village life gravitated towards the Common, it was decided that a new parish church should be built, one that was more suitable for Clapham's rapidly expanding population. And so Holy Trinity on the Common was built in 1776 as the new parish church. The old parish church here was demolished, however, it later became evident that Clapham's expanding population needed a second church, so St Paul's was constructed in 1815.

St Paul's contains many fascinating memorials from the old parish church, including those erected for the Atkins family (one was Lord of the manor). There is also a portrait medallion of William Hewer who originally worked with Samuel Pepys, and whom Pepys – as an old man – went to live with during the last few years of his life. Look out also for the memorial to heroic Major Willoughby Montagu, who fought at Waterloo in 1815 and was made Knight of the Russian Order of St Vladimir.

The graveyard is worth a wander around. In the past plague victims were buried here as well as Roundhead soldiers killed during the Civil War. The ㉒ **Eden Community Garden** along Matrimony Place is a tranquil spot for a break.

Walk back down Rectory Grove. Number 8 is a fine looking Georgian building that was used to house the ㉓ **African Academy** from 1799 to 1805. The academy was the brainchild of members of the Clapham Sect mentioned earlier. Members of the sect were involved in the foundation of Freetown in Sierra Leone. The aim of the academy was to educate the children of prominent Africans in the same region. It must have been extraordinarily difficult for African children to arrive in Clapham during an age when slavery was still legal.

Sadly what was clearly a well-intentioned act if philanthropy, ended in tragedy as several of the boys died of the measles, and the survivors were returned home to Sierra Leone in 1805.

Continue along, bearing right, passing **24** **Turret Grove** – once the site of an Elizabethan manor house in Clapham. The name Turret Grove refers to the turret that was visible on the old manor house that was demolished in 1837.

After a short while, turn right down **25** **Rectory Gardens** – an unusual, narrow little road of small Victorian cottages. The Gardens became run-down in recent decades, with many cottages taken over by squatters in the 1970s. This was the last great age of the London squatting movement, all connected to an alternative way of life that has largely disappeared in recent years. One squatter during the period recalled singer Ian Dury coming here to visit one of his band members who lived in a squat. Another resident was musician Andrew 'Thunderclap' Newman, best known for the 1969 hippy-themed hit 'Something in the Air'. In recent years there has been considerable controversy as Lambeth Council has sought to evict long-standing residents and sell off the properties in order to cash in on Clapham's property boom.

Shortly on the right is a charming old Clapham school building, and then further ahead on the left (opposite Lydon Road) is **26** **The Metalworks** – a former Victorian metalworks converted into warehouse flats. Arts & Crafts pioneer William Bainbridge Reynolds (1855-1935) set up his business here in 1904 (he lived on Rectory Grove) – a reminder of Clapham's history of small scale manufacturing.

Follow the map to bear left into the Old Town, passing some superb **㉗ Queen Anne era buildings** on the left. Number 43 is where the architect John Francis Bentley (1839-1902) lived, as marked by a blue plaque. He is best known for the Byzantine style Roman Catholic cathedral in Westminster.

On the right, you pass **㉘ The Polygon buildings**, with three surviving houses dating from the original construction of 1792. Just after this you will see, standing on its own, the **㉙ Old Fire Station**. It was built in 1868 for the Metropolitan Fire Brigade.

Skirt around the back of The Polygon and follow the map along to the **㉚ Omnibus Theatre**, housed in the old Clapham Library that dates from the 1880s. Outside, by the entrance, is a 1st AD Roman plinth, discovered in 1912 in the grounds of a house on Clapham Common South Side. It has an inscription remembering a Roman named Vitus Licinius Ascanius.

The area along from here is Clapham North Side which, from the 18th century, became a popular place for wealthy people to build grand houses overlooking Clapham Common. The writer **㉛ Graham Greene** lived at number 14, but was forced to leave after his house was badly damaged during the Blitz. Clapham features heavily in his novel *The End of the Affair*. **㉜ Architect Charles Barry** (1795-1860) lived at number 29, and is best remembered for his work on the Houses of Parliament and Trafalgar Square. His house is now part of Trinity Hospice whose origins go back to 1899.

From here you head towards Clapham Common, the great expanse that is valued so highly by Claphamites. Head in a south-westerly direction across the Common, aiming for the **㉝ bandstand** at its heart.

The Common was a marshy place until it was drained in 1722. It has always had a certain reputation for violence. In the 18th century, it was plagued by robbers and highwaymen, with attacks reported in papers throughout the country.

One report, from September 1752, describes how a Mr Sharply 'was attacked on Clapham Common.. by two highwaymen mounted on grey horses with crapes over their faces...they ordered Mr Sharpley to stop or they would blow his brins (*sic*) out; one of them stood..with a pistol cock'd, whilst the other took a Guinea and some silver, and then they rod off towards London'.

The Common has long been a cruising spot for the gay community, some of whom have fallen victim to homophobic attacks. One tragedy occurred in October 2005 when Jody Dobrowski (b.1981) was murdered on the Common. It later transpired that the two men convicted of his murder had committed a string of similar attacks. The crime inspired Channel 4's drama entitled *Clapham Junction* (2007) which focused on the lives of Clapham's gay community.

Soon you reach the bandstand which dates from 1890. It is associated with another grim murder story, notable for helping popularise the term 'Teddy boy' in British culture. During the evening of 2nd June 1953 'The Plough Boys' (a local gang of Teddy Boys who took their name from a historic Clapham pub) started a fight here with some other boys. Their victims ran from the Common and tried to get on a bus to escape, but The Plough Boys caught them. One victim, seventeen-year-old John Beckley, was stabbed to death as he tried to run towards the Old Town.

The excitable British press had a field day – 'Flick Knives, Dance Music and Edwardian Suits' – 'Clapham 'Gang War'. One of the attackers was later convicted of Beckley's murder and narrowly

Clapham Common

escaped the death penalty. The Edwardian styling of the youths led to the 'Teddy Boy' moniker and this particular youth subculture became public enemy number one (at least in the eyes of the media) until fights between Mods and Rockers a decade later.

On a happier note, walk on to **34 Mount Pond**. Today it is one of four ponds on the Common, although in the past there used to be about a dozen. Some were formed naturally but others resulted from efforts to dig up gravel for use in the construction of local roads. Mount Pond dates from 1746 when gravel was dug for a new road in Tooting.

Benjamin Franklin (1706-1790) – one of the founding fathers of the United States – stayed in Clapham in the late 1760s, before he helped frame the Declaration of Independence. Famous for his scientific interests, he conducted experiments at Mount Pond relating to the impact of oil on water. Franklin stayed in Clapham at the house of his friend Christopher Baldwin. Known as The Grange, the house was situated on the West Side of the Common and was demolished around 1900.

From here head eastwards to **35 The Windmill pub**, named

after two local windmills that once stood near here. The pub's origins go back to the early 18th century when it was a coaching inn, and much of the current building dates from the 1790s. Today the Windmill is a very popular pub with views across the Common. The renowned chef Michel Roux Jr described it as his favourite London pub.

In 1796 it was reported that a group of people 'discovered the body of a man on Clapham Common, which from its putrid state, must have lain there for days. He was found near the Windmill, with his brains blown out. There lay at his side a brace of pistols and from his dress he appeared to be a mariner, his head laid on a tuft of grass, that made him appear as he were still asleep'.

Visiting the Common up to 1914 you would have enjoyed the sight of sheep grazing. This rural aspect had disappeared by World War II but resumed when the Common was converted to allotments as the authorities tried to make up for the shortage in food supplies. Much of the area was also covered by huge anti-aircraft guns, searchlights, and bunkers. In the post-war period housing shortages saw 'prefabs' line parts of the Common and they continued to serve as homes here until the mid-1950s.

Continue along the edge of the Common, looking over to the right where at 50 Clapham Common South Side **36** **Noel Coward** (1899-1973) lived in a modest apartment with his parents during World War I. Their flat overlooked the Long Pond which has always been a popular place for model boat enthusiasts since it was created in the 1870s.

235

37

Take care when crossing the road, and then head for **37 Holy Trinity church.** As mentioned earlier, the original Holy Trinity that stood where St Paul's church now stands, was the earlier heart of Clapham village. However it was decided to build a new Holy Trinity church here, and it opened for worship in 1776. Several members of the influential Clapham Sect lived in grand houses overlooking the Common, and they regularly met at Holy Trinity.

There were probably less than twenty key members of the Sect, the best known being William Wilberforce (1759-1833), Zachary Macaulay (1768-1838), Granville Sharp (1735-1813), Henry Thornton (1760-1815), Henry Venn (1725-97) and his son John (1759-1813). Thornton and Wilberforce were also cousins and lived together in Broomwood House on the West side of the Common. Evangelical minister Henry Venn was one of the founders of the Sect, and his son John would continue his work as rector of Holy Trinity. John was also closely involved in running the African Academy mentioned earlier.

The Clapham Sect were influential in British society, and not just because of the pressure they applied to abolish slavery in Britain and its Empire. They sought to apply their religious and moral standards to many other activities – be it factory conditions for children or

37

standards of behaviour for politicians. The sect did a good deal to set the moral agenda in public life that was to gain prominence in the later Victorian Age. Names of key members of the Clapham Sect are listed on a plaque at the church. Look out on the outside for evidence of shrapnel damage caused by German bombs in World War II – a very rare sight in London.

From the church, head eastwards to join the Pavement, walking along with the Common to your right Look out for the stylish

236

37

38 **Windsor Court** that dates from 1935. You pass lots of upmarket shops and sturdy Georgian buildings. Clapham Books is certainly worth a stop and if you pause by number 17 you can see another great **39** **ghost sign** – this one for Deane & Co. Chemists. Hand-painted advertising signs were popular between the 1900s and the 1950s, and now many people dedicate websites and blogs to tracing the few that have survived. This sign relates to Henry Deane who opened a pharmacy here in 1837 and was a gifted photographer responsible for many of the best images that survive of Victorian Clapham. The chemist shop remained in operation here until 1886.

Follow the map around to the branch of Waitrose. Above the shop is a **stone tablet** commemorating the fact that this was once home to **40** **Zachary Macaulay**, a key member of the Clapham Sect and also a founder of London University. His experience as governor of Sierra Leone, and also onboard a slave ship, was useful to the Clapham Sect when taking on those opposed to abolition. His son, Thomas, became famous in his own right as one of the most respected historians of the Victorian age. Continue on to reach the underground station where this walk ends. ●

VISIT...

Eden Community Garden
(see p.229)
Rectory Grove, SW4 6DZ
www.edengardenclapham.org

St Paul's Church (see p.227)
Rectory Grove, SW4 0DZ
www.stpaulsclapham.org

Holy Trinity Church (see p.236)
Clapham Common North Side,
SW4 0QZ
www.holytrinityclapham.org

EAT / DRINK...

The Railway Tavern (see p.222)
18 Clapham High Street, SW4 7UR
www.therailwayclapham.co.uk

Clapham Tap (see p.225)
128 Clapham Manor St., SW4 6ED
www.the-clapham-tap.business.site

The Windmill Pub (see p.234)
Clapham Common South Side,
SW4 9DE
www.windmillclapham.co.uk

Granada Cinema

9 Tooting Walk

DORNTON ROAD

Tooting Walk

1. Tooting Bec Station
2. The Wheatsheaf
3. St Anselms's
4. Nettle's Ghost Sign
5. Former Picture Palace
6. Former Telephone Exchange
7. Numbers 68-72
8. The King's Head
9. Sikh Gurdwara
10. Tooting Islamic Centre
11. Former Royal Arsenal
    Co-operative Society (RACS)
12. Mirch Masala Restaurant
13. St Swithun Mission
14. Former Manor House
15. Former Chapel Building
16. Tooting Market
17. Broadway Market
18. Ghost Sign
19. The Castle
20. Tooting Broadway Underground
21. John Hunter Gate
22. Former Cinema
23. Granada Cinema
24. Tooting Library
25. Monument to Tooting Parish Pump
26. St Nicholas Church
27. Old Village School
28. Brick Pillars
29. Former Clock Tower

TOOTING
COMMON

Tooting Walk

Start: Tooting Bec Station
Finish: Tooting Broadway Station
Distance: 1.9 miles

This walk begins at ❶ **Tooting Bec Station**. Tooting is a strange district, really two places – Tooting Bec and Tooting Graveney – each of which can trace its origins back to Saxon times. However, it was only in the late 19th century that the places you will see today began to emerge, and any remaining gaps between the 'two Tootings' disappeared as it became a continuous route of shops and restaurants, flanked by uniform residential streets.

Tooting is on the up! This multi-cultural, vibrant district has always been the poor cousin of nearby Balham or Wimbledon, however, in the last decade it has become increasingly trendy and gentrified – particularly as young people priced out of previously more desirable areas have moved here. Indeed, Lonely Planet has even described Tooting as one of the 10 coolest neighbourhoods on earth. Whether it really is the 'new Shoreditch' remains to the seen.

Tooting Bec station dates from 1926, and the continued extension of the underground further south out of central London changed once relatively isolated places such as Tooting, Colliers Wood and Morden fundamentally as they each became part of the commuter belt. The station was designed by the prolific architect Charles Holden (1875-1960). He is perhaps best known for Senate House in Bloomsbury, and 55 Broadway, but also worked on several underground stations in London, including seven stations between Clapham and Morden.

Holden also designed dozens of War Commission cemeteries after World War I, and there are parallels between the clean lines of his work there and the underground stations in London. The renowned architectural expert Pevsner described one of the latter as 'an outstanding example of how satisfying such unpretentious buildings can be, purely through the use of careful details and good proportions.'

Outside the station look out for ❷ **The Wheatsheaf public house**. This great Victorian beast of a pub was threatened a few years ago with being replaced by a supermarket, but local pressure – including from Sadiq Khan (then an MP) – helped save it. Khan was reported as saying 'When I was growing up, it was an IRA pub and I used to run past it'. It is one of many traditional establishments in Tooting that have been turned around by new arrivals, catering for a younger, cooler clientele.

On the north side is the striking red-brick Catholic church of ❸ **St Anselm's** that dates from 1933. The Roman Catholic faith is very central to the history of Tooting Bec. Originally known as the Manor of Totinges in Saxon times, the manor was given by William the Conqueror to Richard of Tonbridge. He later gave it to the Benedictine Abbey of Bec in Normandy, hence Tooting 'Bec'.

St Anselm (c.1033-1109) was Abbot of the Abbey of Bec, and later became Archbishop of Canterbury. The Abbey in Tooting stood to the east of here where Tooting Bec Common is today, and it seems almost certain St Anselm would have visited his monks there. Bec Abbey in Normandy – incredibly – is still in use, occupied by Olivetan monks who are well known for their pottery. In medieval times you would have seen monks and more violent scenes in this area as a public gallows stood near here.

Start to walk down Upper Tooting Road, lined with a typical mix of late Victorian and Edwardian red brick buildings. At the corner of Noyna Road spot the ❹ **ghost sign** above the pharmacy – 'Nettle's Tussodyne' and 'Buy Meggezones'.

On the next corner with Fircroft Road is a **⑤ former Picture Palace** – one of many built in Tooting during the craze for such establishments in the early decades of the 20th century. In 1910 this was originally called The Central Hall Picture Palace, later becoming the Classic Cinema. As the area's South Asian community grew, it began showing Bollywood films before closing in 1983.

Originally silent films with live music would have featured here. Now you can learn how to dance to Kizomba, Salsa, Freestyle Waltz ('West Indies Style') and enjoy the Caribbean fusion restaurant.

Continue along, with evidence of Tooting's diverse community all around, from the people on the street to the varied local shops. Tooting's influence even extends beyond our own planet as there is a crater on Mars named after it. The Tooting impact crater was named in 2006 by a former local and astronomer named Pete Mouginis-Mark. At the time, Mayor of London, Sadiq Khan said: 'This is getting a lot of attention, not only because of its twinning to our fantastic area, but also because this is probably the youngest large meteorite crater on Mars'.

On the left by Topsham Road look out for the **⑥ former Telephone Exchange**, a grand, Art Deco building dating from 1939.

Opposite the Exchange at **⑦ numbers 68-72,** you find a much earlier architectural style, described by Wandsworth council as 'rare examples of early **Georgian development**, some of the earliest domestic buildings in the Borough'.

Continue along and next up is ❽ **The King's Head**, another flamboyantly-fronted Victorian pub dating from 1896. It was designed by W.M. Brutton, also responsible for the famous Fitzroy Tavern in Fitzrovia whose Bohemian regulars included Dylan Thomas and George Orwell. The interior has been described as one of the most lavish amongst any pub in South London, and is a must see.

In the 18th century Tooting became known as an attractive countryside location where the wealthier residents of London could build mansions. Although by 1801 it still only had just over 1,000 residents. The old road through Tooting was part of a major route for horse-drawn coaches travelling back and forth from London, however as an area it remained largely resistant to the creeping sprawl of London.

Even in the 1870s, Tooting was described in *Handbook to the Environs of London* as 'a region of villas and nursery gardens, very pleasant'. However, the arrival of the railway in the 1860s brought with it commuters. By the time The King's Head was up and running many of the old houses once surrounded by fields had been replaced by the residential streets that run off the road you are on now. Beside it is the ❾ **Sikh Gurdwara** – or assembly place – housed in on old Royal Mail sorting office. The building still has the Royal coat of arms above the entrance, including the England lion and Scottish unicorn (note the unicorn is chained as it was seen as a dangerous creature).

Continue southwards, roughly following the route of the ancient Roman road that ran 56 miles between London and Chichester and was later known as Stane Street.

You will now see shops selling sarees, halal meat and Islamic books. Ahead on the left is ❿ **Tooting Islamic Centre**, housed in another magnificent former cinema building. This was originally the Mayfair, which ran from 1932 until 1979. The Art Deco style stands in sharp contrast to the redbrick Edwardian era cinema passed earlier. One doorman who worked there in 1970 later recalled 'we told people the place was haunted and the ghost flicked peanuts from the Balcony to people below...The truth was as underground trains travelled underneath the building, the vibration made an isle seat pop down and bits of plaster from the ceiling fall off and hit people...'. Interestingly the Mayfair Tavern is part of the Islamic centre building complex.

Shortly on the right is the ⓫ **former Royal Arsenal Co-operative Society (RACS)** building, dating from 1923. This iconic building was once a department store and later became a Hindu temple. Look for the square motifs and tiles that are typical of the Art Deco style. Due to recent redevelopment, only part of the façade is now visible

as the ground floor is now dominated by a branch of LIDL. The RACS name is derived from a consumer co-operative established in 1868 by workers from the Royal Arsenal in Woolwich. It was munitions workers at the same place who a few years later would found what became the famous Arsenal football team (which only moved from Woolwich to Highbury in 1913). With a motto of 'Each for All and All for Each', RACS was affiliated to the Labour Party and housed refugees during the Spanish Civil War. The RACS co-operative eventually had 500,000 members but financial difficulties in the 1980s saw it merge with the Co-Op.

The RACS store in Tooting provided members with everything from wedding dresses to funeral services, and acted as a hub for locals with activities such as boxing and choirs.

Continue on. Whilst there are dozens of good Asian restaurants in Tooting, one that is frequently recommended is up on the left – ⑫ **Mirch Masala** (213 Upper Tooting Road). The Indian-inspired cuisine here has been recommended by Tooting resident Sadiq Khan (particularly the chilli paneer and nihari), and another well-known figure who has dined here is Imran Khan, the famous cricketer and Pakistani politician.

Now turn left onto Kellino Street, stopping at the junction with St Cyprian's Street to see the old ⑬ **St Swithun Mission**. In 1916 a wooden church and hall were built here, which was eventually replaced by the current building in the early 30s. It closed in

1945, and was later used by Tooting Boys Club. If you had stood on this spot in the 1890s you would be standing upon fields, the whole area to the east covered by Totterdown Fields.

Retrace your steps to Upper Tooting Road. To get a sense of how much this area has changed in a relatively short period of time, continue down to stand opposite Broadwater Road and Gatton Road on the right. In the 1890s you would have faced a grand ⑭ **Manor House**, and looking back to where you started the walk, fields stretched out behind the buildings facing the road. All this open space had been filled in by new residential streets by the start of World War I. Just by Totterdown Street is another frequently recommended Pakistani restaurant – the Lahore Karahi.

Next up on the left is the elegant ⑮ **former chapel building**, built in 1776 for a Methodist congregation. It was called the Defoe Chapel, perhaps indicating a local connection with the author Daniel Defoe (1660-1731). In the late 19th century the other side of the road was dominated by a brewery, with cottages for its workers nearby.

Next to the former chapel is the brightly-coloured entrance building to ⑯ **Tooting Market**, completed in 1930. Describing itself as 'South London's Hippest Market', this is worth spending some time in, offering everything from nail salons to food and fashion. This market and nearby Broadway Market (running since 1936), have been a central fixture of life in Tooting for over 80 years. Some family-run butchers, cobblers and watch repairs shops have been here since the 70s, but as Tooting becomes trendier, new hipster businesses are flocking in.

One of the new arrivals is Graveney Gin that runs a 'nano bar' inside Tooting Market, selling its organic handcrafted batch gin using 'punchy Juniper Berries, Pink Grapefruit, Gogi Berries, Baobab, Fresh Orange, Orris Root & Angelica Root'. Needless to say the mix between older traders and newer arrivals is an interesting one, explaining Lonely Planet's praise of the area's 'multiculturalism and originality'.

When finished, visit ⑰ **Broadway Market** (the entrance is just 20 metres away). Alongside the more traditional London market offerings, this is home to Craft Tooting – the first craft beer shop in the

area. There are plenty of independent shops and eateries to explore in this unique indoor market with the long-established Japanese Food Bar (Hinata) a strong recommendation.

When finished look above 49 Tooting High Street for another ⑱ **ghost sign**.

Opposite is ⑲ **The Castle**, founded in 1832 and the area's oldest pub. It has recently been modernised and offers a great menu.

You now reach ⑳ **Tooting Broadway underground**. This is Tooting Graveney, which – like Tooting Bec – also has links to historic religious houses. The lands in Tooting Graveney were held by Chertsey Abbey and also Westminster Abbey. They later came into the hands of the De Gravenells, hence where Graveney derives from.

The station was opened in 1926, and – like Tooting Bec – was designed by Charles Holden. If you are over a certain age you probably remember the late 70s BBC television series *Citizen Smith* set in Tooting. The station appears in the opening credits. 'Wolfie' Smith – played by Robert Lindsay – is a Marxist urban guerrilla who seeks to emulate Che Guevara and likes to declare 'Freedom for Tooting'. It is hard to imagine today that the BBC would make a prime time comedy programme about a Marxist revolutionary in increasingly gentrified Tooting.

Impossible to miss, outside the station stands a monument to **King Edward VII** which dates from 1911 (the year after his death). Despite his short reign, Edward was a popular figure and there are a number of monuments in his memory in the capital.

Pass Tooting Broadway station on your left, and keep walking for several minutes until you reach Hoyle Road on your right. Turn down it, and continue until you reach the end of the road. Go down the steps on your left to enter the St. George's Hospital complex. Turn right immediately after the steps and you will be able to see the ㉑ **John Hunter Gateway**. It consists of a bust of the celebrated surgeon, John Hunter, atop the entrance gate to the former site of St. George's Hospital. St George's was founded in 1733 and was based near Hyde Park Corner until moving here in 1980. John Hunter was a renowned surgeon and teacher at the hospital, and in his spare time took on resident pupils at his privately-owned teaching museum. It featured nearly 14,000 specimens of plants and animals, including rarities like kangaroos from the voyage of James Cook in 1768-71. This bust is a replica of the original bronze sculpture made by Sir Alfred Gilbert, which also resides in the medical school foyer of the hospital. Retrace your steps along Hoyle Road and back to Tooting Broadway station.

In the 19th century, Mr Drouet's school for pauper children was based near the site of the underground station, at a place called Surrey Hall. Drouet was by all accounts a monster, and treated the children terribly. Other parishes in London sent their paupers out to Mr Drouet, and during a cholera outbreak in January 1849, 180 children died even though no one else in Tooting was infected. News of the tragedy began to emerge, coming to the attention of Charles Dickens, who would go on to write four highly critical articles about the case in *The Examiner*. Drouet was tried for manslaughter but managed to escape punishment. He died a few months after his acquittal.

Dickens wrote of the incident 'The cholera, or some unusually malignant form of typhus assimilating itself to that disease, broke out in Mr Drouet's farm for children, because it was brutally conducted, vilely kept, preposterously inspected, dishonestly defended, a disgrace to a Christian community, and a stain upon a civilised land'. Real life tragedies like this influenced Dickens's fictional accounts of the realities of London life in his time, something that began to change the way the general public looked upon institutions like workhouse and orphanages.

Turn right at the station and follow the map down Mitcham Road, passing an old lamp outside the station, with signs to places such as Croydon and Wandsworth.

There are two more old cinemas along here. The first is hidden behind the 'Sam 99p' and Specsavers, the façade is all that is really left from a ㉒ **cinema** dating from 1912. These early cinemas were much smaller and plainer than what would follow during the glory days of

the picturehouse in the 1930s. An example of which is found a little further along, now a huge bingo hall.

This began as the ㉓ **Granada Cinema** in 1931, and has one of the most fantastic interiors of any building in South London. The building was also used to host concerts by famous stars such as Eddie Fisher, The Andrews Sisters, Carmen Miranda, Frank Sinatra, Jerry Lee Lewis, Little Richard, The Rolling Stones and The Beatles. The Bee Gees played their last ever concert here in 1968, and it closed as a cinema just five years later. If you are over 18 you can enter the Bingo theatre if it is open and see the interior.

You can finish the walk here and return to Tooting Broadway. But if you have time to go a bit further, continue on, looking out for the fine-looking ㉔ **Tooting Library** on the left, dating from the early 1900s, as well as the Players cigarette ghost sign right beside it.

After a few minutes walk you reach Church Lane, continue along it, passing a ㉕ **monument** from 1823 that marks the spot of **Tooting Parish Pump**. Linked to an artesian well, it was used right up until the late 19th century.

Stop at ㉖ **St Nicholas Church**, Tooting. The first church on the site was built over 1,000 years ago. The current Gothic-styled church dates from 1833 when the old Saxon church was demolished.

Carry on down the lane, passing ㉗ **the old village school** on the left. The earlier of the visible memorial stones dates from

1828 and records the rebuilding of the school. Before the arrival of the railways, underground and construction of cinemas, markets, pubs and row after row of terrace houses, this would have been a rural area. Kids would go to this local parish school and play in the fields nearby, no doubt going to the local pump to bring back water for their parents.

Keep going, until you see the ㉘ **brick pillars** by the entrance of Hawthorn Crescent. This was part of St Benedict's Hospital and if you go through the gates and turn left up Limetree Walk you can see some remaining pillars from the old hospital and the ㉙ **former clock tower** as well.

The site was originally dominated by a Roman Catholic College named St Joseph's, completed in 1888. To the east stood Furzedown Park Farm. Just before 1900, the College was repurposed as workhouse accommodation and known as the Tooting Home, with 605 inmates. Later, a military hospital during World War I, it became St Benedict's from 1930 until its closure in 1981. It was eventually demolished to make way for the modern housing you see today.

Having seen these remnants of village life and the workhouse in Tooting, retrace your steps back to Tooting Broadway, marking the end of this walk. ●

SHOP...

Tooting Market (see p.253)
21-23 Tooting High Street,
SW17 0SN
www.tootingmarket.com

Broadway Market (see p.253)
29 Tooting High Street, SW17 0RJ
www.bmtooting.co.uk

EAT / DRINK...

Wheatsheaf Pub (see p.245)
42 Upper Tooting Road,
SW17 7PG
www.thewheatsheafsw17.com

The Kings Head (see p.249)
84 Tooting High Street, SW17 7PB
www.greeneking-pubs.co.uk/pubs/
greater-london/kings-head/

The Castle Pub (see p.255)
38 Tooting High Street, SW17 0RG
www.castletooting.com

Mirch Masala (see p.251)
213 Upper Tooting Road,
SW17 1TJ

10 Peckham Walk

Peckham Walk

1. Copeland Park & Bussey Building
2. Holdron's Department Store
3. John the Unicorn (number 157)
4. Parkstone Road
5. Girdlers Cottages
6. Peckham Islamic Centre Mosque
7. Old School Signs
8. Peckham Rye Common
9. Blenheim Grove
10. Peckham Rye Station
11. Art Deco Buildings
12. Peckham Levels
13. Rye Lane Market
14. Methodist Chapel
15. The Kentish Rovers
16. Site of Hanover Chapel
17. M.Manze's Eel & Pie House
18. The Greyhound
19. Peckham Library
20. Mountview Drama School
21. Old Grand Surrey Canal
22. Willowbrook Bridge
23. Burgess Park
24. Glengall Wharf Garden
25. Bridge-to-Nowhere
26. Chumleigh Gardens
27. Passmore Edwards Library
28. St George's Church
29. Historic Lime Kiln
30. Addington Square
31. Evelina Mansions
32. Steptoes and Sons
33. Calypso Crescent
34. Damilola Taylor Centre
35. Mieux
36. Peckham House Lunatic Asylum
37. Persepolis
38. Wilsons Cycles
39. Site of Tramway Depot

Ruskin Park

Peckham Rye 🚆

Peckham Walk
Start/ Finish: Peckham Rye Station
Distance: 4.5 miles

This walk around Peckham and its surrounding areas – including remnants of the Surrey Canal – explores a part of London that has likely changed more than any other in recent years due to gentrification.

Peckham has traditionally been looked down upon by many Londoners. Indeed many residents of the capital have never visited the area, their impression of it tainted by the television series Only Fools and Horses (whose main characters Del and Rodney live in a dingy Peckham tower block named Mandela House).

However, in the last few years, rising property prices have resulted from an influx of newcomers to the area, and significant investment has been made to improve a number of the poorly maintained and troubled housing estates. You will see much of the old and new Peckham on this walk.

From the station turn right down Rye Lane, heading south towards Peckham Rye Common. Rye Lane is one of the most vibrant thoroughfares in London; with shops and markets serving the area's diverse communities with all manner of goods and services. Almost immediately on the left is the entrance at 133 Rye Lane to the ❶ **Copeland Park and Bussey Building** complex. This is one of the places that has transformed Peckham into such a popular destination in recent years. The vast complex hosts an almost bewildering variety of bars and food outlets, the CLF Arts Café, a fantastic cinema, as well as art studios and small businesses that offer everything from yoga classes to vintage records. It is like Camden in the old days, before it was spoilt by redevelopment.

The red brick Bussey building dates from the 19th century and was originally used to manufacture sports equipment. The named 'Busey' refers to the company's owner, George Gibson Bussey. Aside from producing cricket bats once used by W. G. Grace, the factory also produced munitions during World War II and may have been

used as an air-raid shelter. It was for many decades one of the tallest buildings in the district and offers amazing views over London.

The complex also incorporates the former Holdron's Department store – an Art Deco gem from the 1930s whose glory days were when it was owned by Selfridges and John Lewis in the mid-20th century. It reflects an age when Peckham had a number of up-market department stores, which have largely disappeared as the area declined during the post-war years.

My recommendation would be to complete the walk, then come here in the evening to see Copeland Park and Bussey building at its best – otherwise you'll risk spending several hours here.

Continue along Rye Lane, which boasts a wide range of architectural styles, until you reach the elegant frontage of the former ❷ **Holdron's department store** building, dating from 1935 and now occupied by Khan's Bargain outlet. The owner of Khan's received an award from Historic England in 2019 after restoring the old department store roof to its former glory. Peppered with Art Deco buildings, it is easy to see why Rye Lane and its surrounding streets are often described as Peckham's 'Art Deco Quarter'. Local

architecture expert Benedict O'Looney wrote:

'The central part of Rye Lane in Peckham has a remarkable cluster of Art Deco buildings, markers of the commercial vigour and enterprise of local business which made Rye Lane South London's premier shopping destination in the late 19th and 20th centuries'.

Continue down Rye Lane where on the left is ❸ **John the Unicorn** (number 157) – one of the best bars to have opened in Peckham in recent years. Just after the pub, on the left is ❹ **Parkstone Road**, which contains some useful wall-mounted information boards about Peckham including photographs of buildings on Rye Lane.

Along Rye Lane you will also notice many of the buildings have flat roofs, mostly dating from the late 19th century. Nearly all have ground-level modern shop extensions, making the street feel narrower than it would have appeared in the Victorian Age.

Walk on and head right at K & K Butchers and Fishmarket for a small detour along Choumert Road, passing locals selling everything from West African groceries to Halal sweets. The influx of Nigerian culture to Peckham in past decades has also given rise to the description of streets like this as being part of 'Little Lagos'.

Stop to see the ❺ **Girdlers Cottages** on the right (opposite the old school buildings). Established in 1852, they are some of the oldest buildings in the area, originally almshouses built by the Palyn charity for destitute men. George Palyn was Master of

the Girdlers Company, and when he died in 1609, he left a charitable bequest to provide accommodation for destitute men. The Girdlers Company still exists and is one of London's historic guild organisations, for many centuries controlling the belt-making trade. The final residents of the alms-houses left in the 1980s and now the pretty houses are privately owned.

Just up neighbouring Choumert Grove is the ⑥ **Peckham Islamic Centre Mosque**, more evidence that this is one of the most ethnically and religiously diverse areas of London. Surprisingly, the first purpose-built mosque in London only opened in 1926.

Return down Choumert Road, looking for ⑦ **Old School Signs** for boys, girls and infants entrances on the late 19th-century school opposite the alms-houses.

Return to Rye Lane. An important part of the area is ⑧ **Peckham Rye Common**. This is a long walk but if you are keen to include the Common, turn right, continuing south for a few minutes, and head towards the north end of the Common. As the road forks, bear right, passing estate agents, cafés and pubs. Keep on the right of a large triangle of grass that leads you to a junction to the north end of the common. Notable facts about the common include that it was once used to house Italian prisoners of war during World War II and one of London's hidden rivers – the River Peck – can be glimpsed on the west side. The influence of the river has defined Peckham since medieval times. The name of the original 'Peckham' village was derived from the river Peck. Peckham – mentioned in the Doomsday Book in 1086 as *Pecheham* – used to be known for its market gardens and orchards, but the Industrial Revolution and advancement of the railways in the 19th century meant the area became increasingly urbanised. The River Peck was largely covered over in 1823. Romantic poet and artist William Blake also experienced visions of angels in trees in this area in 1767.

Once you have explored Peckham Rye Common, return to Rye Lane. Alternatively, if you opted for a shorter walk, turn left onto Rye Lane and head north.

Follow the map, taking a small detour left down ❾ **Blenheim Grove** to see some more Art Deco buildings on the right-hand side of the road. Larry's Café is a good example of this and also a great place to stop for a coffee. Whilst not visited on this walk, if

you carried on down Blenheim Grove you would reach Bellenden Road – described as the 'artisanal heart of Peckham' and where the gentrification of this district is at its most obvious. The transformation of Peckham in recent years is evidenced by the fact that in 2019 the price of houses had risen here faster than any other district in the UK since 1995.

Return to Rye Lane and continue north, passing under the bridges outside ⑩ **Peckham Rye Station**.

The station behind the Art Deco façade dates from 1865 and is an impressive design from Charles Henry Driver, one of the most prominent architects of the Victorian era. Driver worked on several railway stations and helped Joseph Bazalgette transform London with the design of the Thames Embankment and pumping stations at Abbey Mills and Crossness.

Continue northwards, passing more ⑪ **buildings of the Art Deco quarter** on the left at the junction with Holly Grove – one a branch of Iceland, the other (at number 72) a McDonalds. The latter was originally a C & A department store building and dates from 1930. By 1934, this style of architecture contributed to Rye Lane being described as 'the Oxford Street of South London'. Many beautiful buildings in this area have become run down in recent years and were due for demolition, however local groups such as *Peckham Vision* have campaigned to save and adapt them for other purposes. Much of the credit for the recent transformation of Peckham goes to the local volunteer groups.

On the right (opposite Elm Grove) walk down the passageway to the entrance of another cultural centre that has in recent years attracted many visitors to Peckham. ⑫ **Peckham Levels** was a disused multi-storey car park that has now been converted as part of a community project. It is home to a wide variety of businesses, restaurants and communities. Frank's bar, on the top floor, offers one of the best free views in London, and was key to establishing Peckham as a 'go to' place for many Londoners and tourists. Again you can visit now, with the risk you will never want to leave, so I recommend you carry on and visit again at the end of the walk. The

Peckhamplex is also one of the best, and cheapest, independent cinemas in the capital.

Return to Rye Lane, where ⑬ **Rye Lane Market** is next up on the left, full of small enterprises from barbers to African fashion, hair braiding and tasty Afro-Carribean food. This is the side of Peckham that has not yet been gentrified.

Opposite is the ⑭ **Methodist Chapel** dating from 1863. The first Baptist place of worship was set up in Peckham in 1818 when it was still a rural hamlet. The chapel later moved to where Peckham Rye train station is today, but had to move again when railway construction began. The current chapel survived serious damage from German bombs in 1943, and the congregation later built this elegant new home which is still used as a place of Methodist worship.

Walk to the north end of Rye Lane to reach Peckham High Street. On the other side is ⑮ **The Kentish Drovers** – named after an 18th-century pub that used to stand on the other side of the High Street. Its name also recalls the fact that for centuries, cattle drivers would stop in the village of Peckham to rest, before travelling on to sell their livestock at the great meat markets of London.

On the corner with Rye Lane is the site of the ⑯ **former Hanover Chapel** that was built in 1819 and – like the Baptist chapel seen earlier –ensured Peckham had a reputation in the 19th century for the number of non-conformist churches that were founded here.

Bear right down the High Street, before turning left and stopping at number

View from Peckhamplex

105, **⑰ M.Manze's Eel & Pie House**. The first M.Manze shop was founded in 1902, when cockneys would regard stewed and jellied eels, and pie and mash with liquor as a regular part of their diet. Tastes have changed, and this is now one of the last remaining traditional eateries to be found in the capital. Manze's is open only at select hours, so plan ahead if you want to stop for a traditional and delicious lunch. Opposite is a old school Peckham boozer – **⑱ the Greyhound** – which dates from the 1880s. Its predecessor of the same name dated back to the 1700s when Peckham was still a rural village.

After Manze's, turn left to reach the dramatic-looking **⑲ Peckham Library** and walk towards it. In 2000 this became the first (and to date only) library to win the prestigious Sterling Prize for architecture.

Bear right, past the library, with the **⑳ Mountview drama school** on the other side. Founded in Crouch End in 1945, the school moved here in 2018, providing a boost to the area's continuing regeneration. The site was originally a canal-side warehouse and later became Whitten's Timber Yard before falling into disuse. The new building is designed by Carl Turner Architects and has helped transform this corner of Peckham, having been shortlisted for the NLA Awards in 2019.

Passing Mountview, you now head north along the Peckham branch of the old **㉑ Grand Surrey Canal**. You will walk for several minutes passing under numerous bridges that once took road users over a working canal. The most notable is the second, ㉒ **Willowbrook Bridge**, a wrought-iron, Victorian delight dating from 1870.

The Grand Surrey Canal is largely forgotten about now, but in its day it was a vastly ambitious, if ultimately unsuccessful, feat of engineering. Parliament approved the building of the canal in 1801, and in the years that followed, the canal was dug out – from Rotherhithe on the Thames, right through South London and ending at Camberwell. Various branches ran off the canal, including the Peckham branch you are now walking along. There were plans to extend the canal as far as Portsmouth, but these were never realised.

The Peckham branch of the Surrey Canal opened in 1826, fifteen years after the main canal to the north of here was completed. The, now cemented over, Peckham branch was once surrounded by wharves, timber yards and other buildings associated with work on the canal. The Mountview drama school, recently visited, is located on the former site of canal-side industrial buildings.

After a pleasant stroll, you reach ㉓ **Burgess Park** – situated on top of the main section of the Surrey Canal. The canal continued to be used right up to the 1940s, but after that, was nearly completely filled in.

On the right is ㉔ **Glengall Wharf Garden**, a peaceful and inspiring community garden and green space that features 10 beehives and chickens. It does a great job of bringing local people together and is situated on the original Glengall Basin where canal boats used to turn before heading down the Peckham branch of the canal. The concrete used to fill in the original canal meant that volunteers had to use this as the foundation for their raised garden.

Now follow the Surrey Canal path left after the garden and over the road through Burgess Park. In the late 19th century, the whole area of the park was dominated by the canal and dozens of commercial streets. In 1917, an attack by Zeppelin bombers killed 12 people and destroyed 3 houses here, and during World War II even worse damage was inflicted by V1 and V2 rockets.

After World War II most of the properties, many run-down, were demolished to make way for the Park, wiping clean what was once a heavily populated part of London. The park was named after Camberwell's first female mayor, Jessie Burgess, in 1973. Check out the informaton boards if you're curious to find out more about the canal and the area's history.

You pass another bridge that once was used to cross the busy canal – the so called ㉕ **'bridge to nowhere'**. Later on the right, you can take a detour to visit ㉖ **Chumleigh Gardens**, another beautiful spot centred on former 19th century almshouses. The almshouses were part of an 'asylum' founded by the Female Friendly Society, whose aim was to help local women. They operated 'by love, kindness, and absence of humbug', and gave small grants to 'poor, aged women of good character'. In the 1800s, before the creation of the Welfare State, benevolent groups such as the Female Friendly Society were all that stood between many local women and the workhouse. Weary walkers might like to note that there is a café, kids' playground and toilet here.

Retrace your steps back to the main path through Burgess Park, and when you cross Wells Way stop to see the old ㉗ **Passmore Edwards Library, Baths and Wash House** that opened in 1903. The Victorian philanthropist Passmore Edwards helped fund the site, aimed at helping the local working-class who had no such facilities at home.

Nearby are the striking columns of ㉘ **St George's Church** that was built in 1824. The church became derelict and in recent years modern housing has been built within, although the impressive façade remains.

Continue through the park where you soon pass a ㉙ **historic lime kiln** dating from 1816. It was once used in the early 19th century to make quick lime that was used in the production of mortar. Coal and limestone were brought along the canal for use in the lime kiln. Many of the historic buildings that you have passed on this walk will have been built with lime produced here.

Reach the western end of the Park, where the Surrey Canal itself ended. Walk south into the picturesque ㉚ **Addington Square**, built between 1810 and 1850 when this area was still largely surrounded by fields and market gardens. The Richardson's – the crime family who competed with the Krays for the title of London's most notorious gangsters – operated out of number 33 on the Square in the 1960s.

Exit the Square on the southeast corner and walk past some bollards to reach New Church Road. Immediately on the other side are the red brick ㉛ **4 Per Cent Industrial**

Dwellings Company buildings, dating from 1900 and known as Evelina Mansions. The Company was founded in 1885 by Sir Nathaniel Rothschild to provide cheap, good quality accommodation to Jewish refugees fleeing persecution in Eastern Europe. Beginning in the East End, more residential blocks were built by the company around the city and were made available to anyone who needed them. Today, they serve as a reminder of how London dealt with its housing crises in the past. The complex is named after Nathaniel's sister Evelina, and four per cent was the expected reasonable rate of return investors in the Company might hope to receive.

Continue eastwards, away from the Park. You will now walk through some of Peckham's many housing estates before returning to Peckham High Street. Just around the corner and on Southampton Way, stop to admire the organised chaos of ⓛ **Steptoes and Sons** – a local institution that sells all manner of second-hand goods and architectural salvage. It is a unique experience visiting the Steptoes and one well worth taking the time to enjoy.

Head left on Parkhouse Street, following it as it winds around to reach Wells Road. Cross over and walk down Coleman Road, with some pretty 19th-century cottages on your right, some covered in ivy. Bear left onto Newent Close and then left again onto Lynbrook Grove. At the end of the Grove, turn right into Chandler Way, and take a left along Burcher Gale Grove (the big school on your left).

You now start to see some of the residential estates that have long been associated with Peckham. The 'five estates' that were built from the 1960s became very run down in following years, the North Peckham estate in particular became a by-word (at least in

the press) for violence, drugs and poor living conditions. In the past couple of decades a great deal of investment, particularly from the European Union, has helped improve things considerably. However, life for many people on the estates is not easy, and in August 2011 this contributed to the anger that erupted during the London Riots, streets in Peckham being among the worst affected.

Turn right (still on Burcher Gale Grove) and along Samuel Street, passing ㉝ **Calypso Crescent**. Continue straight at the bend to join Cronin Street then stop at the junction with Commercial Street. Just to the west of here is Blakes Road, where in November 2000, occurred one of London's highest-profile killings – the stabbing of 10-year-old Damilola Taylor. The two boys convicted of his murder were part of the *Peckham Boys* – a gang that terrorised, and still terrorises the North Peckham Estate and contains an incredibly complex number of 'sub gangs'.

The murder of such a young boy caused national outrage and Damilola is still remembered so many years later by the ㉞

Damilola Taylor Centre just along from here up East Surrey Grove. Sadly, in recent years, knife crime in London has increased. However, few individual tragedies have remained in the public consciousness as the death of Damilola that terrible November day.

Walk east along Commercial Way and then south down Sumner Road until you reach Jocelyn Street Park. Follow the path here to pass along a final stretch of Sumner Road to reach Peckham High Street again.

On the other side of the road look for the vintage pub signage for 35 **'Meux's Famous Stout and Ales'**. Meux was initially based in Tottenham Court Road but moved to Nine Elms in 1921. Despite the dominance of much larger brands in the beer industry, the company continued in business until 1999.

In the late 19th century the ㊱ **Peckham House Lunatic Asylum** stood approximately behind the former pub. It was demolished in 1954 and the site is now occupied by a school.

Turn left along the High Street, looking out for two local institutions – ㊲ **Persepolis**, followed by ㊳ **Wilsons Cycles**. Persepolis is famed for its Persian groceries and restaurant and is run by Sally Butcher, who has written a number of excellent cook books. If you are vegetarian this is a great place to eat.

Wilsons is thought to be the oldest business in Peckham, having opened its doors in 1870.

Continue east, passing the junction with Bellenden Road. Now an open space and a Lidl, this was the ㊴ **site of a major tramway depot** in the late 19th century, when the tram system was a major feature of Peckham High Street.

Continue to reach Rye Lane where you can retrace your steps back to the station, where, if you have time, you can visit some of the attractions mentioned earlier on in the walk. ●

VISIT...

Copeland Park and Bussey
(see p.267)
133 Copeland Road, SE15 3SN
www.copelandpark.com

Glengall Wharf Garden
(see p.278)
64 Glengall Road, SE15 6NF
www.glengallwharfgarden.org.uk

Peckham Levels (see p.273)
F1-F6 Town Centre Carpark,
SE15 4ST
www.copelandpark.co.uk

Peckhamplex Cinema)
95A Rye Lane, SE15 4ST
www.peckhamplex.london

EAT /DRINK ...

M. Manze's Pie and Eel House
(see p.277)
105 Peckham High Street,
SE15 5RS
www.manze.com

The Greyhound (see p.277)
109 Peckham High Street,
SE15 5SE
www.thegreyhoundpeckham.co.uk

Larry's
Unit 5,
12-16 Blenheim GroveSE15 4QL
www.larryspeckham.co.uk

SHOP...

Wilsons Cycle (see p.286)
32 Peckham High Street,
SE15 5DP
www.wilsonscycles.uk

Persepolis (see p.286)
28-30 Peckham High Street
SE15 5DT
www.foratasteofpersia.co.uk

Steptoes and Sons (see p.282)
Southampton Way, SE5 7SW

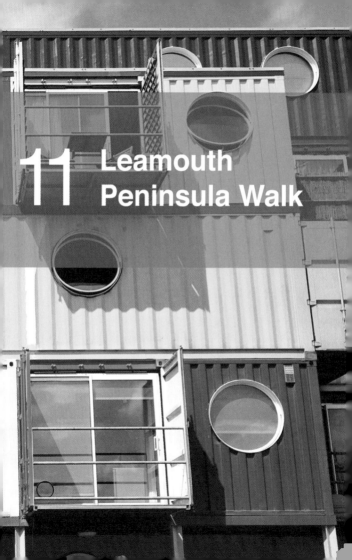

11 Leamouth Peninsula Walk

Leamouth Peninsula

1. Canning Town Station
2. Bow Creek Ecological Park
3. The Blue Bridge
4. Eastern side of Import Dock
5. Great Eastern Railway Co. Wharf
6. Former Dock Walls
7. East India Dock Basin
8. Path
9. Blackwall Station
10. Virginia Settlers Memorial
11. Dock Basin Lock Gates
12. Millennium Memorial
13. Orchard Place
14. Trinity Buoy Wharf
15. Fat Boy Diner
16. Faraday Effect Museum
17. London Graving Dock
18. Former Thames Ironworks & Shipbuilding Co.
19. London City Island
20. English National Ballet
21. Footbridge

FORDS PARK ROAD

Town

SILVERTOWN

ROAD

VICTORIA DOCK ROAD

SILVERTOWN WAY

Leamouth Peninsula Walk

Start / Finish: Canning Town Station
Distance: 2.2 miles

This walk explores one of the most isolated parts of London and much of it is spent walking by the water and around the two peninsulas that stretch out into the River Lea and Bow Creek.

It starts at ❶ **Canning Town Station**, where you exit to see the waters of Bow Creek to the south, and behind you, an undeniably horrible mass of road, rail and other transport-related infrastructure. Also to the south, over the water, are the looming towers of London City Island. This is a recent development that has changed this part of London forever, and bills itself as 'A twelve-acre micro-Manhattan'. You will walk through this development in the second half of this walk.

Before you start walking, look back towards the station. Until the 19th century, the area now called Canning Town was largely covered by boggy marshland. Then there was the rapid industrial

development of Leamouth Peninsula, with shipbuilders, docks, chemical, iron and glassworks all needing to be connected to the railways. Thousands of workers came to live here, near their place of work, and speculators built row upon row of terrace houses to accommodate them. The area is thought to have been named after Lord Canning, a Governor-General of India who was involved in the suppression of the Indian Mutiny in the 1850s.

Maps dating from around 1900 show that the area to the north and east of the current day station was already heavily residential. The narrow, terraced streets were occupied largely by the working-class who frequented the dozens of local pubs. They also visited the nearby Royal Albert Music Hall, opened in 1875 (as Relf's Music Hall) that could hold 2,500 people. Like many other buildings in this area, the music hall (having become a bingo hall) was pulled down in the 1960s to make way for the busy fly-overs and other roads you see today – a community lost to history.

From the station follow the map, passing the footbridge leading to River City. The River Lea starts near Luton and reaches the Thames near here, the last meandering stretch known as Bow Creek. You are now entering another peninsula shaped by the course of the river that has been transformed into ❷ **Bow Creek Ecological Park**. Take the left-hand entrance into the park (not the covered walkway) and start to head south along this peninsula.

This strange place, in the shadow of a DLR bridge, is one of the most secluded spots in London. I have been here on three occasions and only met one single dog walker. This peninsula has never been occupied for residential purposes, so if you

are looking for 'hidden' London, this marooned piece of land may well hit the spot.

Walk down the length of the Park, with the DLR bridge up above. You will see tidal mudflats and wild flowers. There are also plenty of birds, including redshank, sand martins and kingfishers. Several information boards dotted throughout the park tell you more about the wildlife and meadows. There are also a few benches if you want somewhere to picnic.

At the time of writing the very southern tip of the peninsula remained closed, so if you reach a locked gate at the southern edge of the park, follow the path which takes you up the west side where on the left you cross over a ❸ **footbridge (called The Blue Bridge).**

On the other side bear left, away from the roaring traffic, until you find the path again that goes right beside the water with great views of the City Island development to your left.

Continue along for a few minutes. To the west of here (your right) are the former sites of the mighty East India Docks complex that once dominated Blackwall. London was once the largest port in the world, and during the 19th century, ever-larger docks were opened to cope with the increasing size of ships, and growth in international commerce.

The East India Dock Company was founded in 1803 and financed by the company of the same name, that then monopolised trade with India and most of that with Asia and the Far East. At this time the East India Company was the single most powerful private commercial enterprise in the world and arguably remains unequalled in its power even by modern-day behemoths including Amazon and Apple.

The East India Docks offloaded the company's ships carrying goods such as silk, Persian carpets, Chinese tea and Indian spices – sourced from across the Empire.

Walking by the water, it's worth noting that if you had stood here in the mid-19th century and looked over to your right, you would have seen over 250 tall-masted sailing ships. The spot marked ❹ on the map indicates what would have been the **eastern side** of the biggest of the three docks here (called the **Import Dock** by 1900).

By the time Victoria ascended to the throne, the various privately owned London docks were caught in a vicious spiral of competition, which impacted their profits. The East India Docks were forced to merge with their great rival the West India Docks in 1838. Eventually, most London docks were amalgamated into the Port of London Authority in 1909.

During World War II floating Mulberry Harbours were built here, famously used to great effect during the D-Day landings. After the war, the docks were again used for domestic shipping but eventually became uneconomic to run and closed. Most of the old East India Docks were filled in and then gradually built upon, except for the Basin you will see shortly.

As you walk along, the area to your immediate right was occupied in the late 19th century by the ❺ **Great Eastern Railway Company Wharf** where railways were built to transport goods from the docks to the granaries and warehouses of the area. Today the site is being redeveloped for new housing and offices, and ironically attracting investment from East Asia, on land once owned by the East India Company.

At the roundabout take a small detour up Leamouth Road to see the substantial ❻ **walls of the former docks** on both sides. Look for the '**stick and snake**' badges which represent trade and medicine – this was part of the entrance to the old East India Docks pepper warehouse.

Walk back to the roundabout, where you are surrounded by evidence of the mass regeneration of the area, beginning in the 1980s after the old docks closed. The best-known development is at Canary Wharf to the west of here, which has thrived as a modern rival to the old City of London. By contrast, Canning Town is one of the most deprived areas of the country.

Now walk down Blackwall Way (at the 6 o'clock position on the roundabout) and then bear left at the sign for East India Dock Basin. Walk around the western edge of the ❼ **East India Dock Basin** – the only remaining substantial part of the old East

India Docks. Real effort has been made to turn this into a wildlife centre, and you can see dozens of birds through the viewing walls. There are many information boards that help identify the animals that can be seen here. It's a tranquil place dominated by wildlife, making it hard to imagine the Basin once crammed full of sailing ships, with hundreds of workers going about their business.

As you follow the map, take the **❽ path** to the right, leading away from the Basin. This takes you down to the edge of the Thames, where you turn right through the gate and continue westwards along the Thames Path.

There are superb views from here – from the Millennium Dome on the other side of the Thames, to the tall buildings of the redeveloped docklands area. To your right where modern houses now stand was once the location of **❾ Blackwall Station** that operated between 1840 and 1926. This was the eastern terminus of the long-vanished Commercial Railway. The poet Sir John Betjeman (1906-1984) wrote fondly of journeys here in his book *First and Last Loves*, recalling 'stagecoaches...rumbled past East End chimney pots, wharves and shipping stopping at empty black stations till they came to a final halt at Blackwall station...When one emerged there, there was

nothing to see beyond it but a cobbled quay and a vast stretch of wind whipped water...'. Travellers used to be able to catch a ferry from the station to continue to Gravesend.

Walk on to reach the **❿ Virginia Settlers Memorial**. For Americans in particular this is an important marker of where, near here, a small group of 105 'adventurers' set sail from Blackwall in December 1606. They established the first colony in Virginia, Jamestown, 14 years before the more famous *Mayflower* would land in Massachusetts.

One of the three ships was called the *Discovery* and captained by John Smith. He was famously saved by Pocahontas after being captured by her tribe whilst on an expedition in the new colony. The Memorial dates from 1928 and was originally part of the wall of a building that stood nearby.

The East India Export dock was a little inland from here. To give you a sense of how long it was, the distance from the gate you just walked through to the Memorial is approximately half the length of the Export dock. All the new housing you see to your right sits on the site of the old, long filled in, dock. Many of the names used for these new residential blocks reflect the area's history – Settlers Court, Pilgrims Mews, Adventurers Court. The area is very quiet and a little soulless. Certainly, if dockers from the 1850s could be

VIRGINIA QUAY

transported through time to this spot, they would have difficulty recognising anything except the Thames itself (and would struggle to find any pubs).

This is not just a joke. For many locals drinking beer after a day's work on the docks was probably safer than drinking the water. One newspaper in September 1849 reports the state of the water supply as 'black and offensive in the extreme, and in 14 houses in that locality there had been no less than six deaths within a few days'.

Walk a few hundred yards more, following the map to stop roughly at the end of the old Export dock. Then re-trace your steps back to the gate to explore the rest of East India Dock Basin, crossing the path leading over ⑪ **the dock basin lock gates** which date from the late 1870s. If you're curious to find out more about the area's history, refer to the information boards. An example being that sailing ships couldn't leave the East India Docks for trading trips after mid-September due to the weather conditions in the Indian Ocean.

There is also an intriguing ⑫ **metal memorial** nearby 'Marking the Year 2000' on which the names and aspirations for the future of several people are inscribed. I wonder how many lived up to their expectations in the years that followed or come back to remind themselves of their promises (M.G Nasreddin 'I will forever be close to my beloved best friend, Shehab Reda').

Continue along the east side of the Basin, again getting a great view of the mudflats, shingle and saltmarshes, exiting through some gates onto ⑬ **Orchard Place**. You are now entering another part of London that has traditionally been very isolated and which is now undergoing extensive redevelopment as part of the River City initiative. Turning right, see if you can spot any ghost signs for industries once based here.

This area was once called Orchard Place, after Orchard House – a tavern or 'tippling house' located here in the late 17th century. Later, shipyards were built here, as well as warehouses for the docks and factories for various industries.

Between 1820 and 1930 there was a village here on Orchard Place, with a chapel, school and several pubs. Everyone in the village worked in the local industries established in this isolated spot. However, it was a difficult place for a community to settle due to frequent flooding from the Thames. This contributed to the village's decline as it gradually degenerated into a slum.

In 1890 a local priest – the suitably named Father Lawless – spoke of locals as 'hardly human...incarnate mushrooms... God must have made a mistake in creating them'. Orchard Place was remote and isolated and inter-breeding was common. In 1930 it was reported that 100 out of the 160 local school children had the same surname –Lammin. The whole village was moved to Poplar in the 1930s – another community confined to the history books.

Continue walking to reach **⑭ Trinity Buoy Wharf**: one of the most unusual places in London. The Corporation of Trinity House was given a charter by Henry VIII in 1514 and had the authority to assist with navigation for sailors, primarily through the provision of buoys, lighthouses and lightships. A workshop was established here in 1803, specialising in the manufacture of wooden buoys. For over 200 years Trinity House had operations here, and in 1910 employed around 150 workers.

London's only lighthouse – often called the **Bow Creek Lighthouse** – is also found here. Built in the 1860s, it was used to test out new technologies and to train lighthouse keepers.

In the late 19th century this area to the east of the Basin was covered by shipbuilding yards, wharves and graving docks.

Today the area is host to a variety of fascinating artistic and commercial endeavours, but those with an appetite might like to make their first stop the iconic American 40's style **⑮ Fat Boy Diner** (which featured in the 1998 film *Sliding Doors*).

15

The buildings that make up Trinity Buoy Wharf are an eclectic mix of old and new. Several of the buildings and seawalls date from the early 19th century and would have been familiar to the famous scientist Michael Faraday (1791-1867), who had a workshop on this spot. It was here that he conducted experiments while acting as a scientific adviser to Trinity House. There is a tiny (as in garden shed sized) sensory museum called the **16 Faraday Effect**, dedicated to the great man and his time here. The Wharf ceased being used by the Corporation of Trinity House in 1988.

The contemporary buildings here imaginatively repurpose shipping containers to form workspaces and offices. There is some irony in the fact that container shipping led to the demise of these smaller docks in favour of bigger, mechanised ports on the coast that could handle the much larger vessels. These contemporary buildings are not unique to Trinity Buoy Wharf, but are particularly colourful and well designed by the architects at Container City and Nicholas Lacey and Partners. The modern complex now looks very much part of the landscape, making it difficult to believe that the initial installation in 2001 took just 8 days.

The studios and workshops are nowadays occupied by ceramicists, blacksmiths, textile designers and artists that have created a vibrant arts community on the banks of the Thames. This emphasis on arts and crafts is further strengthened by courses run by The Prince's Youth Trust for secondary schools in these much neglected traditional skills.

Among the innovative and unusual businesses to be found here, is the country's first Parkour Academy: dedicated to teaching a form of acrobatics using street furniture and buildings. The academy provides a safe

environment to practice the skills needed for Parkour, and minus the bumps and bruises that leaping through the cityscape often cause.

Trinity Buoy Wharf also boasts one of the UK's largest collections of public art with works by some leading artists and a busy programme of exhibitions which are all free to view. Among the unusual sights, look out for the old London black cab that has given its last ride and now takes pride of place on the roof of one of the container units. There

is also a Dutch-built, tugboat called the *Knocker White* that is now permanently moored here awaiting renovation.

Before leaving Trinity Buoy Wharf, take time to admire the strange bright red ship. The 550-tonne Lightvessel 95 (LV95) is permanently moored here and has been adapted into a recording studio. The vessel was one of several designed on this site as a floating warning to ships in the absence of a more permanent lighthouse. It spent a good deal of its working life alerting mariners to South Goodwin Sands, whose shallow waters had claimed many ships and thousands of lives. The ship served its stationary but essential duty for many years and was only withdrawn from service in 2003. The brightly painted LV95 is a remarkable sight and, having been built to withstand the harshest of maritime conditions, seems destined to remain a permanent feature of the industrial landscape.

If you go to the south side and walk out over a footbridge leading to a boat docking station and look back, you can see the bulging gate of the old ⑰ **London Graving Dock** – one of two dry docks on this side of Orchard Place used to hold ships that required maintenance. The gate is hollow and at high tide would float open and then

be refilled with water to close it again. Orchard Place was home to the shipyards of Perry, Wigram & Green, The Thames Ironworks and many other small yards.

When finished at Trinity Buoy Wharf start to retrace your steps. Look over to the other side of Bow Creek to see an area that was once the main home of the ⑱ **Thames Ironworks and Shipbuilding Company**. It was founded in 1837 and operated until 1912. During that time it mainly produced ships but also iron needed for the building of Kingdom Brunel's Royal Albert Bridge and mass-produced items like cranes and motor cars.

HMS Warrior: the world's first iron-hulled, armour-plated warship was built here, and launched in 1860 (you can visit it in Portsmouth). The ship revolutionised warship design, much in the same way as jet fighters replaced prop planes from the late 1940s. The slipway had to be reinforced because of *Warrior's* enormous size. Charles Dickens wrote of the *Warrior*, 'A black vicious ugly customer as ever I saw, whale-like in size, and with as terrible a row of incisor teeth as ever closed on a French frigate'.

The original company was founded in Orchard Place on this side of Bow Creek, but as the firm prospered, it moved to a much larger site on the opposite bank. A workforce of around 3,000 men built ships for many foreign navies and produced 144 warships – making it the largest shipbuilder on the Thames and one of the biggest employers in the East End. A major tragedy took place here in June 1898 when *HMS Albion* was launched. A huge wave created by the launch swept onlookers into the water and 37 people were drowned.

The Thames Ironworks closed in 1912 due to a lack of new ship orders and competition from shipbuilders in the North – ironic perhaps given World War I was just two years away.

A newspaper report of the closure from 23 December 1912 commented on how 'this important news..will cast a gloom over Christmas festivities in Canning Town'. Another compared how the company 'treated its employees with conspicuous generosity..', suggesting the shipyards of the North-East and the Clyde were succeeding because they paid their workers less and offered very few of the same benefits. It would become a familiar tale in decades to come when the British shipbuilding industry as a whole succumbed to cheaper yards in Asia and elsewhere.

When Crossrail dug a tunnel through the area in 2012, it discovered remains of the Ironworks and Shipbuilding Company complex and archaeologists were called in to document the site: uncovering the railway, forges and a furnace. It is a rare legacy of a time when Britain really did rule the waves – in the 1890s its yards together produced 80% of the world's commercial tonnage,

and the Thames Ironworks was critical to this dominance.

The workers' football team was called Thames Ironworks F.C and played in the FA Cup. Founded in 1895, it was later re-founded as the famous West Ham United – known as 'the Hammers', after the tools used in the yard.

Retrace your steps, passing where you came through the gate from the basin, and continue north under the road bridge to reach the heart of ⑲ **London City Island**. There is not a great deal to see here of historic interest as everything is brand new and very shiny. In the 1860s the Thames Plate Glass Works dominated this northern part of the peninsula, with around three-quarters of locals working here. By 1900 the peninsula was covered with residential housing, a school, pubs, a sugar refinery, iron works and oil mills.

Even until the 1970s this peninsula remained heavily industrialised, with a galvanised ironworks operating on the east side. However this had all been swept away before the recent development began and today you see expensive apartments, a gallery, and new arrivals such as the ⑳ **English National Ballet** (and school). It brings some hope the wider area can benefit from all the new money being attracted to a once highly industrialised backwater of London.

When finished, exit on the north end of River City over the ㉑ **footbridge** and back to Canning Town station where this walk ends.
●

VISIT...

Bow Creek Ecological Park
(see p.293)
E14 oLG
www.visitleevalley.org.uk

Trinity Buoy Wharf (see p.303)
64 Orchard Place, E14 oJW
www.trinitybuoywharf.com

EAT / DRINK...

Fatboy's Diner (see p.304)
Trinity Buoy Wharf
*www.trinitybuoywharf.com/
food-and-drink*

12 Lost City Walk

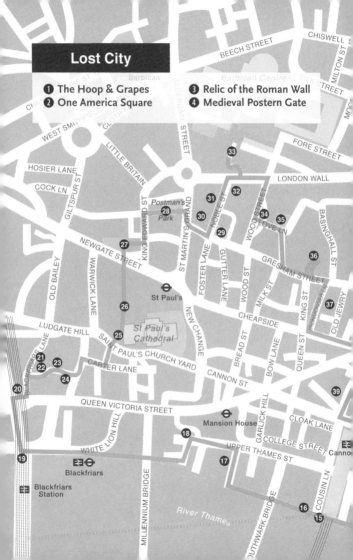

Lost City

1. The Hoop & Grapes
2. One America Square
3. Relic of the Roman Wall
4. Medieval Postern Gate

CHISWELL

BEECH STREET

MILTON ST

Barbican

Barbican Centre

FORE STREET

LONDON WALL

BASINGHALL ST

West Smithfield

HOSIER LANE

COCK LN

GILTSPUR ST

LITTLE BRITAIN

CLOTH

Postman's Park

NEWGATE STREET

OLD BAILEY

WARWICK LANE

KING EDWARD ST

ST MARTIN'S GRAND

FOSTER LANE

GUTTER LANE

NOBLE ST

WOOD ST

WOOD STREET

LOVE LN

GRESHAM STREET

KING ST

HENRIQUEBETH

OLD JEWRY

St Paul's

St Paul's Cathedral

SAINT PAUL'S CHURCH YARD

NEW CHANGE

CHEAPSIDE

BREAD ST

MILK ST

BOW LANE

QUEEN ST

LUDGATE HILL

BLACKFRIARS LANE

CARTER LANE

QUEEN VICTORIA STREET

WHITE LION HILL

Mansion House

GARLICK HILL

CLOAK LANE

COLLEGE STREET

Cann

UPPER THAMES ST

COUSIN LN

Blackfriars

Blackfriars Station

MILLENNIUM BRIDGE

SOUTHWARK BRIDGE

River Thames

5 All Hallows by the Tower
6 Mark Lane
7 St Dunstan-in-the-East
8 St Mary at Hill
9 Company of Watermen & Lightermen
10 Roman House & Baths
11 Old Billingsgate Market
12 St Magnus the Martyr
13 London Bridge
14 Hanseatic Walk
15 Old Steps
16 Walbrook Wharf
17 Queenhithe Dock
18 St Mary Somerset
19 The Fleet River Outflow
20 Blackfriar
21 Apothecaries' Hall
22 Playhouse Yard
23 St Anne Blackfriars
24 The Cockpit
25 St Paul's Cathedral
26 Temple Bar
27 Christchurch Greyfriars

28 Postman's Park
29 Churchyard of St John Zachery
30 St Anne and St Agnes Church
31 Roman and Medieval city wall
32 St Olave Silver Street
33 Remains of Roman Fort
34 St Alban, Wood Street
35 Site of St Mary Aldermanbury
36 Guildhall Yard
37 Tower of St Olave Old Jewry
38 St Stephen Walbrook
39 The London Mithraeum
41 All Hallows, Staining
42 East India Arms
43 Aldgate Pump

Lost City

Start/Finish: Aldgate Underground Station

Distance: 4 miles

St Dunstan-in-the-East

This epic walk starts at Aldgate Station and focuses on the ruins, lost rivers, and relics in and around the Square Mile. The main financial district of the capital is so awash with money, so fast-moving and full of scuttling workers and tourists, that the rate of change and evolution is breathtaking. Every year new skyscrapers alter the horizon, seemingly every week a new bar or restaurant pops up. This is not normally a place to pause and look to the past, but this walk will hopefully reveal some of the overlooked history of this area.

Near to the station is ❶ **The Hoop & Grapes** public house (47 Aldgate High Street). It claims its origins go back to the 1590s and the structure you see today is most likely from the late 17th century. The Great Fire of London of 1666 stopped just short of here, making this timber-framed building an extremely rare example of what many of London's pubs once looked like. However, compared to some of the places you will visit along this walk, it is relatively new.

Walk westwards, heading left down Minories, then right at India Street and onto Vine Street, following the map to America Square. On the corner is an office block named ❷ **One America Square**. Just past the entrance on the left-hand side (along Crosswall), look down from ground level and you'll see a section of the Roman wall which runs through this building. If you are here during the week you can ask to see the wall and if they are not too busy in the conference centre, you should be able to access it.

The Romans occupied London for nearly 400 years, leaving in around c.410 AD after their Empire entered its final

period of decline. As the Roman Empire became increasingly unstable, a fortified wall was built around Londinium between 190-225 AD. It stretched for 3 kilometres and enclosed around 330 acres. The boundaries set by the Romans would determine the shape of London for centuries after the Romans left. Along the wall, the Romans built 20 bastions and a 12-acre fort on the north-eastern corner.

Follow the map under a bridge and immediately after, turn right and continue walking along the path. You will soon see a substantial ❸ **relic of the Roman wall** – it gives a sense of how vast it must have been. Leave by the entrance of the hotel onto Cooper's Row, and turn left to reach the entrance of Tower Hill underground. Just past here down the steps is another section of the Roman wall, beside a statue of Emperor Trajan. The statue was installed here in 1980 and dates from the 20th century. Very little is known about its sculptor or why Trajan was of interest in this part of London – the emperor is unlikely to have even visited Britain.

Continue down the steps towards the Tower of London. You pass the rare remains of a ❹ **medieval postern gate** that once served as an entrance through the city wall that once stood here.

The Tower of London was founded shortly after the Norman conquest of England in 1066, and if you wish to visit it, now is the time – although it takes a few hours to see all the many sights. Turn right and continue along the edge of the Tower of London on the pathway, parallel to the road on the right.

Aim for the spire of the church of ❺ **All Hallows by the Tower.** This church was founded by the Abbey of Barking in 675 AD, so

is therefore much older than the Tower of London. Inside you can see the arch of the original Saxon church, and also, if you go down into the crypt, the remains of a Roman pavement. Samuel Pepys watched the Great Fire of London from the tower here, and John Quincy Adams – sixth president of the United States – was married here.

Opposite the church is an All Bar One that occupies what was originally an underground station named **❻ Mark Lane**. This 'ghost' station operated between 1884-1967. The arches you see today would once have had commuters piling through them on their way to and from jobs in the Square Mile. If you look under one arch you can see the faded name of the station.

Follow the map along Great Tower Street then left down St Dunstan's Hill. Shortly on the right, you see the beautiful remains of the first 'lost' city church on the walk, **❼ St Dunstan- in-the-East**. Built around 1100, this church was one of the dozen destroyed in the Great Fire of London. Sir Christopher Wren rebuilt many of these ruins, as was the case here, until it was once again damaged by German bombs in 1941. After World War II, the authorities had to make difficult decisions about which of these city churches to restore, and for St Dunstan-in-the-East they decided to keep the shell and create the public garden you see today.

On the north side of the church ground, walk through narrow St Dunstan's Alley, turning left down Idol Lane and then right on St Dunstan's Lane to join a street named St Mary's At Hill. Turn right here to reach the church of **❽ St Mary-at-Hill** (look out for a door marked 'Entrance to Church'). This is not a ruin, but does have a small, hidden churchyard that is worth a visit and is possibly the quietest spot in the Square Mile. The churchyard is tucked away down streets, giving an impression of how claustrophobic many parts of medieval London would have been. The church was founded in the 14th century and is another example of the rebuilding undertaken by Sir Christopher Wren after the Great Fire. The poet Sir John Betjeman described it as 'the least spoiled and the most gorgeous interior in the City, all the more exciting by being hidden away among cobbled alleys, paved passages, brick walls, overhung by plane trees'.

Return to St Mary at Hill and walk down it. On the right is the **❾ Hall of the Company of Watermen & Lightermen** of the River Thames. This company was one of many guilds that once dominated London's trade. For centuries, when the Thames was a public highway for people and the transport of goods, the watermen controlled the 'taxi' service for passenger traffic on the river, whilst Lightermen organised the carrying of goods from larger ships. In 1598, 40,000 men worked the river and the company was one of the most influential in the city. The Hall dates from 1780 and is the only Georgian building of its kind in the Square Mile. It remains a well preserved example of this kind of architecture, but the company – whilst still fully functional and concentrating on charitable aims – is a relic of a bygone age.

On Lower Thames Street turn left, stopping at number 101. This anonymous-looking building is home to the **❿ Billingsgate Roman House & Baths**, discovered in 1848. You can visit it on a 45-minute tour which needs to be booked ahead of time (see page 339 for details). Tours are normally three times a day on each Saturday between April and November.

Whether you can take the tour or not, after this point continue westward along Lower Thames Street, passing **⓫ old Billingsgate Market**. The market building belongs to a time when several markets were located in the Square Mile. This site was home to the world's biggest fish market in

the 19th century. The market started here in 1850, and this building was constructed in 1875. The fish market sadly moved out to the Isle of Dogs in 1982.

A little further long is the ⓬ **Church of St Magnus the Martyr**, whose foundation may have been as early as the 11th century. It stands by the north entrance of old London Bridge, and those crossing that bridge at the time would have continued up Fish Street Hill opposite. When in 1831 a new London Bridge was built further up the river, the church lost its prominent position and is now rather marooned by the busy road.

The old church here was one of the first to be destroyed during the Great Fire (which began 300 yards away on Pudding Lane). Outside the church look out for a decayed column of dark wood – said to be from the Roman dock located here and possibly the oldest item you will see on this walk. Inside the church there is a fantastic model of the old London Bridge.

Walk to the right of the church entrance and continue along the Thames Path with the river to your left. Continue under the current ⓭ **London Bridge** – you will now get a clear understanding of how far away the original bridge was located when it touched the west

13

14

15

16

side of St Magnus. The original port of London – before the grand docks were built to the East of the City during the 19th century – was along this stretch of the Thames. Numerous wharves and inlets dominated the river's edge which are now all gone except for a rare exception seen later.

Walk along ⑭ **Hanseatic Walk**, its name recalling the Hanseatic League that was based here. The League comprised merchants principally from Northern Germany whose trade activities were hugely important in European trade from the 13th to 15th centuries. They established trading posts in many ports in Europe, and in London their base was called the Steelyard – a walled community within the City that was largely independent from the rest of London. Hans Holbein the Younger painted many of the merchants of the Hanseatic League in the late 16th century.

Follow the map, passing along Steelyard Passage under the bridge leading to Cannon Street station. You will see The Banker pub, a good place for a stop if you are nearing lunchtime, and beside it a nice set of ⑮ **old steps down to the Thames**. These are the sort of steps that would have been seen much more frequently alongside the river in past centuries, when people used small boats to cross the river and transport goods.

Continue along to ⑯ **Walbrook Wharf**. One of the main natural features of the original city in Roman times was the River Walbrook. Starting in Shoreditch, it runs right through the Square Mile until reaching the Thames at a point just by this wharf (there is an outflow spot down below). For the Romans, the Walbrook was an important source of fresh drinking water and was probably being used for religious purposes. It was also used to dump refuse, and a large number of skulls from the Roman period have been found in the old river bed during excavations – perhaps gladiators, or residents slaughtered by Queen Boadicea, or remains washed down from a burial ground.

During the 16th century the Walbrook was covered over, and during the 19th century channelled into a brick sewer system.

Carry on along the river path, heading up by ⑰ **Queenhithe Dock**. This was once an important dock, or harbour, possibly in use

Millennium Bridge

during Roman times. It was certainly used after London – having been abandoned for centuries – was reoccupied by Saxons during the reign of Alfred the Great. This 'lost' dock was used for bringing corn into London, and Charles II came here whilst observing the Great Fire of London. It is the last example of its kind on this stretch of the river, and there is an extensive modern mural illustrating many of the major events in London's history.

Head inland, rejoining Upper Thames Street and bear left. Shortly you will see over to the right, on the north side of the busy road, the tower of ⑱ **St Mary Somerset**. It is one of nine church tower relics in the City that have been left standing when the rest of their building has been destroyed or demolished. The original church was built here in the 12th century, and St Mary's was one of fifty-one churches rebuilt by Wren after the Great Fire. However, like several other Wren churches, it was mostly demolished in the late 19th century due to a combination of decreasing number of people living in the Square Mile, combined with increasing pressure to clear space for new commercial buildings. Arguably developers, in the name of progress, have done as much damage to the City's architectural history as the Blitz during World War II.

Follow the map back to the river path, passing under the famous Millennium Bridge and continue under Blackfriars railway bridge and the road bridge. Under the second is the outflow of another ⑲ **'lost' London River – The Fleet**. Starting at Hampstead Heath, this was a large, open river that was converted into a canal by 1680. During the 18th century the Fleet was covered over section by section, and today there is nothing visible. If you lean out under Blackfriars Bridge you can see the

drainage outlet where it empties into the Thames. Note the three rows of cast-iron columns that once held Blackfriars railway bridge until the bridge was eventually demolished in the 1980's.

From here use the stairs or lift to get up to street level – see if you can spot a statue of Queen Victoria – and then head north away from the river, bearing right past Blackfriars station. If you have time, a visit to the **20 Blackfriar pub** on the corner is worthwhile. Dating from 1875, this Art Nouveau triumph has one of the most interesting pub interiors in London. The pub stands on the grounds of the Old Dominican Monastery. The name 'Blackfriars' stems from the dark clothing or 'habits' of the Dominican Friars.

Just after the pub, head up Blackfriars Lane, stopping at **21 Apothecaries' Hall**, home of The Worshipful Society of Apothecaries. The inner courtyard is one of the City's best-kept secrets. The Society was founded in 1617 to regulate those who were involved in making and selling medicines and other pharmaceutical products. This has been home to the Apothecaries since 1632, although the current building dates from 1672 after the original was destroyed in The Great Fire. Unlike many other City livery companies, it is still involved actively in practical aspects of the profession, for example running diploma courses in subjects such as forensic medical science.

Retrace your steps to enter ㉒ **Playhouse Yard**. This quiet place was the site of the Blackfriars Theatre, famous for being where William Shakespeare and the King's Men performed in an indoor theatre during the winter months (the warmer months were spent at The Globe in Southwark). You are literally walking in Shakespeare's footsteps, as he owned lodgings close to here.

Another long vanished feature of the City's past lies to the south of Playhouse Yard. This was where The Times' printing office stood for many years, when this area, and nearby Fleet Street, were at the heart of the British newspaper industry. In the last forty years all the papers have moved from the area.

Continue along, stopping by the ruins of a very old church – ㉓ **St Anne Blackfriars**. It was founded within the complex of the Blackfriars monastery that had been closed during the Reformation of the 16th century. Just by the entrance, you can see a remnant of the monastery building. The congregation of St Anne's fought against Shakespeare and his fellow thespians opening a theatre here after they were forced to leave Shoreditch. This led to the founding of the Globe theatre. St Anne's was a victim of the Great Fire and was never rebuilt.

Continue along, passing another fine pub – ㉔ **The Cockpit** – that stands approximately where Shakespeare owned a house, also located in a ruined part of the old monastery.

Follow the map up St Andrew's Hill, turning into Carter Lane and up Dean's Court to reach **㉕ St Paul's Cathedral**. Of course, this is Wren's greatest achievement, built after The Great Fire destroyed most of the city. On the theme of relics and ruins, seven funerary monuments from the old St Paul's survived the Great Fire. The effigy of poet John Donne contains evidence of damage from the fire itself.

On this walk we continue north, passing through **㉖ Temple Bar**. It once stood as the western entry point into the City on Fleet Street, not far from Temple Church. During the medieval period the original 'bar' was probably just a chain across the road. In the late 17th century the humble chain was replaced by this imposing entry gate, built by Wren. In the 1870s the bar was dismantled as it was creating a bottleneck for traffic and was rebuilt in the grounds of a mansion house in Hertfordshire. It was later renovated and brought back here in 2004, the only old entrance gate into the City that survives.

Walk through Paternoster Square to reach Newgate Street and cross over to the tower and other ruins of **㉗ Christchurch Greyfriars Church**, and the neighbouring garden.

The origins of the church date back to a medieval Franciscan monastery whose friars wore grey habits. It was later dissolved during the Dissolution in 1538, and a new parish church was built here, as well as a new school called Christ's Hospital. After the destruction caused by The Great Fire, Wren built a new church here, however his structure – and eight of his other churches - were gutted during a single night of German bombing on 29 December 1940. Sadly the authorities decided not to rebuild the church and it remains one of the finest Wren ruins in London.

Continue up King Edward Street, turning right through **㉘ Postman's Park**. It is neither ruin nor relic, but the site – dating from 1880 – does occupy the former burial ground of St Botolph's Aldersgate nearby. It is famous for its *Memorial to Heroic Self Sacrifice* which contains 120 tablets commemorating acts of courage. The artist G.F. Watt was the driving force behind the creation of the memorials.

Walk right through the park, and right on Aldersgate Street, and then left into Gresham Street. Just ahead on the left – on the other side of Noble Street – is the former **㉙ Churchyard of St John Zachery**. This 12th-century church was destroyed in The Great Fire but never rebuilt. This is another rare physical reminder of the destruction that took place in 1666.

Continue up Noble Street, passing the **㉚ St Anne and St Agnes Church**, a 12th-century foundation rebuilt after the Great Fire by Wren. However, as this walk is more concerned with ruins, keep walking on to find a striking section of the **㉛ Roman and Medieval City Wall**. This once formed the western edge of ancient Londinium. It was only rediscovered in 1940 due to damage caused by German bombs.

At the top on the right look out for the ruins of **㉜ St Olave Silver Street**. This is another 12th-century church that was destroyed in 1666 but not rebuilt. It is special because it is documented that Shakespeare lodged in a house on Silver Street in the early years of the 17th century. He even gave evidence in a court case involving a dispute over a dowry between his landlord and his daughter and son-in-law. The playwright was also recorded as being fined for not attending church in London. It's possible to imagine the busy playwright avoiding Sunday worship after a late night out at the Globe or Blackfriars Playhouse.

Take care crossing over London Wall road. You are now standing within the site

31

of 12-acre Cripplegate Fort, built around 120 AD, and home to a garrison of around 1,000 men. Follow the map into Barber Surgeons' Garden, where you can see the ㉝ **remains of the bastion of a Roman Fort** dating from around 300 AD and later remains from the Medieval period. There are information boards explaining the history of the ruins.

There is also a Physic Garden, containing medicinal herbs and other plants, that belongs to the Worshipful Company of Barbers nearby. It has looked after the interests of barbers and surgeons for over 700 years. In the past, barbers often conducted minor surgical procedures for clients and this side of their activities developed into a trade body for those who began to specialise in this field. The Garden stands on the site of one of the twenty-one bastions in the Roman wall built during the reign of Emperor Hadrian in around 122 AD. Just a little further on you will see one of the tranquil water features of the Barbican complex which is worth a brief detour to admire.

Retrace your steps, following London Wall road and crossing at the junction into Wood Street. Ahead of you is the free-standing tower of ㉞ **St Alban, Wood Street**, another medieval church that was rebuilt by Wren but did not survive the Blitz of 1940. It was recently converted into perhaps the most unusual private residence in London.

Turn left down Love Lane – so named because this was a red light district in Medieval times. Ahead is a garden that occupies the ㉟ **site of St Mary Aldermanbury**. This church has had an extraordinary history. Built in the 12th century, it was destroyed in the Great Fire and rebuilt by Wren. It was then gutted during the Blitz - so far, not so unusual. However in the 1960s the ruins were taken down and reassembled in the grounds of Westminster College in Fulton Missouri as a memorial to Winston Churchill. He had given his famous *Iron Curtain* speech at the College in 1946.

The remaining garden contains a bust of Shakespeare and a memorial to his fellow actors Henry Condell and John Heminges. They lived in this parish and were responsible for assembling their friend Shakespeare's plays after his death. Printing the famous First Folio in 1623, they contributed a great deal to the preservation of Shakespeare's reputation.

From here follow the map into the courtyard of Guildhall – home of the City of London Corporation for over 800 years. On the east side of ❸❻ **Guildhall Yard** is another extraordinary reminder of the City's past – remains of an ancient Roman amphitheater, rediscovered here in 1988. Gladiators, wild beasts and criminals would have died here and it is possible to step inside and get a sense of what life was like for Londoners 2,000 years ago.

Continue down Gresham Street then turn right down Ironmonger Lane, stopping on the left to see the **37** **tower of St Olave Old Jewry**, dedicated to St Olaf, patron saint of Norway. Neighbouring Old Jewry is named after the Jewish quarter of Medieval London, although the Jew population were forcefully expelled from England in 1290. Whilst Wren rebuilt the Medieval church after the Great Fire, it was demolished in the 1880s. Just the tower was allowed to remain, that is now used as an office.

Follow the map along Cheapside towards Bank, and then turn right along Walbrook – named after the Walbrook stream mentioned earlier. You are following the course of the river itself now, and pass the magnificent church of **38** **St Stephen Walbrook** – worth a visit just to see the Henry Moore altar.

Just ahead at 12 Walbrook is **39** **The London Mithraeum**, the new home of the Roman Temple of Mithras. The temple, built in around 240 AD, stood beside the Walbrook river and was at the heart of the Roman mystery cult of Mithras the bull slayer. The cult was particularly popular with Roman soldiers, although no one knows what sort of ceremonies would have been performed here. The temple was discovered in the post-war ruins of the City in 1954, and Sir Winston Churchill got involved in stopping the company that owned the site from demolishing the remains. Now located in the Bloomberg building, recent excavations on this site also discovered 2,000-year-old Roman wood tablets which are the oldest handwritten documents ever to be found in this country. Until a few years ago, the remains of the temple were located a short way from here and were open to the elements. The museum is free to visit but tickets must be booked in advance from their website: www.londonmithreaum.com.

Follow the map along Cannon Street. **40** **The London Stone** is kept on the north side opposite Boots. A block of limestone, it was first recorded in the early 12th century, and possibly has a Roman origin. It has been a well-known landmark in London for centuries. In 1450, popular rebel leader Jack Cade struck his sword against it and claimed to be 'Lord of this city'.

You can choose to end the walk here – near to Monument Station or central stations. However, if you wish to return to the starting point, follow the map up Gracechurch Street, then onto Fenchurch Street.

Further along on the right take a brief detour down Mark Lane to see the remains of ❹ **All Hallows, Staining**. The church was first recorded in the 13th century, and it survived the Great Fire but later collapsed before being rebuilt. However, it was demolished in the late 19th century, leaving just this relic – the medieval tower.

Walk back up Mark Lane to reconnect with Fenchurch Street, passing the red-brick ❷ **East India Arms** at number 67. Serving beer since 1828, this is the original building and a reminder of the East India Company whose headquarters were based very near to here (originally Philpot Lane, later Leadenhall Street). Founded in 1600, the Company came to dominate huge swathes of the British Empire, practically governing India until the Mutiny there in 1857 caused the government to take back control. The pub is, therefore, a rare legacy of an enterprise that from a modest base in London had an impact on the lives of hundreds of millions of people around the Empire.

Up ahead at the junction is the ⑬ **Aldgate Pump**. This historic water pump was first recorded in John Stow's Survey of London (1598) but was no doubt used for centuries before then. The current pump dates from 1876. It is often spoken of as marking the beginning of the East End.

From here, continue eastwards along Aldgate High Street, reaching Aldgate Station and the end of this walk. ●

VISIT...

Guildhall (see p.335)
71 Basinghall Street, EC2V 7HH
www.guildhall.cityoflondon.gov.uk

Billingsgate Roman House & Baths (see p.322)
101 Lower Thames Street, EC3R 6DL
www.cityoflondon.gov.uk

London Mithraeum (see p.337)
12 Walbrook, EC4N 8AA
www.londonmithraeum.com

EAT / DRINK...

The Blackfriar Pub (see p.328)
174 Queen Victoria Street, EC4V 4EG

The Wren Coffee
within St. Nicholas Cole Abbey, 114 Queen Victoria Street, EC4V 4BJ
www.thewrencoffee.com

Byward Kitchen and Bar (see p.338)
All Hallows, EC3R 5BJ
www.bywardkitchenandbar.com

Index

Symbols

O2 Forum, Kentish Town 55
4 Per Cent Industrial Dwellings
    Company 282
100 Club 84, 85

A

Abbey Tavern, The 41
Abbey Road Studios 146
Abercorn Close 151
Adam and Eve Court 84
Adams, John Quincy 321
Addington Square 281
African Academy 229, 236
AIR Studios 81
Aldgate Pump 338
Aldgate Station 316, 339
Al-Fayed, Mohamed 198
Alfred the Great 227, 327
All Hallows by the Tower 319
All Hallows, Staining 338
All Saints Church 132, 212
All Saints Fulham 205
All Saints Parish church 195
Alma Square 148
American School in London 153
Ancient Order of Druids 118
Anderson Shelters 48
Anne, Princess Royal 18
Anne, Queen of Great Britain 231
Annunciation Marble Arch 68
Anti-imperialist movement 25
Apothecaries' Hall 328
Arch of Constantine 64
Armstrong, Louis 84
Asher, Jane 143
Assembly House 52

B

Bailey, David 104
Baird, John Logie 73
Bakewell, Dame Joan 122
Banksy 109
Barber Surgeons' Garden 332
Barrow Hill Reservoir 117
Barry, Charles 231
Bartlett, Thomas 19
Battle of Inkerman 48
Bazalgette, Joseph 195, 273
Beachcroft Academy 133
Beatles, The 81, 89, 94, 97, 116,
    142, 143, 145, 146, 148, 153, 259
Bee Gees, The 259
Belgrave Dock 24
Benedictine Abbey of Bec 246
Bennett, Alan 104, 111, 122
Bentley, John Francis 231
Best, George 198
Betjeman, John 44, 298, 321
Betjeman, Sir John 44, 298, 321
Bevin, Ernest 94
Billingsgate Market 322
Billingsgate Roman House and
    Baths 322, 339
Bishop Beibly Porteus 202
Bishop Bonner 209
Bishop Henry Compton 202
Bishop of London 68, 195, 197, 201,
    202, 205
Bishop's Garden tea house 200
Bishops Park 192, 197, 198, 205, 206
Bishop Stopford 201
Blackfriar Pub, The 328
Blackfriars Bridge 327
Blackwall Station 298
Blake, William 89, 94, 115, 118, 271
Blériot, Louis 73

Blitz, The 11, 78, 89, 136, 220, 231, 327, 334
Bloomfield, Sir Arthur 205
Blue Bridge 295
Blue Plaque 9, 25, 56, 94 109, 113,, 135, 143, 165, 169, 173, 174, 183, 184, 191, 231
Blustons Store 41
Boltons, The 174, 176, 177, 185
Bond, James 18, 153
Booth, Charles 47
Booth, William 92
Boris the Cat 51
Bousfield Primary School 174
Bow Creek 292, 293, 295, 303, 308, 309, 311
Bow Creek Ecological Park 293, 311
Bow Creek Lighthouse 303
Bowie, David 120, 138, 183, 221
Boyd, Joe 85
Bradley's Spanish Bar 85, 97
Bramham Gardens 173, 176
Bridge to nowhere 280
Brinsmead Piano Factory 48
British Circus 145
British Union of Fascists 40
British Zionist Federation 134
Britten, Benjamin 169
Broadway Market 253, 261
Brompton Cemetery 179, 184, 185
Brompton Library 177
Brown, Errol 138
Brown, Ford Maddox 57
Brown Hart Gardens 95
Brunel, Isambard Kingdom 308
Buckingham Palace 64
Bull & Gate Pub 52
Burgess, Jessie 280
Burgess Park 278, 281

Bush, Kate 146
Bussey, George Gibson 267
Butts, Sir William 205
Byron, Lord 79, 140, 148

C
Cabinet War Rooms 32, 212
Cabman's Shelter 9, 92, 139
Cade, Jack 337
Cambridge Boat Race 192
Campbell, Bobby 198
Canning, Lord 293
Carden, George 116
Carey, Lucius 58
Carlos the Jackal 134
Carroll, Lewis 151
Carter, Howard 173
Castle's Pie and Mash 43
Cavendish Avenue 142, 143
Cavendish, Lady Margaret 77
Cavendish Square 77, 79, 82
Cecil, William 56
Central Hall Picture Palace 247
Chalcot Square 109, 113, 114
Chalk Farm Tavern 104, 122, 124
Chandler, Raymond 153
Charles I 58, 170, 202
Charles, Prince of Wales 12, 176
Chelsea Creek 184
Chelsea Waterworks Company 20, 23
Chertsey Abbey 255
Christchurch Greyfriars church 330
Christ Church (Oxford College) 40
Christ's Hospital 330
Chumleigh Gardens 280
Churchill Gardens estate 19, 23
Churchill, Winston 19, 23, 24, 29, 72,, 148, 335, 337

Index

Church of Christ 51
Citizen Smith 255
Clapham Books 239
Clapham Common 218, 231, 232, 234, 235, 239
Clapham Library 231
Clapham Manor Estate 227
Clapham Picturehouse 220
Clapham Public Hall 222
Clapham Sect 219, 220, 229, 236, 239
Clapham Tap Brewery 225
Clarke, Lady Dorothy 205
Clash, The 85
Clergy Orphan School for Boys 142
CLF Arts Café 267
Cockpit Pub, The 329
Coldplay 52, 151
Coleherne Court 176, 177
Coleridge, Samuel Taylor 84
College Francais Bilingue de Londres 48
Condell, Henry 209, 335
Coo, Jimmy 79
Cook, James 256
Copeland Park and Bussey Building 267, 268
Corbyn, Jeremy 28
Corporation of Trinity House 303, 305
Counter's Creek 183
Coward, Noel 235
Craig, Daniel 104
Craven Cottage 198
Craven, William 198
Creation Records 124
Creation Studios 43
Crick, Francis 12
Crimean War 48, 145

Cripplegate Fort 332
Cromwell, Oliver 170, 202
Crossrail project 86
Cubitt, Thomas 11, 223, 227
Cumberland Hotel 67
Cundy, Thomas 11, 27
Czernin, Hazel 77, 78
Czernin, Peter 78

D
Damilola Taylor (and Centre) 284, 285
Danubius Hotel 142
Dark Side of the Moon, The 183
Darwin, Charles 151
Davies, Mary 10
Davies, Ray 55
D-Day 296
Deane, Henry 239
Decca Records 94
Defoe Chapel 253
Defoe, Daniel 253
De Vere family 166
D'herard, Antonio 89
Dickens, Charles 92, 257, 308
Dobrowski, Jody 232
Dolphin Square 16, 17, 18, 19, 20
Dominican Monastery 328
Donne, John 330
Doomsday Book 271
Dracula 12
Driver, Charles Henry 273
Dublin Castle 104
Duckworth, Canon Robinson 151
Duke of Cumberland 68
Duke of Newcastle 77, 79
Dukes of Portland 82, 132
Duncan, Isadora 27
Duque-Tunjano, Maria 182

Dury, Ian 55, 230
Dwight, John 211
Dylan, Bob 67, 178

E

Earl of Shaftesbury 139
Earl's Court Exhibition Centre 183
Earl's Court Hotel 184
Earl's Court House 185
East India Arms 338
East India Company 142, 295, 297, 338
East India Dock Basin 297
East India Docks 295, 296, 297, 300
Ebenezer Strict Baptist Church 225, 226
Ecclestone Square 27, 28, 29
Eden Community Garden 229, 239
Edinboro Castle 104
Edward III 211
Edward VI 202
Edward VII 109, 256
Eight Bells Pub 211, 212
Electric Alhambra 51
Electricity substation 95
Electric Picture Palace 220
Electric Telegraph Company 107
Edward Elgar 94, 146
Elizabeth Regina, Queen, 143, 151
Elizabeth I 56, 202
EMI Records 81, 143, 146
Emperor Hadrian 334
Emperor Trajan 319
Engels, Friedrich 119
Engineer Pub, The 107, 125
English National Ballet 310
Epstein, Brian 94, 153
Evans, Mary Anne 133

Evelina Mansions 282
Execution site 66
Eyre Court 131, 132
Eyre, Henry Samuel 132

F

Fairbanks, Douglas 174
Fairy-tale of New York, A 138
Faraday Effect 305
Faraday, Michael 305
Fat Boy Diner 305
Father Lawless 302
FBI 25, 184
Female Friendly Society 280
Festival of Britain 91
Fiddian-Green, Nic 66
Fielders Meadow 198
Figg, James 84
First and Last Loves 298
First Folio, The 209, 335
FitzRoy 109
Fitzroy Tavern 249
Fleet, River 39, 40, 44, 51, 52, 55, 56, 327, 329, 330
Fleming, Ian 18, 153
Flying Horse Pub, The 87
Ford, Edward Onslow 146
Frampton, Sir George 135
Frankenstein 41, 196
Franklin, Benjamin 234
Frank's Bar 273
Fraser, Robert Richard 182
Freud Museum 117
Freud, Sigmund 117
Friars 330
Fulham F.C 197, 198, 200
Fulham Football Club 198
Fulham House 211
Fulham Palace 195, 197, 202, 212

Fulham Pottery Kiln 211
Fulham Theatre 208
Fulham Vestry Wharf 192
Fury, Billy 143
Furzedown Park Farm 260

G

Gaisford, Thomas 40
Gallagher, Liam 119, 138
Gallows 67, 69, 87, 246
Garibaldi, Giuseppe 118
GCHQ 25
Gee's Court 75
George Eliot Primary School 133
George I 92
George II 68
George IV 48, 81
Ghandi, Mahatma 25
Ghost signs 43, 124, 165, 223, 239,
    256, 255, 259
Gielgud, John 174
Gilbert, Alfred 256
Ginsberg, Allen 115
Girdlers Company 270
Girdlers Cottages 269
Glengall Basin 278
Glengall Wharf Garden 278, 287
Globe Theatre, The 329
Godfrey, Edmund Berry 117
Godwin, George 176
Golden Lion Pub, The 209, 212
Govinda's Restaurant 89
Grade II Listed 21, 103, 207
Grafton Square 226
Granada Cinema 259
Grand Surrey Canal 278
Grant, Peter 138
Graveney Gin 253
Great Expectations 94

Great Fire of London 317, 321, 323,
    327, 328, 329, 330, 332, 334,
    337, 338
Great Portland Estates 82
Greek Orthodox Cathedral of St
    Andrew 43
Grafton, The 47
Greatest Showman, The 174
Greene, Graham 231
Green, Leslie 39, 43, 91, 103
Green, Philip 81
Greyhound Pub, The 277, 287
Grosvenor family 10, 11, 13, 15, 20,
    21, 24, 27, 30, 70
Grosvenor, Gilbert 24
Grosvenor, Hugh 13, 30
Grosvenor, Sir Thomas 10
Guevara, Che 255
Guildhall 335, 339
Guildhall Yard 335
Gunter, James 170, 176

H

Hadid, Zaha 168
Hall of the Company of Watermen
    & Lightermen 322
Hall, Sue 47
Hamilton, Patrick 164, 168, 169,
    177, 182
Hampstead Heath 40, 327
Handbook to the Environs of
    London 249
Hand in Hand Fire & Life Insurance
    Company 207
Hangover Square 164, 165
Hanover Chapel 274
Hanover Square 92, 176
Hardwick, Thomas 140
Harrison, George 89, 97

Harrods 198
Haynes, Johnny 198
Heller, Zoe 108
Heminges, John 209, 335
Hendrix, Jimi 67, 178
Henry Holland pub 75
Henry VII 104
Henry VIII 205, 208, 303
Hepworth, Barbara 79
High Commission of St Lucia 173
High Commissions of Tanzania and Botswana 76
Highwaymen 52, 232
Hill, Octavia 75
Hinata Japanese Bar 255
Hitchcock, Alfred 169, 177
Hitler, Adolf 78
HMS Albion 309
HMS Warrior 308
HMV 94
Holden, Charles 245, 255
Holdron's Department Store 268
Holles, John 77
Holliday, Billie 84
Holloway, Stanley 32
Holly, Buddy 67
Hollywood 28, 169
Holy Apostles Catholic Church 24
Holy Trinity church 220, 236, 227, 229, 236, 239
Home for Unconvicted, Destitute Boys 124
Hoop & Grapes Pub 317
Hope Chapel 51
Hopkins, John 'Hoppy' 47, 85
Horme, Charles 123
Horse Shoe Brewery 86
Hospital of Saint John and Saint Elizabeth 145

Hot Chocolate 138
House of Lords 18
Houses of Parliament 97, 239, 261, 339
Howard de Walden Estate 70, 77
Howard, Harriet 145
Hughes, Ted 103, 109, 113
Hunter, John 185, 256
Hurlingham Books 212
Huskisson, William 15
Hyde Park 89, 118, 256

I

Ice skating 92
Imperial Works 47
Inbetweeners Movie, The 221
Indian Mutiny 293
Infernos nightclub 220
IRA 245
Ireland, Colin 178
Iron Curtain 335
Isle of Dogs 323
Ivy, The 139, 155

J

Jackson, Michael 138, 198
Jacques, Hattie 183
Jazz 84, 90
Jellied eels 43, 277
Jesus Christ Superstar 174
John, Elton 154, 178
John Lewis 75, 78, 79, 81, 97, 268
Johnson, Boris 107, 108, 114, 120, 143
Johnson, John 20
John the Unicorn 269
Jolie, Angelina 16
Joyce, William 18
Junction Tavern, The 57, 58

K

Kean, Charles 83
Keeler, Christine 18
Kelly, John 44
Kentish Delight kebab shop 52
Kentish Drovers 274
Kenyatta, Jomo 25
Khan, Sadiq 245, 247, 251
Khan's Bargains outlet 268
Kingfishers 295
King's Arms Pub, The 208, 209, 212
King's Head Pub, The 163, 165, 249
King's Men, The 329
King's Scholars Pond Sewer 15, 30
King William IV Pub 20
Kinks, The 55
K & K's Butchers & Fishmarket 269
Knight, Maxwell 18
Knights of St. John of Jerusalem 69
Knights Templars, The 131
Knocker White boat 307
Kray twins 281
Krishnan, Ananda 135

L

Labour Party, The 28, 29, 94, 108,
    142, 250
Lahore Karahi Restaurant 251
Lamb & Flag Pub, The 75
Lansdowne 105, 125
Larry's Café 273
Law, Jude 104
Lea, River 292, 293
Lear, Edward 76
Led Zeppelin 138
Legh, Margaret 205
Leitch, Archibald 198
Lennon, John 73, 82, 143

Lighthouse 303
Light Ship 307
Lillington & Longmoore Estate 30
Limehouse 107
Limekiln 281
Lind, Jenny 174
Little Lagos 269
Lloyd-Webber, Andrew 173
Lockyer, Norman 184
London Beer Flood 86
London Bridge 195, 323
London City Island 292, 310
London College of Fashion 60, 79
London Graving Dock 307
London Kabbalah Centre 76
London Mithraeum 337, 339
London Stone 337
Lonely Planet 245, 253
Lord's Cricket Ground 142
Lord, Thomas 131, 142
Lotus Automobiles 124
Louis XIV 208
Louvre, The 131
Lucrine, Mary 92, 94
Lupo, Michael 178
Lupus, Hugh 24
Lutyens, Robert 91
Lutyens, Sir Edwin 91
LV95 Boat 307
Lyon, John 148

M

Macaulay, Zachary 236, 239
Mackenzie, Compton 11
Macmillan, Iain 146
Madonna 67, 76, 120, 176
Maltese religious order of the
    Franciscan Sisters of the Heart
    of Jesus 29

Manor House 251
Manor of Ebury 10
Manor of Fulham 205, 208
Manor of Marylebone 77
Manor of Totinges 246
Maple Building, The 55
Marble Arch 64, 66, 68, 70, 97
Marilyn 47
Mario's Cafe 44
Market 11, 21, 27, 32, 82, 161, 176,
    181, 182, 200, 220, 255, 268, 271,
    274, 281, 322, 323
Mark Lane 321, 338
Marks, Michael 70
Marks & Spencer 70, 90, 91, 134,
    221
Marley, Bob 120
Marquee Club 89
Mars 247
Matilda, Queen 95
Martin, George 81, 94
Marx, Karl 119
Marylebone Cricket Club 142
Mayfair Recording Studios 120
Mayflower, The 299
McCartney, Paul 82, 85, 116, 138,
    142, 143
McCartney, Stella 67
McColl, Kirsty 138
McDonalds 221, 273
McGee, Alan 124
McLaren, Malcolm 73
Mears, Gus 200
Mears, Joseph 200
Mellor, David 179
Memorial 23, 51, 55, 146, 153, 196,,
    205, 229, 260, 298, 299, 300,
    330, 335
Menchik, Vera 222

Mendes, Sam 108
Mercury, Freddie 136
Metalworks 230
Methodist Chapel 274
Metropolitan Fire Brigade 231
Meux's Famous Stout and Ales 285
Mews 29, 40, 51, 120, 151, 166, 168,
    170, 171, 173, 225, 299
MI5 170
MI6 25
Michael, George 67, 120
Miliband, Ed 108
Millennium Bridge 327
Millennium Dome 298
Miller, Glenn 84, 146
Mithras the Bull Slayer 337
M. Manze's Eel & Pie House 277
Moat 201, 202
Modernism 79
Montagu, Major Willoughby 229
Monument 256, 259
Morton, Charles 87
Mosley, Oswald 18, 40
Mosley, Sir Oswald 18
Moss, Kate 81, 104
Most, Mickie 138
Mother Shipton 118, 119
Mount Pond 234
Mountview Drama School 277, 278
Moya, Hidalgo 19
Mulberry Harbours 296
Murdock Supply Company 200
Mutiny 293, 338

N
Napoleon 89, 139, 145
Napoleonic Wars 135, 145
Nash, John 64, 81
National Trust 75

Index

Nelson, Lord 44
Newgate Prison 66
New London Synagogue 151
News of the World 85
Newton, Bruce 164
Nilsen, Dennis 178
Nine Elms 15, 285
Nkrumah, Kwame 56
NLA Awards 277
Nobel Prize 12
Notting Hill 67

O

Oasis 85, 119, 124, 138
Obama, Barack 154
Oddfellows friendly society 225
Oddfellows Hall 225
Odeon 85
Old Eagle Pub, The 43, 58
Old Fire Station 231
Old Manor Yard 184
Oliver, Jamie 104
Olivier, Laurence 10, 107
O'Looney, Benedict 269
Omen, The 196, 206
Omnibus Theatre 231
One America Square 317
Only Fools and Horses 266
Ono, Yoko 73
Ora, Rita 182
Orchard Place 302, 308, 309, 311
Ordnance Arms 136, 155
Orwell, George 78, 82, 154, 249
Oswald's Stone 66
Owl Bookshop 41, 58
Oxford Circus 79, 81, 91, 92
Oxford Market 82
Oxford Music Hall 87
Oxford Tavern, The 39

P

Paddington 107, 114
Paddington Bear 114
Page, Jimmy 178
Palace, The 41, 201
Palyn Charity 270
Palyn, George 270
Pamlico tribe 32
Pankhurst, Emmeline 179
Pantheon 90
Paolozzi, Eduardo 6, 9
Parkour 305
Passmore Edwards Library, Baths
    and Wash House 281
Patel, Priti 120
Peabody Estates 13, 23
Peabody, George 23
Peach, Stanley 95, 286, 287
Peck, River 271
Peckham Boys 284
Peckham House Lunatic Asylum
    286
Peckham Islamic Centre Mosque
    270
Peckham Levels 273, 287
Peckham Library 277
Peckhamplex 274, 287
Peckham Rye Common 267, 270,
    271
Peckham Vision 273
Pembroke Castle 103, 104, 125
Pembroke Pub, The 178
Pembroke Terrace 133
Pennant, Thomas 69
Penny Bazaar 70
Pepys, Samuel 227, 229, 321
Persepolis 286, 287
Physic Garden 334

Piano Makers 44, 107, 111
Picture Palace 220, 247
Pie and Mash 43, 277
Pilgrims 299
Pimlico, Ben 32
Pimlico Poisoning 19
Pimlico Primary School 11
Pineapple Pub, The 57, 58
Pink Floyd 85, 120, 138, 146, 148,
    183
Plant, Robert 104, 178
Plath, Sylvia 109, 113
Playhouse Yard 329
Pleasure gardens 90, 123
Plough Boys 232
Pocahontas 299
Pogues, The 138
Police station 52
Police telephone box 161
Polygon buildings 231
Potter, Beatrix 174, 181
Pope Clement V 131
Portland, Duke of 77, 138
Portland Estate 77
Portland Town 138
Portman, Christopher Edward
    Berkeley 70
Portman Estate 69, 70, 77
Portman Square 69, 70, 71
Portman, Sir William 69, 70
Portnoy, Suzanne 51
Port of London Authority 296
Powell, Philip 19
Powell, William 206
President of the United States 15, 77
Primal Scream 85
Primark 87
Primrose Hill Community
    Association 111

Primrose Hill Community Library
    122
Primrose Hill Primary School 107,
    108
Primrose Hill Studios 111
Princess of Wales 109, 125
Princess's Theatre 83
Private Eye 164, 165
Profumo 18
Punk movement 55, 84
Putin, Vladimir 136
Putney Bridge 190, 191, 192, 194,
    195, 207, 212

Q
Quebec Chapel 68
Queen Mother , The 143, 151
Queen's Pub, The 119
Quincey, Thomas de 83

R
Rackham, Arthur 111
Radha-Krishna temple 89
Radiohead 120
Railway Tavern, The 222, 239
RAK Studios 138
Rank Foundation 28
Rank, James Arthur 28
Ray, James Earl 184
Rectory Gardens 230
Reformation, The 132, 329
Regent Circus 81
Regent Hall 92, 93
Regent's Canal 107
Regent's Park 81, 103, 114, 119, 120,
    122, 124, 125
Regent Street 81
Reid's Brewery 51
Reynolds, William Bainbridge 230

Index

Rice-Davies, Mandy 18
Richardson's crime family 281
Rizal, Dr José 113
Robeson, Paul 25, 146
Robinson, Peter 81
Rocque, John 77
Rolling Stones, The 85, 90, 116, 259
Roman and Medieval city wall 332
Roman Empire 319
Roman Fort 332
Roman pottery 86
Romans, The 317, 319, 325
Roman Temple of Mithras 337
Roof garden/terrace 47, 78
Ross, Diana 67
Rotherhithe 278
Rothschild, Nathaniel 282
Roux, Michel 234
Royal Albert Bridge 308
Royal Albert Music Hall 293
Royal Army Clothing Store 16
Royal Arsenal Co-operative Society
    (RACS) 250
Royal Horse Artillery 64, 135
Rushton, Willie 165
Rutherford, Margaret 32
Rye Lane 267, 268, 269, 270, 271,
    273, 274, 286, 287

S

Saint Espresso & Kitchen 52
Saint Etienne 44
Salvation Army 92
Sancha, Antonia de 179
Sanchez, Ilich Ramirez 134
Security guards 134
Selfridge, Harry Gordon 72
Selfridges 70, 72, 73, 75, 97, 268
Sex Pistols, The 73, 85, 221

Shaftesbury, Lord 9
Shakespeare, William 83, 114, 118,
    205, 209, 211, 222, 329, 332, 335
Shakespeare's Tree 114, 118
Sharp, Granville 206, 236
Shelley, Mary 41, 196
Shelley, Percy 41, 89
Shoreditch 245, 325, 329
Sieff, Edward 134
Sierra Leone 206, 229, 239
Sikh Gurdwara 249
Simms, Frederick Richard 191
Siouxie and the Banshees 85
Sir William Powell Almshouses 206
Situationist Movement 73
Smith, John 299
Socialist Party Office 222
Southcott, Joanna 140
South, Robert 40
Spanish Civil War 196, 250
Spencer, Lady Diana 12, 29, 67, 176,
    177, 183
Spencer, Thomas 70
Spender, Stephen 153
Spiro, Robert 75
Spy 18, 25
Square Mile 316, 321, 322, 325, 327
Stanton, Lt-Sgt Alfred 55
Starbucks 86, 122
Starr, Ringo 82, 143
Stephenson, Robert 15
Steptoes and Sons 282, 287
Sterling Prize 277
Stevens, Rachel 79
Still Water Sculpture 66
Stoker, Bram 12
Stow, John 339
Stratford, Edward 76
Stratford House 76

St. Albans 66
St. Alban, Wood Street 334
St. Anne and St Agnes Church 329, 332
St. Anselms 246
St. Benedict's Hospital 260
St. Botolph's Aldersgate 330
St. Christopher's Place 75
St. Cuthbert with St Matthias Primary School 182
St. Dunstan 321
St. Gabriel's Church 27
St. George's 9, 12, 27, 28, 108, 113, 120, 256, 281
St. George's Church 281
St. George's Hospital 256
St. George's Square 9, 12, 27, 28, 108, 113, 120, 256, 281
St. George's Square Garden 12
St. James the Less 31
St. John's College 56, 58, 211
St. John's Wood Barracks 135
St. John's Wood Church 140
St. John's Wood Clique 135
St. John Zachery 330
St. Katharine Docks 16
St. Magnus the Martyr 323
St. Mark's, Hamilton Terrace 148
St. Mary Aldermanbury 334
St. Mary-at-Hill 321
St. Marylebone Almshouses 136
St. Marylebone Borough Council 133
St. Mary Somerset 327
St. Mary The Boltons 176
St. Nicholas Church 259
St. Olave Old Jewry 335
St. Pancras Church 39

St. Paul's Cathedral 229, 236, 239, 330
St. Paul's Clapham 227
St. Saviours 9, 10, 11, 27
St. Stephen Walbrook 337
St. Swithun Mission 251
Suffragettes 68, 179
Surrey Canal 266, 278, 281
Surrey Hall 257
Survey of London 339
Swift, Taylor 52, 58
Swinton, James Rannie 27

T

Talacre Gardens 47
Tale of Peter Rabbit, The 174
Tate Britain 32, 58, 155, 212, 239, 287, 311, 339
Teddy Boys 232
Telegraph, The 19, 20, 107, 108
Telephone Exchange 247
Temperance Billiard Hall 207, 221
Temperance Pub, The 207
Temple Bar 330
Terry, Ellen 83
Thames Ironworks and Shipbuilding Company 308
Thames Ironworks F.C 310
Thames Plate Glass Works 310
Thatcher, Margaret 143, 154
Thomas Parade 20
Tooting Boys Club 251
Tooting Islamic Centre 250
Tooting Library 259
Tooting Market 253, 261
Tooting Parish Pump 259
Tower of London 95, 319, 321
Townshend Estate 138
Trafalgar Square 40, 231

Index

Trinity Buoy Wharf 303, 307, 308, 311
Trinity Hospice 231
Trinity House 303, 305, 307
Troubadour, The 178, 185
Trump, Donald 15
Tsar Nicholas I 76
Tudor 104, 209
Turret Grove 230
Tutankhamun 173
Tyburn, River 14, 15, 30, 66, 67, 69, 75, 76, 77, 133
Tyburn Tree 66, 75

U

Ukrainian Catholic Cathedral 95
US Embassy 15
Utopia Village 108

V

V2 rocket 75
V&A 131
Van Buren, Martin 77
Vanity Fair 153
Vassall, John 18
Venn, Henry 219, 236
Ventilation Shaft 6, 10
Vicious, Sid 85
Victoria, Queen 170, 328, 339
Violet Hill Gardens 151
Virginia Settlers Memorial 298
Vitus Licinius Ascanius 231

W

War of the Worlds, The 111, 117
Waterhouse, Alfred 95
Waterhouse, Keith 177
Waters, Muddy 84, 90
Watt, G.F. 330

Wek, Alex 79
Weldon, Fay 48
Welfare State 225, 280
Wellington, Duke of 16, 76, 139
Wells, H.G. 111, 117, 154
Western Pumping Station 21, 22
West Ham United 310
Westbourne, River 67
West Indian Ex Services Association 225
Westminster Abbey 32, 212, 239, 287, 311, 339
Westminster Boating Base 16
Westminster, Duke of 10, 27, 28, 30
Westminster, Marquis of 30
Wheatsheaf Public House 245
Whitley, John Robinson 183
Whyte, Thomas 211
William Wilberforce 220, 236
Williams, Gareth 25
William the Conqueror 24, 246
Willowbrook Bridge 278
Wilson, Harold 18
Wilson's Cycles 286
Windmill Pub, The 234
Windsor Court 236
Wingfield, Mjr. Walter Clopton 9, 11
Wise, Henry 30
Wolfe, General 68
Wollstonecraft, Mary 196
Wood, Henry 111
Worcester Park 197
World War I 48, 55, 68, 87, 163, 181, 211, 235, 245, 251, 260, 309
World War II 13, 18, 19, 24, 31, 48, 55, 72, 75, 84, 118, 124, 134, 140, 163, 168, 174, 182, 191, 220, 227, 235, 236, 267, 271, 278, 280, 296, 321, 327

World War II Pillbox 191
Woronzow, Count Simon 136
Worshipful Company of Barbers
    334
Worshipful Society of Apothecaries
    328
Worzel Gummidge 177
Wren, Christopher 321, 327, 330,
    332, 334, 337, 339
Wyatt, James 90
Wyatt, Petronella 143
Wyatt, Woodrow Lyle 143

Y

Yeats, WB 109
Young England Kindergarten 12

Z

Zoo (London) 125

2nd Edition "What a great book"
Joe Swift

The
**LONDON
GARDEN
BOOK** A-Z

Abigail Willis

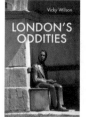

Vicky Wilson

**LONDON'S
ODDITIES**

**LONDON
ARCHITECTURE**

MARIANNE BUTLER

ANDREW KERSHMAN

**WALKING
CAMBRIDGE**

1,000 YEARS OF HISTORY IN 8 WALKS

VICKY WILSON

**WALKING
OXFORD**

1,000 YEARS OF HISTORY IN 8 WALKS

**EDINBURGH'S
HIDDEN WALKS**
*WALK, EXPLORE,
DISCOVER...*

**LONDON'S
CEMETERIES**

**LONDON'S
MARKETS**

ALL THE CAPITAL'S BEST LOVED MARKETS
VINTAGE FAIRS, FARMERS' MARKETS
& CAR BOOT SALES

STEPHEN MILLAR

**LONDON'S
CITY CHURCHES**

FIND THE SIDNEY MARKS OF THE GREAT FIRE
OR VISIT AN ALTAR BY HENRY MOORE

**LONDON'S
HOUSES**
*FROM WORKHOUSE
TO ROYAL PALACE,
COME IN, CLOSE THE
DOOR AND STEP
BACK IN TIME*

**LONDON'S
MONUMENTS**
*FROM BOUDICCA
AND BYRON TO
GUY THE
GORILLA*

**LONDON'S PARKS
AND GARDENS**
*COVER MORE
THAN TWENTY-FIVE
PERCENT OF THE
CAPITAL – THAT'S
A LOT MORE GRASS
BETWEEN TOES
THAN ANY OTHER
CITY IN EUROPE*

About us:

Metro is a small independent publishing company with a reputation for producing well-researched and beautifully-designed guides. To find out more about Metro and order our guides, take a look at our website: **www.metropublications.com**

London's Hidden Walks Series

"A wonderful way to explore
this sometimes secretive city."
Robert Elms, BBC London 94.9FM

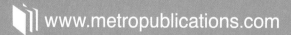

www.metropublications.com

'You once said that if I ever needed a favour, I simply had to ask,'

Luke told Callie.

'Well, you have some nerve, Luke Parker. Calling me in on a long-ago favour!'

'My father is set on me taking over the family business.'

Callie didn't need to hear the steel in his tone to know his take on that. Years ago, something bad must have happened between father and son, something that left Luke vehemently determined to do nothing to increase his father's fortune.

'Just how do you expect me to help you?' She wanted to sound aloof and uncaring, but she was curious.

'Way I see it,' Luke said carefully, 'I need to make myself so undesirable, he'd never let me run the business. And that, darling, is where you come in.'

'Forget it, Luke. I've got better things to do than playing your girlfriend again so you can annoy your father.'

'I'm not asking

'No, Callie, I'm

GW00501430

Dear Reader,

Welcome to Special Edition!

Bestselling author Sherryl Woods brings us
Courting the Enemy, the second book in her special
mini-series THE CALAMITY JANES—where the
life-long friendship between five women is
strengthened as they tackle their problems…and
their love lives…together. Look out for Gina's
story in *To Catch a Thief* next month.

The wealthy Bravo family makes another welcome
appearance with *The Marriage Conspiracy*, the next
book in the always-satisfying Christine Rimmer
series CONVENIENTLY YOURS.

Our THAT'S MY BABY! story is an amnesia tale
with a twist in *Surprise, Doc! You're a Daddy!* by
Jacqueline Diamond and popular author Susan
Mallery also brings us one of her poignant family
stories with *Shelter in a Soldier's Arms*.

There's a powerful marriage-of-convenience tale by
Barbara Benedict, *Solution: Marriage*, and Victoria
Pade's *Baby Be Mine* makes a tough, handsome
bachelor an instant dad.

Happy reading!

The Editors

Solution: Marriage

BARBARA BENEDICT

SILHOUETTE®
SPECIAL EDITION™

DID YOU PURCHASE THIS BOOK WITHOUT A COVER?
If you did, you should be aware it is **stolen property** as it was
reported *unsold and destroyed* by a retailer. Neither the author nor
the publisher has received any payment for this book.

All the characters in this book have no existence outside the imagination
of the author, and have no relation whatsoever to anyone bearing the
same name or names. They are not even distantly inspired by any
individual known or unknown to the author, and all the incidents are
pure invention.

All Rights Reserved including the right of reproduction in whole or in part
in any form. This edition is published by arrangement with Harlequin
Enterprises II B.V. The text of this publication or any part thereof may not
be reproduced or transmitted in any form or by any means, electronic or
mechanical, including photocopying, recording, storage in an
information retrieval system, or otherwise, without the written
permission of the publisher.

This book is sold subject to the condition that it shall not, by way of trade
or otherwise, be lent, resold, hired out or otherwise circulated without the
prior consent of the publisher in any form of binding or cover other than
that in which it is published and without a similar condition including
this condition being imposed on the subsequent purchaser.

Silhouette, Silhouette Special Edition and Colophon are
registered trademarks of Harlequin Books S.A., used under licence.

First published in Great Britain 2002
Silhouette Books, Eton House, 18-24 Paradise Road,
Richmond, Surrey TW9 1SR

© Barbara Benedict 2001

ISBN 0 373 24392 8

23-1102

Printed and bound in Spain
by Litografia Rosés S.A., Barcelona

BARBARA BENEDICT

Weaving a story has always been part of Barbara Benedict's life, from the days when her grandfather would gather the kids around his banjo, to the nights of bedtime tales with her own children. To Barbara, starting a story should be like saying, 'Come, enter a special new world with me.'

For my dad,
who showed me and everyone around him
what love truly means.
We'll all miss you.

Chapter One

Lucky Parker was back in town.

The news ripped through Mamie's Main Street Styling Salon like a midsummer tornado—Tuesdays always drawing the biggest crowd for the cut-and-curl special—but Callianne Magruder didn't need the buzz of small-town gossips to alert her to that man's appearance. Long before the ladies of Latour, Louisiana, began their clucking, she'd felt he was coming.

Thing was, she'd always had this sixth sense when it came to Lucky Parker. Or maybe she might better call it *no* sense, since it invariably led her to trouble.

Trying to appear calm, if not altogether indifferent, she kept working at Mrs. Pendergast's thinning gray hair, but her gaze had this way of sliding back to the window where she could watch Lucky swing his long legs out of his fancy BMW sedan. Locking the vehicle—no doubt a habit from his many years away in New

York City—he pocketed his keys and turned in the direction of the salon.

Callie's heart skipped a beat. Given their past, he'd have no reason to come anywhere near her, she told herself, but her sixth sense insisted *where else?* She wanted to look away, needed to actually *be* indifferent, but she continued to follow his progress with an almost morbid fascination. At half past three on a July afternoon, Main Street shimmered with pavement-buckling waves of heat, but Lucky sauntered with the same cool arrogance he'd displayed when turning his back to it a good ten years ago. Blond hair still slightly long and glinting in the sun, his tall, athletic body honed by years on the football field, he remained Latour's Golden Boy, the conquering hero returning home.

Looking at him, Callie felt that old familiar stab, piercing her heart.

She turned her back, fixing her focus on pulling the curlers from Mrs. Pendergast's hair. She might better use her time earning a good tip from her wealthiest customer. As Gramps used to chant, thinking about that boy would only bring heartache.

And how could it ever be otherwise with the bad blood between their families?

Way back when, Gramps had eloped with the woman Ben Parker wanted to marry, setting off a feud lasting nearly forty years. In a town like Latour, the line separating the haves from have-nots was a distinct one and no Magruder could mess with a Parker and hope to emerge unscathed. Callie had learned the hard way that only a fool tempted fate by spinning dreams about Ben's sole remaining heir. She might have made the mistake once, but she darned well wasn't about to repeat it.

Yet her traitorous gaze kept returning to the long

plate-glass window with a full view of Main Street. She should know heaps better by now, but she couldn't stop staring at the ghost from her past, half dreading yet half hoping his destination was indeed Mamie's salon.

And, oh, wouldn't the tongues start wagging at that.

Acid churned in her stomach as she thought of what she could say to silence the gossips. Or more important, what she'd say to *him.* Latour being such a small place, she should have known this moment would come eventually—and heck, she'd had ten long years to practice—yet with each step Lucky took closer, she grew more aware of how ill prepared she was to face him. Where was her anger, her righteous indignation? Why, in the name of all justice, must the mere sight of that man turn her resolve to mush?

Not this time, she swore again.

She forced herself to remember how it had once been. It would be just like Lucky to stroll in here, as casual as you please, expecting her to fall all over herself in gratitude. Let him grin once, with that wicked gleam in his eyes, and she'd let him have it with both barrels. Contrary to past performances, Callie Magruder wasn't anybody's doormat, and now was as good a time as any to prove it.

Getting herself primed and ready was one thing. Watching him stride past the shop was quite another.

Stunned, she just stood there, staring out the window for a full minute as Lucky continued on down the street. And wasn't that typical? she thought as a wave of embarrassment swept through her. One way or another the Parkers always managed to get the last laugh. There he went without a care in the world, and here she stood, all angered up with nowhere to release it. Darn her sixth sense for lying to her.

Mrs. Pendergast whimpered a protest, forcing Callie

to realize how roughly she must have been brushing the poor woman's hair. Styling the springy gray curls, she fired off a swift round of hair spray and sent her customer off before she could inflict further damage. As she pocketed her tip, she found herself agreeing with Mrs. Pendergast's frowning assessment. If she couldn't keep her mind on the job, Callie Magruder had no business cutting anyone's hair for a living.

Not that it had been her first choice, mind you. At one time she'd had far grander plans for her future. Bright, lively, ambitious Callianne Magruder had been at the top of her class at Latour Central, a student destined to go somewhere, be somebody.

All, of course, pre-Lucky Parker.

Reaching for the broom, she told herself she should be grateful he didn't approach her. She had enough on her plate; she didn't need any more tests of resolve, thank you all the same. Paying off their debts and keeping a roof over her son's head was her foremost concern; not some youthful, torrid love affair that ended all too quickly.

All too painfully.

Marshaling the remaining gray wisps of hair into a dustpan, she reminded herself of the infinite reasons she had to hate the Parker name. Grief, that's all they'd ever caused her, both father and son. If she never had to hear of either man again, she could die a happy woman. The past had long since passed; she had to let it go. She had problems enough with the present, not to mention the future, to expend one more ounce of energy on something she could never change.

Let him keep on walking by. Let him stay out of her life forever. She refused to waste one more thought on a ghost from her past.

* * *

Luke Parker paused, turning back to stare at Mamie's salon. Who did he think he was fooling by heading toward the Fare-Thee-Well Tavern? He could call it what he wanted but deep down he knew he was merely stalling, running away from what he had no stomach to face. The story of his life, up to now.

Staring at the shabby storefronts of the town he'd grown up in, he agreed wholeheartedly with the adage that you should never go home again. Some might find comfort in familiar names and landmarks, but all Luke saw was a slew of unpleasant memories. Given the choice, he'd have gone anywhere else *but* Latour, yet here he nonetheless was, and there was no going back.

Frowning, he turned and marched to Mamie's, not liking himself much for what he was about to do. Make no mistake, he was a veteran of selfish acts, but none of his prior misdeeds could hold a flaming Roman candle to this.

Couldn't be helped. He had to go through with it. The end justifying the means and all that. In a clear case of damned if you do, damned if you don't, you just had to pick the side with the least "damn-age."

He didn't like it, though. Using people was something his father excelled at, and lying always made Luke uneasy. Most folks thought him an amoral playboy, but he had his own code of ethics, however jaded, that he tried his best to live by. And what he was aiming to do now went against just about everything he'd ever put on his list.

Yet the old man was right in one thing. Time came in every man's life when you hit a crossroads and you had to choose one path or the other. After thirty-two self-absorbed years of playing it solo, after an adulthood wasted on boozing, gaming and womanizing, Luke had one last chance to redeem himself. He could seize it or waste the rest of his life with more of the same.

For once he could do something right, make a difference.

Unbidden, the image of Callie Magruder flitted across his mind, looking every bit as young and innocent as the last time he'd seen her—shoulders back and chin up, doing her best to fight the tears misting her eyes as she watched him drive out of town.

Banishing the vision with another determined frown, he yanked open the door to the salon. Over the years Ben Parker had offered little of value when it came to parental guidance, but he had managed to impart one useful piece of advice to his son: if there's an unpleasant task to be done, it's best to get instantly to it.

Luke stepped inside the shop. Seven chairs sat between the long mirror and large window fronting Main Street, six of them swiveling as heads snapped in his direction. Ignoring them, his gaze went instantly to Callie at the far end of the line. Some girls were like that, he'd discovered over the years. They had a presence, an aura, that grabbed hold of you right off and kept your attention. Funny, but he'd never before realized that Callie could be one of them.

She was busy sweeping, her spine stiff, straight and aimed right at him. The way she attacked the floor with the broom, you'd think she was beating back an army of invading insects. He could feel the anger coming off her in waves. In such a mood, Luke knew from experience, she would be a force to reckon with. On the flip side, he also knew a softened, smiling Callie could be any man's dream.

Swallowing his distaste, wishing he had any other way to do this, he went over to Mamie Saunders to cajole her into giving Callie a short break. Luke had never much liked Mamie, with her shrill voice and sharper tongue, but she, like most females in this town, tended to melt like butter in August when he flashed the patented Parker grin. It wasn't his looks or charm that caused the phenomenon, he knew, but rather his single status, backed up by the obscene heap of cash Ben Parker kept in Tyler Fitzhugh's First Fidelity Bank.

Though clearly surprised by his request, Mamie proved no obstacle, gesturing grandly to the back of her shop. Luke could hear the whispers behind him as he made his way to Callie, but he'd learned long since to ignore what the ladies of this town had to say about Ben Parker's sole surviving son. His focus was on the mission before him.

On the woman before him.

He felt like a kid approaching a girl to ask for his first date, knowing he had no guarantee of the outcome. Callie wouldn't refuse him, he'd taken care to make certain of that, but a good deal of both their futures could hinge upon what was said in the next fifteen minutes. Callie Magruder, he thought with an odd tightening in his throat. The girl he'd left behind.

She'd filled out some in the past ten years, the promise of youth blossoming into all the right curves and softness. Nothing to write home about maybe, not after the movie stars and models he'd dated in New York, yet there was an air about her, a blend of common sense and genuine caring that made a man linger. You could talk to Callie. What was more important, she listened.

"Callie?" he said quietly, trying not to startle her.

No such luck. She went still—no, more like rigid—her knuckles turning white where she gripped the broom. Slowly she turned to face him, her features as pale as if she'd just seen a ghost. He noticed that she still wore her brown hair long and straight. The jeans

hugging her slim hips, as threadbare as her sleeveless
denim shirt, looked like they might have survived some
other era. So much about her was exactly the same, yet
something he couldn't quite put a finger on made Callie
seem suddenly a stranger.

An angry stranger.

He told himself that it was no real surprise that she
wasn't overjoyed to see him, but for some reason, her
scowl really bugged him. Maybe she felt she had issues
with him, but then, don't forget, he had some of his
own with her. He was here on a mission, he told himself
sternly, and he had to get to it. By fair means or foul,
he'd get her consent. "Got a minute to talk?"

"Leave me be, Lucky Parker," she said calmly
enough, and all too coldly. "Go spread your mischief
on your side of town."

A far-from-auspicious start.

Still, Luke wouldn't be where he was today if he ever
backed down from a challenge. "Luke," he corrected.
"Nowadays, folks have taken to using my given
name."

She gave him a look as if he'd just made the speech
in a foreign language.

"I'm thirty-two years old," he said with a shrug.
"Being called Lucky was kid's stuff. It's time I grew
up, don't you think?"

Callie wasn't about to tell him what she was thinking.
She held tight to the broom, half to prop herself up but
more to hide how her limbs were trembling. All well
and good to forget the man when she didn't have to see
him, but here he stood, all six foot two and broad, mus-
cled shoulders of him. Lucky—excuse me, Luke—Parker in the living, breathing flesh. Lord, but she'd let
herself forget how truly gorgeous one man could be.

Judge a man not by how he looks, she could hear Gramps chiding, *but rather by what he does.*

"Besides," he added, a hard edge creeping into his tone, "I can't say I'm feeling particularly lucky these days, anyway."

She tilted her head to the side to study him. "You have your youth, money and health. How much good fortune does one man need?"

"You could say luck is in the eyes of the beholder." He shrugged, glancing back over his shoulder. "Listen, Callie, can we go somewhere else to talk?"

Following his gaze, she noticed every eye in the shop was on them, each female reduced to speechlessness, their mouths formed in frozen, silent *O*s. They all knew who Luke was, of course, but few could hazard a guess as to what he could want with Callie. The brief time she'd spent with him that long-ago summer had been as clandestine as it had been idyllic. His approaching her now, right here and like this, must come as a shock to virtually every man, woman and child in the parish.

And make no mistake, it would be all over town in an hour.

"You've got nothing to say that I want to hear," she told him, hoping he'd take the hint and leave before he made matters worse.

But she'd forgotten that this was Luke Parker. Left to run wild as a boy, he'd never quite gotten used to heeding the word *no*.

"You may want to hear *this,*" he said, this time with his usual cockiness. "Don't worry, I talked to Mamie. She said it's okay for you to take your break now."

Turning her back to him, Callie busied herself with sweeping imaginary hair. "Yeah, well, no one asked *me* if it was okay."

He laughed, a sound she'd once lived for, but which

now made her as bristly as the broom in her hands. "Some things never change, Cal. You always did want to do things the hard way."

"Everything changes," she told him through gritted teeth as she propped the broom against the wall. "Even silly little Callie Magruder."

He eyed her speculatively. "Nah, I'll bet my last nickel you're still the same good sport you've always been."

Good *sport?* After so many years of absence, of silence, this was what he came to say? Not wanting him to see her resentment—or worse, her hurt—she busied herself with shoving the combs and brushes into her station drawer. "What do you want, Luke?"

"Ah, that's my Callie. Right to the point. No time to waste on pleasant social discourse."

"So that's what you call this? Pleasant discourse?" She didn't bother to keep the sarcasm from her tone.

"Why, I imagine it could be just about anything you want it to be. You set the tone, Cal. I'll take my cue from you."

Her fingers curled around a brush handle, the urge to fling it at him nearly overwhelming. He had to know what his presence did to her. Heck, danged near every lady in the salon, with their front-row seats to the action, had to know she was fit to bursting with unreleased tension.

Yet there he stood, acting as if the past ten years had never been.

Loosening her grip on the brush, she carefully set it in the drawer. "I'm real busy," she said in what she hoped was a calm, measured tone as she slid the drawer shut and turned to face him. "Surely there's some other girl in this town you can bother."

"Five minutes. I swear it. C'mon Callie, what can be the harm in that?"

Plenty, she knew, yet she found herself staring back at him, even while knowing better. Lounging against the chair, hip propped against it and his arms crossed casually at his chest, he wore his patented grin, that come-on-you-know-you-want-to call to mischief she'd found so hard to resist.

"Why are you badgering me?" she asked abruptly. "What are you up to now?"

He shook his head, his blue gaze clouding. "To find that out, I'm afraid you'll have to come with me."

Chapter Two

Callie *was* curious, as he'd no doubt anticipated, but she had no time for his shenanigans. "I've got two more customers, then the long trek home and supper to get on the table," she told him, betraying her exasperation. "I mean it, Luke Parker. You just move on now and leave me be."

He held up a hand, fingers splayed. "Five minutes?"

"You're not gonna let this go, are you? You'll just keep at me and at me until you get what you want."

She'd expected a grin—vintage Lucky Parker at his disarming best—but Luke stared into her eyes, his steady, grim expression startling her into wondering what the ten-year absence might have done to *him*.

"I can say my piece right here if you want," he said at last, looking pointedly around them. "That way, I can satisfy everyone's curiosity."

Noticing the heads craning in their direction, Callie

visibly shuddered. Not knowing what Luke meant to say, could she take the chance of them being overheard? "Why are you doing this?" she hissed at him. "Haven't you done enough as it is?"

She thought she saw him wince, but his tone was as implacable as ever. "Just hear me out, Callie. Trust me, I wouldn't ask if it wasn't important."

Important for whom? she wanted to scream at him, but that would only prolong an already uncomfortable situation. Better to let him say what he wanted and then get rid of him. She hated being at the mercy of gossips, and she sure didn't think fondly of Luke for putting her in this position, but she couldn't see how she had much of a choice. "Five minutes," she snapped as she turned to march of out the salon. "Not one second more."

She could feel the stunned stares following her progress across the room, as if all twenty eyeballs were glued to her back. She supposed she should be grateful that none of these gossips could relate the scene to Gramps. The late Zeke Magruder wouldn't have enjoyed hearing she was "consorting" with the Parker boy. Oh no, he wouldn't have liked it one bit.

It took her ten strides to reach the door, but Luke made it in less, there in plenty of time to hold it open for her. Passing under his arm, she felt that awful ripple in her midsection again, the intense awareness that he was a man and she was a woman.

A stupid woman, it would seem, wherever Luke Parker was concerned.

She scooted past him, wishing the motion didn't make her seem quite so skittish, yet determined to maintain a healthy distance. Once outside the shield of air-conditioning, the brick wall of heat made it easier. Dense, moist and stagnant, the air hovered between them like a stubborn chaperon. As if she needed to be reminded of the perils in getting too close.

They walked in silence toward the town square, but once out of earshot of the salon, Luke turned his head to study her. "You look great, Callie," he said, making the words sound like some grand pronouncement. "A real fine sight for these sore eyes."

Standing there in her worn jeans and shirt, brown hair frizzing in the humidity, she knew she should take his praise with triple the customary grains of salt. The sad fact was, though, she couldn't remember the last time she'd been paid any compliment. Like a cleansing rain after a long, hard drought, his words soaked into her, revived her. Oh, she knew better than anyone that it was Luke's way to make a woman feel valued—part of his charm and a skill he practiced shamelessly—but in that moment, he made her *feel* pretty, and she wanted to relish the sensation a teeny bit longer. What could be the harm in that?

And wasn't it just such thinking that had gotten her in trouble in the first place?

"Don't waste your sweet talk on me, Luke Parker," she told him firmly. "It isn't nearly as convincing without the drawl, anyway. You sound like a Yankee, you know. Is that what life in the big city does to you?"

He shrugged. "A man's got to survive the best he can."

"Yeah, I bet." Callie could remember newspaper accounts about how much of his surviving had been done in nightclubs with a long string of female celebrities. "From what I heard, you seemed to be managing just fine up there. What I don't understand is what on earth would bring you back home to Latour?"

He hesitated a second before answering, as if unsure of his answer. "I blew out the shoulder, overstayed my welcome.'' He said it glibly enough, but Callie again caught a hard edge behind the words. ''Let's just say I had my five minutes of fame. New York wasn't nearly as much fun without it.''

At least he got to have fun, she thought. And that was the major difference between them. Spoiled by his money, looks and family position, Luke didn't know the first thing about responsibility, while for Callie, it might as well be her middle name.

Looking up, she noticed they'd reached the large patch of grass in front of the town hall that served as Latour's Central Park. Come winter and spring, the area was the town's oasis, but under the hot summer sun even the Spanish moss was wilting, drooping from the oaks like overcooked pasta. Small wonder the place was all but deserted.

''Fun, huh?'' she said, gesturing at the empty square. ''You're not expecting to find any here in Latour, I hope.''

''No, ma'am, that I'm not.'' He herded her along the path to a single stone bench in the far corner. ''But then, life has this way of rarely living up to expectations. I imagine I'll have to wait and see what happens.''

He looked at her pointedly, leaving her with the feeling he knew something that she did not—a private joke, maybe, that he was holding out on. Avoiding his gaze, Callie realized that a great deal more than the heat and humidity stood between them—that in truth, the man was a virtual stranger.

She had the sudden, strong urge to be back in Mamie's shop.

''You said five minutes, Parker,'' she said abruptly. ''And two of those are already up. Why not just come right out and tell me what you're after.''

He glanced at his watch as if checking her time assessment. "Actually, er, well, it's a bit complicated."

"Then we can do this when you have more time." Taking the cue for an easy exit, she turned to walk off.

He reached for her wrist, grabbing it gently, stopping them both in the middle of the path. On her part, Callie could scarcely breathe, with his mere touch reviving far too many memories. Time was…

Not that Luke seemed aware of his effect on her. "Just hear me out," he said, his tone betraying a tension of his own, maybe even impatience. "I'll make it worth your while, I swear it. What I'm offering is, well, let's just call it a business proposition."

She didn't bother to hide her skepticism. "A Parker, playing fair with a Magruder? Now why do I find that so hard to believe?"

Releasing her wrist, he didn't answer, letting the silence stretch between them as he ushered her along the path. Stiff and withdrawn, he acted as if he were the one with the right to be angry. As if it were her family that had tormented his.

"What are you doing cutting hair at Mamie's?" he asked suddenly, the change in subject catching her off guard. "Last I heard, you were aiming to be a nurse practitioner. What happened to going to college?"

"Life happened. Like you said, it rarely lives up to our expectations." She took in a breath, then let it slowly out, determined not to reveal any more to this man. Not that she felt any compunction about burdening him with her troubles; it was more a matter of salvaging her ego. Pride might be a useless commodity in most respects, but when it came to dealing with the Parkers, it was pretty much all she had left.

"I've got a kid now," she said on a higher note,

letting every bit of the proud mother shine through in her tone. "A boy, named Robbie."

That said, Callie watched him carefully. He still wouldn't look at her.

"Yeah, I heard you married Reb Jenkins." His distant gaze implied indifference to the topic, but she nonetheless sensed a continued rigidity about him. "Talk about your spur-of-the-moment decision," he added with the same studied nonchalance. "You were what, three months out of high school?"

And there it was, the zinger she'd been dreading, hitting too close to the bone. "We were in love." She meant to sound firm, but her tone bordered on defensive. She tried again, determined to keep it calm and logical and free of buried emotions. "At least, we thought we were. When we realized…well, we tried to make the best of things."

"You mean, you tried and Reb took advantage."

Of course he'd view it that way. Luke and Reb had never gotten along. They'd always competed for the same things—girls, grades, football scholarships—with Luke generally walking off with the prize.

"Reb and me, we were the proverbial oil and water," she said, glossing over the uglier truths. Actually, they'd made each other miserable. "We lasted barely a year before he lit off downriver to New Orleans. That's where he filed the divorce papers, so I'm supposing that's where he went."

"You didn't nail him for desertion?"

And who are you to pass judgment? she wanted to ask him, but it sounded like a woman scorned, and she sure didn't want him thinking that. He was watching her far too intently as it was. "You can't milk a stone," she said, trying to sound offhand. "Besides, who needs Reb? Me and Robbie are doing fine without him."

"Oh, yes, Robbie. Your son. He must be what now, nine? Ten?"

Underneath the seemingly casual question lay a good dozen emotional land mines, all waiting to blow up in her face. "Robbie just turned nine," she said, hoping to defuse them. "Me and Reb had him right off. He didn't want to wait to start a family."

"Good old Reb," he said angrily, his gaze burning into her. "Always great at starting things, never there to finish them."

Callie had her own edge. "Yeah, well, you know what they say. Only the innocent get to throw stones."

"Biblical references, Cal?" he said, his tone betraying his annoyance. "Now you sound like my old man."

"Don't you ever compare me to Ben Parker." Callie had reached her limit. She'd never claimed to be perfect, but putting that snake's name and hers in the same sentence went beyond what she could accept. "Let's get to the point, shall we? Just why *did* you drag me out here, Luke?"

He seemed startled by her bluntness, but he recovered quickly, his gaze narrowing considerably. "Okay. You once said that if I ever needed a favor, I simply had to ask."

"Well, you have some nerve, Luke Parker." She knew she should keep her mouth shut, but the words came bursting from her like the kernels in a microwave bag of popcorn. "One minute you're insulting me by likening me to Ben, and in the next breath, as casual as you please, you call *me* in on a long-ago favor?"

He looked past her, his jaw going tight. "Ben is set on me taking over the family business."

She didn't need to hear the steel in his tone to know his take on that. Years ago something bad must have happened between father and son, something Luke never talked about, but which had left him vehemently determined to do nothing to increase Ben's fortune. Back in high school, spending his father's money never seemed to pose a problem, but for as long as she'd known him, Luke had refused to lift a finger to keep Parker Industries alive and thriving.

"So you and Ben are banging heads again," she told him, crossing her arms at her chest. She wanted to sound aloof and uncaring, but her curiosity kept getting in the way. "I don't get it, Luke. Just how do you expect me to help you?"

His expression eased a bit, as if he'd sensed a crack in her resistance and meant to bulldoze his way through the opening. "Way I see it," he said carefully, "is that the man will keep wheedling and coaxing and bullying me straight through to doomsday if I don't soon take action. I need to make myself so undesirable, he'd rather have Bozo the Clown run the business. And that, darlin', is where you come in."

"Well, thank you. Do I have to wear the orange wig and oversize shoes?"

"Not exactly." A tiny grin played at his mouth. "I don't want a clown. I was thinking more along the line of Jezebel."

She froze, wary about where he seemed to be going with this. "Forget it, Luke. I've got better things to do than play your girlfriend so you can annoy your father."

"I'm not asking you play my girlfriend," he said, the grin vanishing. "No indeed, Callie, I'm asking you to be my wife."

Chapter Three

"No!" Staring at him in absolute astonishment, Callie felt as if he'd knocked the stuffings right out of her. Of all the idiotic things Luke could have suggested, marriage had to top the list.

"It's the only solution," he said firmly, as if neither of them had a choice. "It's the one sure way to get Ben off my back."

She wanted to make more of a protest, but, reeling from Luke's unconventional proposal, she could barely process the words. The doctors must have slipped him some hallucinatory drug for his injured arm, she decided. It was the only explanation for such a preposterous suggestion. She and Luke Parker, husband and wife? Oh, granted, there had been a time when she'd have gladly died for this moment, but she'd come a long way from the dewy-eyed schoolgirl she'd been then.

"You're out of your mind," she told him, shaking

her head in disbelief. "Can you truly be so vain, you actually thought I'd jump at your offer?"

If so, she'd apparently yet to convince him otherwise. "Hear me out," he said, taking her hands in his own. "You might actually find this to your benefit."

"Right." She yanked her hands free, remembering only too well what his touch could do to her resolutions. "Me and mine always get the better end of any deal with you Parkers."

She expected him to argue, but he merely nodded. "No one will be getting the best of anyone. I'm not pretending I'm Santa Claus. I stand to gain from this, too. As I said, it's a business proposition."

"Funny way to do business. Taking on a wife and another man's son—tell me, who's getting back at who? Wouldn't it be simpler just to tell your father no?"

"Ben Parker?" He looked disappointed in her. "You, of all people, should know he'll never take no for an answer."

"Must be a family trait."

He shook his head as if exasperated, but he didn't back down. "Look, I'm in a real bind here. If you can think of another way to make Ben lay off, I'm eager to hear it, but presenting Zeke Magruder's granddaughter as my wife will do the job clean and quick. No offense intended, but you know how Ben feels about you and your family. If he has to worry about a Magruder whispering in my ear at nights, he won't let me within fifty miles of his precious company."

He was right about that much. Ben Parker had no more love for her than she had for him. Still, she couldn't help but wonder why Luke would so adamantly pursue this course. Marriage was such a major— not to mention permanent—solution.

"Your stint up north must have robbed you of what

little good sense you had," she told him. "We tried a relationship, remember? It barely lasted five weeks."

He stared at her, his blue eyes probing into her. "We weren't really trying for a relationship, Callie. I told you up-front that all I wanted was a friend."

So he had. At least, those were the words coming out of his mouth. The way he'd acted, the way he'd held her and made her feel was another story altogether. "And now all you want is a wife," she countered, getting angrier by the moment. "I guess what I want never factors into the equation."

"What *do* you want, Cal?"

The question caught her so off guard, she nearly blinked. If she were to say the first thing in her head, it would be that she wanted him to stop stirring up all these unwanted memories and emotions.

"I don't want anything from you, Luke Parker," she told him defiantly.

He ignored her. "People always want money. Help me out, Cal, and I'll take care of you financially. You can quit your job—"

"I'm not quitting my job." Working for Mamie might be a far cry from what she wanted to do in life, but she could take pride in making the ladies of Latour look prettier, and in the fact that she was earning her own way. "And I refuse to take one cent of Ben Parker's money."

He looked almost insulted. "We're in total agreement then. I wasn't exactly a bum up in New York, Cal. Trust me, I have more than enough money of my own. Money I've learned to put to good use, so I know what's a good investment." He glanced over his shoulder at the salon. "You don't belong at Mamie's, and we both know it. Keep the job, if it's that important to you, but you belong in college. That's why, along with the legal documents making sure you and your son will be well provided for, I'm including a trust fund to finance your education.''

She could feel herself bristling. Magruders didn't take handouts, especially from a Parker. ''I can pay my own way through college, thank you all the same.''

''I know that.'' The concession, coupled with his solemn nod, unruffled a few of her feathers. ''But in a way,'' he went on smoothly, ''what I'm offering is a job. This will be part of your salary. And I'm not just talking about your schooling. I'm offering to finance your son's education, as well.''

Trust Luke to find her Achilles' heel. Robbie meant everything to her; she'd do just about anything to make his life better.

''And as proof of my good faith,'' Luke went on, ''I'll talk to the doctors at the hospital, get them to release your grandfather to our care. If we can keep him from badgering my father any further, I'm sure there's no need to keep him confined in a strange place.''

With a sudden, painful lump in her throat, Callie remembered the desperation in her grandfather's eyes, his steely grip on her wrist as he pleaded with her to get him out of that awful institution. She'd felt so helpless, uttering hollow reassurances about trying her best. Sad fact was, her best hadn't been good enough. She'd exhausted what little savings she'd had, filing appeals and hounding the parish welfare system, only to discover that nobody cared about the Zeke Magruders of this world. Money, that's what did the talking, and having so darned much of it, Ben Parker talked louder than most.

''You're too late,'' she said, swallowing the lump to make sure her voice sounded even. ''Gramps died last winter.''

"Ah, Callie, I'm sorry. I know how much he meant to you."

Yes, he did, and Luke's sympathy was almost her undoing. All that grief, so close to the surface, had her saying far more than was wise. "They said it was old age, that they couldn't find a more specific cause, but up until your father had him committed to that terrible place, Gramps stayed as young as you or I. I know it was wrong, the way he kept harassing your father, but those little mischiefs kept him going, helped him hold tight to the belief that he'd one day get our home back. By locking him away, Ben Parker robbed him of far more than his freedom, Luke. He took away my grandfather's reason for living. I had to watch that proud old man wither away, powerless to save him, knowing your father's spite was to blame."

"Wait a minute, I'm not sure you can call it spite—"

"I call it as I see it, Luke." She cut in before he could utter one more syllable in defense of his father. "Ben hounded him to death. All because my grandmother chose Gramps and Ben couldn't handle it. You'd think he would be content with owning half this town, but no, he had to go and take away the one thing of value Gramps had left. Don't tell me you don't know that he stole the farm out from under us."

His blank expression told her he didn't know about the rather nasty battle they'd fought with his father. "I never heard anything about Ben taking your farm."

"Gramps took out a mortgage years ago and neglected to tell me," she went on. "Your father knew about it though. He bought out the savings-and-loan that held the deed. Within a month of the takeover, they served our eviction notice, which was what started Gramps on his harassment campaign. Ben threatened to build a factory there, you see, some smoke-belching monstrosity guaranteed to ruin the land. It is, I believe, his version of having the last laugh.''

"I swear, I didn't know, Cal.''

"But you do now. And I hope you can understand why I might feel indisposed to trust anyone bearing the Parker name.''

"I'm not my father,'' he said quietly. He stared at her a long moment, visibly pleading with her to believe him. "Your beef is with Ben, not me. And quite frankly I can't think of a better way at getting back at him than by agreeing to this marriage.''

In that much, Luke had a point. It would do her battered heart good to see Ben's face when his son brought Zeke's granddaughter to his big old fancy house and introduced her as his wife.

Still, she thought in a flash of sanity, it would be remarkably shortsighted to marry for revenge. Marriage to Luke, even in name only, would be like making a pact with the devil. Short-term, she'd get what she wanted, but in the end there'd be a helluva price to pay.

As if he were indeed Lucifer, Luke didn't leave the tempting at that. "The fall semester starts in a month. We can get you signed up for some classes right away.''

"You've given this a lot of thought,'' she said slowly, wondering when careless, take-it-as-it-comes Luke Parker had gotten so methodical. "You must really be serious.''

He took her by the arms, forcing her closer. "Never more so. C'mon Callie, what's left to consider? No matter how you look at it, we both stand to gain.''

Watching him as he talked, her mind flashed back to that long-ago summer when she'd swallowed each and every word his sweet, coaxing lips had uttered. She'd given herself completely to the youth he'd been then—her hopes, her sympathy, her trust. Even now she could feel a softening as the well-remembered yearnings rose up from deep inside her.

She caught herself up short. What was she thinking? Insanity, to even listen to this man.

"Help me out here," Luke continued, applying gentle pressure to her arms, "and I promise you won't regret it."

Something snapped inside her, turning her insides into cold, hard steel. "You're real glib, Luke Parker. We've been down this road, only now I know better than to listen. It's all just words to you. You use them like water but you give them no meaning, no substance." She poked a finger into his chest. "Around here, around *me,* don't you dare go making promises you don't mean to keep."

He grabbed her hand, encircling it with his own and holding it tight against his chest. "We've got this past and we can't hide from it. Neither of us." He towered over her, his gaze just as heated, seeming more than ever a stranger. "But where's the sense in letting it mess up our futures? I'm offering you and your son a chance at a better life, Cal. What will it take to get you to say yes?"

What would it take?

Money, schooling, security—no question that these things might tempt her, but if she couldn't get them herself, she could learn to do without. In truth, there was only one thing she craved, only one thing beyond her reach, and that was the house she'd grown up in. Generations of Magruders, laughing and loving and working together—that was the legacy she wanted so desperately to pass down to her son.

"All I want," she answered without hesitation, "is my family's farm."

He stared at her a long moment, then shook his head.

''What you're asking is close to impossible. There are two things Ben *never* does. One is to give in to my requests, and the other is to back down from a fight with a Magruder.''

She pulled her hand free. ''Then I guess we've got nothing more to talk about.''

''I didn't say I wouldn't do it.'' This time he took her by the shoulders, forcing her to look at him. He seemed tense and grim, a far cry from the grinning youth who always used charm to get what he wanted. ''Marry me, Callie, and I promise I'll find some way to get your farm for you.''

For an instant she could almost believe him. He seemed so sure of himself, so sincere, but then, so much of what he'd seemed in the past had proved to be mere illusion. She'd be a fool to trust in his good intentions.

Still, in the long run, did it matter? If she considered this—and insanely enough, she *was* considering this— Luke's motives needn't concern her at all, not as long as she got what *she* needed out of the bargain, the wherewithal to buy the farm back herself. This would be a business arrangement—nothing less, nothing more. As he'd pointed out, she wouldn't be taking his money, she'd be earning it. On her terms.

''If I agree to this,'' she started slowly, ''I'd have certain conditions.''

He released her arms, eyeing her warily. ''And those would be?''

''Well, for one thing, I want to make it clear that this will be a marriage in name only. No honeymoon, no sharing a bed.''

He raised a brow, but didn't comment.

''Even so,'' she went on, warming to the subject, ''I'd still expect you to honor our vows as if they were real. No carousing with the boys and no sleeping around

with other women. Not here in town. I won't have me
and my boy being the subject of Monday morning's
gossip.''

''Dammit Callie, you can't expect me to be a monk
for the rest of my life.''

''You're right. I don't expect any such thing from
you. I've read the papers, Luke. And I've seen firsthand
how you are with the ladies. Actually, what I was thinking is that it would be to both our advantage to set a
time limit on this marriage.''

He stiffened. ''A time limit?''

She could feel a slight breeze, stirring the warm air
around them. It didn't cool her down any, but it helped
steel her resolve. ''Yes, I think next August should be
more than sufficient time.''

He narrowed his gaze, his expression far from
pleased. ''A year?''

''Let's face it, Luke. If you can't convince Ben to
leave you alone by then, you're not likely to ever convince him.''

''But I had in mind that—''

''Doesn't really matter what you had in mind, Luke.
If we do this, for once we'll be doing things my way,
not yours.''

Overhead Callie could hear the sighs as the Spanish
moss stirred in the breeze. Could be a storm brewing,
she thought inanely—both in the air and in the stranger
glaring back at her. If it were at all physically possible,
his eyes looked ready to spit.

She felt a sudden, strong need to stand her ground.
''Those are my terms,'' she told him, crossing her arms
over her chest. ''Take them or leave them.''

For a moment she thought he might just do that, take
his ridiculous proposal and stomp away, but with dis-

arming abruptness, he shook his head and laughed softly. "You drive a hard bargain, lady."

"Not at all. I'm just looking out for me and mine."

He nodded, sobering instantly. "Okay, then, I agree to your terms. Do we have a deal?"

He held out a hand, no doubt expecting her to shake it, but she couldn't bring herself to reach out and make contact. Some might call it fear, but she preferred to call it practicality. It was such a big step, after all, such a major decision.

"You won't regret it," he said softly. "I'll make certain of that."

The words set off a rage in her. How like Luke to think he could come back here and wrap her around his little finger. "No, *I'll* be the one making certain," she told him, making it plain that she was no longer the trusting teenager she'd been back then. "Play false with me again, Luke Parker, and this time, *you* can live with the regrets."

He stared at her for a long moment, his hand still extended between them. The fact that he didn't flinch, that he met her gaze and held it, had her tentatively reaching out to meet his grip halfway. It was an unsettling sensation, shaking hands with him. She felt suddenly as if she'd had the rug yanked out from under her feet, the walls containing her life pushed back in all directions. She could make all the vows and stipulations she wanted, but in that instant she knew that where she and Luke were concerned, virtually anything could happen.

"C'mon," he said, his voice and expression solemn. "Let's get this show on the road."

Following Luke back to Mamie's, she was left wondering if she had indeed made a pact with the devil.

Chapter Four

"Till death do us part."

A dazed Callie repeated the words because it was expected of her, not out of any real conviction. Until *one year* do we part, she corrected in her mind, as if it could make up for lying to the well-meaning justice of the peace. An elderly version of *The Wizard of Oz*'s scarecrow, Malcolm Fry beamed down at her, tightening her sense of guilt. You'd think he'd be bored, having conducted this ceremony countless times for countless others, but Mr. Fry actually seemed eager to bind them together. His kindliness, his obvious happiness for them, left Callie feeling an utter fraud.

Standing close beside her, Luke betrayed no such difficulty with mouthing the vows. Then again, hard to imagine a Parker battling any last-minute attacks of conscience.

At least she could be grateful that no one she knew

was here to watch them enact this parody of a wedding.
The only witnesses were two female clerks, a pair of
senior citizens in faded gingham shirtwaists, pressed
into service for the brief ten minutes the deception
would last. Tittering as if they were the bride instead
of Callie, the women seemed perfectly happy to over-
look the fact that she carried no flowers, wore no veil
or special outfit. Even the ring was a loaner. Luke had
taken the friendship ring once sent by a fan off his finger, but she supposed the semigold band was a close
enough imitation to prevent any undue eyebrow-raising
by the staff here at City Hall. Besides, she kept telling
herself, it wasn't as if this ceremony meant anything to
either of them.

Except that it was her second time at this. A complete
stranger prompting their vows instead of the family
minister, someone else's grandma serving as her maid
of honor—it was a far cry from how she'd always imagined her wedding. Under the circumstances, she supposed she could forego the fancy reception and frantic
rice throwing, but given that she tried this before, she
could have hoped the word *love* could figure into it
somewhere.

Oblivious to her doubts, Mr. Fry turned to smile at
Luke as he asked for the ring. Callie's guilt swiftly slid
into trepidation as Luke took her left hand to slide the
band onto her finger. Stupid, to have forgotten how it
felt to have his hand cover hers. It came rushing back
in a flood, how swiftly she'd responded to the dangerous heat they'd generated between them. It was all she
could do not to yank her hand free.

It's just a mockery, she wanted to tell the beaming
Mr. Fry, but of course she did no such thing. She had
to get a grip. None of this was about her, anyway. She
was here for Robbie. This marriage, fake or otherwise,

meant they could stop struggling to make ends meet. One short year and she could make sure her son would have all that he needed, all that he deserved. That was what was important here.

Robbie, she thought with a catch in her throat, glad that he was safely tucked away at day camp and unaware of what his mother was now doing. He wouldn't understand, and how could he? To him Luke was a stranger. Not the man who biologically, at least, happened to be his father.

It wasn't a new thing for Callie, this wrestling with the moral dilemma. Had Luke been around at the beginning, things might have been different, but he'd gone and left her, and really, wasn't it a bit late now to be opening that can of worms? For ten long years she'd been virtually alone with her secret, telling no one but Gramps, and through necessity, Reb Jenkins. In all that time her only thought had been to protect the life she and Luke had forged between them, to give their boy the best that life could offer. For Robbie's sake she would marry Luke and let him take care of her son's education, but she had no intention of now relaxing her vigil. Technically the boy might be a Parker, but in all ways that counted, Robbie was *her* son, raised to think, act and breathe like a Magruder. For her son's sake and future well-being, she had no choice but to continue living her lie.

Busy convincing herself, she was startled out of her thoughts by the words, "I now pronounce you man and wife." But that particular death knell didn't frighten her nearly as much as the ensuing "You may now kiss the bride."

She had to face Luke then, had to face what she'd committed herself to for the one year's duration. Oh, she might have felt dread before, the same what-on-earth-am-I-doing sensation when saying her vows with Reb Jenkins, but this was far worse. She'd had no history with Reb, no experience of how *his* lips could turn her bones to mush. Only one man had ever held such power over her—Lucky, always Lucky—and he was leaning down to melt her resolve again.

She fought the urge to run from the room screaming, far too conscious of Mr. Fry and the two old ladies watching them. Of Luke watching her. I can do this, she told herself fiercely. I can touch him and kiss him and feel absolutely nothing.

Half dying inside—and yet, half coming alive—she lifted her face to his.

Luke saw her hesitation and felt a nasty tightening in his gut. Could she actually fear he'd ravish her here on this dusty floor for his own gratification? Did she think so little of him? Gazing down at her uplifted face, he saw the answer in her wide, wary eyes.

Reassure her, a tiny voice coached inside him. *Show her how much you've changed in the ten years you've been gone.*

He leaned down and touched her lips with his own. He meant the kiss to be gentle, perhaps even reassuring, but the instant their lips met, his own started tingling. A sensation that resonated downward throughout his body.

Startled and uneasy, he'd pulled back. Despite all his careful planning and good intentions, he'd never bargained on that—how, even after ten long years apart, something hot and demanding could still spark between them.

He didn't need to see the fear and accusation in Callie's expression to know how this could mess up his agenda. Sobered, he moved away from her, going with Mr. Fry to finish the paperwork. From now on he had to keep his distance, had to keep things simple, to stir up the minimum fuss and heartache. Clearly, if he hoped to achieve his goal, kissing Callie couldn't figure into the equation.

Yet as they finished up the details and left the courthouse, he couldn't seem to take his gaze from her mouth. She tastes like peaches, he now remembered, so sweet and fresh and ready for plucking. And just as it had been ten years ago, he found himself wanting more.

Not that it seemed likely she'd ever again let him near enough to try. Sitting on her side of the BMW, huddled against the door as she clutched the handle, his new wife looked ready to bolt at the slightest provocation. It bothered him that she seemed so afraid of him. It bothered him a lot.

"You don't have to hug the door because of one little kiss," he said, noticing how her entire posture stiffened at the mere sound of his voice. "You didn't feel anything, did you?"

"Of course not."

Of course not. "So what's the big deal? I wasn't putting any moves on you, Cal. The kiss was expected. Didn't you hear those ladies giggling? If I hadn't made it look good, they'd have gone home disappointed and who knows what stories they would spread? Don't worry, I won't be forcing my attentions on you. I promised to be a monk and I will."

She didn't say anything, just nodded, keeping her gaze trained on the road ahead.

Luke hid his impatience with a sigh. "Listen, Callie, I know we have our past, and it's not easy to get over it, but—"

"I'm not thinking about the past," she blurted out, panic ringing loud and clear in her words. "I'm more concerned with the future. You rushed me through this so fast, my mind's in a blur. Here we are heading home, and I haven't the slightest idea where or what that home will be. Shouldn't we discuss how we mean to go about conducting day-to-day life? Really, Luke, don't you think this is all just the slightest bit insane?''

Her voice cracked a little on that last. If she gripped the door handle any tighter, her bone-white knuckles would turn to silver steel.

In his opinion the only insanity was the way she was acting, as if she were the only one with a right to anger. ''I said I'd take care of you, and I will.''

''It's not me I'm worried about,'' she went on. ''I have a son, remember? Robbie will be coming home from day camp soon, and I'm gonna greet him with the news that I went and married a stranger. And if that's not enough to rock his sense of security, I have to admit that I haven't the slightest idea where we and this stranger are going to eat, drink or sleep.''

''The 'stranger' has an apartment over on Elm Street,'' Luke told her angrily. ''Contrary to popular opinion, I'm not completely irresponsible. Granted, my place is a bit sparse on furnishings—needs a woman's touch maybe—but it will do until I can find us a house.''

''I thought you were going to get me my farmhouse back.''

She put the words out there like an accusation. And perhaps she was justified in this, since he'd momentarily forgotten his promise, but he was no less angry at her for pointing it out. ''Until we get the farmhouse, then,'' he said through gritted teeth.

''No.''

Startled by her adamant tone, he glanced over at her. She'd relinquished the grip on the handle and now clasped her arms across her chest instead. ''No, what?''

"No bachelor apartment," she said with a steely edge to her tone. "Robbie and I have a place over on Park Street. The two bedrooms may be small and a far cry from what you're used to, but my boy has already lost one home. I'm not going to make him give up another. The only disruption he's going to face is our move back to the farmhouse."

"Okay. But if there are only two bedrooms, where the heck am I supposed to sleep?"

"The couch. You said yourself you have a lot of business trips planned. You'll be out of town as much as you're in it for the next few months."

Maybe he shouldn't have confided his plans to sell his restaurant in New York and open a new one in New Orleans. "Fine," he told her, not really caring where they stayed. "The couch it is, then. You do intend to allow me a pillow?"

She ignored his sarcasm. "You're headed the wrong way for my apartment," she said, gesturing ahead. "You need to take the next right."

When he drove past the street she'd suggested, she turned to face him with a huff. "Are you ignoring me?"

"Not at all. We'll go to your apartment," he told her with forced patience. "After we're done talking to Ben."

"No!"

Who was this woman? The Callie he remembered had been soft and pliable, more than delighted to go along with all of his suggestions. This more recent version couldn't be more rigid, more combative and ready to fight him at every excuse. "That's the whole purpose of this exercise, isn't it?" he asked, not bothering to hide his exasperation. "Throwing the fait accompli in his face?"

"I meant not yet." She softened her tone. "Robbie

will be coming home soon, expecting me to be there. He's going to be confused enough by the situation. He'll need time to adjust before we subject him to anything more. I certainly don't want him coping with any nonsense from Ben Parker.''

She said the words firmly, but Luke could hear the plea behind them. He turned to glance at her, unsettled to find her studying him. He'd forgotten how deeply that gaze of hers could probe, how it could wriggle all the way in to stir up his conscience. How could he object? was her obvious message. All she wanted was to protect her son.

A perfectly laudable objective. As long as the one she was protecting him from wasn't himself, the boy's rightful father.

She didn't know—nor was he going to tell her just yet—about his little heart-to-heart with her ex-husband.

To say that Luke had been at loose ends that day was an understatement. Having been cut from the team, he'd learned how shallow and temporary his lifestyle in New York had been, how quickly he could lose so much more than a mere job. In what seemed like overnight, he'd gone from superstar to pariah, condemned by the media who once called him their darling, deserted by people he'd thought were friends. Going to New Orleans to lick his wounds, he'd plopped down on a bar stool planning to drown his sorrows. Trust Reb Jenkins to show up at his darkest moment.

Reb had heard all about Luke's meteoric fall from grace. The media hadn't been kind, and anybody who even casually followed sports knew the story, but Reb, who hung on to their boyhood rivalry the way old women cling to the family album, had savored the tale more than most.

''Maybe you got the scholarship and life in the big

leagues,'' he'd gloated, his whiskey-soaked voice slur-
ring over the words, ''but look where it got you.''

It was then that Luke learned how Callie had married
him so soon after Luke left town. Two shots later and
increasingly belligerent, Reb began to gripe about his
marriage, how and when it had all gone sour. ''A bun
in the oven,'' Reb had grumbled more to his shot glass
than to anyone in the room. ''Do the arithmetic, and
it's as clear as air someone got there before me.''

I am that someone, Luke had realized instantly. Even
without doing the arithmetic, he knew Callie, knew she
hadn't been with anyone else.

Reb might have ranted on, but all Luke heard,
thought or felt were the ramifications of Reb's pronouncement. He had a kid out there, a kid who didn't
know he existed, an innocent left to believe his dad was
this hopeless drunk on the bar stool beside him.

Filled with a rage he never could have imagined, he'd
left the bar to roam the street for hours. All too well he
could picture Callie's face the day he'd left her. She
must have known, even then. And still she'd said nothing.

The more he'd thought about it, the more it had fueled his anger. Knowing Callie, she probably felt she
was protecting the kid. All well and good if she'd given
him the chance to sink or swim, but she'd taken the
decision right out of his hands. Now, none of them
would ever know what Luke might have done with the
knowledge. And the one who would suffer most for this
was their innocent son.

So don't talk to him about protecting Robbie.

He took a long moment to swallow his resentment,
aware that he would do far more harm than good by
giving vent to his anger at this particular moment. Taking the next right, he headed to her apartment, willing

to give the inch if it eventually got him the mile. He was by nature the impatient sort, the kind who preferred to have things out in the open, but Callie was nothing if not stubborn, and she'd clung too long to her secret to give it up to the man she felt had abandoned her. Nothing would be gained by forcing her to tell the truth. She had to tell him of her own free will for there to be any real hope for the future.

"Fine, no visit to Ben today," he told her, trying to keep his tone light. He didn't really care about facing down his father, anyway. It was just an excuse, the only one he could think of to coax Callie into marrying him. Just for the record, she wasn't the only one interested in protecting their boy.

"Doesn't it bother you?" She was still staring at him, a slight frown creasing her face. "Our situation, that ceremony? I mean, Mr. Fry and those ladies seemed so tickled to death for us. But it was just a lie and we kept it going."

It was one thing to cultivate patience, but he didn't like being called a liar. "Our marriage is the means to an end," he said curtly, unable to keep the irritation from his tone. "That's all there is to it."

"But it feels wrong to me. Play-acting about love is like…like we're playing with fate. Gramps always said love was a gift that should never be taken lightly."

"I thought you wanted a marriage of convenience. If we're going to make it one of those arranged contracts, like between royal families, love needn't enter into it at all."

"I know. It's just…" She frowned, as if she were groping for the right words and couldn't quite find them. "I saw how it was with my grandparents…and my folks before they died. They meant everything to each other. Just watching them together made you smile, made you want to be like them. That's what I want someday, Luke. Not this…this travesty we call a marriage.''

Barely an hour into married life and already she was looking for the exit?

Pulling to a stop in front of her apartment, he told himself it shouldn't come as a surprise. In his experience it was always this way. Maybe others could find real and enduring emotion, but all his relationships inevitably flat-lined somewhere along the way. Sooner or later the woman admitted that what she'd thought was love actually wasn't.

Even Callie.

Not that he had let it deter him. He'd come back to Latour for his boy, and he wasn't about to let any misconceived notions about love—or the lack thereof—stand in his way. "We made a bargain," he said, turning to face Callie. "Are you going to keep your end of it, or what?"

She blinked, as if startled by the question. "Yes. For the one year I promised."

"That's that, then," he told her. And in his mind, it was.

Getting out of Luke's car, Callie didn't feel nearly as settled. Ever since Luke had kissed her, her mind had been whirling out of control. It had been a mere peck, over before it had begun, but the man's lips had lost none of their power. Even now she could feel the old longing, the same bittersweet acknowledgment of what could never be. Dangerous, that's how she'd always described Luke Parker. Looked as if she would have to be twice as careful, twice as wary.

She risked a glance at him as they entered the run-down three story building, catching his ill-concealed look of dismay. Climbing the rickety stairs, noticing its threadbare carpet, she viewed her current home through his eyes. He was a Parker, accustomed to the very best money could buy; he couldn't possibly enjoy learning, firsthand, how the other half-existed.

And he'd be even worse inside the apartment. Her nicked and battered furniture, the little messes left behind by the rush to get Robbie to school on time, the overall shabbiness of the place—what a sharp contrast to the slick and glittering world Luke normally strolled though. He'd take one look at the place and want to make changes. The next thing she knew he'd be sweeping her and Robbie into the pampered life he took for granted.

No, she wouldn't let that happen, she thought, as she led Luke to apartment 2B. She liked her world the way it was and what was more important, so did Robbie. Okay, maybe this hall was a little dingy, but she had neighbors who watched out for her and her boy—good, honest, caring people who stuck around through thick and thin.

She stopped before her door, suddenly realizing that those same good people would wonder about this stranger she'd unexpectedly brought into their midst. Gramps had constantly warned of the many ripples you could cause with a single action. Marrying Luke, it now seemed, had been like setting off a tidal wave in the tiny pond that had once been her life.

"Maybe it's not such a good idea, your staying here," she said, thinking out loud as she glanced back at him. "Maybe you should stay at your place tonight. Or even a motel."

He reached down to take the key from her hand. "What is this, Cal? Cold feet?"

Actually, with her new husband now towering over

her, she felt the chill from head to toe. "Don't be ridiculous. I just thought that if we're going to do this thing, we should start it off right."

"Then in that case," he said, slipping the key in the lock and shoving open the door, "allow me." Giving her no chance to protest, he slipped one arm under her knees, the other under her back, and in one fluid motion swept her up against his chest.

"What on earth do you think you are doing?" she gasped.

"Starting out right. The groom is supposed to carry the bride over the threshold, I'm told."

"This is ridiculous, Lucky. You put me down, right this minute."

"It's Luke, not Lucky. Remember?"

Held captive in his arms, she could remember far too many things—the stolen moments, the hot, steamy nights they'd shared ten years ago. And as she gazed into his eyes and saw the sudden intensity there, she realized he was remembering, too.

She could feel the pull between them, as if some magnetic force urged their heads closer. Inches away from touching his lips, she heard footsteps through a haze, then the all too clear and startled, "Mom?"

"Ohmigod," she said, all but leaping out of Luke's grasp. "It's Robbie."

Chapter Five

Setting Callie on her feet in what felt like slow motion, Luke turned to face the boy. His sole reason for coming back home, his main motivation for marrying Callie, stared up at him with a nine-year-old's suspicion. Frowning, Robbie stepped protectively in front of his mother.

Something sharp and ugly jammed its way into Luke's chest.

Callie put her arms on the boy's shoulder. ''Robbie, this is Luke,'' she said slowly, as if feeling her way. ''Luke…Parker.''

Luke extended a hand in greeting, but Robbie had already turned away to go into the apartment. With a what-can-I-do shrug, Callie followed after him.

Luke let his hand drop to his side. He'd been picturing this moment for some time, but nothing in his imagination could have conjured up anything so awkward or unsettling. Clearly the boy didn't want him there. Robbie couldn't have made it any plainer.

Determined to change his son's mind, Luke followed them into the apartment. As he closed the door behind him, he heard Callie asking questions while Robbie chattered on about his day. Luke felt oddly uncomfortable, as if he were eavesdropping on a private conversation. Most parents did this after-school ritual every day, he realized. Callie and Robbie, all these years, sharing the little moments that added up to so much, little moments Luke himself had never known.

Robbie plopped his backpack on the dining table in the corner of the living room and began to unload it to show his mother his artwork. From a distance Luke hungrily watched his boy, taking in every detail—the tousled blond hair, the scraped elbows and grass-stained knees, the untied shoelaces. Luke knew a sudden strong urge to lean down and tie those scuffed sneakers, but knew his son wasn't ready for such a gesture. As hard as the concept might be to him, he would have to bide his time and patiently wait for the boy to adjust to having a stranger in the house before he could hope that Robbie would warm toward him.

Backing off, Luke surveyed his surroundings, feeling more than ever like an intruder. Between the dining set, the overstuffed sofa and two matching chairs, the various stands cluttered with knickknacks and the countless photos on the walls, Callie had crammed so much into such a confined space, he couldn't help feeling claustrophobic. And of course the place wouldn't have air-conditioning.

Crossing the room to open a window, he stopped before a row of photographs, his attention snagged by a photo of a young, pregnant Callie, her dark eyes wide with fear. Yet how serene she looked, how happy, in the next picture as she held her new baby in her arms.

It was all there on that wall—his son's life from the start of Callie's pregnancy to the present day, a freckled, happy nine-year-old in the shorts and long socks of a soccer player. Luke couldn't tear his gaze from that last picture. Callie's eyes might stare out at him from the photo, but it was Luke's own mouth grinning back at him.

He turned away, going to the window, swallowing the sudden tightness in his throat. Gazing at those snapshots brought into painful focus how much he'd missed by not being part of it. And how much he might have kept on missing had he not happened upon Reb Jenkins in that dreary French Quarter tavern.

He took a moment to lean on the sill, looking out at the park. Behind him, he could hear Robbie talking excitedly to his mother. Given the circumstances, Luke supposed he could grasp why someone like Callie would choose to exclude him. It still wasn't right, though, keeping the truth from the boy. Robbie shouldn't have to think his father was Reb, some no account bum who lit out when the going got tough. Nor should he ever have to believe his true father didn't want to acknowledge him. No one knew better how it felt to grow up unloved and unnoticed by your father, and Luke was determined not to pass that on to his own flesh and blood.

Yet Callie was nothing if not stubborn, and her pride would never let her son be raised as a Parker. Luke could stake his claim, and he'd no doubt win, but the battle between them would be an ugly one, and it would be poor Robbie who would come out the ultimate victim.

Hence, the wedding. A drastic step, but Luke could

see no other way to show Callie he was ready, willing
and able to be a good father to their boy. His plan was
to become such an integral part of his son's life that
Callie would have to see reason. Once she understood
all the good he could do for Robbie, she would admit,
both publicly and legally, that Luke was her son's father.

What Luke hadn't figured into the equation was Robbie's resistance. In his mind he'd envisioned the warm-
and-cuddly reunion of a television commercial, his son
more a concept than a person in his own right. Face-to-
face with him now, Luke realized Robbie was his
mother all over again. His wide, dark gaze was just as
all-knowing, just as wary and uncompromising. What
would it take, he wondered, to win over this child?

"Him?" Robbie said suddenly, drawing Luke out of
his thoughts. Whirling, he found the boy pointing an
accusing finger in his direction. "*He's* gonna stay
here?" Robbie added, his face a picture of shocked
disbelief.

"I told you," Callie said patiently, tucking a stray
lock behind the boy's ear. "Luke and I are now married.
Of course he'll stay with us."

"But Mom, he's a *Parker*." He said the name as if
it were linked to a serial killer.

"Yeah, honey, and by marrying Luke, I'm now one,
too."

The boy frowned; the thought obviously hadn't occurred to him. "But, Mom, Gramps said the only good
Parker is a—"

"Never you mind," Callie interrupted firmly.
"Gramps had a lot of colorful opinions but we needn't
take them all at face value. Do yourself a favor. Get to
know Luke and then form your own opinions." Her
gaze slid between them, growing stern as it focused

again on her son. "Even Gramps would expect no less from you."

Robbie looked at Luke as if he were a glass of curdled milk. "If you say so."

"I do. Most folks have something to offer, if you give them half a chance. For example, did you know Luke was once a professional quarterback? He played in the Pro Bowl eight of his ten seasons in New York."

He was surprised she'd know that. As he recalled, football had been Callie's least favorite subject. "I still throw a mean lateral," he told the boy. "If you want, maybe you and I could toss a ball around. I could show you some tricks of the trade."

Robbie's eyes widened before he turned, almost guiltily, to his mother. "Mom doesn't want me playing football. She says it's too dangerous."

"Dangerous? Heck, a boy's got to be a boy."

The comment earned him the tiniest grin from Robbie, but Luke got nothing but glares from his mother. "Luke seems to be forgetting his injury," Callie said tightly, placing a proprietary hand on the boy's shoulder. "The one that ended his career."

He backed off, knowing it was too early in the game to be challenging her as to how their child should be raised. Besides, she had a valid point. It made him sick, thinking of his boy laid out on a stretcher, going through the operations and rehabilitation he had endured. "Your mom's right," Luke conceded. "I nearly lost the use of my arm playing the game. But you know," he added on a sudden inspiration, "I used to play soccer, too. I had a coach who showed me all kinds of great tricks. I started out on the bench, but I soon got to play center because I could dribble right up to the goalie and snap the ball right past him."

"I never scored a goal last year."

Hearing the yearning in the boy's voice, Luke nodded behind him out the open window. "I can teach you a few things, I bet," he offered. "I noticed there's a park across the road. If you want, we can go over there and kick the ball around a bit."

"Yeah? You mean right now?"

And suddenly there it was, all the interest and animation he could have hoped for from his son.

Trust Callie to jump in between them. Taking Robbie by the shoulder, she pointed at the door to her right. "You know the rules, young man. No going outside to play until you finish your homework."

"Aw, Mom."

Luke's sentiments exactly.

"Never mind," Callie said sternly, looking over Robbie's shoulder to direct the message at Luke. "Our routine has been disrupted enough today. You have your chores and I have mine, and we'd both best get to them."

Luke knew a cue when he heard it. "Your mom's right. We can practice when you're finished. And maybe it won't be so hot outside then, so we can keep at it longer."

For an instant Luke thought he'd lost him, but with a reluctant grin and an "I'll hurry," Robbie raced to his bedroom.

Shaking her head, Callie turned to Luke. "Sorry about that. Robbie usually has better manners, but he and Gramps were real close. He's a little touchy whenever the Parker name is mentioned."

"A lot of that going around."

She eyed him sharply. "Yeah, well, you and I have a truce at the moment. As long as you keep to your promise to get back our farm." With a tight smile, she turned and marched into the kitchen.

Luke stared after her, annoyed that she would be so persistent. As if the most important issue between them was getting her house back. In his mind, four walls and a roof couldn't possibly compare to making sure their son had a mother *and* father.

"If you're looking for something to do," Callie called from the other room, "I could use some help getting supper."

Luke followed into the tiny kitchen, finding Callie piling vegetables on the narrow counter. "So soon?" he asked, accustomed to dining later in the evening. "When is it that you folks eat?"

"Gumbo takes a while," she said distractedly, pulling pots from a cabinet. "But by and large, we keep to farm hours. The others tend to eat early, too."

"Others?"

"Some of the older folk in the building can't be counted on to cook for themselves. Every now and then I make extras, to help carry them through the week."

She said it matter-of-factly, as if it were perfectly natural to worry about the welfare of strangers when she herself barely kept food on the table. "So what do you do?" he asked. "Feed the entire neighborhood?"

"Just Mrs. Boyle in 2C and old Henry down in 1A. And on gumbo night, we can generally count on Sam Wylie, the maintenance man, stopping by for a bowl or two."

"So you're running a soup kitchen. And any leftovers, I bet, go to the stray cats and dogs in the area."

"It's not a soup kitchen," she snapped. "Nobody here is looking for a free handout."

Ah, yes, the Magruder pride. How well he remembered her stiff-necked refusal to take anything that even remotely smacked of charity. "Really. Do any of these friends of yours chip in for expenses?"

She shrugged as she yanked open a drawer to pull out two knives. "Where I come from cash isn't the only way of doing business. I feed them and they make up for it by looking out for Robbie. Many a night I have to work late."

"Well, that's going to stop."

She whirled around to face him. "Let's get one thing clear. Our bargain doesn't give you leave to march in here and change how I do things. These folks are liable to starve if I don't cook for them. They've got no one else. So if you don't mind, move aside and let me start fixing supper." Face flushed and eyes flashing, she looked like a vengeful warrior brandishing her knives.

"Relax," he said, sliding one of them from her grasp. "I was talking about you quitting your job, not your habit of taking in strays."

"I'm not quitting my job, either." She reached out and snatched the knife back. "I told you that. All I changed with that ceremony is my name." She started chopping vegetables, so furiously it was a wonder she didn't slice off a finger. "And at the end of the year, I'll be changing even that back to what it was."

We'll see about that, Luke thought, reaching for his own knife and pile of vegetables. It went against the grain, but for the time being, he'd hold his peace and bide his time. Before the year was up, though, he'd draw his line in the sand. Robbie was his son, too, and he deserved to bear the name of Parker.

Working in awkward silence, he watched this woman who was his son's mother, bustling about her kitchen as she prepared enough gumbo to feed an army. He found himself comparing her to the women he'd dated in New York. She had none of their poise and polish yet somehow she seemed more worthy of his admiration. The others dallied with their charities, perhaps, but they'd never have involved themselves in something so hands-on and personal. He couldn't imagine a single one of his prior dates even knowing the people in their building, much less going out of the way to make sure they had proper nutrition.

Luke kept thinking about Callie, long after he left her kitchen. Taking Robbie outside for soccer practice, hearing the boy's polite *please and thank-you*s, Luke acknowledged she'd done a fine job with their boy. He'd always imagined the mother of his children to be much like his own mom, a perfumed cloud of cool elegance, innately prepared with the proper words and image for any occasion. Callie might speak like a hick, and wear cast-offs from bargain basements, but somehow or another, people gravitated in droves to the warmth with which she surrounded them.

He had further proof of this at dinner that night as each of her neighbors dropped by with wedding gifts. Luke's former acquaintances would have scoffed at the odd assortment of cheap little trinkets, but Callie reacted to each with genuine joy. Each visitor was urged to join them, plates were added, until they sat ten at a table for six.

Luke couldn't remember the last time he'd had a home-cooked meal, much less enjoyed a family sit-down dinner. As a youth, the other kids had envied his big house, the fancy cars and expensive clothing, but he'd always wondered what it would be like to be surrounded by the warmth and obvious caring he found at her table.

After the meal Sam Wylie regaled them with stories about their landlady, Mrs. Clarke, and her procession of seven husbands. He kept everyone in stitches, even Callie, and Luke couldn't help but respond to his son's infectious laughter. I could get used to this, Luke thought with surprise.

On the other side of the table, Callie caught Luke's contented expression. Watching him smile at her son, she knew a cold, sick dread. If Luke should ever guess the truth…

No, she told herself firmly. As long as she kept quiet and didn't admit anything, Luke couldn't do a thing.

So she kept a smile pasted on her face, not letting it slip even as one by one her guests drifted home. Soon it would be time for Robbie to go to bed, and then what would she say to this man who was now her husband?

Certainly not the truth.

Logically she understood that it was wrong to keep silent. Luke probably had a right to know and what was more important, so did Robbie. But in her heart, the place where she had to face life on an everyday basis, she couldn't bear the consequences of relieving her conscience. If it came down to a custody battle, she knew only too well that she hadn't the resources to ensure her victory. And since the Parkers had taken just about everything from her *except* her boy, she simply couldn't risk losing him, too.

Robbie was *her* son. She'd raised him, and she wasn't about to let all that Parker money screw him up.

Only here was Luke, so up close and personal, charming the socks off their son. She was beginning to suffer very strong, and very real, doubts that she could pull this off. How would she ever get through the next twelve months, living a lie, always fearing she might let something slip?

A little late to be thinking of that now, the voice of logic insisted. Not after living that same lie for the past ten years.

Glancing at Robbie, noticing his enthusiasm as he

described his practice session with Luke, she swallowed the tightness in her throat. Robbie was the issue here, she had to remember. Her personal fears and anxieties didn't matter. She'd do whatever it took, however it had to be done, if it meant protecting her son.

Suddenly restless, she stood up. "Look at how late it is," she said abruptly as she stacked the plates. "Robbie, you'd better go brush your teeth and hop into bed. I'll come tuck you in when I'm done with the dishes."

"Aw, Mom, it's too early to go to bed."

"Your mom's right," Luke said beside her. "You've had a long day. Run along to bed, and I'll help in the kitchen so she can get there that much sooner to tuck you in."

To Callie's surprise—and dismay—Robbie didn't argue with Luke. And to add to her consternation, Luke kept true to his word by standing up next to her and helping to clear the table.

"No, sit," she snapped, appalled at the thought of him joining her in that tiny kitchen. "Please," she added, trying for a more reasonable tone, "you're our guest."

Luke merely continued stacking dishes. "Actually, what I am is your husband. And after such an incredible feast, the least any husband can do is help to clean up."

She tried to protest, but he followed her into the kitchen, rolling up his sleeves and insisting in that butter-would-melt-in-his-mouth way of his that he'd dry the dishes while she washed them. Never had she been so conscious of how confined her kitchen was, or how close to the sink the dish drain sat. Standing shoulder to shoulder as they performed the domestic task together, they seemed more like a happily settled couple than the uninvolved groom and edgy bride they were in truth underneath.

"Not much of a honeymoon, is it?" Luke asked, again seeming to pick up on her thoughts as he reached for a glass and dried it.

"What do you expect?" Annoyed, she made great business out of rinsing a plate and setting it in the dish drain. "It isn't much of a marriage."

"Yeah." Going for the plate, he brushed against her arm, seeming completely unaware that he'd touched her. "Ever think that maybe you wouldn't feel like such a fraud if we'd made more of an occasion out of it?"

She gave him a disbelieving stare. "What do you suggest?" she heard herself asking sharply. "That we have music? French champagne? This is a business arrangement, remember."

He blinked, tilting his head to study her.

Realizing how harsh she must have sounded, she hastened to remind him—and herself—where her priorities lay. "I can't see any sense in making a big deal out of a date that won't ever be repeated. We might better start out the way we mean to go on."

"Doing dishes?"

"Among other things. I told you at the start, this marriage isn't about me, or even you. I'm only going through this for my boy."

He paused, dish in one hand, towel in the other as he studied her. "He's lucky to have you," he said at last, reaching for another plate. "Nice touch, giving him the extended family. Not many people can pull it off. My folks couldn't deal with even the three of us spending time together. I can't remember ever sitting down to a meal with my parents."

He got real busy with the plate, continuing to rub it long after it was dry. "C'mon," Callie said, realizing that it was now her, studying him. "All families eat together. At least once in a while."

He shook his head. "Not us. After Matt died, my parents pretty much gave up on the family thing. Life in the Parker household wasn't the same without him. He was...well, let's just say my big brother was a hard act to follow."

His tone was even, his face expressionless, but Callie nonetheless sensed the pain behind his words. She was reminded of her first view of Luke Parker, back when she'd started kindergarten. Flanked by her mom and dad, she'd assumed the other kids would also be accompanied by doting parents. Most were, but unlike the other third graders, Luke had stood by himself in the corner, completely alone, completely aloof. That was when she'd first started dreaming about him, she supposed. It had been a potent combination, his loneliness and proud determination not to show it.

As if he, too, was lost in thoughts of the past, Luke fell silent then, and she was content to let him. She might have probed once, being intensely curious about anything connected to Luke Parker. But he'd always been reluctant to talk about his brother, and only a fool would tread into personal matters now. Not when she had so much to hide.

She had 364 more days of this, she mustn't forget. Twelve months of living on the surface, keeping it cool and casual, and protecting her son from heartache.

Whatever she did, she mustn't let Luke get anywhere near her far-too-soft heart. That, she'd learned from experience, was the sure path to disaster.

Luke sensed the change in her and guessed at the reason, but he wasn't about to give in to her wishes so easily. For the time being he'd let her coast, get used to the idea of having him around. But the time would soon come when he would press his advantage.

With this in mind, he started out slowly, bit by bit involving himself in their daily routine over the next two weeks. He made certain he was home each day to help Robbie practice soccer and then help Callie feed the neighborhood. Wherever necessary, Luke filled in the blanks of their existence, paying bills, carpooling Robbie to school and watching the boy when his mother had to work. People back in New York would never recognize this domesticated version of "Lucky" Luke Parker, but helping his son do math homework filled Luke with a satisfaction he'd never before known in his life.

This was where he should be, what he was meant to be doing. Yet two weeks into the marriage, here he sat, late at night, alone on this uncomfortable sofa, not one step closer to convincing Callie.

He had to find a way. With Robbie's great-grandfather gone, it was painfully obvious that he was starved for male guidance, and who better to offer it than his rightful father? The boy needed him, but Callie stubbornly refused to acknowledge this, much less confess the truth to either of them. A proud and unyielding icicle, she had yet to thaw a drop.

She remained determined to call it quits at the end of the year. She kept a calendar in the kitchen, for crying out loud, on which she marked off the days with a bright red X. She treated their marriage like a prison sentence, or a time of penance, all the while doing everything in her power to keep her distance.

That was the problem, as far as Luke was concerned. All that distance. Callie had her issues, and maybe she even had a right to them, but she sure wasn't doing anyone any good by clinging to her pride so doggedly. Why, there had been a time...

As if it were yesterday, he could picture her in his

mind, smiling as she had the first time he'd noticed her, that long-ago day in the Thunderbird Diner. Home for his mother's funeral, he'd been in a miserable mood that day. Ten minutes in the house, and already Ben had been at him, badgering Luke about what he meant to do with his useless life now that he'd graduated from college.

Luke had been sitting there, still stinging from his father's tirade, when all at once there was Callie, stepping up to take his order, the light in her expression breezing through him like a gust of fresh air. The way she'd looked at him, as if he were worth far more than his father's assessment, had been a balm to his battered spirits.

And maybe that was what he now found so different about her, he suddenly realized. Her glorious smile was gone, at least where he was concerned. Nowadays, all he got from her was wariness and suspicion, if she let him see anything at all.

Annoyed by this, he rose from the couch to pace across the room. Eyeing the home-sewn curtains, the hand-painted lamp shade, all the homey, cozy touches she'd added to this shabby apartment, he knew she was still in there somewhere, the girl who offered warmth without weighing the consequences or worrying over what it might cost her. Her unstinting passion, that's what he'd found so appealing. He just had to find some way to bring the old Callie forward.

After all, she'd wanted him once. Surely if he handled this right, he could revive old feelings. The kiss in the clerk's office, the look in her eyes when he tried to carry her over the threshold—maybe she wasn't as immune to him as she wanted him to believe. After all, they were older now, mature adults capable of reaching out and attaining common ground. Besides, who said you had to be in love to know mutually satisfying passion? Physical release could be just the thing to relieve the tension between them.

All he had to do was stir up some memories and let nature take its course.

With a broadening smile, he decided he would begin his campaign tomorrow.

Chapter Six

Callie approached the Thunderbird Diner with a great deal of trepidation. She'd just enrolled in nursing school and her mood should have been a festive one, but she kept fretting about why Luke had chosen this, of all places, to celebrate. He couldn't know—she hoped—of the countless hours she'd spent here in the past watching him and his friends living the good life, taking their money and leisure for granted. Or the countless dreams she'd spun, wishing that just once she could be the girl seated beside Lucky Parker.

She'd been eighteen then, a kid with nothing but dreams to drive her, and she'd been dreaming about the Parker boy so long, it had become an aching, deep inside. It wasn't just his good looks that hooked her—though just glancing at him could set her heart aflutter. No, it was more the way he could be standing in the middle of a crowd and yet somehow not be part of it.

In her private fantasies, she'd always pictured herself filling up the emptiness that haunted him.

So she'd been no better than a sitting duck waiting for the shotgun blast of reality, the day he'd asked if he could drive her home. Oh, deep down she'd known that it wasn't Callianne Magruder he was after, and that Gramps would have a conniption fit if he learned she'd been "consorting" with a Parker, but there was Luke, looking lost and lonely, and she'd been hoping for this moment so long. How could she possibly consider refusing him?

Well, she couldn't, any more than she could have stopped herself jabbering her head off on the ride to the farm. Good old Lucky, ever charming, ever polite, asking all the right questions until it seemed the most natural thing in the world to be confiding her dreams for the future.

She'd had two major ambitions back then—one to become a nurse, and the other to be Mrs. Luke Parker. The first she had told him about; the second she'd kept to herself for the time being. She'd heard him insist that he only wanted friendship, but hers was the fervency of youth, the cocky, stubborn certainty that if she tried hard enough and put all her heart in it, she could one day make him love her.

More fool her.

Though she'd waited, hoping and praying every day for the following week, Lucky never called. Nor had he stopped by the Thunderbird Diner. Over and over, she'd replayed the afternoon in her mind, hating herself for not being able to shut up, for having cheap, unattractive clothing, for being born on the wrong side of town. But most of all, she'd despised herself for being such a hopeless dreamer. Anyone with half a brain would have known, going in, that she hadn't the means or know-how to attract a boy like Lucky Parker.

A fact brought home when five days later, getting off work, she'd seen him go into the movie theater with Amy Ann Masters, his rich, gorgeous girlfriend from high school.

Should have learned my lesson then, Callie thought as she yanked open the door to the diner. But no, she'd gone on to bigger and bigger self delusions. Some folks had to be hit on the head with a sledgehammer.

And here she was, entering round two, determined to prove that the last thing she needed was another bump on the head.

As if he'd been watching for her approach, Luke rose suddenly from the rear booth, flashing his full-voltage smile. She couldn't help it; her heart did a little flip-flop in her chest.

Stop that right now, she told herself sternly. The inexperience of youth was one thing but she had no such alibi as an adult.

"Congratulations," Luke said, stepping up to take her hands in his. "How does it feel to be a college student?"

Flustered by his touch—and proximity—she yanked her hand free. "Actually, it feels kind of strange," she said, moving over to slide into her side of the booth. "I guess I still can't believe it will happen."

Pretending that she hadn't just left him there with his hands extended, Luke slid into the bench opposite. "It will happen. I sent off the tuition check this morning."

She couldn't stop the frown. "It's just that I've been dreaming of this for so long, and dreams have a way of evaporating, you know?"

He nodded, as if he did indeed know, and for an instant he no longer seemed so much like the enemy.

"You're going to school," he told her, leaning over the table to get right there in her face. "You have my word on it."

"Okay." Against her will, her lips curved slightly upward.

"So," he said, leaning back. "Now can we celebrate?" Not waiting for an answer, he turned to gesture for the waitress. "Paula, help me out. We've got us a special occasion here. Do you think you could bring your chef's special dish and a bottle of your finest cola?"

The poor kid tried to explain that they didn't have a chef, much less a special, but before long she, too, fell victim to Luke's charm and was playing along. Callie, who'd forgotten how much fun he could be, found herself slowly unwinding enough to answer his friendly questions with more than mere monosyllables. After a time she even posed a few of her own. By the time Paula delivered their overcooked hamburgers and soggy fries, the conversation had veered into the years he'd been away.

She tried to keep things focused on his experiences in New York, but every now and then he'd slip in a question about her and Robbie. Though she didn't mind talking about the good times, every time the conversation strayed into darker, more personal areas, she steered it back to his days on the football field.

"I admit I was a bit of a playboy," he told her straight-faced as he signed the check for their lunch. "But it was expected of me. Part of the image, you know? The first year or so I suppose I liked being the media darling, but seeing your name in the papers gets old real fast. Especially when a lot of what was printed was outright distortion."

He looked so genuine as he said it, leaning over the

table to take her hands. Yet as much as Callie found herself wanting to unbend, she couldn't forget the past, no more than she could stop wondering if this, like everything else, was just a game to him.

That was the trouble with Luke in a nutshell. On or off the field, he played the angles, went with the percentages. Given their past history, was it any wonder that she could never quite tell when he was revealing how he truly felt and when he was just saying what he thought she wanted to hear?

Callie was spared making a comment when Paula came by to take the check, the girl pausing a few extra moments to flirt with Luke. Watching him, Callie decided he just couldn't help himself. The Parker charm was in his blood; it didn't matter if he cared about you or not, he had to exert it. She would be wise to keep that in mind each time he turned those baby-blues on her.

The instant Paula left, Callie made great business of glancing at her watch. "Will you look at the time?" she said as she slid out of the booth. "We've been sitting here chatting for almost two hours. I should head home." Leaving him no chance to protest, she marched to the door.

Battling confusion, Luke hurried out of the booth after her. For a moment he could have sworn he had the old Callie back. Talking about Robbie, she'd gone all soft and gentle, but then her gaze had suddenly turned wary, and there it was again—the wall of distrust and hostility standing firmly between them.

Not this time; he wasn't going to let her get off so easy. "This was fun," he told her, stepping up to open her door and help her into the car. "We should try it again some time."

"Hmm."

Hmm, indeed. Sliding into the driver's seat, he tried again. "I've got this trip to New York tomorrow, but when I get back…"

He let it dangle, leaving it a question she had to answer.

She took her time. "As I recall," she said at last, "entertaining me isn't part of our agreement."

She could have been colder, he supposed, but then she'd be frozen to the seat. "You make it sound as if taking you to lunch is some obligation on my part," he said, unable to keep the irritation out of his voice.

"Isn't it?"

"No, dammit, it isn't. I had fun. So did you. What's wrong with the two of us having a good time together?"

"Nothing's wrong." Her delivery of the words was quick and sharp, like sniper fire. "I just don't think it's wise to make a habit of it."

"Is that what you're afraid of? You think I'll become a habit?"

"Of course not," she said, but the fact that she wouldn't look at him implied otherwise. "Oh, Luke, let's face it. Living together for the next eleven months will be hard enough without adding complications. If you ask my opinion, I think we'd be smarter to avoid each other whenever possible."

"I see," he told her, but he didn't think it should be hard at all. *Especially* if they indulged in those complications. "What you're saying is we're supposed to live under the same roof, eat from the same table, but never cross over the line marked personal."

"Yes. That's what a marriage of convenience is."

She held up her chin, all prim and self-righteous. Clearly, this was going to be harder than he'd first thought. He would have to rethink his strategy, it would seem, something he'd have plenty of time for, in the two weeks he'd be in New York.

But before he left, though, he had something important to get out of the way. "As long as we're keeping to the letter of the law in our bargain," he said slowly, turning to face Callie with a solemn expression, "I need to ask you a favor."

"*Another* one?" She went stiff again, a North Atlantic iceberg parked in his BMW.

He swallowed, stifling the urge to snap back at her. "Actually, you could say it's all part of the same package. It's Ben—"

"It's getting late. I need to start thinking about dinner."

"The masses won't starve in the next hour." Realizing he'd let his annoyance show after all, Luke tried again, with a deliberately calmer tone. "This is important to me, Cal. I wouldn't ask if it wasn't."

"Hmm."

He was beginning to hate that sound. "Ben's been calling the office most every day, bugging me to come to work for him. I can't stand it anymore. If you come with me now, we can tell him we're married and get it over with." He didn't add that he was worried about her and Robbie, afraid his father might confront them while he was gone. "I want things settled before I leave for New York."

She took in a solid breath, as if needing the extra air to get through her speech. All she said, though, was, "Now?"

"Is there any real reason why not?"

She pursed her lips, stared out the side window. "I suppose there's no sense in putting it off," she said on a sigh, sounding as enthusiastic as if she were facing a double hip replacement. "Robbie is probably as adjusted as he's ever likely to get."

Before she could change her mind, Luke started up the car and put it in gear. "It'll only take a few minutes," he assured her. "We can just pop in, say our piece, and you'll never have to deal with him again."

She nodded with a weak smile that let Luke see how much she dreaded this.

"I imagine you'd rather be facing a root canal," he told her, "but trust me, I'm not all that ecstatic about it, either."

"But it's your father." She tilted her head, as if wondering what could possibly make him tick. "After all this time, he's bound to be happy to see you. And after ten years, at least some part of him must be looking forward to welcoming you home."

"You ever been to Ben's house?"

She shook her head. "We both know Ben Parker wouldn't let a Magruder anywhere near the place."

"You're right. Only the crème de la crème get invited inside his showplace. He had a writer from *Town and Country* once. 'Immaculate and impeccably furnished,' that's how he described it. He didn't mention that it was also a mausoleum, as cold as the stone it's built from. Trust me, you'll find little emotion inside those walls. No father-son camaraderie between me and Ben, no trust or loyalty, much less something as frivolous as a welcome. To that man I'm just another possession, one more trophy to hang upon his walls."

She frowned as though she thought he was exaggerating. As if anyone in his right mind would make something like that up.

"Let me do the talking," he said irritably as he headed to his father's house. "I know how to handle my father."

Callie sat on her side of the car, partly resenting his smug assessment, but equally happy getting out of having to talk to Ben Parker. Hating him as she did, she was liable to say something she'd regret.

Besides, she didn't really have to say a word. All she needed to do was stroll into that palatial estate on his son's arm, acting as if she owned it. That, coupled with Luke's announcement, should just about do the trick.

And a tiny part of her couldn't wait for the moment Ben realized a Magruder had married his son. Heaven knew, he deserved every last second of shock and horror the news would bring him. "Life holds some ugly truths," he'd pontificated at her the day she'd begged for Gramps to spend his last few days at home. "Zeke did the crime and now he'll do his time. Learn to live with it."

Remembering poor old Gramps, lying helpless and scared in the psychiatric hospital where Ben's vindictiveness had confined him, made her pretty darned eager to watch Ben face some "ugly truths" of his own.

Yet, ushered into the stuffy, ostentatious cavern Ben called his study, standing while he sat silent and judgmental at his desk, Callie found no surprise on his autocratic features, no shock at all about seeing her beside his son. From his trim white hair to his slick Italian loafers, Ben was a study of utter disdain.

He kept them waiting, frowning as if he were the principal and they, about-to-be-expelled students. "You've been busy," he said at last, sneering at his son, speaking as if Callie wasn't even in the room. "But then, so have I."

With the same cool contempt, he flung a stack of papers across the desk in front of Luke. "Read those. They should make my position plain."

In Luke's position, Callie would have been sputtering, but he eyed the papers with his own unique brand of distaste. "Let me guess," he said, making no attempt to pick them up. "You're cutting me out of the will."

Ben shifted slightly in the chair, but his cold, mocking smile never wavered. "You married beneath you. You can go to the hell of your own making if you're so determined, but I refuse to have my good name dragged through the mud by some money-grubbing wanna-be after my fortune."

"You don't say."

"I do." With cold, blue eyes locked on his son, Ben delivered his ultimatum. "Get rid of her. Or you stand to lose it all."

Luke leaned over the desk, facing his father with an eerily similar smile. "You don't get it, do you old man? Callie is my wife. Till death do us part. You can learn to accept and respect her, or you can keep your damned money and rot in hell with it."

Turning to grab Callie by the arm, Luke dragged her out of the room and out of the house, ignoring Ben's bellows that he get his ungrateful butt back in there.

"That went well, don't you think?" he said, once they were both settled in the car.

Appalled, Callie didn't know what to think. She couldn't imagine ever having had such a scene with her parents, but had it been possible, she certainly would have been too devastated to joke about it afterward. "It was awful," she sputtered. "Y-you can't leave it like this. You've got to go back in there and discuss things rationally."

"We both know there's no reasoning with that man."

"But he was serious, Luke. It wasn't a bluff. He really, truly means to cut you off."

Luke shrugged, looking back to the house. "Yeah? So what?"

"So what? He's your only remaining family. You can't just cut off all ties with your past. You're a Parker. What about your birthright?"

He looked at her then, his blue eyes electric, glittering with suppressed rage. "All my life that man has dangled his money in front of me, using it to bend me to his will. Well, let me tell you, I'm sick to death of it. I don't care if he offers a hundred times the fortune, Ben has no right to talk about you that way. Contrary to the world-according-to-Ben-Parker, there are some things more important than money."

Callie couldn't have spoken if she'd wanted to. All her life, she'd been waiting for someone to step up in her defense like that, and for it to be Luke Parker, after all these years, well, it near took her breath away. Not to mention her wits.

She had the sudden urge to reach out and stroke his arm. In her own small way, she wanted to comfort him, to give back a part of what he'd just given her. "Well, I sure don't care about his money," she finally said. "I say the heck with Ben Parker. Let him take it to his grave."

Luke just looked at her, long and hard, as if he could actually see inside her for the very first time. "You're something else, Cal. Where were you when I was growing up?"

"I've always been right here, Luke. Though I imagine it was hard to see me, way over there on the other side of the tracks."

With a rueful grin he started the car. "Maybe you haven't heard, but I'm living on your side of town myself these days."

"Only temporarily. Once we get back the farm…" It struck her, with sudden, painful clarity, that with Luke now estranged from his father, her chances of ever seeing her family home again had gone from poor to virtually none.

In her pause, Luke apparently saw it, too. Hitting the wheel with his hands, he told her he was sorry. "I got so angry at him, I didn't think about your property. I shouldn't have lost my temper like that, but at the time all I could think was that someone had to wipe the smirk off his face."

And wasn't that always the case—Luke Parker thinking of himself, first, last and foremost. "I'm glad you feel better now that you've vented your anger," she told him through gritted teeth. "I, of course, don't have that luxury. I have to figure out some way to tell my son he won't ever get his old bedroom back again."

"Dammit, Callie." Luke scowled as he jammed the car in gear and drove away. "I said I'd get that land back for you, and I will."

She started to call him on it but, really, what was the sense? In his mind, at this precise moment, Luke no doubt believed what he said. So had she, for an instant, but that was dangerous thinking. Hadn't she learned by now that if she wanted something done, she had to do it herself?

She would save up her own money with what she made at the beauty parlor. It should add up a lot faster now that Luke was paying the rent. When the time came, if Ben still hadn't mellowed, she could have someone else pretend to be buying the place. Old Henry, maybe, or Mrs. Boyle. Someone she knew she could trust.

Because that was the bottom line, wasn't it? Trust was what was needed here, and it was something she knew better than to give Luke.

Hugging her side of the car, she was grateful for the

silence that sprang up between them. Distance, that's what she needed, not all these reminders of the past.

All things considered, she thought it a good thing that Luke would be gone for the next two weeks.

Chapter Seven

Barely a week later Callie sat on the empty sofa in her empty apartment, wondering why she'd wandered out here in the middle of the night. It wasn't the heat—though Lord knew it had certainly been oppressive this August—and she hadn't been disturbed by any unusual sound.

Something felt off—out of kilter. Something, somewhere, was missing.

For some reason, her gaze focused on the football sitting by itself on the center shelf of her bookcase, bathed by a swath of light from the streetlamp outside the window. Half-aware that she was doing so, she rose from the couch and approached the football, with its frayed laces and scuffed surface. Luke had asked if he could put it there, saying it was from his brother. She'd thought at the time that it was unlike him to be so sentimental. After the things he'd said, that long-ago day at the cemetery, she wouldn't think he'd be the type to carry around a memento wherever he went.

Reaching out, she touched the football, seeing Luke as he'd been that day at the cemetery, tall and strong and handsome, golden hair rippling in the gentle breeze. It was a week after he'd driven her home from the diner, and she'd just about made peace with the fact that she'd never talk with him again. She'd been tending the family graves—a monthly ritual she practiced to this day—and was tugging at weeds when she glanced up. There she'd been, struggling to speak, to think, even to breathe while Luke stared down at her, the conquering hero in his lettered varsity jacket. When she finally summoned the wits to ask what he was doing, he'd said curtly that he was there to say goodbye to his mother.

"You're going away?" was all she could utter, betraying what of course was her greatest fear at that moment.

"Not much to keep me here," he said, removing his jacket to sling it over his broad shoulders. "But that's not what I meant. I'm saying goodbye because she's dead. Adios. It's over. Time to move on."

Callie, who spent every fourth Sunday making certain this last link with her loved ones was *not* severed, thought it the coldest thing she'd ever heard. "But you just buried her," she protested. "It must be the shock talking. You'll see, Luke. You can try to move on, but in here," she added, gesturing at her heart, "surely you'll always miss her."

He stared at her, his face devoid of all emotion. "I doubt it. My mother was gone long before she ever got cancer."

Callie didn't know what to say to that. Rising to her feet, wiping her muddy hands on her jeans, she stood helplessly by, watching as Luke stared off into space.

Then all of a sudden he shrugged as if shaking free of his inner demons. "Didn't mean to be morbid," he said, looking down at the pansies she was about to plant. "Looks like you have enough to deal with. This for your folks?"

Something hard and tight caught in her throat. "My whole family. My folks, sister and little baby brother."

"Jeez, Callie, that must have been tough." He focused on her, his gaze softening.

"Yeah." She still found it hard to talk about, but in the face of his compassion, it felt wrong, leaving it like that. "We were coming home from a vacation in Florida," she explained, "and Dad was too tired to be driving. I don't think he even saw the truck until it was too late. My sister and I survived the crash, but Bobby and my folks didn't make it. Saralynn died of complications a week later." Even after eight years, talking about the accident still made her voice quiver. "I think about them every day, though. I can't imagine saying goodbye to them forever. They're too much a part of me, of my memories, who I am."

He nodded as if he understood, but his next words left her wondering if he ever could. "You ever get blamed for surviving, Cal? Ever blame yourself?"

"Jeez, no," she blurted out before reconsidering. "Maybe at first I felt a bit guilty, but Gramps won't allow it. He says that my parents lived their lives for me, and it would break their hearts to see me moping around. People die, Gramps insists, and there's nothing we can do to stop it. He told me to concentrate on living the best life I can."

"And have you?" He stared at her, as if her answer were truly important.

"I try."

"I bet you do." He sighed. "But then, you're one of a kind, Callianne Magruder."

"Is that a good thing or bad?"

His lips curved slightly, as he was trying to grin, but couldn't quite get his heart into it. "Good, definitely on the plus side. Indeed, if I were even half as decent, I'd say goodbye now and walk away from you."

Heart completely stopped, she struggled to find her voice for her next question. "But you're not going to, are you?"

He studied her face for another long moment. "I'm not a stay-at-home kind of guy, Callie. I'm your proverbial rolling stone, gathering no moss. The minute I get a pro contract, I'll be taking off and not looking back."

Callie could remember blushing from head to toe, embarrassed that he'd read her hopes so accurately. She could remember a great many things about that moment—the clean, fresh scent of newly turned earth, the warm breeze stirring about them, the lure of his lips hovering so close above hers. What she failed to recall was his warning.

She'd been quite adept at hearing only what she wanted to hear in those days, she thought as she lifted up the football. But then, Luke had made it easy. He hadn't said goodbye that day, hadn't walked off as he'd threatened. Instead, tossing his jacket to the ground, he'd rolled up his sleeves and taken the trowel from her hands. He'd stayed to help her, and he'd asked her to meet him after work the next day.

Staring at the football in her hands, Callie realized he was doing it again, getting right there in her face and clouding her judgment. With the slightest of shudders, she set the ball back on the shelf and backed away from it. Two short weeks Luke had lived here, and yet after only five days his absence was so noticeable he could have been sleeping in the apartment for years. Even Old Henry had been asking just this morning when the "Mr." was coming home.

Luke had a way of filling up a place, she should have remembered, and leaving a vacuum when he was gone.

The realization struck her in a cold, rippling wave. *Luke* was what was missing, what her insomnia was about. Could she truly be foolish enough to be losing sleep over a man like that again?

She glanced back at her bedroom door, remembering her twisted sheets and blankets. Embarrassed, she switched her gaze back to the living room, but it fell instantly on the football. Pacing anxiously about the room, she tried to find any other reason for her restlessness, but marrying Luke had dealt with most of her money worries, and her son was doing just fine. The only problem with Robbie, at the moment, was his daily nagging about when she thought Luke would come home.

Luke, Luke, Luke. Was there nothing left in her life where his name didn't enter into it?

She came to an abrupt halt in front of the couch. A slow flush rose to her cheeks as she remembered a similar sleepless night, last week when Luke had still been here. Stumbling past the couch on the way to the kitchen for a late-night glass of water, she'd been made vividly aware of the fact that her new husband didn't sleep in pajamas.

The sight of him sprawled out on her couch, clad only in his shorts, had stopped her dead in her tracks. Whatever other complaints she could lodge against him, she'd never claimed he was any less than a magnificent male specimen, and there he lay, all six foot two of hardened muscle, sleeping like a babe. While Callie had retreated to her room to toss and turn until morning.

So it wasn't just the man himself that was keeping her up, she thought, not at all pleased with the observation. She appeared to have a good, old-fashioned case of lust. After all this time, with all she'd been through, she could have hoped she'd be immune by now. At the very least she should be able to control her physical yearnings.

I can handle this, she told herself firmly, moving away from the couch to prowl across her living room. If indeed she was having problems with her libido, she'd take care of it the same way she'd dealt with every other hardship that came her way. Calmly, methodically. Using her brain instead of her emotions.

Logically she couldn't blame a piece of furniture. It wasn't the couch's fault that Luke slept here where she could happen upon him most any night. Of course, she could stay in her bedroom until morning, but then she'd be a prisoner for the next eleven months, and that would make this a marriage of major *in*convenience.

Luke couldn't be happy about having to sleep here either, she told herself. The chipped dropleaf table, the battered brass lamp, all the little knickknacks she'd brought from the farmhouse—these things might be valued mementos to her, but raised in the pristine, picture-perfect Parker house, Luke must feel hemmed in by what he must consider sentimental trash. It was a wonder he even got to sleep at night.

It didn't help at all to picture him tossing and turning here, while she did the same in her bed.

Shutting off such thoughts, she told herself that he simply couldn't continue to sleep on the sofa. The man was their guest, and they owed him a decent night's rest.

Even as she made the rationalization, an idea began to form, gathering steam. Her grandfather's bed was gathering dust in the storage room. How hard would it be to lug it up from the basement and move Robbie's belongings to her room? Then she could offer the smaller bedroom to Luke, thereby getting him off this couch.

Excited about the prospect, she was ready to tackle the job at once, until she realized it was three in the morning and Robbie was fast asleep in the room she wanted to dismantle. No matter. She didn't have to work tomorrow; she could tackle it then. First thing in the morning, she vowed as she slipped back into bed, she'd get Luke out of her living room—and out of her thoughts.

The next afternoon, surveying the new bedroom, she admitted that the project had been harder than she'd originally envisioned. The iron bed frame proved quite heavy, the mattress unwieldy, and it had taken several hours to clear out Robbie's clutter.

Still, she was pleased with the results. Digging into the cedar chest filled with her grandfather's belongings, she'd found the navy-blue bedspread and drapes to give the room a more masculine feel. Her own had been stripped of all femininity, giving way to Robbie's things, the *Star Wars* posters and sports equipment. A small price to pay, she felt, for peace of mind.

"You gotta be kidding," Robbie suddenly sputtered behind her, arriving home a good ten minutes early. "You moved my things in here with you? How could you?"

"Quite easily. I just picked them up and carried them here."

Normally, this would have teased a grin, but Robbie

was clearly too upset for any attempt at humor. "I'm nine years old, Mom," he protested indignantly. "Too big to be sharing a room with my mother." He made the title sound like a four-letter word.

Callie tried to pretend that it didn't matter that she'd spent all day changing her room to make it more appealing to him. "I know it's not the ideal situation, but we need to be fair. We can't make Luke sleep on the couch."

He gave a look that said, *what do you mean, we?* "Then let him sleep with you," he insisted. "Jason's mom and dad sleep in the same room. He says that's the way it's supposed to be with married people."

Great. So Robbie was discussing her marriage with his buddies at school. "Luke and I aren't like other couples," she tried to explain, carefully picking her way through what felt like a mine field. "We're sort of taking our time, feeling our way."

Even to her own ears the excuse sounded lame, but Robbie was too concerned with his own situation to care. "It's not fair, Mom. I don't want to be in your room. Jason's gonna tease me. He'll say I'm having nightmares, or wetting the bed, or even something worse. Before I know it, the other kids will be calling me a big baby."

Callie began to regret ever starting this. "Robbie—"

"Why do I have to move?" He didn't put the emphasis on the word *I* but on *move*. "Why can't I stay with Luke in my room?"

"I can't let—"

"We can talk, every night," he went on, gathering steam. "And when he isn't too busy with his own stuff, he can help me with my homework."

"I can talk to you." She tried unsuccessfully to keep

the pleading note out of her tone. "I can help with your homework."

"Yeah, but he's a guy."

Bald and honest, the truth of that statement pierced her heart. No matter how hard she tried, there were some things even the most loving mother could never provide. Boys needed a man to talk to, and ever since Gramps died, Robbie had been searching for a replacement. Along came Luke, with his football stories and boyish charm, and was it any wonder Robbie thought he'd found the male role model he'd been missing?

But does it have to be Luke? she thought. She didn't want her son experiencing even a fraction of the pain she'd known when that man walked out on her.

"You have to understand," she told Robbie, trying to find a way to cause him the least hurt. "Luke isn't used to sharing a room. He's always had his privacy."

"So have I, but I don't mind sharing. He might not, either. Can't we at least ask?"

"Robbie…"

Again he ignored her. "Tonight, when you talk to him, just ask what he thinks. I bet you anything he'll say it's a great idea."

He would, too. That was Luke. He liked sweeping in and playing the hero. The trouble was, he rarely stuck around when things got too hard to handle.

"Don't depend on Luke for too much," she warned. "He's a great guy, I know, but he's not all that reliable. All his life he's never had to worry about anyone but himself."

Robbie tilted his head, eyeing her with suspicion. "If you don't like him so much, why did you marry him?"

"I do like Luke," she started to protest, tempted to brush off the question, but her son's shrewd gaze told her he wasn't buying any of it. "Luke and I didn't get married because we're in love,'' she said on a sigh, reaching over to put an arm around his shoulder. "He's trying to make up for what his dad did to Gramps. We never meant our marriage to be permanent. Just long enough so you and I can get on our feet financially.''

She expected to see his disappointment or shock, perhaps even disapproval, but Robbie merely nodded and took the news in stride. "Okay, so what's the big deal then?'' he asked with a nine-year-old's practicality. "Why can't he stay in my room?''

Why, indeed? "It's not really my decision to make,'' she said, temporizing, wondering how to tell him that people were not always what they seemed.

He pulled away, clearly not pleased with her. "Then you'll ask him? You'll let him decide?''

Busy formulating excuses, Callie nearly jumped when the phone rang behind her. "That's probably Jason, asking me to spend tomorrow night at his house,'' Robbie said as he raced to answer it. "Can I?''

"Robbie, we're not done talking—''

"Aw, Mom, you gonna say yes or what?''

Clearly, he'd moved on to the next topic. Callie found it somewhat reassuring that sharing a room with Luke was no longer as important to Robbie as being able to spend the night at a friend's house. Perhaps she'd made too much of his protest, projecting her own feelings and fears onto her son.

Moving to the phone, she decided she would let him stay at Jason's, provided she talked with his mother first.

Robbie was chattering on as she held out her hand to take the receiver. His sudden animation should have clued her in, but it wasn't until she heard him mention his bedroom that she realized he wasn't talking to Jason.

Inside, she went cold, then hot. She couldn't tell

which emotion had the upper hand—surprise, dismay or excitement. When Robbie finally handed her the phone, all she knew for certain was that she wasn't ready to deal with Luke Parker.

"Sounds like you've got your hands full," Luke said. "I gather there's some disagreement about where I should sleep?"

Over the phone his voice seemed twice as deep, and unbelievably sexy. Her treacherous heart skipped a beat when she heard it.

"You shouldn't have to sleep on that awful sofa," she stated baldly. "I tried to solve the problem by putting you in Robbie's room and him in mine, but apparently, sharing a room with me makes him a baby."

Robbie flashed her a look before announcing that he was going to *his* room to do his homework.

"He's going through a period of transition, Cal. Rob is—"

"Since when do you call him Rob?" Callie interrupted, her maternal antennae up and running.

"Since he asked me to." She could hear the tension in Luke's voice, as if he had to work hard not to snap back at her. "It's perfectly natural for the kid to want to be thought of as a young man, to separate himself from anything that makes him feel like an infant."

Even his mother? Callie thought, going stiff inside. "And since when have you become such an expert on *my* son?"

She heard silence on the other end, though the strain of Luke's struggle for patience was nearly audible. "I might have been a business major, but I took psych in college," he said at last, exasperation creeping into his tone. "All kids go through this. It's part of the maturation process. Make an issue of it and you'll only alienate him further."

Though his words made sense, she resisted them emotionally. How could she possibly call her boy Rob? She cradled him in her arms, nursed him at her breasts. In her mind, in her heart, he would always be Robbie.

"Do we really have to argue long-distance, Cal?" She heard a new note in Luke's voice. Not quite pleading, but she sensed a certain weariness, perhaps even concession.

"I'll raise my boy as I see fit, Luke," she felt compelled to say, anyway.

"I know you will." His was a statement of fact, not words of understanding. "As far as the room, do whatever's easiest for you," he added, again betraying exasperation. "I'll survive on the couch if you don't want me bunking with Rob. Whatever you decide is fine by me."

"We should wait and discuss this when you get home," she offered, not wanting to sound like the rat in the piece.

"Okay. If you come pick me up at the airport, we can talk about it on the ride home. Which, by the way, will be tomorrow evening."

"Tomorrow?" She couldn't keep the alarm from her tone. "I thought you said you'd be gone for two weeks."

"Disappointed?"

"No, of course not," she told him quickly. She wasn't disappointed, exactly, but she couldn't deny the frisson of alarm. One more day and Luke would be back in her tiny apartment, towering over her, addling her wits with his overwhelming presence.

No, she definitely *wasn't* ready for Luke Parker. "I had the impression you had a lot to do there."

"Things wrapped up sooner than expected. I sold the

restaurant. I'm meeting the buyer soon to iron out the final details.''

''Congratulations.'' Even she could hear how flat that sounded. The truth was, she wasn't sure she was happy about the news. With nothing to tie him to New York, Luke would be around that much more.

''About tomorrow night. We don't need to hurry home, do we?'' he asked, cutting into her thoughts to offer a reprieve of sorts. ''Rob mentioned that he'll be sleeping at Jason's. Why don't you and I go out to dinner?''

''Dinner?'' she repeated, taken by surprise.

''You know, the last meal of the day? After all the cooking you've done for me, the least I can offer is a night where someone else cooks for you.''

Callie couldn't remember the last time she'd been taken somewhere for dinner. Reb hated going out anywhere, and after the divorce she'd been too busy with Robbie, Gramps and earning a living to indulge in anything as frivolous as dating.

''I have to work tomorrow,'' she told him, hoping that would be the end of it.

Not with Luke. ''My flight doesn't get in until after seven. You're not working overtime, are you?''

''No, but—''

''Wear something special,'' he went on in his coaxing tone, giving her no chance to argue. ''Let's make a night of it, dinner and dancing, the works. It's not like we have any real reason to rush back to the apartment.''

He had her there. When she stopped to think about it, she realized it might be better to spend the night out in public than alone here with Luke. What would she do with all those vast, yawning silences—or worse, quiet intimacies—that sprang up when two people shared the same roof?

Besides, she wasn't completely opposed to the idea. It might be fun to get out, dress up nice, be somebody other than Robbie's mother for a change. "I suppose I—"

"Come pick me up at the airport, and we can go from there." He gave her his flight time and number, once again talking past any opportunity for her to object. "I'm looking forward to it," he added. "It's funny. Here, I'm surrounded by faces and places, but still, I've been darned lonely. I miss you guys."

Callie was stunned speechless. Careless words, the sort of thing Luke could declare without meaning any of it. But the way his voice caught at the end, she thought she heard real emotion behind the admission. Especially when he hastily tried to gloss over it. "Jeez, look at the time," he said in almost the same breath. "I've got ten minutes to get to my meeting. Gotta run, but I'll see you tomorrow at the airport, right?"

"I guess so."

If he heard her reluctance, he chose to ignore it. "Great. See you then," he said before severing the connection.

Staring at the receiver as she slowly set it back in its cradle, Callie was left wondering if she'd merely imagined the "I miss you guys." Typical Luke, sandwiching the emotion in between his need to celebrate, and the "Gee, can you pick me up?"

Not that that mattered. Moving away from the phone, she reminded herself that all she'd agreed to was a night out with the man. It wasn't a date, or anything special. They'd be sharing a meal, and that was that.

Alone in his hotel room, Luke frowned at the phone, wishing he hadn't had to break the connection. Hearing Rob's voice, then Callie's, had brought into focus how

lonely he'd felt here in New York. Still, he couldn't
believe he'd told her he missed them.

He had no meeting to go to; the details had been set
that afternoon, and all he had to do was sign on the
dotted line tomorrow. No, he'd made a spur-of-the-
moment excuse to get Callie off the phone and thinking
of something else.

He'd made a mistake, broken the rule about stepping
over into the personal. All too easily he could picture
her face as he'd said it, going all skittish and wary as
she searched for the nearest place to hide from him.
Okay, so maybe she felt justified in keeping Luke at
arm's distance, but Luke would be damned before he'd
let her take their boy into hiding with her.

Her son, she'd said, as if Luke had absolutely no say
in it.

He'd almost lost it then. Only the force of sheer will-
power had kept him from blurting out his claim, but
once his anger cooled and sanity prevailed, he'd recognized how such an impulsive act would get him nowhere. With the miracles of modern science, he could
stake a legal claim on his son whenever he wanted, but
not without destroying the fragile remnants of his relationship with Callie. And two separate parents—with
two distant households—was not what he wanted for
his son.

He'd already decided that divided custody would
only make everyone miserable. Luke's own parents had
never divorced, but they might as well have, with his
mom keeping to her side of the house, with Ben, on the
rare occasions he was home, keeping to his. Growing
up, stuck somewhere between them, Luke knew first-
hand what part-time parenting could do to a kid. Rob
deserved a father who would be there for him one hun-

dred percent, not some stranger who seemed bent on taking him away from his mother.

So Luke had come to the conclusion that the best solution for them all—the only solution—was for him and Callie to *stay* married. And all that remained was to convince Callie of this.

Hence, his plans for tomorrow night.

Surely it was more than a stroke of luck that Rob would be gone for the night. Luke preferred to think of it as a sign, a nod from the powers-that-be giving him the go-ahead. Still, either way, he'd be a fool not to take advantage of the openings life offered him.

Inhaling deeply, he settled back on the bed to stare up at the ceiling. He might have carefully omitted certain details about their date, but he'd been straight up about one thing. Oddly enough, he *had* missed her.

Odder still, he couldn't wait for tomorrow.

Chapter Eight

Straightening his tie as he made his way down the aisle of the plane, Luke realized he was nervous. He certainly had a great deal to accomplish. Somehow, he had to remind Callie how good it had once been between them—certainly too good to continue sleeping apart. Maybe they could never find the deep, enduring love she claimed her parents had shared, but all things considered, they could do far worse. At least he'd make sure she always had food on the table and a roof over her head. And the nights...

Thinking about what they could do with those nights, he felt an unexpected tightening in his groin.

The rush of excitement faded, though, as he emerged through the gate and found no Callie—smiling or otherwise—waiting in the crowd.

He glanced at his watch to make sure the plane hadn't landed early, only to find it was eleven minutes later than his scheduled arrival. Not a good sign, that Callie wasn't here. If she'd decided not to meet him, all his planning would amount to nothing. To less than nothing, because he'd be back at square one.

Clenching his jaw, he fell into step with the other passengers, meandering like herded cattle toward the baggage carousel. This was a mere setback, he told himself, not the end of the war. Callie wouldn't be Callie if she didn't wage a good battle.

Still, he'd been so certain she would show tonight. She'd said she would, and it wasn't like Callie to leave anyone stranded.

Except maybe a Parker.

"Luke?"

Her voice rang out in the crowded airport, grabbing hold of him, stopping him in his tracks. With a burst of elation, he turned on a heel to face her, and she nearly bumped into his chest.

"Wow, Cal," was all he could manage as he held her by the arms and took in the sight of her.

He'd been expecting a jazzed-up version of her customary shorts and T-shirt, or an inexpensive sundress perhaps, with straw bag and sandals. Yet her simple black sheath was the epitome of elegance…and incredibly sexy, the way it clung to her every curve. Dainty black pumps made the most of her long, slim legs, while the low, swooping neckline kept him aware of her glorious breasts…and twice as eager to explore them. She wore her dark hair swept up, laying bare her slim neck and shoulders, exposing tiny diamond studs in her earlobes. A mixture of refinement and blatant sexuality, she could easily be a supermodel, except for the shy, almost uncertain expression in her eyes.

"Is it too much?" she asked, slipping free of his

grasp. "I don't know what women wear on dates anymore."

"You look like a million dollars."

"You sure?" Frowning, she glanced around them. "People seem to be staring."

"They're probably wondering how a chump like me could interest someone like you." He actually felt like a chump, the way he couldn't pull his gaze away from her.

She eyed him as if he'd said she had a wart on her nose. "Right. Mr. Football Superstar, groveling at the feet of a Louisiana farm girl. You really don't need to waste your charm on me, Luke. Save your lines for the girls who need them."

"It wasn't a line," he said sharply, beginning to get annoyed. "I meant what I said. You look terrific."

"Yeah, well..." Her voice trailed off as the color rushed into her cheeks. "Thanks, then. I guess."

It was so like her to bristle one minute and blush the next. Hard to get a handle on what to say to her when he could never quite predict how she'd react. Studying her, noticing her fingers playing with the strap on her purse, it struck him that she might be as nervous as he, though of course, for far different reasons.

He wished he could tell her to relax, that he wouldn't force her into anything she didn't want to do, but that would be tipping his hand. Instead, he tried to put them both at ease by sticking to neutral ground. Leading her downstairs to the baggage area, he asked about Rob and kept her talking about the boy as they made their way to the car. Luke truly wanted to know everything that had happened to his son in his absence, but his questions served the dual purpose of unwinding Callie and making them both feel comfortable with each other.

And Callie did relax. Under the encouragement of

Luke's comments and timely laughter, she let herself get caught up in her anecdotes about Robbie and her "strays," as Luke called the people in her building. It wasn't until the car stopped that she realized she'd kicked off her shoes and was not only facing Luke as she rattled off her stories, but leaning far too close to his side.

When he turned to face *her,* however, the words dried up in her throat. He looked suddenly so serious, so intense, she thought for a dizzying moment that he meant to kiss her.

Instead, he merely said, "We're here," and turned to get out of the car.

Her lips continued to tingle as if he had indeed touched them with his own. Blinking to yank herself back to the here and now, she took several moments to notice the neon sign blinking in the same rhythm above their heads.

Bayou Moonlight Cruise it declared in gaudy Vegas fashion.

"What are we doing here?" she blurted as she scrambled out of the car, recognizing the site of their first real date.

"Remember? Dinner, dancing?"

That was the trouble; she remembered far too well. "Here? In *this* place?"

He shrugged. "After a week in New York, I've got a hankering for all things Louisiana. The food and music, the sounds and smells and peace of the bayou."

She looked up at the sign, not bothering to hide her skepticism. "Ten years ago, you called it a tourist trap. Or don't you remember this is where we went to celebrate me passing my finals?"

"Is it?" He too gazed at the sign, as if seeing it for

the first time. "Funny, all these tourist traps seem the same to me."

"You didn't want to take the cruise. As I recall, you said it was hokey, a far cry from the true Louisiana experience."

"As *I* recall, we still had a great time. Didn't we?"

Yes, and that was the trouble. She'd had an incredible night. To a sheltered, inexperienced eighteen-year-old, dancing with Luke Parker under the stars had been nothing short of magical. Perhaps part of the enchantment came from the fact that it was just the two of them, with no one aware that he was a Parker and she a Magruder. What a heady feeling, standing on equal ground with the man she adored beyond all reason.

Making it all the more painful to be brought back down to earth.

"C'mon, Cal," Luke said now, taking her hand. "We're here, let's make a night of it. Tell me you don't want to have fun."

How ironic, Callie thought, the way their roles had reversed. Last time she'd tugged Luke onto the boat. This time he did the coaxing while she resisted. The trouble was, he had a point. She did want fun. Heck, no one needed it more.

All in all, maybe it was a good thing the place was so familiar. Already knowing the danger spots, she would be prepared to avoid them. She could go and dance her heart out, knowing better than to take any of his nonsense seriously, knowing beforehand that the magic didn't last in the cold light of day.

"You're right," she told Luke, pulling free of his grasp. "Come hell or high water, I'm having a good time tonight."

And strolling onto the boat with him, she did her best to keep true to her word. Not that she found it hard in the carnival atmosphere. Pushing off from the dock with the band playing and Christmas lights twinkling, it was as if the entire boat had made a silent pact to suspend reality for the next few hours. The battered planks and tired rigging became a glittering pleasure barge, with everyone aboard abandoning their cares to enter a world of fun and laughter. It wouldn't last, make-believe never did, but for the cruise's brief duration, Callie meant to make the most of it.

She made a point of trying every dish at the buffet, even the collard greens she normally detested. Though rarely a drinker, she let Luke refill her champagne glass whenever she drained it and she danced each dance, from the sedate two step to the more boisterous polka, not stopping until she was breathless.

After one too many sessions, Luke held up his hands to beg for mercy. Insisting that they needed a breather, he led her to a quiet, empty area at the back of the boat.

It was an incredible night, crystal clear with a thousand stars and a pale moon just clearing the horizon. In the distance she could hear the mournful call of a hoot owl, the steady churn of the motor and the slapping of water against the boat. Soon the band would again start playing, but right in this moment she knew it was as close to serenity as she was liable to get.

She breathed in the warm night air, letting it calm her.

"Can't catch your breath?" Luke asked, leaning an elbow on the rail.

"Just reminiscing." She smiled, feeling mellow. "Back when I was a kid, I used to get these breathing attacks. I would get so panicky, I'd start wheezing. The only way I could stop was if my mom took me outside to the porch swing, sitting close so I could breathe along with her. All through it, calm as you please, she'd talk about the day she'd had, or what was going on in the world, anything to get my mind off breathing. Oftentimes, she'd talk about the air having a life of its own, like some character in a movie, and she'd make me figure out who it was playing that particular night. A stormy evening and I'd say the air was Hamlet, or Scarlett O'Hara.''

"And a night like tonight?"

"Oh, that's easy. Tonight, it's a siren, like Salome or Cleopatra. You feel it, how it's all soft and sultry?"

"Yeah, I feel it." His voice went low and sexy again. His gaze, focused on her lips, made her suddenly uneasy.

"Kinda makes it hard to get enough oxygen," she said, looking away. "Especially after all that dancing."

"Really? I'd never have guessed you were having a problem." He gave a low chuckle. "If you ask me, you were a whirling dervish on the dance floor. I felt like a broken puppet, trying to keep up."

"Oh, really? And who suggested the limbo?"

"I was kidding and you know it." He shook his head. "As I remember, you danced me ragged last time, too. It's been so long I'd forgotten how much fun twirling around like that can be."

"Oh, right. You never went dancing in New York."

"Well, there's dancing, and then there's dancing."

"How profound." She didn't mean to sound so sarcastic, but there was no taking the words back.

"The women I was with up north acted as if we were on-stage," he continued anyway. "Always looking around to see who was looking at them. With them I was just going through the motions, but tonight…I don't know, it was different watching you so obviously enjoy every moment."

He was doing it again, flirting without thinking, and

she had half a mind to call him on it. Unfortunately, with all the wine she'd been drinking, half a mind was pretty much all she had left.

Sighing, he turned to lean over the rail and watch the river glide by. "Actually, much of my life has been a matter of going through the motions. I feel like this cruise—running the same course night after night, clocking a lot of miles, getting nowhere."

"What is this?" she asked, surprised by his observation. "Luke Parker, turning philosophical?"

"Maybe I've changed."

"Yeah, and maybe I'm gonna win the state lottery."

He looked up at her, tilting his head to study her face. "Everybody changes, Cal," he said flatly, turning his attention back to the river. "Even me."

"To paraphrase, there's changing and then there's changing. I'm thinking your philosophy is more likely influenced by all the champagne you've had to drink."

He continued to stare at her. If she hadn't known better, she might have thought he looked hurt. "Ever-practical Callie. You're probably right. It might be the wine talking."

"Yeah," she conceded, "and maybe it's the wine listening, too. I sure had more than my fair share. I don't remember ever feeling this light-headed and giddy."

Straightening, he turned to stand before her, gently pushing a stray tendril of hair behind her ear. "You said it yourself. Not enough oxygen on the dance floor."

In truth, she was wondering if the lack of oxygen might be caused by his touch. Her heart was beating so fast and loud it was a wonder he couldn't hear it, standing as he was mere inches away.

"Speaking of which," he said huskily, "isn't that our song the band's playing?"

Bemused by his proximity, she hadn't heard music

until he mentioned it. Even then, it took some moments to identify the tune "Always," the last song they'd danced to that long-ago night. It was an oldie, a favorite of her grandparents, but the words had lodged themselves in her heart. Ten years ago, clasped tightly in his arms as Luke whirled her about the dance floor, she'd fervently believed she would love this man forever.

Silly little Callie Magruder.

But he was doing it again, not taking no for an answer, sweeping her off into a never-never land where music directed her footsteps and logic was no longer needed. Right there on the empty upper deck, with only the stars and moon for company, Luke made certain she savored the sheer joy of the moment.

And, oh, what a moment it was, dancing in his arms.

Everything conspired against her. Ever the siren, the air swirled around them, weaving a silk cocoon of sensation, shutting out all discordant sound. The voices, the clink of glasses, even the engines melted into the sweet, flowing music that now shaped her world.

A world that became smaller and tighter as the ripe scent of the river blended with Luke's sandalwood and musk, as the light from the stars above zoomed down to fuse with his probing blue gaze. All physical reality concentrated itself in the strong shoulders beneath her fingers, the warm, solid form cradling her own. Her entire existence was Luke, all Luke, holding her as if he'd never let her go.

The more they danced, the more desire rose up in her, that bone-deep yearning he'd always inspired. With an allover shiver, she sensed his awareness of her, and helpless to stop it, she waited breathlessly for his kiss.

The entire world halted as slowly, oh, so slowly, his lips approached and then found hers. She might have moaned—she certainly felt as if she had—as her mind acknowledged how badly she'd been missing this feeling. Every bone in her body seemed to melt, every care floated away. The things he made her feel in his slow, gentle exploration of her mouth were a revelation. For Callie, it was magic, pure and simple.

"C'mon, let's get out of here," he whispered into her mouth.

Stunned, she pulled back to stare into his eyes, his soft-blue focus anchoring her through the breathless ride as reality intruded. Too late she realized the music had stopped, that the boat's engines had ground to a halt.

How long had she stood there, lost in his arms?

Horrified, she turned away from him, appalled further by her sense of loss. Fantasy hour was over, she told herself sternly. Time for Cinderella to give back the gown and slippers.

"Wow," Luke said behind her. "Didn't mean to do that."

She almost asked, "Didn't you?" but what would be the sense? All things considered, she'd betrayed too much of herself as it was.

"I don't know," she said instead, still refusing to face him. "The stars, the music, all that wine. Don't you think it was inevitable?"

"I guess. Maybe."

"You'd have kissed a crocodile in that moment, Luke. And so would I. No sense making a big deal about it. It's not like it will ever be repeated."

"No?"

"No!" All she could think of was that she had to get away from here, from him. "We're docked," she said to change the subject. "We should get going."

He eyed her strangely but followed her lead as they made their way to the lower deck. Both of them remained silent and subdued as they got in the car and drove off, a fact for which Callie told herself she should be eternally grateful. She had no wish to discuss her irresponsible behavior with the man who had caused it. What she really wanted was to go home and hide in her room.

But she was no longer in fantasy land, and in the real world wishes were rarely granted. She understood this fully when Luke again stopped the car at a familiar landmark. Only this time the flashing sign read Sleepy Bye Motel.

Anger rushed over her. The cruise was bad enough, but this was way too much of a coincidence. They'd come here, too, that night. For far more than just dancing.

"What is this, Luke Parker?" she asked with an undeniable edge to her tone. "What in tarnation are you up to now?"

Chapter Nine

Hearing the anger in Callie's voice, Luke knew he'd made a mistake. Making the arrangements back in New York, he'd thought it a stroke of genius to bring her here, the perfect culmination to a night of romance, but after her reaction to a simple kiss, he realized it hadn't been a good idea at all.

However, it would have been better to know this *before* he'd started drinking.

"Listen Cal," he told her patiently, " I'm really not trying to pull anything on you." At least, not anymore. "But we've got a good half-hour drive home, and after the wine I had, I won't risk our lives weaving down the highway. You feel up to driving?"

She stared straight into him, her expression not thawing a bit. "I matched you glass for glass, Luke Parker." Biting her lip, she looked ahead out the windshield. "I have a son, you know. I can't be gadding about, staying out all hours and then rolling in like something the cat dragged home.''

"Rob is at Jason's house, and not due home until tomorrow. By then, we'll *both* have plenty of time to make ourselves presentable.''

She heaved a sigh, a far-from-happy sound. "Well, I'm not staying *here*.'' The way she said it, and the look she gave the place, you'd think he'd suggested bedding down with cockroaches. True, the Sleepy Bye Motel might have seen better days, and couldn't provide the implicit guarantees of a chain motel, but it was nonetheless clean and respectable, a mom-and-pop establishment that had been there for ages.

"Look around us, Cal.'' Luke tried again, trying to contain his exasperation. "This isn't exactly a metropolis. What you see is pretty much it for local lodging.''

She kept her gaze straight ahead, as if that tight tone of hers was directed at the motel rather than him. "You must take me for all kinds of a fool. Are you really going to sit there and pretend you don't remember what happened in this place?''

"Is that what's bothering you?'' In some ways he was glad to hear she did remember. The whole purpose was to spark such memories, after all. Still, it wouldn't help his cause if he made her even angrier. "Of course I remember,'' he told her gently. "I had too much to drink that night, too, and this was the only place available. Relax, Cal. I promise I'll get separate rooms.''

"That's what you said last time.''

Yes, he had, but the place had only one vacancy that night. "If they're full up,'' he further reassured her, "I'll sleep in the car. Scout's honor.''

He made the offer, hoping she'd say that she wouldn't hear of him making the sacrifice, but her frosty expression killed that hope. She even insisted upon coming to the office with him while he booked the rooms.

Deciding that he could be stubborn, too, Luke gave it another try as they paused by their individual doors, taking care to flash his most disarming grin. "It's not that late, you know. Wanna come in and talk, maybe catch some late-night TV?"

"I don't think so."

And like that she disappeared into her room.

He stood by his own door for a full five minutes, staring at where she had been with a vague, empty longing. He tried to tell himself sex was what he wanted, that its deprivation caused the uneasy void, but deep down he sensed it was no longer that simple. Then again, nothing about Callie would ever be simple.

Something had changed as they'd glided around the dance floor. Something he couldn't quite define, but couldn't deny, either. He'd swept her off in a waltz, hoping to bring her back to the starry-eyed kid she had been, but somewhere in the process their roles had reversed. Holding Callie in his arms, her lovely face shining with joy, it had struck him how insanely happy he'd been that night. As he gazed at her moonlit features, breathing in her delicate scent, he'd been mesmerized by an overpowering urge to kiss her, the *need* to kiss her, certain that if he could just absorb even a whiff of her sweet essence, somehow he would be saved.

Shaking his head, he pushed open his door, the impersonal hotel room a stark contrast to his fanciful thoughts. Surrounded by the utilitarian furnishings—the dated brown shag rug, worn tweed spread and drapes, the cracked placard on the door detailing the rates—Luke put a more practical spin on the night's events.

Frustration was what bothered him, he told himself as he tossed the key on the battered dresser. For the past week, alone in another empty hotel room, he'd put too much imagination into the planning. What had he expected, that he could take Callie to some mystical plane and wipe away the past? If so, he'd neglected to enter two prime factors into his calculations. One being reality, and the other, Callie herself.

Kicking off his shoes, he flopped on his back to the bed. Where had it gone so wrong that she would reject him completely? He'd been a perfect gentleman; she could have no complaints there. It hadn't been easy, either. All night long he'd been unable to draw his gaze from the delicate column of her neck, aching to trail his tongue over the exposed flesh to the tiny diamond studs in her earlobes. Had he acted on it? No. Nor had he reached up to free her luxuriant hair, knowing from experience that it would settle like silk around them. And not once had he given in to the urge to slide his eager hands up and down the smooth, satiny curves of that sinfully wicked dress.

All he'd actually done was kiss her.

He jumped up from the bed to pace the narrow confines, but he paused by the door connecting his room to hers. It would be locked up tight on her side, he knew, much like the woman herself. There must be a key to both somewhere, but he sure didn't have it. If he did he'd be in that room with her now and not standing here like some horny teenager, wondering what might be gained by giving in to the temptation to lay shoulder to wood.

All too vividly he remembered their last stay here, right down to each tiny detail and nuance. He knew, for example, that Callie was in the room they'd shared that long-ago night. He could picture her lying on the same bed, maybe even hugging the same pillow to her chest. He'd been the perfect gentleman that night, too, she should have recalled, dropping a chaste peck on her head before rolling over to his side of the bed.

But being Callie, she would probably focus instead on what had happened the following day. In that respect, he supposed he could almost understand her panicked retreat. After the kiss they'd shared tonight, she had living, breathing proof of the lust they still generated between them.

Unconsciously he reached out to touch the door separating him from his wife. How cold it felt to the touch, how unyielding. Just like Callie.

Yet, she hadn't always been that way. Once, he'd been on the other side of that door, enveloped by the softness and warmth Callie invariably gave to just about everyone else.

Only, he'd walked away without looking back.

Feeling suddenly uncomfortable with his thoughts, he pulled his hand back and jammed it into a pocket. He was tired and he'd had too much to drink. No wonder he couldn't think straight.

Muttering under his breath, he kicked off his slacks and climbed under the covers. Rather than continue on this tangent to nowhere, he might better save his "philosophical" musings for the morning when his head was clearer.

Tomorrow he could figure out what to do next.

Callie lay in the dark, eyeing the connecting door as if it were some crazed stalker waiting to pounce. Luke was on the other side, she couldn't stop fretting. Luke, who by kissing her, awakened all sorts of feelings she'd hoped she'd long since killed and buried.

Clutching the pillow to her midsection, she screwed her eyes tightly shut, trying hard not to remember. But images came rushing at her, flooding her, making her relive each intense moment. Luke had obviously failed to notice, but this was the very same room they'd shared ten years ago.

That night she'd paused at the threshold, frightened to enter, while an equal part of her hummed with ex-hilaration. This was it, her moment of truth. She was alone with Lucky Parker, the boy she'd dreamed of for so very long, but she wasn't hopelessly blind and stupid. She knew he had a reputation for having his way with the female population and had a pretty good idea of what he expected of her that night.

Or so she'd thought. Imagine her surprise when he so very sweetly kissed her on the forehead and then rolled over to go straight to sleep.

A wiser girl would have been grateful, but young and inexperienced in such matters, Callie had felt let down and unfulfilled. She'd lain awake in this bed until the wee hours of morning, wondering what she'd done wrong, what she could be lacking, that the local Romeo would feel no need to seduce her.

As a result she'd been asleep when Luke rose the next day. Opening her eyes at half past eight, she'd been startled, then horrified to find the bed empty. A quick, desperate search of the room yielded no sign of him. In her mind this could mean only one thing. Waking to the clear light of day, he'd regretted whatever impulse drove him to bring her here. Certain that he'd deserted her, she'd burst into tears.

But it hadn't taken long to realize that it was now up

to her, and her alone, to get herself home. She had enough money for bus fare—if she could find a station in this middle of nowhere—but before she took step one, she'd have to make herself more presentable. Stumbling into the shower, she'd turned the cold water on full force, letting the sharp needles of ice beat some sense into her.

Time to face facts, she'd told herself sternly. She had to let go of the silly fantasy she'd been building in her brain. Last night might have seemed magical, but the fact remained—some girls had the power to make a man lose touch with reality, but she was not, and never would be, one of them. Not where Lucky Parker was concerned.

Only, just as she was emerging from the bathroom, skimpy towel clutched to her chest, who should stumble into the room but Luke. One look at his startled expression, and the combination of fear, surprise and utter relief started her sobbing again.

Concerned, he'd run over to reassure and comfort her. Cocooned in his warm, strong grip, she'd felt something crazy snap in her brain. Even now, it seemed all hazy and out of control, but at that moment she hadn't wanted to be "practical Callie" anymore. All her life she'd yearned for a chance like that. She had to take it, make the most of it while it lasted.

So when the towel slipped in the middle of their kiss, she'd done nothing to retrieve it. She'd heard Luke's sharp intake of air and recognized the warning, but she merely moved closer, every inch of her tingling with anticipation and yearning. It had been wild and impulsive, and so unlike her, but she'd given herself up to the moment without a second's hesitation.

Seemed like a good idea at the time, Callie thought

now as she stared into the darkness. What a ninny she'd been, so ripe and eager for heartache. Being held in Luke's arms was all she'd ever dreamed of and more, but when they were finished, and the urgency left him, the reality of what she'd done sunk in. Especially when Luke so pointedly turned away from her.

It wasn't as if she hadn't known, going in, that she couldn't count on him. Sex couldn't hold a man, especially not one like Luke. What she hadn't been aware of, though, was that it could sure do a number on a woman.

Staring at the door between them, she felt a bone-deep gratitude that it was locked securely, that Luke couldn't get to her, charm her, tempt her into continuing what they'd started with one mere kiss. Were they in the same room…

No, she told herself firmly, no more falling into that trap. Punching her pillow into shape, she visualized the calendar as her lifeline, imagining the eleven months, four days and fifteen hours remaining as bowling pins, each with Luke's face on it. One by one, she would knock them down, so that this time when he took off, she'd be standing tall and proud with her heart intact.

At half past seven the next morning Luke knocked on Callie's door, fighting a sense of déjà vu. Ten years ago he'd gone to the same little shop for coffee and doughnuts, even carried a similar bag back to the room with the same assortment of sugar, stirrers and napkins. Would they actually eat the doughnuts this time, he couldn't help wondering, or could he convince her that there was another, more interesting exercise to kick off the day?

Apparently not. No skimpy towel today; Callie wore

the somewhat-worse-for-wear black dress, her pearl-white cardigan buttoned to the neck and a forbidding scowl on her face. "Let's go," she announced, brushing past him.

"But what about breakfast?" he asked, holding up the bag.

"We can eat on the way."

She didn't look back, nor falter a step. Trailing her to the car, lugging the coffee and doughnuts, Luke felt cut off at the knees. It wasn't that he'd expected to toss her on the bed and have his way with her, but he had hoped that by sitting and talking in the all-too-intimate setting, Callie would relax around him and not feel the need to panic. It annoyed him that she'd not only anticipated his strategy but taken steps to prevent it.

"What's the hurry?" he asked irritably when they were settled in the car, the bag of doughnuts sitting like a referee between them. "Scared to be alone with me?"

Advantage, Luke.

"Of course not." Her snippy tone said otherwise. "I'm just anxious to get back to Robbie."

Back to deuce. A cheap shot, using their son as an excuse. "Rob isn't there, remember."

"Yeah, well, I should be there waiting. I'm *always* there when he gets home."

Advantage, Callie, with yet another blow beneath the belt. "We'll be there," he said, putting the emphasis on the *we* as he started the car and backed out onto the road. "The hell with breakfast."

The bag went flying as he peeled out and Callie barely managed to catch it. Eyes wide and tone considerably less certain, she asked him what he thought he was doing.

"Getting you home," he growled, refusing to look at her. "Isn't that what you wanted?"

"I'd prefer to get there in one piece."

Silence settled over the car, though Luke thought it was a wonder she couldn't hear him fuming. Who did she think she was, calling him on being a lousy father, when she'd never even told him he was one? Just what did she expect from him, anyway? How was he supposed to have the slightest idea what made a good dad? Ben sure hadn't fallen into that category, and without a substitute to model himself after, Luke was winging it and bound to make mistakes. And there Callie sat, a self-appointed judge and jury, the vigilant critic eager to pounce.

He stole a glance at her. Callie sat hugging the bag to her chest, if not frightened then certainly concerned as she stared at the road ahead. Aware that he'd put that expression on her face, Luke slowed the car, his temper cooling with each mile per hour their speed decreased.

What was wrong with him, losing his temper that way? This wasn't how he'd envisioned their little getaway ending. In his mind he'd pictured her laughing, her face glowing, eyes dancing with anticipation for the day ahead. Much like she'd been on that day ten years ago.

Until he botched that up, too.

Wincing, he too stared at the road, seeing Callie again as he'd barged into the room to find her clad only in a towel. When he'd seen her tears, all he could think of was that something bad must have happened to her and he had to fix it.

But when he'd held her, a sense of the inevitable had come over him. In that moment he'd have gladly tilted at windmills in her behalf, yet when she'd looked up at him with her dewy, doelike eyes, his last hope of playing the gentleman flew out the window.

He'd been sorry afterward, though. He could try to defend himself—Lord knew the tension had been building between them to a fever pitch—but, all evidence to the contrary, he'd never planned to take her to bed. He had been incapable of driving, the motel truly didn't have an extra room, and he'd valued her friendship far too much to screw it up with sex.

But there she'd sat on the other side of his truck, looking at him as if he'd just handed her the moon, and he hadn't the stomach or guts to set her straight. While she bubbled on about how magical the night had been, he'd tried to find some way to announce that they had to stop seeing each other. No more easy companionship, no more helping him work through his feelings of loss and self-doubt. Even Lucky "Me First" Parker knew you couldn't be friends with a girl when every time you looked at her, you itched to get her in bed.

He'd decided there and then that he couldn't ever be alone with her again. Not when he couldn't trust himself not to touch her.

Wincing again, he pictured her shocked expression that morning as he'd dropped her off on the road to the farm. With no warning, and even less finesse, he'd blurted out that he wouldn't be coming around anymore. He couldn't have been crueler. Thinking back, his truck had probably even kicked up gravel in her face in his haste to peel away.

And if that hadn't been enough, he'd rammed the point home by taking Amy Ann Masters to the Bonfire Bash the next night. His intent had been to make the break clean and distinctive, but when he noticed Callie dancing with Reb Jenkins, Luke had been the one with second thoughts. All night he'd barely heard a word Amy Ann chattered, his attention focused on Callie. He couldn't bear to watch that grease monkey's hands on her, pawing her, marking her. All Luke could think of was that he had to put a stop to it, yet how much better off they all would have been had he just walked away.

"Luke, wait," she called out suddenly from the seat beside him. "Turn here, please?"

Luke automatically applied the brake, his thoughts snapping back into focus in time to recognize the road to the Magruder farm.

Nothing like returning to the scene of the crime.

Chapter Ten

Bouncing along the rutted lane, Callie battled with her own memories. She didn't know why she'd asked Luke to take this little detour. Was she a masochist, bent on reliving the pain of all she'd lost in the past ten years?

Driving down this lane, though, hadn't been something she and Luke had done together back then. Trying to keep their meetings a secret from Gramps, she'd always made Luke drop her off at the highway. He'd never been near the house—except for the night of the Bonfire Bash.

Wincing, she remembered how she'd let Reb drive her home that night, mostly to make Luke jealous, but partly because Reb's attention was a salve to her bruised ego. She'd even let Reb kiss her, hoping he could stir her to mindless, forgetful passion, but Reb had never been tall enough or blond enough or…face it, he just wasn't Lucky Parker.

The fact had been brought home when she'd stood watching Reb drive off and Luke emerged from the shadows. She'd been shocked to see him, and maybe even a little angry, but deep down, where that sixth sense of hers functioned, she supposed she should have known it was inevitable.

"Don't sell yourself short," Luke had snapped. "You can do heaps better than Reb Jenkins."

She lost it then, shouting back that he was nothing but an uncaring snob. "From where I stand," she ranted, "Reb looks like a fine prospect. He has a steady job, and he generally stays out of trouble. I'm just a farmer, remember, and worse, a Magruder. What more can a girl like me ask for?"

"This!" he growled, yanking her into his arms for a mind-numbing kiss.

"Callie?"

Suddenly conscious of Luke calling her name, Callie was jolted rudely out of her thoughts. Glancing over to his side of the car, she found him watching her intently. Slowly she realized her fingers were touching her lips.

She dropped her arm, appalled. Unwilling to sit there one instant longer, she yanked open the door handle and spilled out of the car.

Watching her go, Luke shook his head, wondering if she, too, was thinking of the night he'd kissed her in this very spot.

Even now he could feel the animal, urgent insanity of it all, not just that night but night after night of seeking her out, day after day seeking some way to break free of her spell. Never before or since had he been so hot for a woman, so immersed in the passion that he couldn't see an hour into the future, much less into the years ahead. Four years older than Callie, he should have been the one with the common sense, the one with the wisdom to apply the brakes.

But he hadn't stopped anything. Not until it was already too late and all for the wrong reasons.

He took his time leaving the BMW, giving her time to compose herself. She wouldn't want him seeing what she would consider her weakness, he knew. Her pride was a valued commodity to Callie, and all things considered, maybe it was the least he could offer.

As he slowly approached her, he realized she wasn't focusing on the spot where they'd embarked on their month of unbridled lust, but rather on the farmhouse where she and her family once lived. Irrationally he felt a flash of disappointment—and then he got a good look at her face.

She held her features tight, as if trying to keep the sadness and grief inside, but she couldn't quite manage to hold the moisture gathering in her eyes. Taking in her stooped shoulders, the single tear dripping down her cheek, Luke had to feel for her, but he still couldn't grasp such depth of emotion for something as replaceable as a house.

Viewing the two-storied structure with its wraparound porch and gabled attic windows, Luke couldn't see the appeal of the place. All he saw was peeling paint and missing shingles, and a lot more work than the worth of the property warranted. "So this is the old homestead," he said, knowing enough to keep his assessment to himself. "I never got around to seeing it in the daylight."

She sighed wistfully, as if he hadn't managed to completely hide his disdain. "I know it doesn't look like much, but I have a lot of fine memories tied up in this house. See that window, over there on the right by that live oak? Inside was the bedroom I shared with my sister. Late at night Saralynn and I used to climb out on those limbs and head down to the river to catch crawdads. Gramps knew about it, and sometimes he even joined us, but I don't think my parents ever guessed the many times we crept out of bed." She forced a smile. "And there, over on the porch, that's the swing my mama and I used to sit in."

Following her gaze to the rickety porch, Luke remembered her telling him last night how her mother would hold her there, soothing and calming her, helping her breathe.

"I keep having a dream about this place," she went on, dabbing at the tear on her cheek. "It's Christmas, and everyone is here, gathered around the tree. My folks, my sister and brother, Gramps and Robbie. Looking at them all holding hands, I feel so happy, so complete, but then I wake up, and reality takes over. I swear, sometimes I get to feeling so cold and lonely I have to rub my arms just to feel them."

Hearing the strain in her voice, he had the urge to take Callie to the porch, to sit on the swing beside her and offer comfort in her mother's place.

He didn't act on it, though. The way things were between them, she was liable to box his ears. "You still have Robbie," he said instead, trying to console her.

"Yeah…" She let the word trail off, as if she'd gotten lost in her thoughts. When she spoke, it seemed from a long way off. "But that's just it. He'll never have any of this. He'll never know."

"So he'll make his own memories. It's just a house, Cal. We can build another one. With a basketball court and swimming pool."

She eyed him as if he'd just uttered blasphemy. "Maybe you can dismiss it as 'just a house,'" she said fiercely, "but this place is far more than four walls and a roof to me. Generations of Magruders lived, loved and died in that house. Over a hundred years of tears and laughter and memories, all of it passed down to me, and I let it slip through my fingers. This farm was all I had left of my family, Luke. All I had to pass on to my son.''

She sniffed loudly and threw back her shoulders. ''So please don't stand there and tell me how easy it will be to replace it. You Parkers think money is always the answer, but you can't buy off someone's heritage with a basketball court and swimming pool.''

She turned away, as if embarrassed by her outburst. Gazing at her, Luke felt his throat go tight. He still didn't understand her obsession with this farm, but for the first time he caught a glimpse at how hard it must have been for her, carrying their child, trying to keep her family going. More often than not, she must have felt the weight of the world on her slim shoulders.

''It's getting late,'' she said suddenly beside him, her voice sharp and crisp, as if the last few minutes had never been. Her stiff carriage as she marched to the car without looking back made her message plain. She didn't want to talk about her farm anymore. At least not to him. In her mind he was still the enemy.

He followed her back to the car, wondering if he would ever be able to change her mind.

''I didn't mean to sound insensitive,'' he told her as he slid into the seat beside her. ''But let's face it. If Ben were to sell the house I grew up in, I'd never count it as a loss. I'd think it a stroke of luck.''

''Well, I'm tired of counting my losses,'' she said quietly. ''Just once, why can't I get lucky?''

Hearing her sound so subdued bothered him. ''I'm here,'' he said, reaching out to gently touch her cheek. ''*Lucky* Parker, in the living breathing flesh.''

He knew the words were a mistake the minute they left his mouth.

"Funny," Callie said sharply. "I can't see where your good fortune ever rubbed off on me."

"Good fortune?" He was getting tired of her thinking he'd had it so good, when in truth she'd had a far better childhood than he had. "Do you really think luck brought me home to play games with my father?"

"No, I reckon poor judgment did that."

He went rigid inside. "And what is that supposed to mean?"

"I can read, Luke. Every sordid detail. The whole fiasco with your coach was there in the papers."

She sat prim and smug, judging him on some news hound's quest for a byline. "For your information," he told her stiffly, "I never touched my coach, much less tried to strangle him. I sure as hell wasn't sleeping with his daughter. We had bad blood between us, I'm not denying that, but it had nothing to do with his kid. We exchanged words, not blows. Angry, ugly words that hurt the team, but that's the extent of my crime. What you didn't read, apparently, was the retraction the papers eventually printed. You're not alone. Not too many ever found the true version, buried as it was in the back pages. And just for the record, contrary to rumor and innuendo, my fight with the coach wasn't why I left the team. My arm was shot. I couldn't throw anymore. It's as simple as that."

"Nothing's that simple, Luke."

Of course it wasn't. And trust Callie to pick up on it. "What do you want to hear? I learned some painful lessons. I learned I wasn't a superhero and nowhere near infallible. And when the chips were down, I discovered the people I thought were friends really weren't."

"So that's why you came home? To lick your wounds?"

Must she always think the worst of him? "Maybe I came home to start over," he said, trying to make her understand, maybe even to help himself understand. "Maybe I knew I had to go back to the beginning to figure out where it all went wrong." Looking at her, he was seized with a sudden inspiration. "Maybe I realized that what I truly needed," he said, reaching out for her, "was to come home to you."

She edged back against the door, holding up a hand as if to ward him off. *"Maybe?"* she said in a high, tight voice. "How stupid do you think I am, Luke? I don't know what game you're playing now, but whatever it is, don't for a second assume that I'll be joining in."

"I'm done playing games," he ground out.

"Oh, really? Then what was last night all about? And our lunch date at the diner. Tell me, what was the next step? Taking me back to that hotel in New Orleans?"

Not liking how squarely she'd hit that nail on the head, Luke cursed silently. "I don't see what's wrong in trying to recapture the past. When I look back, those were the best days of my life."

"If it was all that great," she asked skeptically, "why did you run from me like a frightened rabbit?"

The words hung between them, forming an unscalable wall. "C'mon, Cal, I was just a kid," he protested, determined to climb it anyway.

"So was I." She shifted to lean back against the seat, arms crossed militantly across her chest. "But I'm not that silly little girl anymore. I can't afford to wander down memory lane with you. I've got my own kid now, relying on me to stay focused on the future."

She sucked in a breath, staring back at him, her wide

brown eyes one huge accusation. "We made a bargain, Luke. If you can't keep your end of it, we might as well end this farce of a marriage."

Arms still crossed, she looked away out the side window.

Stunned by her threat, stung by her accusations, Luke gazed out his own window in the gathering silence. For once in his life he had no clever quip, no carefully turned phase to toss back at her. She was right. They had made a bargain, and he wasn't living up to his end of it.

How blind he'd been, thinking he could seduce this woman into compliance. Maybe he could placate the other females he'd dated with soft caresses and whispered murmurings, but Callie could see right through him. All he'd accomplished with their trip down Memory Lane was to prove what he'd let slip through his fingers. How ironic, that he should be the one to fall deeper into all the old yearnings, while Callie slipped further away.

He wanted her—he could still taste her there on his lips—but he realized he wanted more than mere physical gratification. He needed her warmth and understanding.

Her smile was what he missed most, he discovered—the way her whole face once lit up whenever he'd walked into the room.

Yet, given what he'd done to her, considering what she'd gone through in his absence, he supposed she had good reason for her current wary looks and skittish behavior. In her position he wasn't sure *he* could trust Luke Parker. Not when he was now so obviously trying to get her in bed.

Yet, until she did trust him, there would be no unburdening of her soul to him, no heartfelt confessions about Rob, no smiles of welcome at the end of the day.

Trust. She'd had ten long years to let her resentment fester, a painfully long interval during which she'd been harassed by his father. What could he do to make it up to her, to prove that not all Parkers were snakes like Ben?

As if in answer he heard the creak of rusty chains as the porch swing moved in the breeze.

He looked up at the house, remembering Callie's steely expression as she told him the one thing that would get her to agree to the marriage. She'd worn the same look today, telling him how tired she was of counting her losses. He might not understand such desperation, but clearly, this farm meant everything to Callie. By keeping his promise and getting it back for her, he could go a long way toward earning her trust.

First thing tomorrow, he thought as he started up the car, he'd be sitting down to have a long talk with Ben.

Callie watched Luke as he gazed at the farmhouse, wondering what he was thinking, wishing he'd just take her home. After last night, and now this morning, she felt like a bundle of emotions, as raw and fresh as a badly scraped shin. All Luke had to do was look at her wrong, she feared, and she was liable to start bawling.

Unfortunately, she was not nearly as immune to the memories as she needed him to believe.

She was glad Luke said nothing more as he started the car and drove them home. She hadn't the strength left to fend off his questions, to keep her fears to herself. The sad fact was that while she could lie to Luke, she could no longer hide the truth from herself.

His kiss last night had stirred far more than her distrust and impatience. It had brought her back to a time when the world had been mystery and magic, when anything seemed possible. The possibility that she could still so easily fall under Luke's spell, however temporarily, just about scared her to death.

She couldn't go through that pain again, she thought, gazing over at his determined profile. She wouldn't.

Slowly it sifted back to her, the memory of their last night together.

It had been so incredibly intense between them. Five blissful weeks in which they hadn't been able to get enough of each other. Somehow, they'd found a way to be together every day, Luke picking her up after work to take her down to the river or out to the back roads where they had made love in his truck. To Callie, it hadn't mattered where they went or what they did, as long as she could see him, touch him, hold him tight.

Lying in his arms afterward, warm and throbbing in the afterglow, she would coax him to talk, sensing something was eating at him. Eventually he admitted his fear that with each day that passed, his dreams of a football career grew slimmer. From what he'd told her, she knew the pro contract was important to him. But she didn't know why it was so vital, and she secretly resented the world that waited to take him away.

So when he confessed one night that he'd given up hope, that he was considering making use of his business degree even if it meant going to work for his father, she'd let herself assume he'd changed and was now ready to settle down. When he began talking about finding an apartment and getting a more reliable vehicle, she'd started spinning dreams of an autumn wedding.

She'd been so deliriously happy, she'd literally walked in the clouds. When Luke suggested sneaking off to New Orleans for the night, she'd truly believed he'd picked that romantic French Quarter hotel to make the occasion memorable. Though they might never have said the words, she didn't doubt that they were both in love, both committed, and she was equally certain that this was the night he meant to ask her to marry him. Making love with him in the huge brass bed, she thought herself the luckiest girl in the world.

And afterward, when he declared that she was the best thing to ever happen to him, the joy in her heart bubbled over. It was then that she made the mistake of saying out loud that she loved him.

Luke had gone deathly still. The entire world seemed to stop as he withdrew from her in a cold, forbidding silence. He might as well have vanished, so remote did he become, so unapproachable.

Watching in numbed shock, Callie would have given anything to have taken the words back, but she'd put them out there, an unintentional test, and the love she'd thought they'd shared failed miserably.

As he did now, Luke had maintained the wall of silence the entire drive home, offering only an abrupt "gotta run" when he dropped her off at the roadside. No kiss goodbye, not even an "I'll call you." Which he didn't. Ever again.

Not until ten years later when he showed up, out of the blue, and asked her to marry him.

Was it true? Had he really changed? she wondered, gazing at his profile. Certainly his features had matured, grown more chiseled. She could see the lines etched into the corners of his eyes, the tightness of the mouth once generous with laughter.

Still, if she'd learned nothing in the past ten years, she had to know by now that you couldn't judge a book by its cover. Not when the book you were trying to read was Luke Parker.

No, before she'd ever believe him again, she needed

actions, not words. He couldn't just tell her he'd changed, he had to show her. And whether or not he cared to admit it, tricking her back into his bed was not the action of an honorable man.

"Recapturing the past," he'd called it, talking as if that time was some trinket he'd misplaced, and not the most heart-wrenching days of her life. It had taken years to get over her sense of betrayal, not to mention the humiliation of being so wrong about their relationship, about Lucky Parker. She'd never told him—mainly because he never asked—but she'd been so crazy in love at the time she'd have gone off with Luke wherever he wanted. She'd have left the farm and deserted her grandfather, and for what? For a boy who didn't even have the sensitivity, the downright decency, to tell her he was going off without her.

And every day after that she'd suffered the guilt of what her selfishness might so easily have done to those around her. Each time she gazed at her stooped and aging grandfather, she'd lived with the knowledge of how she'd been so ready to abandon him to face Ben Parker alone. And there was Reb Jenkins, who she'd used to make Lucky jealous, and later to keep Gramps from getting suspicious. The way Reb would moon after her with his puppy dog eyes made her cringe inside, knowing she'd led him on, that it was her fault and not his if he now expected more from her than she could ever give him. Part of the reason she'd agreed to Reb's impulsive marriage proposal was a misguided attempt at atonement. The other reason was that by then, she'd discovered she was having a baby.

She'd told Reb the truth, but at that point he was so desperate to have her, he insisted it didn't matter, that he'd be honored to give her baby his name. She and Luke had been so discreet, no one in town had any reason to suspect he was the real father, so she saw no reason to burden Reb with the knowledge. It didn't matter, anyway. The day Robbie was born, Reb figured out what she had known months ago, that he just wasn't cut out for the job of raising another man's son. Two days after that he'd left her and her boy to fend for themselves.

No, she decided on a sigh as she turned away from gazing at Luke. She couldn't listen to any more promises, and she wasn't sitting idly by with only hope to sustain her. She'd learned the hard way that the only one she could rely on, the only one she could trust ultimately, was herself.

If Luke couldn't see that—and worse, if she couldn't get her traitorous heart to listen—then she meant what she'd told him. She couldn't risk Robbie getting hurt and she'd sure had her own fill of suffering.

Better, in the long run, to put an end to this marriage.

Chapter Eleven

Luke unpacked his suitcase, placing his things in the drawers assigned him, marveling at how such a simple act could make him feel as if he'd come home. He'd only stayed two weeks at Callie's apartment before his week up north, yet he'd missed this place, with its mismatched furniture and unconventional decorations. He couldn't wait to sit on the lumpy couch to watch television, to help Callie cook dinner in her postage-stamp kitchen.

Then again, maybe he might better avoid the kitchen tonight, considering how Callie herself had done little to welcome him back. Except for pointing him in the direction of Rob's room and stating tersely that he could put his stuff in the dresser, she'd maintained the uneasy silence that had sprung up between them in the car.

You're here on borrowed time, mister, he muttered to himself. One false move and she'll have you out on the street.

Her attitude still annoyed him, but he was trying to be patient and understanding, to learn how to see things from her perspective. He'd done her wrong, and there was no getting around it. To get back in her good graces, he'd have to pass her test, survive her trial by fire. Proving himself to Callie would never be easy, but perhaps it was long past time he took the first step.

He had to make plans, establish solid, concrete actions to show her he was serious about making a life here with her and their boy. That way, when he handed her the key to her farm, she'd have no doubt that he'd meant every word of his promise.

And the path to proving himself, he knew, began with his son.

As if on cue the front door opened and Rob's youthful voice rang out, "I'm home!" A rush of emotion swept through Luke, a combination of joy and self-doubt, mixed in with his eagerness to see the boy. So anxious was he, in fact, that he rushed out of the room with a pile of shirts still in his hands.

Stepping into the living room, he found Rob hugging his mother. Watching them, Luke knew his decision to work at his marriage was the right one, the only one. Only a certified creep would consider separating this pair, even for the occasional holidays and two-week stint in the summer.

Luke set the shirts on the stand beside him, and Rob looked up suddenly. "Luke," he cried out, wriggling free of his mother. "I didn't know you were going to be here."

Faced with Rob's big, beaming smile, Luke would have cashed in his last penny to have been here for the boy from the beginning. A man could spend millions and still never get the rush, the sense of completeness, Luke got from his son's welcome. Humbled considerably, he knew he'd been wrong to gripe about his lack of good fortune. Being hugged by Rob made Luke feel incredibly lucky.

Until he looked up and saw Callie frowning at him.

He could almost hear her thoughts. Who was he to sweep in here and steal her boy's affections? One more item for the list, he decided. He'd have to show Callie he deserved to be hugged by their son. From this day on, he vowed, he'd work doubly hard on learning to be a good father.

"I told you I'd be back as soon as I could," he told Rob, tousling the boy's hair. "You and I have to practice soccer."

"I got the greatest news." The boy was practically bouncing, he was so excited. "Coach picked me for the team. He says he wants me to play center."

A fierce pride surged through Luke. "You deserve it, Rob. No one could have worked harder."

The boy puffed up with his own pride. "You made it happen. I didn't know anything until we started practicing."

Luke roughed up his hair again. "Whatever the case, such great news requires a celebration. I vote we go out tonight for dinner."

Rob whooped and hollered, but you'd think Luke had suggested debauchery, the way Callie scowled at him. "Not tonight," she pronounced primly, moving up to place a hand on Rob's shoulder. "You need an early evening after your late night at Jason's."

Luke instantly got the message. This had nothing to do with their son getting enough sleep; she'd had her fill of "celebrating" with Luke over dinner.

"Besides," she went on, "you haven't finished your homework. There's more to life than playing soccer, Robbie."

Knowing how the boy felt about the sport, Luke could have warned her that it was the wrong way to put it, long before the boy shot a look at his mother. "Jeez, Mom, just once you could try to understand. And why can't you call me Rob like Luke does?"

Watching Callie, Luke caught the surprised hurt in her expression before she could hide it. "Because she's your mom," he intervened before she could dig her hole deeper. "All moms have their own special name for their kid."

Rob tilted his head, clearly amazed by this information. "Yeah? What did your mom call you?"

Luke tried to remember his mother ever using an endearment. Mostly what he recalled hearing was "scrape your feet" or "keep your voice down" or the all-too-frequent "not now, I'm busy." None of which would convince Rob, or cover for Callie. "She called me Lucky," he fibbed. "After a while, most everyone did."

"Yeah, well they don't now." Again, Rob flashed a look at his mother. "Now that you're a grown-up, everyone calls you Luke."

"Maybe that's because my mom isn't here anymore. I'm not lucky like you."

Callie's surprise, Luke noticed, was now directed at him. Mixed in with it, though, was a bit of suspicion as if she were wondering what his angle might be now.

Glancing back at his mother, Rob gave her a sheepish grin. "Okay. I guess you can call me Robbie. But just here at home, okay? Not in front of Coach, or my teacher."

Clearly considering the matter settled, Rob looked at the pile of shirts, then at his bedroom. "Were you putting those in my room?" He spun to face Callie. "You did move my bed back in there, didn't you?"

Luke, knowing full well that she hadn't, tried to

change the subject. "As soon as I put these away, what say you and I go across the street to the park?"

"Not yet," Callie interrupted. "He has five pages of math to do first."

"I can't believe you're being mean about this, too." Rob looked ready for a full rebellion. "You don't want me doing anything with Luke."

"That's not true, Robbie. You're pushing. Don't you think you should first ask our guest what he wants to do."

"I did. On the phone the other night. He'd said he'd be happy to share a room with me, didn't you Luke?"

They both looked up him, Rob pleading, Callie pursing her lips. "I also said I'd be just as happy on the couch," Luke offered as a compromise, placating neither.

Rob's snort proved what little stock he put in that statement. "He can't sleep on the couch, Mom. It's falling apart. You're the one who says a Magruder doesn't ever stint on their guests."

"Fine," Callie said, tossing her hands up in the air. "Share the room, then. I'll move the stupid bed this very minute."

She started stomping toward her bedroom, but Luke intercepted her, grabbing her wrist. "*I'll* move the bed. It's the least I can do."

For a minute he thought she meant to argue, but giving a pointed glare at his hand gripping her arm, she wrenched away from his grasp. "Fine. Whatever. I'll go fix dinner then."

"What's with her?" a mystified Rob asked when she left the room.

A sentiment Luke might feel inclined to echo, but he knew better than to admit it to the boy. "I think we hurt her feelings," he told Rob instead, giving him his first lesson in the vagaries of women. "It's a new thing for her, seeing you growing up. Give her time to get used to it. She loves you, you know, and wants only what's best for you."

"Yeah, I guess."

"No guessing involved. You just think back to how many times she was there when you needed her." Even as he thought the words, Luke realized he should be heeding his own advice. More times than not, Callie had been there when he needed someone to talk to, and how had he repaid her?

"You think I should go apologize?" Rob asked, glancing back at the kitchen door. "Think that will make her feel better?"

Nodding, Luke wished a mere apology would work for himself. "I think it's a good plan, Rob. Tell you what. I'll go move your bed while you talk to your mom. Then we can work together on that math homework."

"What about soccer?"

"Only if there's time before dinner."

Rob looked as if he was going to argue, but he apparently thought better of it, holding his head high as he marched to the kitchen. Watching him, Luke marveled at what a great kid he was, all thanks to Callie.

He'd had a rocky start today, he told himself as he headed into her bedroom, yet he'd managed to recover. By keeping his temper in check and his mind on the game plan, he could eventually make headway in proving to Callie that he wasn't the enemy. At least she hadn't yet repeated her threat about ending their marriage.

All things considered, he told himself, he'd made a good beginning. Keep on this way, and things were bound to work out fine.

*   *   *

Having Luke live with them wasn't ever going to work, Callie thought later as she washed the dishes. Every time she turned around, it seemed, he was with Robbie, the two of them united against her. Bad enough they shared a bedroom and their obsession with soccer, but Luke was now helping her son with his homework.

"He's better than you at math," was the boy's explanation. It was true, she supposed, but seeing Luke beside Robbie at the dining room table, she had this fierce, irrational urge to order him out of the house. If he was using her son to get to her, she'd have him strung by his thumbs from the roof.

She was in the middle of a huff when Luke strolled through the door. "We just conquered fractions," he announced, absentmindedly rubbing his shoulder. "Now I'm ready to tackle the dishes."

Heaven forbid. The last thing she needed in her confused state was to make small talk with Luke in this claustrophobic kitchen. "Go rest your arm. You probably re-injured it moving that bed."

It would be no more than he deserved, she felt, but she didn't vocalize the sentiment. She had no wish to argue; she just wanted him out of her kitchen.

"Nah, it's just a little stiff," he said, reaching for a towel. "I think I can manage to lift a couple of plates."

"Well, it's not necessary," she insisted. "I'm practically finished, anyway."

"I'm happy to help." He reached into the dish drain as if she hadn't even spoken. "I told Rob we'll all have to pitch in more, with you starting school next week."

Having him stand so close made her nervous. Worse, she felt *edgy*. Oblivious to this, he reached behind her to stack the plate he'd dried on the counter. As he did, she caught a hint of his aftershave, a spicy pine blend that reminded her of Christmas. For a brief, unguarded moment, she flashed back to the way it had been between them, a time when she'd live for that scent, never guessing the ugliness that would soon spring up between them.

"In fact," he went on, dispersing the memory, "I've decided that from now on, I can drive Rob to and from school."

"Absolutely not." All her worries and resentment exploding to the surface, she whirled to face him, spraying a healthy dose of dishwater on his clean white shirt.

"Jeez, Cal," he said, dabbing at it with the dishrag. "What did I do wrong now?"

"You're taking over, Luke. That's what. First it was soccer, then doing his math, now you're playing his chauffeur?"

"You're mad at me because I'm trying to help out with your son?"

Put like that, she did sound irrational. Stabbing her hands back into the dishwater, she yanked out a plate and rinsed it. "I don't think it's a good idea, you and Robbie spending all this time together."

Luke sighed as he reached behind her to put the last of the dishes on top of the pile.

"I'm serious, Luke," she insisted. "He can get *too* used to having you around. What will happen to him when you go? Kids don't understand people leaving them. All they know is how much it hurts."

Reaching for the pile, he paused mere inches behind her. "Are you sure we're talking about Rob?" he asked, having no need to add the implied *and not you?*

Callie froze as the truth behind his question slammed into her. Could she honestly claim that her fears were solely for Robbie?

"Besides," Luke added as he moved away to shove

the dishes into place on the shelf, "who says I'm going anywhere?"

He could have said a few things to stop her in her tracks, but none as effective as that. And to punctuate the question, he slammed the cabinet shut.

She turned to find him leaning back against the counter, staring at her, his features tight with suppressed emotion. "I saw his face, Cal," he said slowly, as if picking his words with care. "I saw his happiness and excitement when he saw me. And you know what? I felt the same about him. Give me a little credit here. I'm not a total monster."

"But there's only eleven months left to this marriage," she protested, wanting to make him see the flaw in his logic. "What happens to all his happiness and excitement when you walk away from us?"

"You put the time limit on our marriage," he reminded sternly. "Not me."

Did he expect her to believe he wanted to stay married? Mr. Luke Gotta-Run Parker?

He must have seen her skepticism. "You told me not to make any promises I don't aim to keep," he said, again speaking slowly. "Well, here's one you can bank on. I'm not running out on Rob, Callie. Whatever might happen between you and me, I'll always be there for that kid."

Once again, she felt robbed of speech. He seemed so intense, so determined and so thoroughly unlike the easygoing, fun-loving Lucky who'd once captured her heart.

"I can't always claim to know what I'm doing," he went on, "but Rob and I have a good relationship and I'd like to keep it going. I know what it's like to grow up without a father's attention, Cal. That's not what you want for your boy."

She stiffened, turning back to the sink to yank out the plug. "Don't tell me what I want," she told him to the accompaniment of gurgling water. "You think it was my choice to make my son grow up without a father?" Pushed by her anger, she began scrubbing the sink so hard it was a wonder she didn't rub off the enamel.

Behind her she could hear him inhale sharply, then let the air out. "Forget the past," he said quietly. "I'm talking about the here and now."

She could hear him push off from the counter, his voice getting louder as he approached. "The boy needs a father, Cal. And I'm here volunteering to take on the job." Stepping up behind her, he reached over her arm to gently remove the scrub brush from her hands. "Give me the chance to prove I'm the man Rob needs in his life. The one he deserves."

She didn't answer; she couldn't even look at him, but she relinquished the brush without a fight.

Gazing down at her averted face, sensing her fear and confusion, Luke knew better, this time, than to assume her silence meant victory. Still, she was listening—not willingly, or happily—but at least he had her attention. What he did with it would determine his fate.

"You asked me earlier today if I'd come home to lick my wounds," he said, stepping back so she wouldn't feel threatened by his presence. "I'd be lying if I said it wasn't partly the reason. Those last few years in New York were a painful experience, but they forced me to take a long, hard look at myself and the selfish life I'd been living. I guess it's not so much a matter of wanting to change as knowing I *have* to change if I want to look at myself in the mirror."

She frowned. "Are you telling me that's what all this

buddy-buddy stuff is with my son? You trying to do something worthwhile with your life?''

Luke leaned back against the counter again, trying to seem relaxed and therefore nonthreatening. ''Something like that. Rob's a real good mirror, Cal. In case you haven't noticed, he doesn't let anything slip by him.''

She didn't melt a molecule. ''Well, I don't want you using my boy to make yourself feel better. He's been through enough as it is.''

''Oh, for crying out loud, I'm not using anybody. Aren't you listening?'' He stopped, dismayed to find himself standing straight and rigid again, and much too close to her. He didn't like that he'd so easily lost his temper after all, but it was just too much for him, listening to her talk about *her* boy, when he was Rob's parent, too.

Still, it wasn't helping his case any by going off on a short fuse. ''I'm trying to do something decent here,'' he added more gently. ''And you're not making it any easier.''

She blinked, as if the possibility of her being even somewhat in the wrong had never occurred to her.

''We can point fingers until doomsday,'' he said wearily, ''but in the long run, what will it accomplish? Can't you at least give me a shot at this?''

''A shot at what, Luke?''

She stood there with her hands on her hips, his judge, jury and executioner. And what could he tell her that could possibly sway her mind?

Tell her the truth, his conscience told him. As the woman said, he might as well start as he meant to go on. ''Making amends. Being what the boy needs, and being there for his mother.'' He held up a hand before she could comment. ''I know. You want results, not promises. So that's what I'll give you. Results.''

And even as he said it, he knew there was no time like the present to get started. Why wait until tomorrow? He'd battle his father tonight.

"Speaking of which," he said, glancing at his watch. "I have to go out."

"Out?" She blinked again, clearly caught off guard. "At half past eight?"

"Trust me, it's important." He walked over to her, taking her by the arms, but it wasn't until he saw her widened eyes that he realized he'd meant to kiss her. Not passionately, just a peck, as if they were a happily settled couple. Callie's horrified expression made it clear that they were anything but.

"I should be home for the late-night news," he said, dropping her arms. "Save a spot on the couch for me."

He could feel her stare, probing him in the back as he left the room, but really, what more could he say to her? No sense getting her hopes up, not when Ben was bound to put up one hell of a fight.

Let him, he thought determinedly. For once in their lives Luke wasn't backing down. It might take a week, and it might take a year, but getting Callie's farm back for her had become his crusade.

Whatever it took, he'd prove to her he could keep a promise.

Casting aside the covers she'd tangled around her, Callie got out of her bed. Might as well check out the apartment to see if Luke had come home yet. He'd gone out over six hours ago, but she'd yet to hear him come in the door.

She might have dozed off and missed him, she supposed, but she had this unsettled feeling in her gut, a sure sign that her annoying sixth sense might be kicking into gear. Just be on the couch, Luke, she thought as she donned a robe and groped her way to her bedroom door. *Be there safe and sound so I can go back to sleep.*

When she didn't find him in the living room, she remembered that he was sleeping in Robbie's room now. Going there, she found Luke's new bed empty. At three in the morning she didn't know whether to be sick with worry or just plain furious.

And just where do you think he is? asked a nasty little voice inside her. Against her will she kept seeing those tabloid pictures of him on the arm of one gorgeous female after another, kept hearing his protest that he wasn't a monk.

Jamming her hands in her robe pockets, she told herself that it mattered little to her where he slept. She certainly didn't want any emotional ties between them.

So why, then, did the thought of Luke with another woman make her physically ill?

It was the vows they'd taken, she insisted to herself. It had nothing to do with personal, more intimate feelings. Luke had sworn to remain faithful, and he should now keep his word, just as she kept hers. That was the way an honest man made amends, the way he backed up his words with action.

Results, he'd promised her. Listening to him, feeling the strength and determination in his hands on her arms, she'd actually wanted to believe him.

"Just come home," she heard herself whisper.

Daunting, how desperately she needed to see him walk into the room. Standing there, staring at a door that refused to open, she was forced to acknowledge that Robbie wasn't the only one who was growing too accustomed to having Luke around. How had it happened that she would be pacing across her living room at three in the morning, mentally begging her errant husband to come home? Hadn't she sworn, years ago, never to let Luke reduce her to such a state again? If she had any backbone, the instant Luke walked in the door she'd tell him their marriage was over.

Only, what if he wasn't with a woman or at a bar or involved in any of the other pastimes that had kept Reb out into the wee hours of the morning? What if there was a logical explanation? Like an accident. She pictured him, trapped in his BMW, unable to call for help.

Luke, please, just come home.

As if in answer, she heard the screech of tires outside the apartment and the slam of a car door. She ran to the window, worry sliding into anger as she saw the BMW. Clearly, he couldn't be hurt, if he was already bounding up the stairs.

Had it all been a lie? His talk about the new Luke, the committed Luke—had it merely been the old Luke telling her what he thought she wanted to hear?

Facing the door, she toyed with the idea of running to her room, but she needed too many answers to pretend a total lack of concern over his absence. It was one thing when she thought him hurt, but her worry had quickly transformed into anger. No, she'd sit here on the couch like an angry parent, demanding an explanation for why he hadn't come home. Then she'd tell him what he could do with his chance at atonement.

Working herself into a state, she was primed and ready when Luke stumbled through the door. ''Where have you been?'' she asked as she leaped to her feet, forgetting her intention to remain angry and aloof on the sofa.

''At the hospital,'' he said wearily. ''Ben's had a stroke.''

Chapter Twelve

For Luke the sight of an enraged Callie came as the last straw. To say he'd been to hell and back was an understatement. It wasn't every day you put your father in intensive care.

"What happened?" Callie gasped.

"We argued. He collapsed. They don't know if he'll ever regain much quality of life or, for that matter, even consciousness."

He could see his own stunned disbelief in her eyes. "Luke, I'm so sorry. Is there anything I can do?"

"You can get me a whiskey if you have it. A tall one. I need something to help me sleep. I've got four—" he glanced at the clock "—make that three hours before the doctors show up for their morning rounds."

"I don't have any alcohol," she said apologetically. "I could make cocoa, though. Warm milk is supposed to help you sleep."

"Then make it a tall cocoa. Thanks, Cal," he said as she turned for the kitchen.

She glanced back at him, mystified. "For what?"

For being you, he thought, but aloud he said, "For not bombarding me with questions. For not biting my head off the minute I walked in the door."

"Sit down and rest," she told him in motherlike fashion. "Once you've recovered your wits, there will be plenty of time for questions."

And head biting, he thought as he watched her disappear in the kitchen.

Taking off his jacket and plopping down on the couch, he was glad to have the time to regroup. He'd had precious little opportunity to process the night's events during the nightmare in the emergency room.

Typically, the visit with his father had started out badly and gone swiftly from worse to worst. After all these years, you'd think he and the old man could manage a civil conversation, but they'd been shouting at each other ten minutes after Luke walked in the door.

Looking back, the warning signs had been there. Ben had looked awful, but since he'd been drinking heavily, and the stench of cigar smoke clung to the air, Luke attributed his bad color to his lifelong vices. Still, he should have paid more heed to the trembling in his father's hands and the way Ben never rose from his chair. Not until his last outburst.

And by then, it had been far too late.

Luke shut his eyes, remembering the ugliness of their argument.

How smug Ben had seemed, sitting like a king on his throne in his plush recliner, not even bothering to offer his son a seat, much less a drink. "What do you want?" he barked, as if Luke were there for a handout.

"I think it's time you and I had a talk," he stated firmly.

Ben merely snorted.

In the fireplace behind them, the flames hissed and popped. The fact that it was too early in the season for such a blaze was another clear sign of Ben's failing health, but all Luke could hear was his father's condemning silence.

"You want to get back in the will," Ben said finally, eyeing Luke over his glass as he took a long pull on his whiskey. "But it's not gonna happen until you meet my two conditions."

"You honestly think that's why I came here? That I care two hoots about your money? Or, God forbid, this house?"

Looking around him, Ben shrugged, as if he considered his son's failure to value his possessions Luke's loss, not his. "Condition one is that you give up the football nonsense," he said, pretending Luke hadn't spoken. "Starting tomorrow, you'll come work for me."

Time warp, Luke thought, recognizing the same words Ben had uttered ten years ago, when trying to talk him out of a sports career. Of course, that was before Ben had heard of Luke's extracurricular activities. Once he'd learned his son had been seeing the Magruder girl, Ben couldn't get Luke to New York fast enough. "You're lucky to escape with your freedom," he told his son over and over. "White trash like that get their tentacles into a man by tricking him into believing she's having his baby."

And just think of the irony in that, Luke thought.

"We've had this argument, Dad," he stated firmly. "We both know I have no intention of playing your puppet. Get used to the fact that you'll have to find somebody else to play Pinocchio. I'm not going anywhere near your damned company.''

''That *damned company* paid for your fancy cars and hoity-toity education,'' Ben ranted back at him. ''It's time you showed it, and me, some respect.''

''I've tried that, for almost thirty years. All things considered, don't you think it's time you showed *me* some respect?''

They stared at each other for a long, heated moment. ''Wasn't right, what happened to Matt,'' Ben said at last, not backing down an inch. ''That boy's my only shot at the future.''

Dread creeping into him, Luke had to ask. ''What boy?''

''Your son. My grandson.'' Ben sighed as he gazed into the fire. ''The only hope I have left.''

''You know about Rob?'' It made Luke sick inside, thinking what his father could do with the information.

''That's the difference between you and me. I make sure I've got all the facts before I go off half-cocked.'' Shaking his head, Ben focused his gaze on Luke. ''I knew there had to be a reason for you to do something as stupid as marrying the Magruder girl.''

''Did it ever occur to you that I might have feelings for Callie?''

''You?'' Ben snorted.

More than the word hovered between them. Luke could feel the past, all the many times he should have shown emotion but didn't, all the reasons Ben maintained he just didn't have it in him.

''I know about your financial arrangement with the woman, so don't bother lying to me about why you came home. It's plain as day you want custody of the boy, and for once we're in agreement. Get his name

changed to Parker and then you can fulfill my second
condition.''

"Oh, really. And that is?''

"Get rid of the mother.''

If Ben hadn't been his father, Luke would have loved
nothing better than to physically wipe the smirk off his
face. Get rid of her, Ben said, as if Callie were some
trash to be dumped at the curb. "I've got a better idea,''
Luke said icily. "Why don't you quit playing Machia-
velli and sell me the Magruder farm.''

"Over my dead body!'' Ben visibly trembled with
what Luke thought was rage. "I've got plans for that
land, and I'm not giving them up for any Magruder.''

"It's not just any Magruder,'' Luke growled back.
"It's your daughter-in-law.''

"White trash.''

Ten years ago Ben had used the same derogatory
term for Callie. Looking at him now, Luke felt suddenly
ashamed for not protesting. "Who are you to look down
your nose at her?'' he asked, standing up for her now.
"In my book, Callie has more honor and decency in
her little finger than you have in your entire self-
righteous body.''

"You think honor and decency was why she married
you? Wake up and smell the greed, boy. All that girl
wants is to get herself written into the will.''

"Not Callie.''

"Not Callie," Ben mocked. "She took your money,
didn't she? Bet your pretty little bride urged you to
reconcile when I threatened to cut you off, didn't she?
Heck, who can blame her? It's human nature to grasp
at the fortune you stand to inherit. Given how she grew
up, I imagine she'd do just about anything for financial
security. Even making up to you.''

Some might find a twisted logic to all Ben said, but

Luke knew for a fact that his father was wrong about Callie. "Here's a news bulletin," he said. "Not everyone is as conniving as you."

Ben leaned forward in his chair, glaring. "You watch how you talk to me, boy."

"I am watching. Weighing every word. So listen up and understand this, old man. I don't care if you're my father, I won't have you bad-mouthing my wife. If I hear you've done one thing to make her even frown, I'll see to it that you don't get within a mile of Robbie."

"You're threatening me, boy?" Ben gave him a nasty, little smile. "I still have her farm, remember. I can still make sure you and your precious wife never step foot on it again."

"Oh, I'll get the farm," Luke swore, "even if it means setting up my own industry in the area and running you out of business."

"Why, you ungrateful twerp," Ben shouted at him. "If your brother, Matt, were here, he'd put you in your place."

"Saint Matt," Luke muttered.

"Don't you dare sneer at his memory," Ben snarled, rising from his chair to stand before Luke. "He was worth ten of you. A hundred. You're not fit to utter his name."

"Matt is dead." Luke knew he was being cruel but he couldn't seem to stop. "You lost him twenty years ago, Dad, and nothing you can say or do now will ever resurrect him. So don't for a moment think I'll sit by and watch you use Robbie as his substitute."

"Damn you!" Ben hissed, tossing the remains of his glass in Luke's face.

And then, with a strange gurgle in the back of his throat, Ben collapsed in a heap at Luke's feet.

* * *

"Luke, are you okay?" Callie suddenly asked, seeming a long way away.

Looking up, slowly focusing on her face, Luke realized how lost he'd been in his thoughts. "Uh, yeah. I'm fine." Sitting up from his slouch, he reached to take the mug from her hands. "Just a little dazed, I guess. I still can't believe he collapsed like that. It all happened so suddenly. One minute he was shouting at me and the next…"

He trailed off, too drained to take it further.

Sitting beside him, Callie filled in the blanks. "You had another fight." She stated the obvious. Turning to face him, she sat with her feet tucked beside her, her arm draped over the couch. "Want to talk about it?"

For an instant he was tempted to unload, but in truth what could he tell her? That he'd lost his temper again and probably cost her the farm? "Not at four in the morning," he said instead, taking a gulp of the cocoa. "Suffice it to say, we had one of our typical arguments. And as usual I said too many things I shouldn't have."

"You're not blaming yourself for your father's collapse, are you?" She stared at him solemnly, a wise little sage in pink pajamas and a white chenille bathrobe. "Don't go down that road, Luke. If Ben had a stroke, you can as easily blame his lifestyle or his temper. No offense, but he was one mean old cuss. All that anger was bound to be his undoing someday."

"Yeah." Luke took another gulp from the mug. "Still, you weren't there, Cal. You didn't see him being loaded onto the stretcher, having tubes inserted everywhere. And then at the hospital, the machines clanking and beeping, all the doctors shaking their heads."

She reached out tentatively, touching his arm. "As you said, it's late and you're tired. In the morning, when you're rested and can think straight, you'll see that Ben put himself in that hospital. Not you.''

"I fought with him.''

She pulled back her arm, as if just now aware of the impulsive gesture. Luke, who had felt warmed by it, wished she could have remained unaware a little bit longer.

"So?'' she said, raising a brow. "You fight with me and I'm not in any intensive care unit.''

He gave her a reluctant grin. "Okay, I get your point. And for what it's worth, I appreciate the pep talk. I'm going to need all the assurances I can get. It won't be easy, getting through these next few weeks.''

"He's that bad?''

"It's still too soon to tell, but the even best prognosis leaves him permanently paralyzed. This wasn't his first stroke, apparently. He'd been warned repeatedly to cut back on work, to stop the drinking and smoking.''

From her expression, he could see how she barely restrained herself from muttering, *I told you so.*

"Even if he did put himself in this position,'' he half conceded, "it still doesn't lessen the nightmare. Whether or not Ben comes out of his coma, a lot of decisions will have to be made. Not just about his health care. There's the company, his estate, that monstrosity he calls a house. As his closest surviving relative, I alone have the responsibility of making those decisions. I never asked for this to happen, Cal. I'm not even sure I can handle it.''

Her hand reached out again, tentatively touching his shoulder. "You're not alone, Luke. Robbie and I are here to help.''

She gave him time to absorb the feeling, to understand what it could mean to have a family behind him, before she hastily withdrew her hand once again. "Not that we can help with major decisions or other important matters,'' she said, plainly retreating. ''But if you need someone to talk to, to sound out ideas…''

She let the words taper off, clearly uncomfortable with her offer. ''Thanks,'' he said simply, reaching out to clasp her hand before she could withdraw any further. ''I'd appreciate that.''

And he did. More than he could ever tell her. Thinking back, talking with Callie had always made him feel better about everything.

Cheeks reddening, Callie stared at their joined hands, then slowly looked up to meet his gaze. For a long moment she looked into him, probing as if taking his measure, before pulling her gaze, and hand, away.

''It's late,'' she said far too brightly as she rose to her feet, tightly clasping the lapels of her robe together. ''You're not going to get the sleep you need if I keep you up chatting.''

As she stood, Luke could feel the warmth leave him. He had the overwhelming urge to pull her back down to the couch beside him, to hold her close until they both fell asleep. Unfortunately, he couldn't imagine her cooperating.

''Yeah, I guess you're right.'' Draining the mug, he, too, rose to his feet, turning toward the kitchen to wash it.

''Here, I'll take that,'' she said, reaching for the mug.

''No, I'm responsible for the mess. I'll get it.'' Luke didn't let go, and she didn't relinquish her hold, either. ''Really, Cal, I'm not ready to turn in just yet, anyway.''

He could have stayed awake for hours, he realized, staring down at her lovely face, for once softened as she gazed back at him. Frightening, how much he longed to kiss her. Yet how exhilarating to sense she just might want the same.

"I'm sorry about your dad," was all she said, though, as she removed her grip on the mug. "And for so very nearly biting off your head when you walked in the door."

"Oh, ye of little faith."

She gave him a rueful grin. "Maybe I jumped to conclusions, but you were gone almost seven hours. In the future call if you're going to be late."

"I'm not some trouble-making teenager, Cal. I shouldn't have to report in."

Her grin all too swiftly became her far-too-familiar frown. "Yeah, well I shouldn't have to worry that you're dead in some ditch, either."

It had never occurred to him that she might be concerned with his safety. He found it a novel concept, that anyone would worry over him. He also found he liked the idea. "Point taken," he told her on a sigh. "This is new ground for me, Cal. I've always been something of a loner."

She nodded, as if she understood and accepted his explanation. "I swear," he went on, placing his fingers, Boy Scout style, over his heart. "From now on, I'll call home for even the slightest delay."

She tilted her head, studying him for a moment, before shaking her head. "We'll see," she said as she turned for her bedroom. "Good night, Luke. And good luck with your dad tomorrow if I don't see you before you leave in the morning."

Watching her go, Luke had another strong urge to grab for her, to keep her close, but he wisely kept his arms to himself. He'd known from the start that Callie Magruder would be a tough nut to crack, and he wasn't risking the small progress he'd made by forcing her to open up before she was ready.

Talking to her tonight, feeling her concern, he'd realized he was tired of being a loner. All his life he'd stood apart. He used to tell himself that he found strength in standing alone, but in truth, all he'd ever encountered was a vast, aching emptiness.

If she wanted him calling home every five minutes, then heck, he'd carry his cell phone wherever he went. He would survive her trial by fire. Whatever it took, he'd prove himself worthy.

Callie lay in her bed, listening to Luke putter around in the kitchen. What an unsettling night it had been, starting with Luke's vow to be there for Robbie, then the news about his father and now this uneasy truce between them. Was it any wonder her head was spinning?

What on earth was she going to do about Luke?

She couldn't quite lose her suspicions—after all, she'd had ten long years to nurture them—yet she couldn't deny that he was going out of his way to be considerate. None of the girls in the salon ever bragged about their husbands doing dishes. If anything, they were always griping because the big louts refused to do anything to help out in the house.

And yet, she mustn't forget that Luke had built a house of cards for her before. The minute she'd felt comfortable in it, the illusion had tumbled down around her. How could she trust him? How could she trust any of this?

Trust in your heart, Gramps would have advised, *but always let your head lead the way.*

All well and good, she thought, but what did you do when heart and head wanted to go in different directions? Emotionally she could share Luke's pain. She could see clearly that he desperately needed a friend. Logically, however, she couldn't ignore his track record. She herself was living proof that Luke had a habit of leaving his friends in the lurch when he no longer needed them.

Of course, he claimed to have changed. She couldn't deny that his time away had altered him, but in what way and to what extent? She wasn't going back out on any limb for that man. She couldn't afford to, not with Robbie to consider.

Are you protecting Robbie? he'd implied. Or are you just trying to save yourself?

A clever tactic, getting her to doubt herself, but either way it made little difference. By leaving her all those years ago, he'd lost all right to question her motivations. His own were at issue here, and the jury was still out deliberating. Until Callie had proof that he could follow through on his promises, she'd be a fool to trust a word the man ever uttered.

But isn't that what he offered? questioned the voice of logic. In her mind she could see his face as he asked for the chance to prove himself. She'd seen it all—his regret, self-doubt and sheer determination. She'd be foolish to get her hopes up, but what if it were true, what if Luke Parker really had changed?

"We'll see," she'd told him earlier, and perhaps that was her own best advice. She could wait, give him enough rope, as long as she made sure she wasn't there to watch while he hanged himself.

This time, she'd be the one taking off.

Chapter Thirteen

The following Saturday, waiting on the sidelines to watch Robbie play his first soccer game, Callie still hadn't made up her mind about Luke. Not because he'd been unable to convince her, but because she'd seen precious little of him to help in her assessment. For the past week Luke had fallen in the habit of coming back to the apartment after midnight and leaving before she rose in the morning, leaving a note that he'd gone to the hospital or off on various errands for his father's estate. She hoped he wasn't overlooking his own business dealings, but since they rarely talked, she had no way of knowing what he did or where he went.

Robbie had seen him, though, she'd learned just this morning. It seemed he and Luke got together in the afternoons when she was either at school or working in the beauty parlor. Whatever else Luke might be neglecting, he made sure to be there every day for soccer practice. And by doing so, he'd scored big points with her son.

She looked down the sidelines at Robbie, the boy hopping on one foot then the other as he glanced anxiously around him. Painful lesson number one, she thought, her heart constricting for him. Getting to the practices was one thing, but apparently Luke hadn't grasped the importance of making it to the games.

Though it was exactly what she'd expected of him, Callie couldn't forgive Luke for disappointing her boy. Even now, with the referee blowing his whistle and the boys taking the field, Robbie continued to glance back over his shoulder, still hoping to find Luke on the sidelines. The poor kid was so preoccupied with looking behind him, he missed the first ball that was kicked his way. Hearing the coach berate him, Callie swore she'd give the same to Luke and more, next time she saw him.

Busy preparing her scathing comments, she didn't realize how soon she'd get the opportunity until she noticed the shadow looming beside her. She was so shocked to see Luke, every invective went flying out of her head.

"Sorry I'm late." Luke said, not looking at her as he waved an enthusiastic hello at Robbie. "The traffic was brutal."

Slowly recovering from her surprise, Callie studied him. Amid the denim and sweats of the other parents, he seemed thoroughly out of place in his unbuttoned suit jacket and dangling tie, and a rumpled white shirt that had seen better days. Still, he remained gorgeous enough to set her pulse racing.

Flustered by her involuntary reaction to him, she tried to recapture her anger and resentment. Seeing her son's happy face, though, she realized she was fighting a losing battle. Clearly, it hadn't been easy for Luke to get here, but he hadn't let Robbie down. And whether she liked it or not, his showing up had scored big points with her, too.

"How's your father doing?" she asked, when what she really meant was, how are *you* doing?

"No real change," he said tersely, obviously having no wish to talk about Ben. "Tell me about the game. Any score yet?"

"They just started," she told him, then couldn't stop herself from adding, "Robbie missed a pass, busy scouring the sidelines for you. I think he was afraid you wouldn't make it."

He'd been shading his eyes as he watched the field, but he turned to her with a fierce expression. "You think I'd miss his first game? I spent too many years scanning the bleachers, hoping my father would be there, not to know how Rob would feel if I bailed on him. I told him I'd be here. And I'll go through hell and high water before I'd ever go back on my word to that boy."

"Okay, I get it. You made your point."

"Besides," he said with a reluctant grin, "I put a lot of time into those practices. I have to see if it paid off or not."

"I'd say so. Look." She pointed down the field where Robbie was running, spindly legs chugging furiously as he charged at the goalie.

"Pass the ball, Rob," Luke coached softly beside her, his gaze riveted on the boy. "Your teammate is wide open."

For a second it looked as if Robbie meant to try and score himself, but at the last minute he side-kicked it across the field to the boy trailing inches behind him. A second later, the ball went sailing into the goal.

Around them, the other parents let out a cheer, but Luke smiled with quiet satisfaction. He's actually proud of Robbie, Callie thought with wonder. He truly must care about him.

"Did you see, Luke?" Robbie shouted to him as the teams came back to set up for the kickoff. "I got an assist."

"Good eye, Rob," Luke shouted back. "You read the field perfectly."

"He's so happy about helping someone else score?" Callie asked, confused. "I thought you were teaching him how to score the goals himself."

Luke looked at her, seeming almost disappointed. "First I want him to learn that the cornerstone of any sport is teamwork," he said, turning his attention back to the game. "Kind of like it should be in marriage."

He slipped that in just as Robbie stole the ball, so she had little time to think about it, much less make a comment. She knew better than to listen to his jibes, anyway. As if Luke "Love-'Em-and-Leave-'Em" Parker knew the first thing about what made a good marriage.

The game heated up, the action fast and furious. Unlike most of the men there—and some of the women—Luke didn't run up and down the sidelines screaming and yelling at Robbie to run faster or kick the ball harder. He stood where he was, smiling his encouragement, watching carefully as if mentally taking notes.

Twice more Robbie got the ball and passed it off, but the one time he was open and able to score, a teammate charged at the goal instead. The goalie made the save and tossed it down the field, creating a quick score for their opponents.

At halftime, Robbie ran straight to Luke while the other boys went to the bench for their drink and snack.

"Sorry, Luke," he said, his face screwed up with regret. "I wanted to score so you could be proud of me."

"Are you kidding?" Luke hunkered down beside the boy, placing his arm on the boy's shoulder. "You're doing great, Rob. Scoring isn't everything. The object is to work together out there, recognizing each other's strengths and opportunities. If your teammate had recognized that you were open, he'd have passed the ball instead. You would have scored that goal, and it would now be two-nothing in your favor."

"You think?"

"I do. You know, Rob, sometimes you can be a little too unselfish. I noticed you keep looking to pass, but you're not following your instincts. Lose yourself, get into the flow of the game. When the opening presents itself, take it. We both know you've got what it takes to score a goal."

Robbie beamed happily. "Yeah, but I'm not nearly as good a scorer as Tommy," he said as the boy who had gotten their only goal wandered over to join them. "I'm thinking maybe we shouldn't let him practice with us anymore, huh, Luke?"

"It's not just the two of you practicing in the park?" Callie asked Luke. "Why do I feel as if my son has suddenly developed this secret life without me?"

Luke looked up at her, half-amused. "It's no secret, Cal. Tommy happens to live in the neighborhood. Sometimes Jason joins us, too." Leaving her to digest this, he turned back to the two boys, who were busy trading good-natured insults. "Is this teamwork?" Luke asked, smiling from one boy to the other. "Do we want to win this game or what?"

He's really good at this, Callie thought, watching the three heads bent together as they discussed strategy for the second half. Unlike their coach, shouting at Robbie's teammates over by the bench, Luke found a positive way to show the boys what they were doing wrong, taking special care also to point out what they were doing right. In her opinion, they might be better off with Luke running the team.

The realization surprised her. A short time ago, had anyone told her that Luke Parker could be good with children, she'd have laughed in his face.

Standing, Luke nodded in the direction of the bench. "You guys better get going. Coach is looking for you. Remember, it's all about teamwork."

As the boys scrambled off, he turned to face Callie with a puzzled expression. "Okay," he said tentatively, "now what did I do to put that frown on your face? You're not mad because you think Robbie and I are keeping secrets, are you?"

She shook her head. In truth, she'd been thinking about his earlier comment, how it took teamwork to make a good marriage. Watching him with Robbie, she'd found herself wondering what it could be like for her son if he had a mother *and* father, working together to make the best life possible for him.

Annoyed to find herself softening toward Luke, she answered his question by bringing up another issue that had been bothering her. "Not deliberate secrets, maybe, but you and he have this soccer thing between you, and I can't help but feel left out. I want to be as good a soccer mom as the next gal, but you two start rambling on about being offside, or running fast breaks and you might as well be talking in Martian."

He flashed his million-dollar smile, the one that got his face on the front pages of the tabloids and never failed to make her heart beat faster. "That's easily remedied, Cal. Ask and I'll tell you. Better yet, why don't I show you as the game goes on?"

As the second half progressed, Luke patiently explained the intricacies of the game to her, including the coach's apparent strategy. He didn't agree with the man's game plan, she could tell, and when the last whistle blew, with Robbie's team losing, she found herself siding with Luke. In her mind, he'd have made a far better coach for these boys. He'd have helped them win but victory or not, he'd make sure they felt good about themselves afterward.

Impulsively, she told him this as they waited for Robbie to complete the ritual of congratulating their opponents.

Luke merely shrugged. "Rob's coach merely uses different methods than I would. That's how it is in sports. If Robbie wants to keep playing, he'll have to learn to deal with all sorts of approaches and personalities."

"Like you did with your coach?" Even before she saw his wince, Callie regretted the question. She hadn't meant it to be snide, but it sure sounded that way.

To her surprise he didn't take exception to it, choosing instead to answer honestly. "I'm a perfect example of what can happen when you don't listen to your coach. I had a swollen head, thought I knew better than everyone else, and I hurt my team by so publicly voicing my opinions. All I can say in my defense is that my coach knew how to push my buttons. I guess he reminded me too much of my father."

Callie could hear the pain behind his remark. "If he was anything like Ben," she offered, trying to make up for her earlier comment, "then I don't blame you for not listening to him."

"I'm afraid the media and fans in New York didn't agree with you," Luke said tautly, staring ahead at the handshaking on the field. "And I can't really blame them. I cost the team a shot at the play-offs with my bullheadedness. I tell you, if I had it to do over, I'd hold a tighter rein on my temper. All those years on the field and I never took home a championship ring.''

Staring at his profile, she saw the tightness in his jaw, heard the wistfulness in his tone. ''You really miss it, don't you?''

''Football formed my life for nearly twenty years. I'm bound to feel a certain loss, and I sure regret not achieving all my goals. Every player wants to wear that ring. It's why we put up with getting our heads bashed every Sunday. Well, I took one hit too many, and the arm is now shot and my last hope for a championship is out the window.''

''But couldn't you still coach a team to a winning season?'' she asked. ''You're obviously very good at it.''

Still staring at his profile, she saw a grin tug at the corner of his lips. ''Thanks for the vote of confidence,'' he said. ''But I'm afraid the league doesn't agree with you. The day I retired, I had my agent put out feelers for the coaching positions then available, but we didn't get any takers. Not a one.''

''I'm sorry to hear that.''

''Don't be. I've already moved on. For me football is over.'' He sounded wistful, almost sad, but he tightened his tone as he shook his head. ''You see, I made the decision to come back to Louisiana, and this time I aim to stay here. After all, I have a new challenge to occupy my time.''

''Your new restaurant?''

''No, ma'am,'' he said, turning to face her. ''You.''

Under the heat of his gaze, Callie fought the urge to start wriggling. ''Luke Parker, what nonsense are you spouting now?'' she asked instead.

"No nonsense." His tone, posture and intense gaze
backed up his words. "I was wrong, leaving without a
word that long-ago summer. Now I have to start all
over, showing you my word can be trusted. And I
reckon that's going to take a long, long time."

A thousand questions whipped through her brain. But
before she could formulate any of them, Robbie raced
up to demand Luke's attention.

And in truth Callie was glad for the distraction. Leaving them to analyze the game, she used the time to
analyze her reaction to this new and unsettling Luke.
Had he said such things to her when he'd first strolled
into town, she'd have frozen up tight as a clam and told
him what he could do with his "challenge." But watching him today with Robbie, she'd felt something subtle
shift inside her and could no longer dismiss him so easily. She didn't completely trust Luke, and she wondered
if she ever could, but she'd grown more willing to at
least hear what he had to say.

Following him and Robbie, she looked up suddenly
and realized they were in the parking lot, headed toward
Luke's car. Soon he'd be driving off, she thought with
a start, dealing with all the other, more important things
claiming his attention. She was surprised—and dismayed—at how much his leaving bothered her.

It's happening again, she thought, angry to realize
that Luke Parker had lost none of his power to get under
her skin.

When they reached the BMW and Robbie scrambled
into the back seat, it felt as if even her son was con-
spiring against her. "Luke has things to do," she told
him through gritted teeth. "C'mon, you and I can take
the bus."

"Don't be silly," Luke said, talking to her over the

roof from the driver's side of the car. "Why take a smelly bus when I can give you a ride?"

If there was one thing guaranteed to get her goat, it was being called "silly." Callie, who had been taking the bus all week to work and school, found herself bristling. "We're perfectly capable of using public transportation."

"Loosen up that Magruder spine, will you?" He seemed suddenly as annoyed as she was. "I'm not offering charity. Rob just played a grueling game in the hot sun, and I'm sure he'd rather be taking a shower than waiting around at some bus stop. So, please, just get in the danged car and let me drive you home."

She glared at him knowing she was being unreasonable, that her reluctance to get in the car had nothing to do with any need to take the bus. She was afraid of him, afraid of herself when he was around.

"Please, Mom?" Robbie urged from the back seat.

She got in the car, but she didn't concede graciously. "This is ridiculous," she told Luke as they drove off. "You're obviously busy. You don't have time to be chauffeuring us around."

"Trust me," he said dryly, "this is the highlight of my day. Being with you and Rob beats hanging out at the hospital or dealing with Ben's problems. After this, I get to go to the mansion. It seems Ben stopped paying his staff a month ago, so they've skipped off, leaving the place empty. I've got to stop by to feed the dogs and leave on a light to discourage vandals."

"I wanna see the mansion," Robbie piped in from the backseat. "Can we come?"

The last thing Callie wished was to return to Ben's home. "What happened to taking a shower?"

"C'mon, Mom, the mansion is between here and

home. We don't want to make him go out of his way, do we?''

Callie looked to Luke, who merely shrugged as if to say, "your call.''

"Besides,'' Robbie continued, "who needs a shower when I can jump in the pool? It's heated, you know. And right next to it is a basketball court, with two hoops and everything.''

Callie bristled at the excitement in her son's voice. "What is this, Luke?" she asked, turning on the seat to watch his face. "What are you two hatching up now?''

"Huh?''

"Don't play innocent with me. You think I can't recognize a recruitment speech? I can't believe you'd stoop to bribing him.''

"Oh, for crying out loud, Cal. He asked where I grew up and I told him. Nobody's been plotting behind your back.''

"Jeez, Mom. Get a little paranoid, why don't you?''

She blinked, unable to believe her son would say such a thing to her, unable to hide the hurt. "Am I paranoid, Luke?" she asked, blaming him for turning Robbie against her. "Tell the truth. Were you or were you not hoping to move us into that mausoleum?''

"I swear to you, the thought never crossed my mind." He took his gaze off the road to stare at her a moment. Gazing into his eyes, she could almost believe him.

Until he ruined it by adding, "Though now that you brought it up, I'm not sure why not.''

"I'd say it's painfully obvious why not.''

"I know how you feel, Cal," he said, returning his attention to his driving. "But let's look at this from a practical standpoint. We'd be closer to everything there. The hospital, Rob's classes and soccer, even your nursing school. And we'd certainly have us a lot more room to move around in.''

Callie stared at him in disbelief. ''You can't expect me to live in Ben Parker's house.''

''He won't be there, Cal. And it's not as if we'll stay forever. If Ben doesn't show improvement soon, I'll have to put him in a long-term-care facility and sell the house.''

''So your plan is to uproot Robbie, knowing we'll just have to move again?'' She'd known it was stupid to hope that he'd ever understand anything. ''We discussed this, Luke. Didn't you hear a word I said?''

''Forget it, okay? I have. It was a dumb suggestion.''

''Wait,'' Robbie called out, leaning forward in the seat to stick his head between them. ''We're not moving?''

''No,'' Luke said firmly. ''We've already got a place to live. Besides, if we leave, who will feed Mrs. Boyle and Old Henry?''

Taken aback, Callie stared at Luke's profile. She hadn't expected that, she hadn't realized Luke would see how leaving her older friends to fend for themselves would bother her. Could he have been listening to her, after all?

''It's not fair,'' Robbie continued to protest. ''Don't I get a say in this?''

''Okay, Robbie,'' Callie said, wanting to show she could be reasonable. ''Just what is it you wish to say?''

''I think we should try living in the mansion. It'd be like staying at some fancy hotel. You and me never go on vacation, Mom. This could be fun.''

Of all the descriptive terms Callie might have used for Ben's house, *fun* would never appear on the list. ''I thought we agreed not to move again until we got back the farm.''

"You said that, Mom. The farm is much more important to you than it is to me. I don't care where I live as long as you and Luke are there with me."

Shocked, Callie gaped at her son, wondering where she'd gone wrong that he could so easily dismiss his heritage. Swimming pools and basketball courts, that's all Robbie could see. What prayer did a simple farm have of impressing her son compared with all the very best the Parker money could offer?

"Don't badger your mom," Luke said firmly. "She knows what she's talking about. Anybody can put a pool in their backyard. You can't buy tradition, or the sense of belonging that comes from living in a house that's been in the family for generations. I bet you take one look at my father's place and wonder how anyone could ever want to live there."

Callie doubted that Luke actually meant what he said. If he did, he'd have kept his promise and gotten the farm for her. Still, he had stepped in to support her, when he could have continued pressing her about staying at the mansion and thereby scoring more points with Robbie.

Sighing, the boy glanced from one to the other of them. "Okay, so we don't live there," he tried again, knowing he'd never win against a united front. "But why can't we go for a visit? It's not just the pool, Mom. I want to see the dogs, too."

This was another source of friction between them, Robbie wanting a puppy and Callie insisting that they couldn't keep a dog in the apartment. Once they got the farm, it would be possible, but being just a boy, Robbie was a bit short on patience.

He had no such deficiencies in perseverance, however. Sensing that he would nag and nag until he got inside the Parker mansion, Callie threw in the towel.

"Fine, let's stop at the mansion, then. I'm tired of being the villain in the piece."

Luke looked at her sharply. "Funny, I thought I was the villain."

"We can share the part," she said flippantly. "I'm sure there's plenty of blame to go around."

It didn't take Luke's puzzled expression to bring home the significance of what she'd just said. She supposed she'd been working toward the concession all week. "Let's face it," she went on. "All this fighting and name calling is getting us nowhere, Luke. Maybe you're right. Maybe it is time for a little teamwork."

He nodded, but his was less a smile of triumph than of satisfaction. "Okay, then."

"Don't think you're the star of the team, though, or even the coach. We're on equal footing or I don't play."

"Feel free to take the lead, Cal. I admit, I'm still new at this and learning as I go."

She felt it only fair to warn him. "I'll still be watching you, Luke, so don't try to pull a fast one."

"Fair enough. I say we call a truce."

"What the heck are you two talking about?" Robbie asked from the back seat. "Does this mean we're going to the mansion or what?"

"Your call, coach," Luke said to her. "The turn into the driveway is coming up."

"Make the turn," she said, "and stop your gloating. Both of you."

They all kept quiet, but then, the drive leading up to the house was nothing if not intimidating. A hundred and fifty years ago, they'd have called the place a plantation, with its many live oaks, the Greek Revival house with its impressive white columns and acres of gardens and manicured lawns. Ben must have loved being master of such a domain. From up on the iron-railed galleries, he must have spent many a happy evening, lording it over the other, lesser mortals. No doubt that was why he'd built his house so huge.

As they left the car and entered the house, she couldn't help but notice the eerie quiet. She felt like Dorothy and her motley crew as they approached the fearsome wizard, dreading what might come next. Ben might not be there, but she could sense his presence in every cold, glittering crystal of the chandeliers, in the slate-gray hardness of the miles of marble tile. Some might be awed by the winding staircase, the opulent display of artwork, but Callie merely felt chilled. Luke was right. One look at the place and she was ready to go home.

She glanced over at him, noticing his frown, and sensed he was as uncomfortable as she was. For the first time she had a sense of what it must have been like for him, growing up here. No wonder he'd called himself a rolling stone. Who would ever feel the need to come back to such a home?

Robbie, though, seemed oblivious to the forbidding atmosphere. Hollering, no doubt enjoying the echo his voice made, he raced across the foyer and up the stairs. Callie called after him to stop, but Luke shook his head. "Let him enjoy himself, Cal. It's time someone had fun in this house."

And there was no denying the boy had a ball, sliding down the mahogany rail, scampering outside with the dogs, diving into the pool after Luke, the two of them shedding their shoes and shirts in their mad dash to the water. Watching them splash, challenging each other to race after race, Callie realized it had been too long since she'd seen her son have such fun. He needed more of it, she decided. For that matter, so did she.

Maybe that's why, when Luke sneaked up behind her

and pushed her in, she didn't pop up sputtering with fury. And maybe it was also why, when he reached down to help her up, she gave in to the urge to yank him back into the water with her. Within seconds they were wrestling and yelling like boisterous teenagers, much to the delight of Robbie.

And for a brief time Callie forgot who and where she was, even how she'd gotten there. All that existed was the three of them and the good feelings they generated among themselves. It wasn't until she and Luke got out of the pool and stood on the deck dripping that reality came snapping back into focus.

It was such a little thing, really. Luke reaching out to lift a wet strand of hair from her face. A reflex action, something he'd done a dozen times when they'd gone swimming as kids, but of course, that was the problem. Back then, she'd invariably ended up in his arms.

Staring at him now, she could see he was no longer the boy he'd been then. For one thing he wore a lot more dents on his broad chest, including the ragged scar from the surgery on his shoulder. She had an urge to trace his scar, to feel this older, hardened version of Luke. And with the urge she grew aware of a sudden, pulsing throb within her.

She became aware of other things, as well. Her wet T-shirt clinging to her skin, her nipples straining against the fabric. Luke's utter stillness, his ironclad control, as he watched her study his body. Once upon a time they wouldn't know an instant's hesitation. Touching each other had been like breathing back then. Neither one could live without it.

And meeting his gaze, seeing all the old intensity and sense of wonder, she had to ask herself if either one of them had truly changed. She still wanted him badly, and looking into his eyes, she knew that he felt the same.

Long before she could have dreamed of dragging her gaze away, she heard the rude jangle of a phone behind her. She blinked, breaking the connection between them.

"Cal," Luke said softly, the name almost a question as he held his hand out to her. Deep down, she ached to take it.

"Isn't anybody going to answer the phone?" Robbie called out from the pool, preventing her from doing anything so foolish.

Muttering an oath, Luke lowered his hand and went to answer the cell phone, hiding amid the pile of shirts on the table.

Standing there shivering, listening to Luke as he mumbled into the phone, Callie fought to regain her bearings. She never would have let him kiss her, she thought frantically. Not at Ben's house and certainly not with Robbie right there watching from the pool.

Who did she think she was kidding? For that breathless second, she hadn't known anything existed but Luke.

She tried to tell herself to snap out of it, to remember the past and all he'd done to her, but found it hard to summon up the old conviction. She kept seeing how it could be if she *could* trust him, how a day like today could stretch happily into the future.

As if to remind her how fleeting happiness could be, Luke clicked off the phone and reached for his shirt. "Party's over, I'm afraid," he said solemnly. "That was the hospital. Looks like Ben has come out of his coma."

Chapter Fourteen

Callie eased Luke's BMW into the last available parking spot, grateful that it wasn't her grandfather's clunky sedan. Old Beauty, they'd called the old boat that had given the Magruders so many years of faithful service—before it, like Gramps, gave up the good fight.

Gramps, she thought, her throat going tight as she glanced up at the imposing hospital. They'd brought him to this very place almost a year ago. Unlike Ben Parker, though, Gramps never came out of his coma.

Walking inside the building, she knew it was small of her to feel resentful, but where was the justice in letting a small-minded, vindictive tyrant like Ben thrive, while her sweet little old grandfather lost everything? She wasn't here to congratulate Ben on his recovery or even to visit. She'd come out of sheer expediency.

After the phone call, they'd both agreed that Luke needed to rush to the hospital to make decisions and arrangements. She'd dropped him off and then driven Robbie to the apartment. Mrs. Boyle was with the boy now, while Callie returned for Luke.

An hour and a half ago, it had seemed a sensible plan, but now, walking into the hospital, assaulted by its smells and sounds, she was no longer certain she should be here. A bundle of mixed emotions, she didn't know what she might do or say, not when she was haunted by memories of her grandfather's stay here, her lifelong feud with Ben and, most daunting of all, the intense moment by the pool she'd shared with Luke.

Taking the elevator to the fourth floor, she acknowledged that she was afraid to face him, afraid of what she'd see in his expression, scared to death of how she would react. All the way home and back she kept asking herself the same question. Was she right to so stubbornly resist the pull he held over her, or in the end was her surrender inevitable?

Nowhere near an answer, she identified herself as a family member to the desk nurse, who directed her to the room at the end of the hall. As she approached, Callie could hear the wheezing and beeping of the machines around her and flashed back to the awful moment when the noises connected to Gramps had stopped. In a rush she felt again the utter devastation of that moment, her overwhelming fury.

That was the way to go, she insisted to herself. Never mind her self-doubt or any inner yearnings. She owed it to Gramps to concentrate instead on all the many reasons she had to hate Ben Parker.

But as she marched into the room, even her anger was taken away from her.

She didn't know what she'd been expecting—Ben sitting up gloating, maybe—but the actuality of his condition hit her square in the solar plexus. Pale to the point of ghostliness, an old, wizened man starcd listlessly back at her, his presence obscenely diminished by the stark, white vastness of the hospital bed. He didn't move, didn't blink. Indeed, she saw more signs of life in the tubes running in and out of him than anywhere on his face.

There would be no more gloating, she realized. No more vindictive posturing and lording it over the rest of them.

Her gaze went to Luke, standing on the other side of the bed. She must have showed the question in her eyes for he shook his head with a grim expression. "He had another stroke," he said quietly, though to Callie it seemed his voice echoed about the room. "This one did him in."

"Then why is he on life support?"

"I had to." Luke sighed, looking down at his father. "It's what he would have demanded."

An odd choice of words, *demanded*. And yet, how telling that at such a time his only son would talk about what the man expected, not what Ben deserved.

"Let's get out of here," Luke said, the words rasping against her nerves.

Callie might share his need to put distance between them and the oppressive atmosphere in this room, but while she knew her own reasons for leaving, she couldn't grasp his. "Aren't you going to stay with him?" she asked, following Luke out into the hall. "Your own father?"

"He can linger like this for weeks, Cal. And quite frankly, I'm too tired and worn to keep the vigil to-night."

Looking at him, she could see the strain in his eyes, the slump in his shoulders. The past hour—this past week—had certainly taken its toll, yet, while her heart might go out to him, she kept thinking of his father's cold, lifeless face. Monster though Ben Parker might have been, no one deserved to be alone in his final hours. "Surely there's someone you can call who will sit with him."

Luke made a sweeping gesture with his arm. "Look around you. Do you see them lining up at the doors? The sad fact is, no one will come because nobody has a reason to. He has a sister in Texas, but he alienated her long ago, just as he's ticked off virtually everyone else in this town. Only Ben's lawyer would show up if I summoned him, and all things considered, that's a tad too ghoulish for me."

Callie couldn't stop herself from glancing back at the solitary figure in that cold and somber room. How different it had been when Gramps lay dying. She'd darned near worn herself out, answering the questions from neighbors and friends expressing their concern and support. She could have picked from a long line of volunteers, but she'd stubbornly stayed at his bedside herself.

But that had been Gramps, and this was Ben, and in her heart she couldn't fault Luke for his decision. She'd made her vigil out of love, not out of guilt.

But Luke was looking back at his father's room, too, she noticed, and for a quick, unguarded moment, she saw the yearning on his face. It struck her that while little affection might be lost between the two, Luke still must be hurting. It couldn't be easy, standing by helplessly while his last link with his family slipped away. All at once she realized how awful he must feel. And how alone.

As if to confirm her realization, he sighed heavily as he made a stab at the elevator button. "Don't worry, I'll be back first thing in the morning. Right now I want to go to the apartment and see Rob, make sure he's okay. I don't want him confused and frightened by not knowing what's going on.''

Who is this man? Callie couldn't help thinking as they made their way to the parking lot. She hadn't expected him to worry about Robbie, hadn't dreamed he would make even the smallest effort to be there for Ben. All the way home she stared at his strong profile, as if seeing Luke, really seeing him, for the first time since he'd returned to Latour. Later, watching Luke patiently explain Ben's condition to Robbie, who stood beside Luke as he helped her cook dinner, she was forced to acknowledge that this man was a far cry from the boy who'd so carelessly broken her heart.

Sitting alone on the sofa, long after he and Robbie had called it a night, she stared at his silly football, wondering if all this time she'd been wrong about Luke. Gramps used to say that we see only what we want to see. Had it been her fault, and not Luke's, that all she had seen was a villain?

Over the next few days Luke sensed a change in Callie. She no longer bristled at everything he said, and he could see a certain softening in her expression when she gazed at him. Being Callie, she probably felt sorry for him, empathizing with what he must be going through with his father.

Another man might have been encouraged by this, but it made Luke feel uneasy. He knew he didn't deserve her sympathy. In his place Callie would have suffered each time she saw the shell of a man who was once her father. But each day he sat by Ben's bedside, or tried to untangle his affairs, Luke was merely going through the motions. He'd long since proven he wasn't capable of grief and sorrow, and he'd certainly never known anything quite as corny as love.

He couldn't tell Callie this, though. He couldn't risk her reaction, didn't want to see her softening expression harden with disgust.

Each day he put in his time at the hospital, but every night he couldn't get back to the apartment fast enough. He would climb the stairs, drawn by the aromas emanating from Callie's kitchen, the distant chatter and laughter of mother and son. When he stepped in the door and saw their smiles of welcome—Robbie's wide and beaming, Callie's a kinder, gentler version—he would shed the ugly emptiness of the last few hours. Helping his son with his homework, he could forget the day's events. Their comfortable routine, the way they let him fit into it, all combined to soothe him, make him feel calm and whole again.

Yet along with the gentler, healing moments came the deepening physical awareness between him and Callie. For Luke each day meant greater and greater torture. Living in such close quarters, he would often brush against her, catch her sweet, floral scent. The need was there, bone deep and throbbing, yet he knew better than to reach out for her, to try to pull her closer. After the moment at Ben's house, he knew she'd seen his lust and maybe even shared it, but she'd made it clear ever since then that friendship and teamwork was all she was prepared to offer. Every time he neared her, she'd skitter off like a frightened mouse. She took care not to be alone with him, using Robbie as a shield between them. Luke knew he could push, and she might even surrender, but he also knew it could destroy the trust he'd been so painstakingly building. And that was a risk he wasn't prepared to take.

No, for the future to have half a chance, he had to wait for Callie to take the first step, when and if she was ready.

On Friday his resolve was severely tested. No sooner had Luke stepped in the door than Jason's mother called, asking if Robbie could go with them to the movies. Luke could see that Callie didn't want to let the boy go: yet, since it wasn't a school night, she couldn't voice a legitimate objection. In the end, though blatantly reluctant, she had to let the boy go.

Luke could taste the tension in the air the instant Rob skipped out the door. "Sure is quiet all of a sudden," he said, hoping to lessen the strain the boy had left in his wake. "Want me to turn on the television?"

Refusing to look at him, she glanced helplessly at the clock, but at ten to eight, it was still too early to hide in her bedroom. "No. Yes. Oh, I don't know."

"I'm not going to bite, Cal. And I swear, I'm not going to try anything." At her startled glance, he smiled reassuringly. "I promised to be a gentleman and I will."

"Maybe it's not you I'm worried about," he thought he heard her mumble as she began to prowl about the room.

Luke patted the sofa. "C'mon, have a seat on the couch. I'll take the chair. You can tell me how Rob did today on his math test."

She stopped by the window to look back at him, her eyes wide and frightened. "It's not going to work, Luke. I can't just sit here, pretending nothing is happening, not when every time I look at you, I remember what it was like when we were kids. What *I* was like. It scares the devil out of me. I can't let myself go down that road again."

Luke searched for the words to reassure her. "This is a new road, Cal, and who says we have to go racing down it? We can take our time, check it out. We're not kids anymore. I'd say we've both of us learned our lessons.''

"Have we?" Sighing, she looked out the window, as if it bothered her just to look at him. "Can we be so sure that what's going on here isn't another case of some good-old-fashioned lust?"

"And what if it is?" Luke asked, suddenly annoyed. Taking a step closer, he knew he was treading on dangerous ground, but he was glad to have this out in the open. "Is it such a bad thing, to want each other so badly? We've got friendship and mutual respect. I know tons of relationships based on a helluva lot less than that.''

She reached out for the drape, clinging to it as if for support. "You can't count on lust. At least I can't. Eventually it burns out and then where will I be? I won't go through it again, Luke. The fear of being pregnant, facing all the gossips, getting through the years ahead alone.''

She still wouldn't look at him, but Luke didn't need to see her face or hear the tremble in her voice to grasp what she was saying. She was right. Not having been there, he could only imagine what it must have been like for a frightened eighteen-year-old, having a baby out of wedlock in a town like Latour. He still couldn't handle the fact that she'd given Reb's name to his boy, but he could no longer swear that in her place he might not have done the same.

"There's this great new invention," he teased gently. "They call it birth control."

"Yeah, well, we used birth control most of the time." She bit her lip, gripping the drape tighter, as if she'd realized what she'd just now admitted.

Say it, Luke coached silently, moving closer. Give

me hell, if you must, but just once let me hear from your lips that Rob is my son.

"I mean, Reb and I tried to use it," she hastily said, "but he wasn't always what you could call reliable."

Luke stopped where he stood, flooded with disappointment. Barely a foot of physical distance might separate them, but in their minds they were still miles apart.

"Reb always was a fool," he snapped, wishing he could find a way to bridge the gap. "I can't claim to know what you two had between you, but that was then and this is now. I'm not Reb Jenkins, Cal. And as I told you, *I'm* not going anywhere. I'll be hanging around, whether or not you're pregnant."

Her knuckles were white where she gripped the drape. "Hanging around?"

"Okay, bad choice of words. I should have come right out and said I'll be your husband, standing by you, whether or not you have another baby."

She let go of the drape, taking the few steps to stand before him. "I don't get it, Luke. You say you want to be my husband, but if you're not looking for love, what can you hope to get out of staying married?"

He shrugged, uncomfortable with the question. Yet he knew she expected, and deserved, total honesty from him. "A home, a family. Someone to cheer me on when times are good and to hold my hands when things turn sour. I guess I want what I've always wanted from you, Callie. A partner. A friend."

"Oh, Luke." She reached up to touch his face. "Can you be so certain that friendship will be enough?"

"We'll make it be enough." He took her hand in his and gently kissed it. "At least for now. I can't begin to predict what the future will do to us, but I can guarantee this. As long as you want me, I'll be here. I honestly can't imagine being anywhere else."

Hearing his voice, watching his face, Callie could feel her resistance melting. She found it hard to doubt his sincerity, to even care what was safe and sound, when she kept getting caught up in memories of Luke touching and stroking her. Being in his arms made her feel so good, so alive. How could it possibly be wrong to rekindle those feelings?

She inched closer, just to the point where their bodies touched. She heard his sharp intake of breath and felt him stiffen, but he made no move to take it further. Instead, he dropped her hand as if it had burned him.

"What is it?" she asked, her voice brittle with frustration. "Don't you want to kiss me?"

He stood statue still, staring down at her, his stormy blue eyes glazed with passion. "If it were my decision, I'd have you flat on your back in a nanosecond. Is that what you want to hear?"

Apparently so, considering the adrenaline rushing through her system. In the back of her mind she could hear a tiny voice telling Luke, *Do it!* while the sensible part struggled to hold on to her last shred of sanity.

"But it isn't my decision, Cal," he went on, his voice taut with suppressed emotion. "It won't work if you walk away from me feeling tricked or coerced. I'll wait until you feel comfortable with your decision. This time it's your call to make."

His words were like a splash of cold water. Luke was right. She couldn't go into this having doubts; she knew from experience how relentlessly regret could haunt her. "Oh, Luke," she said raggedly. "I do want you…"

"But?" he prompted when she let the words trail off.

"Physically, I'm almost sick with the wanting." She stared up at him, needing him to understand. "But I'm not sure I'm emotionally ready. I can't go on all my life repeating the same mistakes."

"Okay," he said, breathing deeply as he stepped back away from her.

Feeling suddenly chilled, Callie fought the urge to reach for him, to pull him back. "I'm sorry, Luke."

"Don't be. I said I'd respect your decision and I do."

She sensed she was annoying him with her apologies and explanations, but she couldn't seem to stop. "It would have been crazy, anyway, to try anything now, here. We could have still been, you know, when Robbie walked in the door."

"I get it, Cal. Tonight's not the night. Listen, this is just going to get more and more awkward, so maybe it's best if I just take off."

He was leaving her? "So it is all about the sex?" she blurted out. "If I don't put out, that's your excuse to leave me?" She couldn't believe how pathetic she sounded, but all at once she felt like that eighteen-year-old kid again, watching Lucky Parker stroll out of her life.

He stared at her coldly. "If it was just about sex, I could have made my move days ago and let us both live with the consequences. I ache for you, Cal, I won't deny it. But give me a little credit, will you? I'm not going to cut out on you to punish you because I feel frustrated. I only meant to give us both a little breathing space. I thought I'd go for a drive to clear my head."

She felt like a balloon that had just been punctured. "Oh."

He ran a harried hand through his hair. "We're both a bit too on edge at the moment. What say we continue this discussion some other time?"

She had to agree, it would have been churlish not to, but as Luke turned and marched out the door, she was no longer so certain she'd made the right decision.

Wrapping her arms around her, she tried to ward off

the sudden chill. All week long she'd been wondering how it would feel to have Luke's arms around her again, but her chance had come and, coward that she was, she'd let it slip out of her fingers.

In her mind she heard Luke suggesting they continue their "discussion" at another time. Did that mean she'd get another shot at this?

More important—what would she do with it?

Chapter Fifteen

The next morning, sitting at the breakfast table with Robbie and Luke, Callie had to wonder if she'd merely imagined the scene last night in the living room. She'd gone to bed early so she didn't know when Luke had returned, but his long drive seemed to have done wonders. Teasing Robbie, gobbling down pancakes faster than she could cook them, he acted—on the surface, at least—as if last night had never been.

She sensed an undercurrent of tension between them, but then, that too could be in her imagination. Lord knew she'd been on needles and pins all morning. She kept fretting about his warning that they would talk about this again. Part of her might be anxious to get the topic out in the open, but unfortunately the other part still hadn't the least idea what she was going to say.

Did she want Luke to make love to her? Could she trust him enough not to walk away afterward?

"Where's my soccer uniform?" Robbie asked suddenly, startling her out of her thoughts. "I hope it's washed. The game starts in an hour."

Glad for the distraction, Callie turned to her son. "I laid out your shorts and shirt on your bed. Though, considering how messy it was, I'm not surprised you couldn't find your uniform. How many times do I have to tell you that life is so much easier when you're organized?"

Robbie made a face. "You know I hate making the bed."

Callie groaned inwardly. This was one argument she rarely enjoyed, and she sure didn't want to go into it today with Luke watching. Still, she wouldn't be much of a disciplinarian if she ignored Robbie's minirebellion.

But before she could force the issue, Luke spoke up from the other side of the table. "I'm not too fond of the chore, either, Rob, but when something has to be done, I've found it's better to get it out of the way. I made mine the minute I left it."

Robbie made a face. "Yeah, well, I think you're *too* neat. You don't even leave a sock on the floor. Sometimes I wonder if Mom only brought you here to make me look bad."

"Now wait a minute, Robbie."

Luke shot Callie a look across the table, silently asking her to trust him to handle this. "It wasn't your mom's choice to put me in the room with you, if you'll remember. Just stop the bellyaching, Rob, and do as she asks."

"But it isn't fair," Robbie protested, anyway. "I don't care about the mess. If it bothers her so much, why doesn't she make the bed?"

Callie stiffened, but again Luke jumped into the fray.

"Because your mom isn't your maid. With all she has to do lately, you should be grateful she took the time to do your uniform. I don't see you doing much to help her."

Robbie blinked, as if the possibility of helping his mother had never occurred to him.

"Finish your breakfast," Luke said, gesturing at Robbie's plate. "And then you can head to your room. You should have ample time to straighten it before you have to get ready for soccer."

"Oh, all right." Though Robbie huffed a bit, he was smiling again before he took two bites of his pancake. "You are coming to the game, aren't you?

It was now Callie's turn to blink as she stared at her son. When it came to making his bed, she'd never known Robbie to back down so easily. She felt a rush of gratitude toward Luke for coming to her support.

Funny. A few short days ago she'd have accused him of interfering.

"Wouldn't miss it," Luke said, and it took Callie a few beats to remember he was talking about the game. "But right after it's over, you and I are taking your mother out shopping for a car."

Robbie hollered his approval, and again it took Callie several beats to catch up. "Wait a minute, Luke. I can't let you buy me anything as expensive as a car."

Luke sighed as if he'd anticipated her objection yet had hoped she wouldn't make it. "Lighten up, Cal. It's not a handout. I'm trying to be practical. Think of how much easier life would be if you had a vehicle to drive around in."

"I don't need a vehicle," she insisted stubbornly. "I can take the bus."

"And drive yourself into the ground trying to make the connections? Twice last week you were late to class.

What's going to happen if I'm called out of town on business? Who's going to pick up Robbie?''

She didn't like to think of her son being stranded, but whatever Luke might call it, in her mind his buying her a car was still a handout.

"This isn't a case of a Magruder having to be beholden to a Parker," Luke went on as if reading her thoughts. "I'm your husband, for crying out loud. If it offends your pride or sense of independence, let me buy the car now, and you can pay me back from your earnings at the beauty parlor."

She didn't want to tell him she was putting that money away to buy back the farm. At the moment it didn't seem political to admit what little faith she had in him getting it for her.

"Be practical, Cal," he coaxed. "Think of Robbie."

"Yeah, Mom, think of me. I want a new car. A big red shiny sports car."

Luke shook his head. "Get a grip, boy. This is your mom we're talking about. I imagine she'd much prefer a minivan or maybe a station wagon."

Robbie shook his head even more emphatically. "Nah, they go too slow."

"Ever think maybe your mom prefers taking it slow?"

Callie bristled, aware of the double meaning behind his words. So she hadn't been imagining the undercurrent of tension, after all. Maybe they'd better have their discussion sooner than later. She was in no mood to put up with him getting in his digs all day.

She looked up to glare at him, but when she met his gaze, she found nothing but patient resignation there.

"It's her car, you know," Luke said to Robbie, though he kept his gaze on her. "Ultimately it's got to be her decision."

Looking into his eyes, Callie realized he wasn't mocking her reluctance to go to bed with him. In his own way he was telling her it was okay.

"And what if she decides not to have the car at all?" she couldn't stop herself from asking.

He gave her a reluctant grin. "I'll try to talk her out of it, of course, but if that's what she truly wants, I guess I'll have to respect her decision."

"Aw, Mom," Robbie said, his face a study of disapproval. "What's wrong with you? He wants to buy us a car, I say we let him."

Callie, who was finding it harder to remember her objections, frowned at her son. "Aren't you supposed to be making your bed?"

At that moment the phone rang in the kitchen. "Saved by the bell," Robbie said as he scampered off to answer it.

Across the table Luke went still. He thinks it's about his father, Callie realized. And if it was the hospital, they both knew the news wouldn't be good.

He rose abruptly, taking two strides toward the kitchen before Robbie came bounding out of it, almost colliding with Luke. "It's for you," he said, holding out the portable phone, another of Luke's additions to the household. "Some guy named Pete Lawry."

"My agent?" Luke said, as if shifting mental gears slowly.

Robbie shrugged. "I guess. He said something about a job in New York."

"This could be important." Luke quickened his pace, the gears apparently moving faster now. "I'll, uh, take it in the bedroom."

Watching him go, Callie knew a sudden, sick dread. A job in New York, Robbie said. Something Luke considered "important."

He said he wouldn't leave, she protested silently. He'd looked her in the eye and sworn that he would be there for her and her son. But she knew, even without being told, that if his agent had called, it must be about the coaching position Luke wanted, or something else to do with football. And really, how could she and Robbie ever compete with that?

Football was his one and only love, Luke had once told her. Of course he'd go back to it. He'd done so before, hadn't he, and for a lot less reason.

Desperate to hear what he said to his agent, Callie strained to listen, but Robbie was back at the table, chattering on about how he was now off the hook. With Luke in his bedroom, he couldn't really clean it, could he? Callie yearned to tell her son to hush up so she could listen, but that would betray her anxiety. Biting her lip to contain her words, she resigned herself to waiting with a forced patience. Sooner or later she'd hear the news, anyway.

In that respect fate was kind, for she didn't have to wait long. Though she didn't think it a good sign that Luke was whistling when he came out of the bedroom.

"Okay, I'm done in there now, Rob," he said cheerfully, gesturing behind him, "You can go in and make your bed."

"Aw, Luke."

"Never mind. Get marching."

Grumbling, yet grinning all the way, Robbie went into his bedroom while Luke returned to the table. He made great business of adding more pancakes to his plate and refilling his cup with black coffee. And when she thought he would finally speak, he began filling his face instead.

"So?" she found herself asking, annoyed that he'd forced her into it.

He looked up, seeming confused, as if he hadn't a clue what she was asking.

"Your agent? The phone call?"

He took a few extra chews, as if he were eating hard-tack instead of pancakes. "Oh, that," he said, reaching for his coffee to wash it down.

"Yes, that. I don't want to pry—"

"Sure you do. And, really, can't say I blame you. It's not every day I get a call from Pete." Setting down his cup, he dug back into the pancakes.

For a frustrating minute, Callie thought he meant to leave it at that. As he chewed, his face took on a thoughtful expression, and she thought, *He's trying to find the way to break the news to me.*

Something hard and lumpy settled in her gut. He was going, and just like before she could do nothing to prevent it.

Setting down his fork, he took in a breath. "As Robbie said, Pete called with a job offer. My old team needs an offensive coach, and they said I topped their list. All things considered, they made an attractive offer."

"I'm happy for you, Luke," she said, hoping she'd managed to put some conviction in her tone.

He seemed surprised, as if he'd expected her to rant and rave. "Well, thanks. I've got to say, it sure helps the old ego. I can't tell you how good it felt to turn them down."

"You what?"

"I believe the concise version would be, I said no."

"But that's crazy." Callie was having trouble processing this. "I thought you said a coaching job was exactly what you wanted?"

"That's right, it was. Past tense, Cal. As I told Pete, my life is in Louisiana now, and I'm not going to leave it.'' He picked up his fork again, acting as if he'd just remarked on the weather and not delivered a bombshell.

It sure seemed like a bomb to Callie, with all her misconceptions exploding in her face. "You're staying," she said in a daze.

"Yup. Looks like you're stuck with me." He poked a section of pancake, but he hesitated with the fork halfway to his mouth. "You think I'm being awfully blasé about this, don't you?"

"I'd have thought you'd take some time to think it over."

"Yeah, I'd have thought so, too." Seeming almost pensive, he set down the fork before leaning toward her over the table. "Don't get me wrong, I was tempted as hell, but then I saw Rob's face, staring back at me from his school picture on his dresser, and I knew I couldn't leave." He shook his head. "Really, Cal, can't you hear that boy now if I announced I was taking off in the middle of soccer season?"

"You're staying for Robbie, then?" That was good—she'd kept her voice low and even, almost aloof.

"Among other things." He held her gaze across the table. "His mother and I, for example, still have a couple of unresolved issues between us."

The heat in his gaze left no doubt about what issue he was referring to. Callie felt as if her bones had suddenly turned to mush. "If you're talking about the car…"

She'd thrown that out, hoping to counteract his effect on her, but the smile he then gave her only made matters worse. "As I recall," he said in his deep, sexy tone, "I still have to talk you out of your decision."

But he didn't, she realized as she gazed back at him, caught up in the dizzying heat that he alone could generate. Not really. She still wanted him. She supposed she'd always wanted him, but she could no longer find the reasons, much less the will, to tell him no.

"I suppose it wouldn't hurt to go looking," she told him, meeting him stare for stare.

He nodded, his grin letting her know he'd caught the double entendre. "I know a great place for minivans."

"Actually," she said breathlessly, "I was thinking I might want to check out the sports cars."

Something flared in his eyes, and for an instant she thought he might leap over the table to get to her, but Robbie picked that moment to burst into the room complaining about the lumps he couldn't get out of his bed.

Callie could almost hear the snap as their gazes disconnected. Before her eyes Luke transformed from the hungry lover into the patient father, offering to go with Robbie to show the boy his own surefire bed-making method.

Taking a lot more time to recover, envying Luke's self-discipline, Callie marveled anew at the change in him. Though she would have to do something about his self-discipline, she decided. And for that, she'd have to find some way for her and Luke to be alone.

But no opportunity presented itself as the day wore on. She'd hoped maybe Jason's mother could have Robbie spend the night, but the woman had company coming to dinner, Callie learned during the game, so she really couldn't ask.

Nor was Luke any help. If anything, he seemed determined to keep Robbie with them. He insisted on dragging the boy along, having Callie and Robbie wait in the car while he stopped in at the hospital to check on his father. And of course the boy went along when they looked at cars, going from dealership to dealership before Callie selected a sensible compact. Robbie was disgusted with her choice, and Luke tried to urge her toward the SUV, but she knew that even after she earned her nursing license, she'd never be able to pay him back.

Afterward Luke suggested celebrating with dinner and a movie. Callie objected, insisting that it would be two late evenings in a row for Robbie, but Luke called for a vote and the males voted her down, two to one. All through dinner, and again in the dark theater, she kept looking at Luke, yearning to touch him, to feel his hands on her. How ironic—no, infuriating—that, now that she'd made her decision, Luke no longer seemed to share her urgency.

It wasn't until he'd carried the sleeping Robbie upstairs to his bed and was carefully closing the bedroom door behind him that she figured out what in truth he'd been doing. Watching him from her position in front of the couch, she felt like a hormone-laden teenager, waiting until her parents fell asleep to sneak her boyfriend into the house.

"Is that what the marathon day was about?" she whispered. "You were deliberately tiring that poor boy out so he'd sleep like a log?"

"Of course." He crossed the room to her. "How else were you and I going to resume our discussion?"

"But you never even looked at me all day."

"I couldn't." He stopped before her, still holding himself in check, but his eyes positively smoldered. "Just once, if you looked back at me like you did this morning, I'd have ripped off your clothes right there in the car lot."

A thrill shot through her, followed by the now-all-too-familiar throbbing.

"I wasn't imagining that look, was I, Cal? I'm not imagining it now?"

All she could do was shake her head, feeling suddenly, overwhelmingly shy. It had been so long, after all, and he'd had so many years experience. What if he took her in his arms and felt nothing but disappointment?

He reached for her hand, squeezing it gently. "What's it to be, Cal? Moment of truth."

Yes, it was. Everything about giving herself to Luke now was a risk, but she'd spent ten long years playing it safe, holding herself in check. All at once she had too many powerful emotions to contain inside her. She wanted this, wanted Luke—she'd never wanted anything more.

Standing on tiptoe, she kissed him quite emphatically on the lips.

With a groan, he wrapped his arms around her, pulling her tight to his chest, deepening the kiss she'd started. Warming to his touch, Callie realized that she'd only been half-alive the past ten years. Everything inside her had been sleeping, waiting for Luke to awaken her again.

And just as she thought she would die of the sheer perfection of it all, Luke eased back to look at her. "You sure about this?" he asked huskily.

"No. Yes. Oh, Luke, just shut up and kiss me."

He sucked in a ragged breath. "I want you so bad it hurts. I can't stop—"

"I know," she interrupted. "Neither can I."

He took her head in his hands, reducing the world to just them, to just that moment. "I've got to warn you," he said, his voice hoarse. "I'm just about liable to devour you whole."

She nodded, and then he was slanting his mouth over hers, kissing her, his tongue swirling deep into the last vestige of her resistance. She felt his arms at her knees, scooping her up against his chest to carry her to her

bedroom. Kicking the door shut behind him, he crossed
the room and lay her on the bed. All through it, Callie
kept kissing him, unable to break away from his honey-
sweet lips.

But he apparently had other plans for her. "You're
so beautiful," he muttered as his lips trailed down her
throat, up past her ears, back to her mouth. All Callie
could do was thread her fingers into his hair, holding
on, as his kisses went on and on, sweet and tender, slow
and throbbing. If he'd rushed her, or been demanding,
she might have had the wherewithal to call a halt, but
he continued to caress her as if she were a valued treasure he couldn't bear to lose. He didn't just call her
beautiful; he made her feel it. Every inch of her glowed,
coming to life as his large, capable hands slid down her
back, her legs, inching slowly, deliciously up over her
breasts, lingering there as his fingers flicked over her
nipples.

"Oh, Luke," was all she could formulate, lost in a
thousand wonderful sensations.

"It's okay," he muttered into her mouth, his hands
trailing across her breasts and then down her back again.
"Let the world go, Cal. Just lie here and let me pleasure
you."

And pleasure her he certainly did. He could be a ma-
gician, a snake charmer, keeping her writhing beneath
his artful touch. He had no need of a reedy pipe; his
song was a whisper in her ear, chanting over and over
about how hot she was, how soft, how perfect. His voice
brushed over her, as sensuous as a cool, fresh breeze
on a hot, humid day.

And just as she thought she could go on like this
forever, he reached down to cup her bottom, bringing
her tight against him. She gasped as their combined
body heat ignited a spark deep within her.

She could scarcely breathe with the intensity of it, but he fanned that spark, sending it raging through her body as his hands shifted to the buttons on her shirt. One by one he slipped them open, so adroitly that a dazed Callie was only half-aware of the movement. His mouth covering hers, working its magic, occupied her attention—until her shirt lay open and he was dipping his head down to trace his tongue across the swells above her bra. She felt like a drowning victim, ready to give up the fight. She couldn't stop him when he kissed her there. She didn't want to.

Without conscious thought, she arched her back, reaching up to meet his nimble touch, urging him to do much, much more.

And he was oh, so obliging. With the same incredible deftness, he unhooked her bra, letting her breasts spill out before his appreciative gaze. He stroked each globe tenderly with a look of wonder, and Callie arched her back even more to meet his tongue, groaning as it flicked over her tight, hardened nipples. Moans of pleasure escaped her lips as he traced the sensitive flesh from one breast to the other, swirling over them, licking, laving, sucking them gently into his mouth. For Callie, it was as if he were pulling her inside out, drawing all the soft, vulnerable parts of her past the protective shell, making her experience what she had so long avoided. What had once lain dormant now sprang to aching, pulsing, vibrant life.

She reveled in the sensation; he left her no choice. Reaching down, he unsnapped her jeans, slipping them off her slim hips. With the same agility he removed her panties until there was nothing left to bar his way. "So damned beautiful," he muttered as he trailed kisses downward, over her belly to her legs, then up to the triangle between them. Grabbing his hair with a groan,

Callie tugged his face back up to hers, her tongue now probing into his mouth. Mindlessly she pulled at his shirt, tugging it up over his head. He smiled down at her as she likewise dispatched of his slacks and shorts.

"Remember, Cal?" he rasped out as their skin met, their warmth fused into one, surging heat. "You, me, the pure magic?"

Oh, yes, indeed, she remembered. She could be eighteen again, so in love it hurt to breathe, so hot for the guy who could push all her buttons. He was pushing them now, knowing all the right spots, using his knowledge to keep her right there on the edge, half-mad with the wanting, the need. Gone was the slow, lazy exploration. She couldn't get enough of him—her gaze, her hands, her mouth roamed avidly over his body—hungrily touching, feeling, tasting every inch.

She didn't need to tell him she was ready; he seemed to know. Slipping on a condom, he slid slowly into her with a slick, fluid motion. He paused there, letting her get used to him, but really, there was no need. They both knew he belonged there. Always had, always would.

She could feel him swell, filling her, making her whole. How had she lived all these years without this, without Luke? He began to move, sliding in and slipping out in a torturously slow, incredibly sweet rhythm, making her dizzy with need. Clinging to him, she wrapped her legs around his, amazed at how easily she fell into sync with his movements, as if no time at all had elapsed. Yes, she chanted silently. Oh, yes.

In the back of her mind she might have realized that her chants were no longer silent, that her murmurs were urging him on, but she was too caught up in the sheer beauty of it to be embarrassed. With each thrust inside her, with each withdrawal, her exhortations grew louder, the pleasure grew fiercer, her needs more demanding. She was arching her back to meet him, opening every pore to welcome him in. As the ride grew wilder, the dance more frantic, she dug her nails into his skin to hang on to him, to keep him close. Their mouths remained joined, even their breaths intermingling as the pressure built. The heat consumed them, the force of passion urged them higher and higher. Up, up, up they climbed, fused together as a single entity, until Callie felt the slow rumble deep within her, gathering momentum, out of control. "Oh, Luke," she cried out as the pressure exploded in a burst of fire, sending spasm after spasm of exquisite pleasure rocketing though her body.

He answered with a series of groans as he, too, climaxed and began thrusting with decreasing urgency, still kissing her, still holding her tight.

Clinging to him, Callie could feel herself start to tremble at the release of ten years of pent-up emotion. Their coming together after so long a time had been so incredible, so perfect, was it any wonder she now felt a need to cry? The only thing that could possibly make it more wonderful was if Luke were to say he loved her.

But he wouldn't, she thought wistfully as he slowly rolled off her to lie on his side of the bed. Perhaps she should stop and consider that fact.

Luke leaned on an elbow, looking down at her with concern. "Ah, Cal, you're not having regrets already, are you?" he asked, reaching over to brush a stray tear from her cheek.

She shook her head. "No. Not at all. It was…it's just… Oh, Luke, I'd forgotten how amazing it can be."

"I know. I'm still throbbing." Smiling, he gently pushed a strand of hair from her eyes. "I forgot how you'd sometimes get teary afterward. You used to say it was because you were too happy to hold it all in."

"I'm surprised you remember."

"Oh, I remember a lot of things, Cal. The taste of you, the sight of you all rumpled and glowing after we made love. Tonight, with you, I feel like a kid again with my whole life before me. Anything seems possible."

Callie knew the feeling; it was what had gotten her in trouble in the first place. "Yeah, I know what you mean," she told him. "Only we're adults now so, hopefully, we won't make the same mistakes."

He seemed to withdraw from her, though he hadn't moved an inch. Frowning, he stared pensively at the door behind her. "You're right. And I suppose we'd better start here at home by talking to Rob."

Callie froze. He knows, she thought in an instant of panic. Somehow he's figured out that Robbie is his son.

Before she could figure out whether his knowing was a bad thing, Luke went on to explain. "We need to tell him what's going on. He's bound to notice sooner or later that I'm no longer sleeping in the room with him."

Just like that, he sent her off on a new worry. "Wait a minute, Luke. Who said anything about you sleeping here?"

He focused on her, his expression puzzled. "So now I'm a one-night stand?"

"No, of course not." She felt strange having this conversation, as if somehow their roles had reversed. "I just think we should be more cautious, take it a step at a time. We rushed headlong into it last time and look where it took us."

"It's not the same," he said fiercely. "We're not the same."

"No, we're not. I'm a mom now, and I have Robbie

to consider. Let's face it, if things don't work out between us, it's going to mess him up.''

''Then we'll have to make sure things do work out, won't we?'' Staring down at her, he challenged her to protest. ''And we can't do that by keeping our distance.''

He was doing it again, she realized. In one way at least Luke hadn't changed. She mustn't fool herself; it would always be like this, him sweeping her along, using his persuasive logic and imposing will to convince her before she was ready to make a decision.

If they stayed together, theirs could be an almost constant battle of wills. And that was just one of her many reasons for her to pause before taking their relationship any further.

After all, there was the matter of Robbie, as Luke had so unintentionally reminded. If they were going to be a family, if Luke was going to act like Robbie's father, surely she owed it to both of them to tell the truth. After all this time, it wouldn't be easy to confess. Gaining their understanding, and forgiveness, would be far harder still.

Although, cowardice wasn't the sole source of her hesitation. She wasn't yet certain she trusted Luke with the truth. He already cared about the boy. Imagine how he would feel once he learned Robbie was truly his son.

That was the trouble. She could imagine it all too clearly. And if things didn't work out between them, she couldn't picture Luke walking off without a fight. He'd want to take Robbie with him, and with all that Parker money behind him, she wouldn't stand a chance. It would be like losing the farm again, only a billion times worse. Like Gramps, she'd lose all her reason for living if Luke took away her son.

She didn't want to believe Luke could be that cruel,

but she hadn't believed he would ever leave her, either, and look what had come of that.

"I'm not talking about keeping my distance," she tried to explain to him. "All I want is to take things—"

But before she could finish, the phone once again interrupted them. Cursing, Luke scrambled out of bed to answer it.

This time it *was* the hospital. And this time Ben Parker was dead.

Chapter Sixteen

Luke stood in the foyer of his father's house, feeling as if he walked in a fog. He'd come to sort through his father's belongings, to see what other little eccentricities Ben might have committed during his diminishing health, but he might better wait until Callie finished driving Rob to school and showed up here to help. Face-to-face with the reality of what lay ahead, he realized he couldn't handle the chore alone.

Thank God for Callie. True to her word, she'd stuck by him, making him feel that he had family to get him through this. She'd been his rock, helping with the arrangements, screening his calls, always there with a meal and a smile when Luke was too tired to think.

It had only been two days since Ben's passing, but they'd been the longest, most grueling days of his life. Every time he turned around, there seemed to be another problem, a greater complication. Yet of all the

unpleasant tasks that had fallen to him, calling his aunt
had to be the absolute worst.

Ben's sister, Emma, had been vocal in her glee and
liberal with the obscenities. "Don't think I won't con-
test the will," she'd ranted immediately. "That son of
a bitch owes me through the nose, and if I get my way,
I'm taking everything."

Aunt Emma had gone on to describe in colorful detail
her disdain for Ben's branch of the family, taking care
to ensure Luke knew that, as Ben's son, he topped the
list. Adding that it would be a cold day in hell before
she would waste time attending her brother's funeral,
she'd slammed down the phone, leaving Luke no
chance for rebuttal.

But then, what could he have told her? Ben had returned her animosity a hundredfold. Many were the
times he'd ranted about how it would be that same cold
day before he ever let his sister see even a cent of his
money.

Only one thing had gotten Luke through the ordeal
of the past two days, and that was the hope that once
the ugliness was behind them, he and Callie would get
the chance to talk. Every hour he replayed in his mind
the one night they'd shared, still reeling with the pleasure, the power he'd felt holding her in his arms. As far
as he was concerned, that night had gone a long way
toward proving they still had the old magic between
them.

He was certain she'd felt it, too, and he couldn't for
the life of him understand her hesitation, but given the
timing he knew enough to be patient. He'd have opportunity enough to force the issue after he'd buried his
father and gotten his hands on the farm. Once he handed
her the keys to the place, when he'd once and for all
proven that he could be trusted, he would get her to

agree about everything—about sleeping together, staying married and, most important, the truth about his son.

If necessary he'd bring up the subject himself. He wasn't looking forward to the inevitable scene, but he also knew their marriage wouldn't last the year with a lie like that between them. He could strive all he wanted to be patient and understanding, but each day the resentment ate deeper and deeper. Each time Luke looked at Rob, he wondered how on earth Callie could have used a sleaze like Reb Jenkins as his replacement. How she could keep on using him, even though he was gone and Luke was there in her house, doing the job.

No, he'd give her time to tell him the truth herself, but before the year was up, they'd have this out in the open.

He nearly jumped when the doorbell chimed behind him. That must be Callie now, he thought, turning with a smile to answer the door.

But when he opened it, he didn't find his wife there waiting, but rather Roger Freehorn, Ben's attorney. Crisp and sharp in his black three-piece suit, not a single strand of his snow-white hair out of place, Roger had clearly come on business. And looked darned uncomfortable about it, too.

Inviting him in, Luke ushered the man into the living room and offered him something to drink. Roger refused politely, primly confirming Luke's suspicion that his was no mere sympathy call. "I assume you're here about the estate?" Luke prompted, gesturing to a chair by the fireplace.

Roger frowned. "Yes." He sat slowly, setting his black leather briefcase on his lap. "I'm afraid I have bad news for you, Mr. Parker."

Not another lawsuit, Luke thought. In the past few

days, he'd been appalled by how many people had a score to settle with his father.

"I urged your father to reconsider," Roger went on, visibly squirming in his seat. "Perhaps he would have eventually, if he hadn't had the stroke. Unfortunately, however, Ben died before he could reverse his latest version."

"Isn't it a little soon to discuss this?" Luke asked, suddenly uncomfortable himself. "I mean, the man isn't even in the ground yet."

"Yes, I quite see your point, but there are…" Roger hesitated, then cleared his throat. "You'll find there are certain limitations, and I thought you might be grateful for the advance notification."

Luke stared at him blankly.

Roger cleared his throat again. "You can read it if you wish," he offered, removing a sheaf of papers from the briefcase. "But I must warn, Ben was vehement in his language. I'm not privy to the entire disagreement between you, of course, but your father made no secret of his displeasure. He was quite explicit in his demands that you were not to inherit a single penny from his estate."

Luke sat there, too stunned to speak. Logically he had no reason to be surprised—Ben had certainly threatened him enough—but really, this was taking spite to a new level. Not that he wanted Ben's estate, especially not with its current financial troubles, but you'd think the old man could have spared a single memento for his only son.

"That's my father for you," he said at last, aware that the lawyer was watching, waiting for him to speak. "It's okay, Mr. Frechorn. I'm not going to toss a fit. There's nothing in Ben's estate that I care about, anyway."

Yet even as he saw the man's trepidation give way to relief, Luke realized there was something he very much wanted. Everything hinged on him getting that farm for Callie. "Just out of curiosity," he asked, feeling his way carefully, "just who does stand to inherit?"

Roger glanced down at the will, as if he didn't already know what was there. "As of this moment it would be one Robert Jenkins."

Robbie? Luke had a moment to be relieved, to think his father had done the right thing after all, before Roger went on in the same crisp syllables. "The inheritance is provisional, however, upon what you choose to do within the next few months."

"Me?"

"According to your father's last wishes, Robert Jenkins will inherit on the condition that you fulfill two stipulations."

Here we go again, Luke thought. Ben and his stipulations.

"The first is that you have thirty days to begin divorce proceedings against your current wife, Callianne. The second is that you establish legal custody of Robert Jenkins and change his name to Parker."

"You've got to be kidding." In his mind Luke could picture his father before he collapsed, sitting like a gloating king in the chair he now occupied.

Roger shook his head. "I certainly wish I was, Mr. Parker. But unfortunately these are the terms of your father's will. I assure you, they are all legally binding."

"I bet they are. Tell me, who gets the Magruder farm if I don't fulfill his lousy stipulations?"

Roger again glanced down at the papers, scanning them rapidly, before looking up to shake his head. "I'm not familiar with that particular property, but if it's part of the estate, it will pass down to Ben's surviving sister, Emma Jane Whitney.''

In his mind Luke could picture the woman dancing her jig of joy, thrilled that she could now save the court costs of contesting. He had no hope that this windfall would soften her thinking, that he could ask for the farm and expect her to just fork it over. No, he'd be lucky if he could get her to sell it to him, and even then she'd soak him for ten times its worth.

But what was the option? Divorcing Callie and taking her son away from her?

Telling the lawyer that he needed time to think this over, Luke led the man to the door and watched him drive off. He was still standing there in a daze as Callie drove up in her new car.

''Who was that?'' she asked, a bit puzzled as she followed him into the house.

''Ben's lawyer. He and I just had a little chat.'' Not trusting himself to say more, Luke turned to the stairs, taking them two at a time to the top.

''Luke, what's the matter?'' Callie asked breathlessly, catching up with him outside his father's room. ''What did that man say to you?''

''Roger?'' he asked distractedly, staring at his father's closed door. ''He came to tell me about the will.''

He felt a strange reluctance to step inside that room with Callie, to poke through the secrets of the cold, unfeeling stranger who had been his father.

And then it dawned on him that he didn't have to go through Ben's things, that his father's estate was no longer his responsibility. All things considered, he might better clear out his own room, before Aunt Emma got her clutches into the few possessions he'd left behind.

"C'mon," he told Callie, leading her down the hall. "Let's talk in my room."

But once there, his throat felt paralyzed. Callie stared at him in bewilderment, but he couldn't bring himself to admit what little his father thought of him. If your own father thought you worthless, so the reasoning went, you couldn't be much of a bargain.

"Just grab everything that isn't nailed down," he told her, "and toss it on the bed. I'll get a box to cart it all off in."

"What is it, Luke?" She put a hand on his arm, her warmth seeping into him. "What's got you so upset?"

"Start on that shelf," he told her as he shrugged free of her grasp. "I'll be back in a second."

On her face he could see her concern shift into worry, but he left the room anyway, needing to think. All the way to the cellar and back he wondered what he could tell her. That his spiteful father demanded their divorce? That his grasping aunt would never let them have the farm? Even if she could accept those things—and being Callie, that was a very big *if*—what did that tell her about his family? About himself?

By the time he'd returned with a box, she'd collected a pile on the bed, but she left her work immediately to put her arms around him. "Talk to me, Luke," she said, brown eyes wide and pleading as she gazed up at him. "Whatever it is, it can't be worse than I'm imagining."

"Don't bet on it." He broke away to walk to the other side of the bed, grabbing up a pile of books and tossing them in the box.

"Luke."

He stared at her across the bed. "He disinherited me, okay?" he said, irrationally annoyed by her persistence. The box shook as he slam-dunked his high school yearbook into it.

"I thought you said you didn't care about the estate, anyway," she said with the same dogged determination. "Why are you upset? Now you won't have the headache of dealing with all its problems."

Trust Callie to get right to the heart of things. Another reason he couldn't tell her everything his father expected of him. "Maybe you forgot, but your farm is part of that estate."

"Oh."

"Yeah, oh. My Aunt Emma will get it. The same aunt as you'll recall, who made it crystal clear that she's not sharing anything with any relative of Ben Parker." He punctuated this by hurling his high school trophies in the box. "Even if we could get her to sell, I haven't got money enough for what that robber baron will fleece us."

Of all the things he regretted in his life, nothing topped the look of disappointment he now saw on her face. "Cal, I'm sorry," he said, knowing he was the one who put it there. He and his snake of a father.

"I know. It's not your fault."

The sentiment was nice, but neither one of them was buying it.

He'd promised her and once again, he'd let her down. "It's what we were arguing about," he said slowly, leaning down to pick up the photographs, the last few items left on his bed. "I was trying to get Ben to sell me the farm that night he collapsed."

"Oh." She could have been carved of marble, the way she stood motionless, staring at him with unblinking eyes.

Luke needed her to understand. "He tried to buy me off, Cal. My own father tried to use me like a pawn to get what he wanted. And all the time he was fully aware that he'd already cut me off from everything. You're right, I don't care about his damned money. I never did. But do you have any idea what it feels like to know your father's last statement to the world was that to him you meant absolutely nothing?''

"Oh, Luke,'' she sighed, her compassion bringing her features back to life.

And for Luke her concern made him feel as if a floodgate inside him had been opened. "Of course, I didn't need him to make a public statement. He made his feelings painfully clear in his last words to me.'' He looked down at the photo in his hands, seeing the face of his brother smiling back. A knot of pain twisted inside him, but he shook it off as he tossed the picture in with the rest of his stuff. "He made sure to tell me, one final time, that I could try until I was blue in the face, but I'd never be able to measure up to Matt.''

"Your brother?''

Luke laughed, a hard, dry bark with not a trace of humor in it. "Saint Matthew in the flesh. Without whom the sun refused to rise and set.''

She looked confused again, tilting her head to study him. "I didn't realize you and your brother didn't get along.''

For some reason he couldn't bear for her to think that. "Oh, no, Cal, I idolized Matt, maybe even more than Ben did. Who wouldn't? He was a guy's guy, the kind of big brother who always made time for you, laughed at your dumb jokes, helped you find ways to avoid a licking when you got into trouble.''

She took a step or two closer, her face drawn with concern. "You've never talked about his death, Luke. It must have hurt a lot.''

All at once he couldn't face her compassion, knowing he didn't deserve it. Turning away, he went to his shelves, acting as if he really cared about retrieving the model cars there. "I never talk about it because I was to blame for Matt's dying."

"No, I don't believe that."

She sounded so earnest, so staunch in her defense of him. "Matt and Ben used to go hunting," he went on as he snatched up the cars and lugged them to the box. "It was a shared passion between them but something I hated. I went once and puked my guts out, which only made Ben more determined to make a man out of me. He set up a trip for my eighth birthday, him and me out in the woods. I dreaded it so much I had nightmares for weeks beforehand. Matt heard me during one of them, and when he figured out what was messing me up, he suggested I play sick to get out of the trip. And to keep Ben off my back, he volunteered to go in my place."

Luke paused, remembering the proud smile on Ben's face as they left that day, and how for an instant, trapped in his sick bed, he'd felt a spurt of envy. It still pricked his conscience, the swift, involuntary hatred he'd felt for his brother. Just once, he remembered thinking, he wished he could do something to make their father look at him like that.

"Ben came home alone, a day later than planned," he went on. "I didn't have a clue what was going on. I was eight and pretty self-absorbed, so it never occurred to me that Matt wouldn't be there sooner or later. He'd promised to help with my homework, you see, and my brother never went back on his word. I was so certain he'd come home that night, I went to Ben's study looking for him. They usually spent an hour or two chatting there before going to bed."

And how he'd longed to be invited, Luke remembered. Once, he'd barged in, hoping they'd ask him to join them, but Ben's glare made certain he never made that mistake again.

"Ben was alone, holding a whisky and staring at the fire." Dropping the cars into the box, Luke spoke evenly, as if it had happened to someone else. "He turned to me when I asked where Matt was, and the look he gave me could have frozen a stone. I wasn't fit to utter Matt's name, he said. His son would still be alive if it wasn't for me."

"He blamed *you?* But that's insane." She crawled onto the bed, scrambling across to kneel in front of him. "It was an accident. You weren't even there. Ben couldn't possibly claim you had anything to do with it."

Luke shrugged. "He didn't say the exact words, but my father made no secret of what he was thinking. If I'd gone along as planned, I'd have fallen into that ravine, and Matt would still be alive today."

The words rang between them. Callie, God bless her, looked horrified for him. "Is that what he said to you the night he had the stroke?"

Luke shook his head. "Not verbatim, but then, he didn't have to spell it out. His every action for most of my life has emphasized his conviction that he'd lost the better son that day, that he was stuck with an inferior imitation."

Callie looked up at him, her hands grasping his arms. "Oh, Luke, tell me you didn't believe his nonsense."

"Why not?" he told her, trying to sound flippant about it. "Ben was right, after all. I knew it even then, standing in that study, witnessing my father's grief and unable to share it. It was like I had this cold, dark void where my heart should have been. I never shed a tear, not even at the funeral. I buried my brother, and that was that."

Wrapping her arms around him, Callie held him tight. "Don't waste your pity on me," he told her, feeling stiff and leaden and unable to hug her back. "It was painfully obvious to everyone I knew that I had something intrinsically wrong with me, that emotionally speaking, I had to be some kind of monster. Ben found me a series of shrinks for a while, but in truth, my parents had already washed their hands of me. By the next week Ben was off busying himself with acquiring bigger and bigger profits. Left alone, my mother retreated into her grief, letting it drain her until she had no strength or even will to fight the cancer."

"You weren't a monster," Callie said fiercely, looking him straight in the face. "You were a kid, practically a baby, looking for a way to deal with your grief on your own. Your parents should have been flogged for being so negligent, so self-absorbed. Don't tell me you didn't grieve, that you're not still trying to find a way to mourn for your brother. I can hear it in your voice, see it in your eyes. You've got to let it out, Luke. It's not healthy to hold it all in."

"Grown men don't cry." He tried to look away, but she wouldn't let him, scrambling off the bed to stand before him.

"Is that the gospel according to Ben?" she asked, holding his face in both her hands. "How could you listen to a thing that man ever said to you? He was the monster, Luke. If he'd spent less time being macho, he could have dealt with his grief in a positive fashion and not used it to scar an eight-year-old boy. Stop listening to him, Luke. Stop bottling up the pain he caused you."

"What do you want from me, Cal?" he asked, taking her hands away. "You expect me to start bawling like a baby?"

"Why not?" She moved forward, getting right there in his face. "I cried for weeks when I lost Gramps. I lost my whole family, Luke. I know how it hurts, how it tears at you, but shouldering the blame for your loss isn't helping anyone.'' She sighed, as if digging deep inside her for what to say next. ''Remember that day at the cemetery, when you asked if I felt guilty for surviving? I told you what Gramps told me, that my parents would be angry if they knew I was wasting my life, wallowing in guilt and misery. Do you truly think this is what your brother would have wanted? That Matt would want you blaming yourself for his dying?''

Listening to her, Luke could hear her logic, but after twenty-plus years of carrying the weight of his guilt, he couldn't so easily put it down. ''Ben would have called this rationalization.''

She looked angry suddenly. ''Forget what Ben might have said. He was a spiteful, bitter man, and you've got to let go of his poison.'' That said, she softened her expression, reaching up once more to touch his face. ''I know it's hard, letting go of your last link with your family, but you don't have to feel so alone, Luke. Always remember you've got Robbie and me in your corner.''

''Do I, Cal?'' he asked hoarsely, every inch of him focused on her beautiful face.

''Like the man said,'' she said with a feeble smile, ''I'm not going anywhere.''

Just like that he could feel something slip inside him, the knot of self-hatred he'd been carrying around for far too long.

Gazing down at her he was amazed anew at how lovely Callie was, how her simple smile could reach inside him and make his chest ache. He leaned down to drop a kiss on her lips, a tribute to her beauty and perhaps an expression of his gratitude. She reached up, her arms encircling his neck, and the impulsive gesture swiftly flared into mutual passion.

For an instant Luke lost all touch with the world, his mind, body and soul awash with sensation. Yes, this was how it was between them. This was why it had never been quite the same with any other woman. Everything about Callie turned him on, her scent, her curves, the skin as soft as her heart.

He heard her murmur, but it was not even close to a protest as she melted into him. Slanting his mouth over hers, he kissed her deep and hard, feeling like a kid again, as eager and ready as if it were his first time. Mouths still joined, he scooped her up and carried her to the bed.

But as he set her down gently on the mattress, she blinked up at him, looking as if she couldn't remember how she had gotten there. "Oh, Luke, this is crazy."

"You want to stop?"

She answered by reaching up to pull his head to hers, and Luke felt as if he might burst with the wonder of having her here, so giving and delectable and eager in his bed. Last time had been a blur of crazed pleasure, but it was different now, deeper somehow, and he meant to make certain they savored every single moment.

He had to stay focused, in control.

But this was Callie, the woman who had always brought him to the edge, and he found it increasingly impossible to resist her. She had her hands under his shirt, sliding across his skin, slipping his shirt over his head. He wanted to undress her slowly, to unwrap her like a long-awaited birthday present, but she was already tugging at his zipper, yanking at his pants. Shoes, socks, underwear went flying in their mad rush to have nothing between them.

"Do you know how it feels?" he rasped into her mouth. "Have you any idea what it does to me, being here with you like this?"

She nodded, drawing his gaze into the depths of her eyes. "It feels complete, like there's a vital part of you that's no longer missing, for at least as long as the kiss lasts."

Luke gazed at her in wonder. Trust Callie to put what had been a vague impression into words he could grasp. Kissing her did make him feel he'd discovered a part of him he'd always been lacking. No wonder he wanted the moment to last.

Unable to stop himself, he slipped back to her mouth, her sweet, melting wonder of a mouth. Yet, as he caressed her, he knew it wasn't just the kissing that made him feel this way. Their entire bodies seemed likewise connected, moving as one, joining as one. And it was up to him now to make the sensation go on forever.

Taking his time to explore her, struggling against the mounting pressure as she stroked him, he understood why it had never been like this with any other woman. Why it could never be like this with anyone else. Only sweet, generous Callie knew how to take him out of himself, how to strip away his guilts and conceits and make him want to strive higher.

And that was why, though he ached to feel every bit of her incredible warmth, Luke reached back for the condoms.

She was ready for him, opening up like a blossoming flower to welcome him in. As he entered her, the two of them joining in one motion, one rhythm, he knew he could happily die right then with the pleasure. Her sweet building moans filled him with a sense of power, of joy, in the clear knowledge that they were in this together.

Callie stayed with him through each pulsing, throbbing thrust, clinging to him, urging him to probe deeper yet. Her tongue was everywhere, twirling in his mouth, on his chest, in his ear until she was crying out his name, over and over. She dug her nails into his flesh as she began to pulsate deep inside her, rippling around him, squeezing him tight. And then it was too late, he could no longer hold back, could no longer want to as her orgasm urged him to spew everything he had into her sweet, welcoming body.

Spent, the urgency leaving him, Luke felt awed by what had just transpired between them. He'd left his mark on her, and she'd left her own on him. After this, not even Callie would find any reason for them to remain apart.

He lay on his side, watching her. Eyes closed, lips curved in a smile, she seemed so beautiful and serene, she could be an angel. *His* angel.

In her own little world Callie felt like anything *but* an angel. Surely it had to be a sin, making love with a man you knew could never love you, but, still vibrating with the utter wonder of it all, she couldn't quite bring herself to care.

Not in the face of her recent discovery. Listening to Luke as he'd talked about his brother, watching his face each time he mentioned Ben, she'd understood for the first time the ghosts that had driven this man. Holding him, feeling him inside her, she'd had no choice but to acknowledge the truth. She still loved Luke Parker with all her heart and she probably would do so forever.

Keeping her eyes closed, she made peace with the fact. She could feel his heat so close beside her, could feel his breath tickling her throat, and she smiled at the thought that even after such a mind-blowing experience, his attention remained focused on her. Okay, so he didn't say the three magic words, but he cared about her and Robbie and he wanted to stick around. Couldn't she find some way to be content with that?

After all, she was resourceful. She might yet turn him around. Maybe it wasn't so much that Luke couldn't love, but that his father made him think he was unlovable. One more case of Ben Parker infecting the world with his poison.

Aching inside, she pictured Luke as a little boy, watching his world fall apart, feeling powerless to stop it. It had to have been awful enough losing his brother, but to have his own parents turn against him when he needed them most...? No wonder he thought he couldn't love. How could he risk another hurtful rejection?

Opening her eyes, needing suddenly to see him, she found Luke staring dreamily at her face. Oh, yes, she could work with this. And if not, well, maybe she had love enough for them both.

Luke saw the softening in her eyes and felt a rush of emotion flood through his veins. "Penny for your thoughts?" he asked gently, suddenly wanting to know everything about her.

"Cheapskate." She smiled, taking the sting out of the word. "You really think my thoughts are only worth a penny?"

"Of course not," he told her, teasing back. "But keep in mind, I've just been disinherited."

Her face clouded, and he feared the reminder had jolted her back to her earlier caution. "I forgot about your father being dead," she said, reaching down to draw the bedspread over her naked body. "He must be turning over in his grave, knowing what we just did here in his house."

"Let him squirm." He reached for her hand, removing it from the bedspread. "I've wasted too much of my life caring what Ben might think. For once I want to worry about what is good and right instead."

And in Luke's mind what was right and good was Callie, and she deserved better than what his father had done to her. Ben might have died thinking he'd had the last laugh over the Magruders, but Luke aimed to prove otherwise. If he had to sell his soul, he'd make certain he got that farm for Callie.

"I want you, Cal," he told her. "And Rob. Can't get any more good and right than that."

She reached up to touch his face. "Is it really what you want?" she asked, her brown eyes a pool of questions.

Bringing her hand to his lips, he nodded, smiling. Naked to the waist, her face drawn in consternation, she was still the most beautiful woman, inside and out, that he'd ever laid eyes on. And by far the most desirable.

"Actually," he muttered into her lips as he lowered the bedspread to her toes. "Now that you ask, I can think of a few more things I want."

Chapter Seventeen

Luke left the florist's, clasping a dozen long-stemmed roses. It was over, he thought with a sense of satisfaction. It hadn't been easy, but he'd done it, and now all he had to do was find the best way to tell Callie.

He hoped she was home, waiting. In the past six weeks since his father's funeral, she'd become quite the gadabout in her new car, though she always managed to make it home for dinner. She liked to tease that she had to be there to feed her "strays," but Luke wasn't fooled. He knew she was drawn by what she and he did *after* dinner—that she looked forward to their nights together as much as he did.

Hurrying to his car, he marveled that even after a month and a half he would still be in such a fever to see her, to spend every possible moment with her. Oh, they'd had their spats, the various adjustments people went through when first living together, but every night they found new and better ways to put their differences behind them.

All except one. He frowned as he thought about what he considered the one sore point in their relationship. Though he'd given her every opportunity, Callie had yet to confess that Rob was his son.

Up until now Luke hadn't wanted to risk rocking the boat, but what he'd done today changed everything. He had to talk to Callie, force the issue. He just had to figure out what he meant to say.

Tossing the flowers in the back seat as he slid into his car, he banged an elbow into the box of stuff he'd carted home from his father's house. That it still sat on the passenger seat where he'd left it was a pretty good indication of where his mind had been the past month or so. On Callie and the future.

One of these days he had to sort through this sad collection, figure out what was junk and what was a keeper. Lord knew he'd been too upset at the time to be aware of anything he'd thrown into the box.

Suddenly curious, he looked inside it, shaking his head at the slew of model cars. Definitely the scrap heap, he thought. Then again, maybe Rob would want them. Luke smiled at the prospect of him and his son gluing and painting their own collection of cars together.

Shaking his head, he was about to give up his cursory inspection when a framed photograph caught his attention. Like a beacon, Matt's face called to him, insisting that Luke remove the picture from the box. Holding it in his hands, he felt the years melt away.

He could see his brother so clearly, grinning ear to ear as the picture was taken. They'd all been pumped that day because Matt's team had just won the high school's first football championship. An all-county half-back, Matt had scored three touchdowns, and everyone in town had been gushing all over him, Ben especially.

Yet Matt took time to pull his little brother aside, confiding that even at seven, Luke was the better athlete. "You'll have heaps of awards of your own someday," he'd said with a grin as he tossed Luke the game ball, "but here, keep this in the meantime."

He'd been right. Luke had gone on to collect his own trophies, but not a single one meant as much as that ball from his brother. He still had it, sitting on the shelf in Callie's apartment. Through the years he'd carried it everywhere, to remind him that his big brother had held such faith in him.

Throat going tight, he stared at Matt's face and the words inscribed at the bottom. "Pals forever," Matt had written, assuring with a wink that whatever happened, he'd always be in Luke's corner.

And all at once Luke could feel him there now, Matt's comforting presence warming him down deep into his heart. Memories crashed over him, all the good times they'd shared, the countless laughs, the middle-of-the-night heart-to-hearts. How often had Matt said that it wasn't their job to live up to their father's expectations? That they had to find their own way in life, using their own unique talents.

A smart guy, Matt. As much as he'd admired their father, he would have been the first to call Ben a jerk for not recognizing his second son's worth. And he'd have called Luke an even bigger one for not realizing it himself.

Callie had. It humbled Luke to know how she'd believed in him when no one else would. And it scared the very devil out of him to think how he could have so easily, so carelessly, lost her forever.

Matt would have liked Callie, Luke thought, gazing

down at his brother's face. He'd have agreed with her, insisting that the idea of blaming Luke for his death was ludicrous. Instead Matt would have shaken his head and demanded to know what his little brother could have been thinking, wasting all these years with self-pity when he could have been loving Callie.

Loving Callie. The truth hit Luke with the force of a blind-side tackle. Far more than mere physical attraction had first drawn him to Callianne Magruder, just as it kept him coming back for more. He loved her. He'd always loved her. He'd just never let himself believe it before.

Feeling every bit the chump his brother would have called him, Luke jammed his car into gear and sped off like a rocket. With all the things he had to say, the secrets to confess, he couldn't get home to her fast enough.

Shaking her head, Callie glanced around the bedroom she now shared with Luke. Robbie might have complained about his neatness, but as far as she was concerned, the man could show a little improvement. True, he didn't leave his socks on the floor, but they often spilled over the hamper, and in her opinion, his "sure-fire method of bed making" left a lot to be desired. And just once she wished he could put his papers back in the drawer of the desk.

She knew she was being cranky, but she'd been up all night studying for an exam she'd had this morning, and she'd then spent the afternoon working at the beauty parlor. Mamie was running a half-off special this week, which meant most folks felt it fair to halve her tip. Stuffing her few dollars and change into the jar she kept on the dresser, she knew that at this rate it would be centuries before she had enough to make a down payment on her farm.

Luke felt bad about not getting the property, she knew, but she didn't blame him. Not really. She knew she couldn't hold it against him that his father was so danged vicious, yet she couldn't seem to get past the fact that Luke had failed to keep his promise. She tried to understand, but it left her feeling...well, disappointed. It didn't change her feelings for him, she would love him to the grave, but the way he couldn't quite grasp how much the farm meant to her remained vaguely troubling.

Troubling? My, but she was in a fine mood today. She was tired, and a bit short-tempered. She would get over it.

But something else bothered her, she knew, some little niggling thing in the back of her head. Nothing she could put a finger on. Just this sort of floating anxiety, as if she could sense a storm brewing but couldn't tell from what direction it would hit.

Her darned sixth sense again, working overtime.

Suddenly impatient with her thoughts, she decided she might better spend her time tidying up. She had no business whining, anyway, she told herself as she jammed the socks back in the hamper and straightened the bed. In all other respects, living with Luke these past few weeks had been a dream come true. He helped around the house, he was incredible with Robbie, and the nights they shared on that bed were pure and utter heaven.

Smiling, she realized the great times weren't just here in this apartment, either. Unlike when they were kids, Luke didn't try to hide their relationship. He took her everywhere, showing her off to his friends and business associates, assuring her with his words, look and touch that he couldn't be more proud of her.

Why couldn't she be happy enough with that?

She was greedy, that's why. Angry at herself, she went to the desk and started gathering the papers into a neat pile. The trouble was that now that she'd had a taste of what Luke could offer, she wanted it all. His respect, his admiration. His love.

Dream on, Callie.

With a weary sigh, she opened the drawer to put the papers inside it, only to be greeted with a jumbled mess. She could see now why he cluttered the top: there was no room in the drawer to put anything away.

All it would take was a little organization to set it right, she thought irritably. He was no better than Robbie, in a hurry to get on to the next thing and unmindful of the havoc he left in his wake.

And as if it were indeed a mess of her son's making, she automatically began sorting through the chaos. What Luke needed was a desk organizer in which to keep his supplies, she thought. Maybe she'd pick one up the next time she went shopping. Putting pens, staples and paper clips on one side, paperwork on the other, she was in the process of joining the pile she'd collected with the papers in the drawer when the single word "Paternity" caught her eye.

She hesitated, the chill of trepidation slicing through her veins. Somewhere in the back of her mind she knew this was an invasion of Luke's privacy, yet she reached for the document, anyway. And the more she read, the more she couldn't stop.

Her hands shook as she gripped it, for she recognized what it was immediately. Not the original document, perhaps, but the copy she held in her hands was a legal petition to establish paternity, the object to be claimed being one Robert Jenkins.

Reading her son's name, Callie dropped the document as if it had burned a hole in her hand.

Like a low-budget soap opera, the past few months played through her mind. Luke, first asking about Robbie, the two of them getting closer, leaving her out. Luke, making it only too plain how much he wanted to play the boy's father.

No, it had to be a mistake, she thought, nausea rising up in her throat. Luke couldn't have been pretending. He'd been such an attentive lover, the very best of husbands, an incredible dad...

She stopped, sick at heart. In truth, Luke had shown too much devotion to a boy not of his own flesh and blood. Taking it further, she could remember the many times when she'd felt he'd been more concerned about Robbie than he was about her. All along had he been lying to her, using her, just to get to his son?

No, she repeated adamantly. It didn't make sense. Marrying her was an awfully elaborate ruse when all he had to do was file the paper at her feet. With all his money and connections he could have laid claim to Robbie in the blink of an eye and never once had to deal with silly little Callie Magruder.

So what in the name of sweet heaven had the past few months been about?

There was but one way to answer the question, she realized as she heard a car pull up to the curb outside and recognized the purr of his BMW. No sense making herself crazy with her suspicions. For all she knew, he could have a perfectly logical explanation. As soon as Luke walked in the door, she merely had to ask him for it.

But when she heard his calm and reasonable voice in

the living room, talking with Robbie, all she knew was
an insane urge to hide. Suddenly she couldn't face him,
couldn't bear to know the truth.

But she had nowhere to hide in her tiny bedroom,
nowhere to run from the truth. Before she was ready—
as if she could ever be ready—Luke burst into the room,
smiling ear to ear, holding a manila envelope and presenting a huge bouquet of roses. "Get dressed, Cal. You
and I are going out celebrating."

She shook her head, refusing to step forward to take
the flowers. Trembling inside and out, Callie looked at
the man who had held her so tenderly in his arms, whispering in her ear, making promises he never meant to
keep. "Who are you?" she asked him, pointing to the
paper on the floor between them. "How could you look
me in the eye and lie to me like that?"

As he glanced down at the paternity claim, the smile
left his face. Dropping the roses on the bed, he looked
at the envelope in his hands. "Maybe it's just as well
to have it out in the open," he started to say, but Callie
had heard and seen enough.

"What, Luke?" she asked, her voice trembling as
much as her limbs. "The fact that you've been trying
to steal my son away from me?"

"*Our* son, Cal. And nobody's trying to steal him
away. That paper…" He glared down at the paternity
claim as if no more happy to see it there than she was.
"I was desperate at the time. I thought I had to—"

"Stop." She put her hands over her ears. "I can't
listen to your explanations anymore. I tried that, and all
the while you were conniving behind my back."

"What is this, Cal?" he asked gently, stepping
closer. One hand still holding the envelope, he used the
other to take hers from her ear. "One little misunder-

standing and you're so ready to believe the worst of me?''

"Little misunderstanding?" Feeling his warmth seep into her, Callie wrenched away, going to the other side of the room to put physical distance between them. He used his touch to get to her, she couldn't forget, and she couldn't let him cloud her judgment.

In some part of her mind she recognized that this was already crazy, that she was letting everything spin out of control. Her emotions were running the show, however, and all they could see was that her very worst nightmare had now come true. "I'd say this runs a little deeper than a mere misunderstanding. And since you knew how reluctant I was to trust you again, I'd have to call this a full-fledged betrayal.''

"For crying out loud, Cal. Calm down. Nobody—''

"I don't want to calm down," she cried, cutting him off. "I want answers. Why did you do it, Luke? Were you that afraid of letting some white trash scum like me raise your son?''

"Where in hell did this come from?" Luke shook his head, clearly exasperated. "I thought we'd gotten past the Magruder versus Parker thing. Ben is dead, Cal. The feud died with him.''

"For you, maybe, but then, you didn't have to go through it. You took off for the worst ten years of my life.''

He gazed at her in disbelief. "You act as if I deliberately abandoned you. I 'took off,' as you put it, because I mistakenly believed that living in the limelight would solve all my problems. I couldn't drag you through all that. Leaving you behind, I thought, was the best for you in the long run. I decided I'd only make you miserable.''

"Listen to yourself, Luke. You knew, you decided.

Doesn't it ever occur to you that I'm capable of making my own decisions?'' She stared back at him, knowing she was making things worse, but she'd held the resentment in for so long, the words spilled out of their own accord. "You could have let me know what was going on. You could at least have given me the option of going away with you.''

"Really. And what option did you give me when you learned you were pregnant? Get off your high horse, Cal. You're not the only victim here. Did it never occur to *you* what you've done to me *and* our son, by keeping your precious little secret?''

"You were gone,'' she lashed out, refusing to let him score that point. "You left town, left me, without ever once looking back.''

He winced, but it didn't lessen his anger. "Yeah, and that's your excuse for tricking Reb into marriage?''

She felt as if he'd slapped her. "I didn't. Reb went into that marriage with his eyes wide open.''

"I see. So it was a reward, then, you naming Rob after him?''

She couldn't believe he'd think so little of her. "Robbie's name has nothing to do with Reb. I named him after my dad, Robert, and my baby brother. I wanted my boy to have something of them, and I wanted a part of the Magruders to pass down to him. A good decision, it turns out, since I no longer have the farm to give him.''

"You and that damned farm,'' he muttered under his breath, running a harried hand through his hair.

His continued inability to understand her longing merely fueled her anger. "Don't worry. I won't nag you anymore about your promise. I've been saving up my money in that jar over there. I'll buy 'that damned farm' myself.''

It was his turn to look as if he'd been slapped. "You have so little faith in me?"

How could he look at her like that? she wondered, acting as if he'd been the one hurt.

But before she could spout back that he'd done very little to earn her faith, Robbie popped into the room, looking from one to the other with obvious consternation. "Can you stop? I don't want you yelling at each other."

Luke looked to her, giving her the chance to answer first, but in truth, what could she tell her son? That she was fighting the battle of her life to keep him? That the man she married, the man she loved so hopelessly wanted to take him away? The man who just so happened to be his father.

She didn't have to say anything; Robbie took it out of her hands. "I heard my name," the boy said, focusing his gaze on Callie. "Is this about me? Are you mad because Luke is my dad?"

A cold chill passed through her. This had to be the ultimate betrayal. "You told him?" she rasped at Luke.

Luke showed no guilt at all; he seemed merely annoyed.

"Luke didn't say anything," Robbie went on. "I'm not dumb, Mom. I can figure things out for myself. Maybe even better than you can. He wants to be my dad, but you're trying to scare him away with all your screaming and yelling."

"Rob, that's enough."

Callie's nerves were so raw she flinched at Luke's stern tone. She couldn't believe her son could talk to her like this, couldn't believe any of it was happening.

"No," Robbie protested, "it's not fair what she's doing. Tell her, Luke. Tell her you're not leaving. That

you'll keep on being my dad whether she wants you to
or not.''

Sighing, Luke went over to put an arm around the
boy, assuring Robbie that he'd always be there for him.
Watching him hug her son, seeing how Robbie hugged
him back, Callie saw it all with heartbreaking clarity.
This was why Luke married her, why he'd taken the
pains to romance her. He needed the time and opportunity to get closer to Robbie. None of it had anything
to do with her at all.

Assuring the boy that his mom and he would work
things out, Luke again embraced Robbie, before urging
him to run down the hall to deliver Mrs. Boyle's dinner.
That should have been my hug, Callie thought bitterly,
though she was too emotionally wrung out to know
which male she resented. Neither one felt any compunction to comfort her. Two against one, with her now
on the outside.

All thanks to Luke's conniving.

The instant Robbie left the apartment, Luke moved
closer, absentmindedly slapping the manila envelope
against his thigh. ''This is stupid, Cal. We need to
talk.''

She held up a hand to halt him. ''No, Luke, the only
thing stupid here is me. Who can blame you for playing
me for a sucker? I was such an easy mark. You'd think
I'd have learned my lesson but no, I let you worm your
way back into my heart, never even guessing it was
Robbie you were after.''

He stopped in the middle of the room, plainly surprised by her attack, as if he'd expected Robbie's in-
terruption to break the ice. ''I thought you'd gotten past
your silly insecurities, Cal. I thought we had the start
of something good here.''

''Something good? Pardon me, but how can what we

have be anything but a sham? And how dare you dismiss what you did to me as my 'silly insecurities.' Look at you, standing there playing innocent when we both know you tricked me from the start.''

He had the good grace to grimace. ''Okay, I admit, maybe I was deluding us both in the beginning. I knew that damned pride of yours and the way you clung to your feud. I couldn't see how you would ever let Rob be raised as a Parker. I didn't know, didn't understand, how it could be between us, but somewhere along the way you got to me, Callie. If you believe nothing else, you've got to know that.''

She held herself taut, clenching her fists so tightly the bones in her hands felt ready to snap. ''What are you trying to say, Luke? That now, just like that, you've discovered you love me? Excuse me if I can't trust it, but I find your declaration too much of a coincidence, seeing as how you've never felt the need to utter the words before.''

''Words, Cal?'' he asked, his tone just as tightly strung. ''Is that what I need to gain your trust? Here, all along you had me thinking what you wanted was action. When, exactly, are you going to start judging me by what I do now, and not on the sins of my past?''

''That—'' she stabbed a finger at the paternity petition, ''—is hardly the act of a trustworthy man.''

He stared at the document, shaking his head. ''Ben's will is in the drawer, too, Cal,'' he said, his tone going lifeless. ''You should have read that, too. If you had, you'd understand why I did what I did. It was a mistake, I can see that now, but that's all it was. A mistake, not a betrayal.''

''Funny, I feel betrayed. You lied to me, Luke. What kind of marriage can we ever have when I can never know if you're speaking from the heart or getting ready to stab me in the back?''

"So what is the bottom line here?" he asked angrily. "You want to call it quits?"

"What is this?" she tossed back at him. "Don't tell me you're actually going to let me make a decision?"

"That's all I've been doing for the past few months, in case you haven't noticed." He looked so cold suddenly, so furious. "So yes, it's your call, Cal. Just say the word and I'm out that door."

"You're not taking Robbie with you!"

He visibly recoiled, as if she'd been the one to insert the dagger. "You really think me capable of taking your son from you?" He shook his head, gazing at her sadly. "Maybe you're right, Cal. We can't have much of a marriage, if all you can think about right now is that I'm capable of being that cruel. Rip up the damned petition and keep your precious little secret. It was never, ever about separating you and Robbie. If you weren't so tangled up in the past, too proud and stubborn to get past it, maybe you'd see all I ever wanted was a place in your family."

He turned and marched to the door. Callie could feel something inside of her dying. *Say something,* an inner voice screamed. *Don't let him walk out of your life forever.*

But she couldn't speak, couldn't get the words past her disillusionment and hurt. She stood frozen to the spot, feeling as cold and lifeless as the first time he'd walked out on her.

He stopped at the door, glancing at the jar on her dresser. "Just for the record, I only toyed with the idea of filing that petition. I tore up the original weeks ago. I would never have considered it if I wasn't so desperate to keep my promise. I knew how important your trust in me would be for our future." Looking back at her, he gave her a grim smile. "Look at us now, though. Seems your trust was all just an illusion." With a sigh, he slapped the manila folder down next to the jar. "Here, you can find something else to do with your money."

He strode through the door then, closing it quietly after him. Callie stared at the door for the longest time, too numbed to move, to even think. How quiet the room now seemed, how empty.

She began to tremble violently as the realization sunk in. This was actually it, the end she'd been dreading. Six weeks of near bliss, and in the blink of an eye it was over.

But it hadn't been a blink, she was forced to acknowledge. It had been a nasty, ugly argument that she herself had started and then dragged out to its fatal conclusion.

Luke was gone. He wasn't coming back. And all he'd left behind for her were the roses on the bed and an envelope on her dresser.

Like a sleepwalker, she made her way to the dresser, staring at the envelope for a long, uneasy moment before finally picking it up. Reaching inside, she pulled out a sheaf of papers, causing a lone, rusted key to tumble out. She reached for it, snatching the key before it could hit the floor. It landed in her hand, warm and heavy, but she didn't need to see or feel its contours to recognize this, the symbol of all she had loved and lost.

The farm, she thought with a painful lump in her throat.

Through a gathering mist of tears, she gazed at the papers in her hands, the deed to the property and a bill of sale signed by Luke and the owner, Emma Whitney. Noticing the outrageous amount he'd paid his aunt for the farm, Callie clasped the papers to her chest. As wealthy as Luke might be, such a sum had to stretch even his limits.

Yet he'd done it, she thought, the lump in her throat growing larger. In the end Luke had kept his promise.

I've got to talk to him, she thought frantically, starting for the door. But outside an engine roared to life, and she heard the squeal of tires as the BMW raced down the road without her.

She sank to the floor, her trembling limbs no longer able to support her. Luke was no doubt on his way to New York again, and who could blame him? His old team still needed a coach, and she'd certainly given him no reason to stay here in Louisiana. It could well be another ten years before she saw the man again. Given what she'd said to him, it might well be far longer.

Her and her insecurities, he'd accused. Her and her stubborn pride.

The tears spilled out of her eyes, down her cheeks, and she could do nothing to stop them. She heard Robbie enter the apartment, calling Luke's name, but she stayed where she was, clasping the papers to her chest, unable to move a muscle.

She could hear her son in the other rooms, searching every nook and cranny for a sign of his father. Any moment he'd come crashing through her door, demanding to know what she'd done to make Luke leave them. Robbie would never give up on him so easily, she realized. Robbie was still young enough to believe in Luke with unblinking trust. If only she could have had just a touch of the boy's conviction.

All too soon her door slammed open and Robbie burst into the room. "He left?" he asked, his tone an accusation.

Looking up at him, unable to stop the tears, Callie could only nod.

Robbie did an amazing thing then. His expression immediately softening, he hunkered down next to her, and as if he were four times his age, put a comforting arm around her shoulders.

"Don't worry, Mom," he told her with a grown man's assurance. "We'll get him back."

Chapter Eighteen

"Did you call his office?"

Callie glanced over at her son, fidgeting on his side of the car. In the day and a half that Luke had been gone, the boy had been nothing if not relentless. "Yes, Rob, and rest assured, I left several messages."

He smiled at her, his way of rewarding her for using the nickname. After the way the boy had comforted her through this, how could she not respect his wishes? Insisting upon calling him Robbie had been just another case of her clinging to the past. And as Luke had pointed out, she'd done more harm than good with her stubbornness.

Blessed with hindsight, she could see that Luke had been right to condemn her insecurities, too. The way Rob had rushed to support her proved how foolish she'd been to fear that anyone could ever separate them. Love, real love, didn't end because something better came

along. It endured, even through misunderstandings—
silly or otherwise.

"Did you try the mansion?" Rob tried again, his
boyish face practically pleading with her.

She had—she'd been that desperate—but she'd been
informed quite rudely that Mr. Parker no longer had any
connection to the house. She'd even tried calling Ben's
lawyer, Roger Freehorn. The poor man had fallen all
over himself trying to express his regret that her son
had not been able to inherit, but Mr. Luke Parker had
been quite adamant about *not* fulfilling his father's stipulations.

Callie had shared the man's regret, though for a far
different cause. By then, she'd read the will in Luke's
desk drawer and understood better why he'd drawn up
the paternity petition. The fact that he'd never filed it,
that he'd found the more honorable—and obscenely expensive—way to fulfill his promise, made her feel twice
as awful for accusing him. And twice as determined to
apologize.

"I called the mansion, but it belongs to Luke's aunt
Emma now," she told Rob gently. "And even if she
did know Luke's whereabouts, she isn't likely to con-
fide in me."

The boy nodded, accepting this with a glum expression. "Maybe he'll be at the farmhouse," he tried next,
his face brightening considerably.

Callie gripped the wheel tighter, not knowing what
to tell him. She didn't want to dampen the boy's enthusiasm, but in her heart she knew Rob was dreaming.
Luke had no reason to be waiting at the farm when they
got there. Between her bitter accusations and blatant
lack of faith, she had done her shrewish best to make
sure he stayed away forever.

Lying in their big, empty bed the past two nights,

tossing and turning and unable to sleep, Callie had
found ample time to relive the ugly scene, to piece together the months leading up to it. The past ten years,
for that matter.

And in those long, lonely hours, she'd acknowledged
that she had been so terribly young when she'd first
fallen in love with Luke, certainly too young to understand all the word entailed, much less know how to
offer it unconditionally to another. Caught up in her
own dreams and fears, she'd never stopped to consider
that Luke might be struggling with his own problems.
He too had been just a kid, after all, with parents who'd
left him with even less of a clue as to what to do with
deep emotion.

Maybe she'd been hurt badly when Luke left town,
but she'd been wrong to blame him because she'd been
alone to raise their son. As he'd pointed out, she never
gave him the option of sticking around to be Rob's father. Had she told him back then that she was pregnant,
he still might have left her, but she'd usurped his right
to make the decision. And by not trusting Luke with
the truth, she'd stolen ten years from him, and she'd
done the same to their son.

Glancing over at Rob's profile, seeing Luke's steady
gaze and determined chin, she wished, yet again, that
she could have it all to do over.

Luke had been right about that, too. She'd been as
bad as his father, letting past hurts infect how she
thought and felt in the present. She'd been so focused
on Luke's leaving her, she'd left no room for a future.
If she could have let go of her pain long enough to
notice that things were different now, that Luke was
different now, maybe she wouldn't have been in such
a hurry to condemn him.

Alone in her bed last night, she'd seen it all too

clearly. Maybe Luke was the one to *physically* walk out the door this time, but not before Callie herself had turned her back *emotionally* on what they'd been building between them.

As he'd said, they'd *both* had their hard lessons, but she needed to start learning from hers, to move on with a new and deeper understanding. It was time to face up to her mistakes, to take the blame for them and start a little of her own atoning.

Which she meant to do at once, if only she could find him.

"There's a good chance Luke went to New York," she told Rob slowly, knowing she had better warn the boy of the worst-case scenario. "He had a job offer, remember, and after what he paid for the farm, the salary he can earn up there must be looking pretty good."

Rob shook his head vehemently. "He wouldn't leave without saying goodbye."

She started to correct him, wishing to spare the boy hurt, but then she turned and saw her son's unswerving conviction. In her mind she could picture Luke that night in the kitchen, wearing the same, solemn expression. *Whatever might happen between you and me,* he'd told her, *I'll always be there for that kid.*

Rob was right, she realized, and the thought filled her heart with its first real hope. Luke *would* return, and when he did, she would have to convince him he had come back for more than his son. That somehow, by talking things out and working together, they could still be a family.

Taking the turnoff, she thought of the day she'd brought Luke here to the farm, how embarrassed and unsettled she'd felt afterward at having revealed so much of herself to him. Looking back, she realized she hadn't shared near enough. Had she let all her doubts and fears and past resentments out that day, maybe she and Luke could have found a way to get past them. Together.

Sighing, she stopped the car in front of the house, overcome by a confusing swirl of emotion as her past and present collided. "We're here," she said to Rob, taking in a deep breath as she held out the key. "Want to be the first to unlock the door?"

He shook his head. "You do it, Mom. I know how important it is to you."

Catching the slight emphasis on the *you,* Callie resisted the urge to insist as they both climbed out of the car. After all, what did it matter who opened the door? They were here, back where both their lives had begun, and could now resume the tradition of all the Magruders before them. Callie hurried up the steps to the porch, her mind on her moment of triumph, unaware that Rob hadn't followed until she turned to see he wasn't standing beside her.

Spinning, she found him still by the car, looking decidedly uncomfortable as he eyed the rear of the house. "If you don't mind," he said hesitantly, "I want to go out back and explore the barn."

"But what about the house?" Callie protested, disappointed that he had no interest in sharing this moment with her. "Don't you want to pick out your bedroom?"

He shook his head. "Maybe later, Mom. First I have to find a reason for Jason to come all the way out here to visit me."

The key felt suddenly heavy in her hands. "You don't want to be here, do you, Rob? You don't want to leave the apartment."

"It's not that. It's okay, wherever we live. But you've got to understand, Mom. It just isn't the same without Luke."

Callie nodded, not trusting herself to speak. She should have anticipated Rob's reaction. He'd only been six years old when they left the farm. Of course he would miss the short time he'd shared with his father far more than some hazy, barely remembered past.

"I know. I miss him, too," she told him, knowing it was inadequate for what they were both feeling, but Rob smiled anyway, letting her know that he understood.

Shooing him off to the barn, she poked the key in the lock and entered the house, determined that one of them at least, would maintain the link with their family. That was the reason she dreamed so long for this, why she'd scrimped and saved and made so many sacrifices.

But strolling about the farmhouse, she discovered that the sounds she heard and felt weren't echoes of long-ago tears and laughter. The only echoes were her own solitary footsteps, going from room to empty room. Rob had tried to warn her weeks ago but she hadn't been ready to listen. Memories were fine in their place, but living, breathing people were what made a home, what made up a family. And the fact was, the most vital cog in both their lives was missing.

It hit her hard, acknowledging how much she'd actually hoped to find Luke here, coaxing and pleading with his devilish grin. Standing in the room she'd once shared with her sister, she was swamped by a wave of longing. Not for the past, but this time, for the future.

As powerfully as if he stood in the room beside her, she could smell Luke's fresh, outdoors scent, could hear his infectious laughter, could feel his strong, capable arms supporting her. *Oh, Luke,* she thought, clasping her own arms for warmth.

It began as the merest sensation, a sort of prickling at the back of her neck. She almost dismissed it as imag-

ination, but then, really, when had her sixth sense ever
lied to her?

She turned to find him standing in the door frame, as
striking as ever in frayed jeans and dusty blue plaid
flannel shirt. Gazing at him, she could feel her heart
swell in her chest.

"I hope you don't mind that I parked in your barn,"
he said without the slightest trace of emotion as he
stepped into the room. "I had to unload some lumber
and shingles. There's a couple of guys coming tomorrow to mend the roof."

"I'll reimburse you," she offered quickly. "You've
done more than enough already."

Seeing his frown, she realized how prim that must
have sounded. She'd meant that he'd done far more than
she deserved, but she seemed to have left the impression
that her pride was wounded. Yet try as she might, she
could think of no way to undo the damage. Planning to
apologize was one thing, she found. Actually facing
Luke was quite another.

"I called your office," she tried. "Didn't you get my
messages?"

But that, too, sounded more like an accusation than
any attempt at reconciliation. "I've been away," he answered curtly. "A job interview. I just got back this
morning."

So he had gone to New York, Callie thought unhap-
pily. He did plan to move away. "You've been busy,"
she said inanely. At his blank expression she added,
"Your interview, the supplies for the roof."

"That's not all I did," he said, seeming suddenly
grim as he went to the window overlooking the backyard. "Before you get angry at me again, I want to
explain that I ran into Rob outside. I had a present for
him. I wasn't planning on giving it to him without talk-

ng to you first, but I'm afraid once he saw it…well, take a look for yourself and see what I mean.''

Callie crossed to the window and saw her son in the yard below, playing catch with a black-and-white puppy.

"It's part shepherd, part collie," Luke explained. "I figured it would make a good farm dog. I also thought it might help Rob make the transition."

What transition? she wanted to ask. Rob's move from the apartment to the farmhouse, or from a family of three to living with a single parent? Yet, as vital as the answer might be to her future, she couldn't bring herself to voice the question.

The conversation wasn't going at all as she'd planned, she thought miserably. Instead of seizing the opportunity to tell him how sorry she was, she stood there like a craven coward, letting the words freeze in her throat. Had she learned nothing, after all? Wasn't it better to take the chance and fail, than let her one small shot at happiness slip through her fingers?

"Luke," she began.

She turned to him even as he turned to her to say, "Callie."

Gazing down at his wife, Luke decided to speak first. He'd grown tired of the forced politeness, the careful skirting around the crucial issues. Having come to do battle, he meant to get at it.

"You might as well know, I have no intention of signing any divorce papers," he told her firmly. "You'll have to fight me in court if you hope to get out of this marriage."

He'd expected a protest, or at the very least a huff, but she merely gaped at him with utter amazement.

"I've had two of the longest days of my life to think about this," Luke went on, "and I came to the conclusion that what we're doing is stupid. Someone's got to put a stop to it. I love you and you love me. What the heck are we doing apart?''

''Wait, back up,'' she told him, grabbing his hand. ''Did you actually say you love me?''

Luke knew this was his moment; he couldn't screw it up. ''You're the expert on the emotion; you tell me. I have this bone-deep yearning to be wherever you are. I'm miserable when I'm not. When I look into the future, I can't imagine you not being in it. I want to be there for every moment, big and small. When you stub your toe, when you graduate from college, when you first learn you're carrying our second baby. Dammit, Cal, I've made a lot of mistakes in my life, but the biggest of all was in giving up when things got tough. Well, I'm not giving up on us, not even if it takes the rest of my life to convince you. It's taken far too long for the truth to sink in, but you *are* my life, Cal, and I'm just no good without you.''

He watched the tears well in her eyes, but still she didn't speak.

''You once called me lucky,'' he went on, encouraged that at least she'd yet to withdraw her hand. ''At the time I thought you were crazy, but I see now that I was the one unable to think straight. How many people get a second shot at life, the chance to do it right? Our chance is here, Cal, staring us in the face. Can you really turn your back on it? Do you really want to?''

Tears brimming in her eyes, she shook her head. ''Oh, Luke, I'm so sorry for the things I said to you. I was angry and hurt and scared of losing you. I should have trusted you more, like Rob did. I could have at least given you the chance to explain.''

Feeling as if a huge weight had been lifted from his shoulders, he tugged her arms. ''There's no time like the present,'' he said, pulling her up against him. ''I'm open for any and all questions.''

''I don't have any,'' she told him, gazing up at him with a look of wonder. ''Not anymore. All I can think of is that I very badly need you to kiss me.''

He took her face in his hands, more than happy to oblige. No doubt about it, he thought as he sank back into the incredible sweetness that was Callie, he was the luckiest man in the world.

Callie clung to him, so overwhelmingly grateful for this second chance, equally determined to make the most of it. Oh, they would continue having problems—she didn't for a moment doubt it—but from now on they would talk things out and resolve them. As long as Luke loved her, as long as he kept kissing her like this, they'd find a way to stay together.

Callie was so immersed in the absolute wonder of it all, she didn't realize they were no longer alone in the room until she heard a distinctive yap behind them.

''Cool,'' Rob cried from the doorway as she and Luke pulled apart. ''Does this mean we get to be a family? Here, in this house?''

Callie hesitated for a second, remembering Luke's interview, but in truth, did it matter to her where they lived, as long as they lived there together? ''Luke might be moving up North, Rob. We'll have to go wherever he goes.''

He smiled down at her. ''I'm glad to hear it, but relax, I'm not going anywhere. Not after the money I sunk into this house. My interview was in New Orleans, Cal. Seems they need a new coach, too.''

''Cool,'' Rob repeated. ''We'd better pick out a room if we're gonna stay here,'' he said to the animal. ''And I guess I'd better pick out a name for you, too, so I can teach you to behave better.'' Turning into the hall, he hesitated, frowning at Luke and Callie. "Come to think of it, what's my name going to be? Do I get to be a Parker now, too?"

Beside her, Callie could feel Luke stiffen, preparing himself for a fight. "Sure, why not?" she said to relieve him of that worry, happy to find that she'd put even that obstacle behind them.

"You're sure?" Luke asked, taking her face in his hands as Rob bounded off down the hall.

"You know me, always 'practical Callie.' I was thinking it will make things far simpler, especially if you meant what you said about that second baby."

Any doubts she had about his feelings were quelled by the look he now gave her. "If you want," he said, nodding at the bed in the corner, "we can shut the door and I'll show you just how serious a man can be."

Ah, yes, Callie thought as she fell back into the magic of his kiss. This was where she belonged.

Here in Luke's arms she'd at long last come home.

* * * * *

SILHOUETTE®
SPECIAL EDITION™

AVAILABLE FROM 15TH NOVEMBER 2002

BABY CHRISTMAS Pamela Browning
That's My Baby!

Rachel Hirsch was astounded to find a baby outside her door on Christmas Eve, and then she met handsome Joe Marzinski. Could he show her the value of romance and family—with a little help from baby Christmas?

TO CATCH A THIEF Sherryl Woods
The Calamity Janes

City lawyer Rafe O'Donnell was in hot pursuit of Gina Petrillo, and he didn't intend to let his sexy suspect out of his sight. But while he was out to catch a thief—Gina just might steal his heart!

CHRISTMAS IN WHITEHORN Susan Mallery
Montana

Worn-out detective Mark Kincaid didn't want to risk getting hurt again, but his adorable neighbour Darcy Montague was *very* appealing. Was she too good to be true or just the woman to make his heart come alive?

THE MD MEETS HIS MATCH Marie Ferrarella

Sexy physician James Quintano had April yearning for everything she'd sworn she'd never need. He hadn't come to town to put down roots—but what man could resist her hot-blooded beauty?

ALMOST A BRIDE Patricia McLinn
Wyoming Wildflowers

Dave Currick had already broken Matty Brennan's heart, but she needed an in-name-only husband. His intimate wedding kiss warned her that he had his own agenda. *Why had he married her?*

A LITTLE CHRISTMAS MAGIC Sylvie Kurtz

Logan Ward needed solitude, not a petite blonde angel and her son. But soon he was listening for Beth Lannigen's knock at his door. Would her plan to make him smile this Christmas bring his heart out of hiding?

AVAILABLE FROM 15TH NOVEMBER 2002

SILHOUETTE®

Sensation™

Passionate, dramatic, thrilling romances

BRAND-NEW HEARTACHE Maggie Shayne
JACK'S CHRISTMAS MISSION Beverly Barton
BANNING'S WOMAN Ruth Langan
BORN ROYAL Alexandra Sellers
A HERO TO HOLD Linda Castillo
ANYTHING FOR HIS CHILDREN Karen Templeton

Intrigue™

Danger, deception and suspense

LASSITER'S LAW Rebecca York
HOWLING IN THE DARKNESS BJ Daniels
GUARDING JANE DOE Harper Allen
ANOTHER WOMAN'S BABY Joanna Wayne

Superromance™

*Enjoy the drama, explore the emotions,
experience the relationship*

WHAT CHILD IS THIS? Karen Young
HUSH, LITTLE BABY Judith Arnold
A CHRISTMAS LEGACY Kathryn Shay
DECEPTION Morgan Hayes

Desire™ 2 in 1

Two intense, sensual love stories in one volume

THE BACHELORETTE Kate Little
RISQUÉ BUSINESS Anne Marie Winston

LUKE'S PROMISE Eileen Wilks
TALLCHIEF: THE HUNTER Cait London

STORMBOUND WITH A TYCOON Shawna Delacorte
WIFE WITH AMNESIA Metsy Hingle

On sale November 15th 2002

*Available at most branches of WH Smith,
Tesco, Martins, Borders, Eason, Sainsbury's
and most good paperback bookshops.*

1202/128/SH33

DELIVERED BY

Christmas

Linda Howard

Joan Hohl   Sandra Steffen

Available from 18th October 2002

*Available at most branches of WH Smith,
Tesco, Martins, Borders, Eason, Sainsbury's
and all good paperback bookshops.*

1102/128/SH41

SILHOUETTE®
SPECIAL EDITION™

*presents six more passionate and
adventurous stories from*

MONTANA

*Welcome to Montana — a place of passion
and adventure, where there is a charming
little town with some big secrets...*

Christmas in Whitehorn by Susan Mallery
December 2002

In Love With Her Boss by Christie Ridgway
January 2003

Marked for Marriage by Jackie Merritt
February 2003

Her Montana Man by Laurie Paige
May 2003

Big Sky Cowboy by Jennifer Mikels
June 2003

Montana Lawman by Allison Leigh
July 2003

1202/SH/LC47

SILHOUETTE

SPECIAL EDITION

presents

Patricia McLinn

with her exciting new series

Wyoming Wildflowers

These women are as strong and feminine
as the men are bold and rugged...and
they're all ready for...love!

ALMOST A BRIDE
December 2002

MATCH MADE IN WYOMING
February 2003

MY HEART REMEMBERS
April 2003

THE RUNAWAY BRIDE
June 2003

1202/SH/LC49

FREE!

2 Books
and a surprise gift!

We would like to take this opportunity to thank you for reading this Silhouette® book
offering you the chance to take TWO more specially selected titles from the Special Edition
series absolutely FREE! We're also making this offer to introduce you to the benefits
the Reader Service™ —

- ★ FREE home delivery
- ★ FREE gifts and competitions
- ★ FREE monthly Newsletter
- ★ Books available before they're in the shops
- ★ Exclusive Reader Service discount

Accepting these FREE books and gift places you under no obligation to buy; you may cancel
any time, even after receiving your free shipment. Simply complete your details below and
return the entire page to the address below. *You don't even need a stamp!*

YES! Please send me 2 free Special Edition books and a surprise gift. I understand that
unless you hear from me, I will receive 4 superb new titles every month for just £2.80
each, postage and packing free. I am under no obligation to purchase any books and may cancel
my subscription at any time. The free books and gift will be mine to keep in any case.

E2ZEB

Ms/Mrs/Miss/Mr ....Initials.................................

BLOCK CAPITALS PLEASE

Surname..

Address..

....

....Postcode ....

Send this whole page to:
UK: The Reader Service, FREEPOST CN8l, Croydon, CR9 3WZ
EIRE: The Reader Service, PO Box 4546, Kilcock, County Kildare (stamp required)

Offer not valid to current Reader Service subscribers to this series. We reserve the right to refuse an application and applicants must be aged
years or over. Only one application per household. Terms and prices subject to change without notice. Offer expires
28th February 2003. As a result of this application, you may receive offers from Harlequin Mills & Boon and other carefully selected
companies. If you would prefer not to share in this opportunity please write to The Data Manager at the address above.

Silhouette® is a registered trademark used under licence.
Special Edition ™ is being used as a trademark.